Kaplan Publishing are constantly finding new ways to make a difference to your studies and our exciting online resources really do offer something different to students looking for exam success.

This book comes with free MyKaplan online resources so that you can study anytime, anywhere. This free online resource is not sold separately and is included in the price of the book.

Having purchased this book, you have access to the following online study materials:

| CONTENT | ACCA (including FFA,FAB,FMA) | | FIA (excluding FFA,FAB,FMA) | |
|---|---|---|---|---|
| | Text | Kit | Text | Kit |
| Eletronic version of the book | ✓ | ✓ | ✓ | ✓ |
| Check Your Understanding Test with instant answers | ✓ | | | |
| Material updates | ✓ | ✓ | ✓ | ✓ |
| Latest official ACCA exam questions* | | ✓ | | |
| Extra question assistance using the signpost icon** | | ✓ | | |
| Question debriefs using clock icon*** | | ✓ | | |
| Consolidation Test including questions and answers | ✓ | | | |

\*      Excludes AB, MA, FA, LW, FAB, FMA and FFA; for all other subjects includes a selection of questions, as released by ACCA

\*\*    For ACCA SBR, AFM, APM, AAA only

\*\*\*  Excludes AB, MA, FA, LW, FAB, FMA and FFA

## How to access your online resources

Kaplan Financial students will already have a MyKaplan account and these extra resources will be available to you online. You do not need to register again, as this process was completed when you enrolled. If you are having problems accessing online materials, please ask your course administrator.

If you are not studying with Kaplan and did not purchase your book via a Kaplan website, to unlock your extra online resources please go to www.mykaplan.co.uk/addabook (even if you have set up an account and registered books previously). You will then need to enter the ISBN number (on the title page and back cover) and the unique pass key number contained in the scratch panel below to gain access.

You will also be required to enter additional information during this process to set up or confirm your account details.

If you purchased through Kaplan Flexible Learning or via the Kaplan Publishing website you will automatically receive an e-mail invitation to MyKaplan. Please register your details using this email to gain access to your content. If you do not receive the e-mail or book content, please contact Kaplan Publishing.

## Your Code and Information

This code can only be used once for the registration of one book online. This registration and your online content will expire when the final sittings for the examinations covered by this book have taken place. Please allow one hour from the time you submit your book details for us to process your request.

Please scratch the film to access your MyKaplan code.

Please be aware that this code is case-sensitive and you will need to include the dashes within the passcode, but not when entering the ISBN. For further technical support, please visit www.MyKaplan.co.uk

# ACCA

# Applied Skills

## Financial Reporting (FR)

## EXAM KIT

PUBLISHING

**British Library Cataloguing-in-Publication Data**

A catalogue record for this book is available from the British Library.

Published by:
Kaplan Publishing UK
Unit 2 The Business Centre
Molly Millar's Lane
Wokingham
Berkshire
RG41 2QZ

ISBN: 978-1-78740-104-4

© Kaplan Financial Limited, 2018

The text in this material and any others made available by any Kaplan Group company does not amount to advice on a particular matter and should not be taken as such. No reliance should be placed on the content as the basis for any investment or other decision or in connection with any advice given to third parties. Please consult your appropriate professional adviser as necessary. Kaplan Publishing Limited, all other Kaplan group companies, the International Accounting Standards Board, and the IFRS Foundation expressly disclaim all liability to any person in respect of any losses or other claims, whether direct, indirect, incidental, consequential or otherwise arising in relation to the use of such materials. Printed and bound in Great Britain.

### *Acknowledgements*

These materials are reviewed by the ACCA examining team. The objective of the review is to ensure that the material properly covers the syllabus and study guide outcomes, used by the examining team in setting the exams, in the appropriate breadth and depth. The review does not ensure that every eventuality, combination or application of examinable topics is addressed by the ACCA Approved Content. Nor does the review comprise a detailed technical check of the content as the Approved Content Provider has its own quality assurance processes in place in this respect.

# CONTENTS

## Section

This document references IFRS® Standards and IAS® Standards, which are authored by the International Accounting Standards Board (the Board), and published in the 2017 IFRS Standards Red Book.

**Features in this edition**

In addition to providing a wide-ranging bank of exam-standard questions, we have also included in this edition:

- Details of the examination format.

- Examples of objective-test, multi-task and constructed response questions that will form part of the examination format.

- Exam-specific information and advice on exam technique.

- An analysis of all of the recent published examination papers.

- Our recommended approach to make your revision for this particular subject as effective as possible. This includes step-by-step guidance on how best to use our Kaplan material (study text, pocket notes and exam kit) at this stage in your studies.

- Enhanced tutorial answers packed with specific key answer tips, technical tutorial notes and exam technique tips from our experienced tutors.

You will find a wealth of other resources to help you with your studies on the following sites:

www.mykaplan.co.uk and www.accaglobal.com/students/

Quality and accuracy are of the utmost importance to us so if you spot an error in any of our products, please send an email to mykaplanreporting@kaplan.com with full details.

Our Quality Co-ordinator will work with our technical team to verify the error and take action to ensure that it is corrected in future editions.

# INDEX TO QUESTIONS AND ANSWERS

## INTRODUCTION

Following the revised exam format, and the addition of IFRS 16 *Leases*, a number of the previous ACCA exam questions within this kit have been adapted to reflect updated standards, and the revised exam format. If changed in any way from the original version, whether due to updates in the IFRS® Standards or due to changes in exam format, this is indicated in the end column of the index below with the mark (A).

The specimen exam and September 2016 full examination is included at the end of the kit.

## KEY TO THE INDEX

### PAPER ENHANCEMENTS

We have added the following enhancements to the answers in this exam kit:

**Key answer tips**

All answers include key answer tips to help your understanding of each question.

**Tutorial note**

All answers include more tutorial notes to explain some of the technical points in more detail.

**Top tutor tips**

For selected questions, we 'walk through the answer' giving guidance on how to approach the questions with helpful 'tips from a top tutor', together with technical tutor notes.

These answers are indicated with the 'footsteps' icon in the index.

## ONLINE ENHANCEMENTS

 **Question debrief**

For selected questions, we recommend that they are to be completed in full exam conditions (i.e. completed to time in a closed book environment).

In addition to the examiner's technical answer, enhanced with key answer tips and tutorial notes in this exam kit, online you can find an answer debrief by a top tutor that:

- works through the question in full

- points out how to approach the question

- shows how to ensure that the easy marks are obtained as quickly as possible, and

- emphasises how to tackle exam questions and exam technique.

These questions are indicated with the 'clock' icon in the index.

Online question enhancements and answer debriefs will be available on MyKaplan at

www.MyKaplan.co.uk

# ANALYSIS OF PAST EXAM PAPERS

The table summarises the key topics that have been tested in recent Financial Reporting exams. A much wider range of topics will now be examined following the introduction of objective-test questions. The information from June 2015 onwards only relates to constructed response questions, as multiple-choice questions have not usually been published. For the September 2016 examination, following a change in the examination format, ACCA published the full examination. This will not be repeated for future sittings.

| | Dec 2013 | Jun 2014 | Dec 2014 | Jun 2015 | Sep/ Dec 2015 | Mar/ Jun 2016 | Sep 2016 | Dec 2016 | Mar/ Jun 2017 | Sep/ Dec 2017 |
|---|---|---|---|---|---|---|---|---|---|---|
| **Group financial statements** | | | | | | | | | | |
| Consolidated statement of profit or loss and other comprehensive income | | ✓ | | ✓ | | | | ✓ | | |
| Consolidated statement of financial position | | | | | ✓ | ✓ | | ✓ | ✓ | ✓ |
| Consolidated SPL and SFP | ✓ | | ✓ | | | | | | | |
| Associates | | | | | | | | ✓ | | |
| **Single entity financial statements** | | | | | | | | | | |
| From trial balance | ✓ | ✓ | ✓ | ✓ | ✓ | ✓ | ✓ | | | |
| Redraft | | | | | | | ✓ | | | |
| Statement of changes in equity | | ✓ | | ✓ | ✓ | | | | | |
| Statement of cash flows | ✓ | | ✓ | | | | | | | |
| **Performance appraisal** | | | | | | | | | | |
| Ratios | | ✓ | ✓ | ✓ | ✓ | ✓ | ✓ | ✓ | ✓ | ✓ |
| Groups | | | | | | | | | ✓ | ✓ |
| **Framework/IFRS** | | | | | | | | | | |
| IASB Framework | ✓ | | ✓ | ✓ | | | ✓ | ✓ | | |
| Accounting principles/ substance | ✓ | | ✓ | | | | | | | |
| Not for profit/specialised entities | | | ✓ | | | | | ✓ | | |
| IAS 2 | | | ✓ | | | | | | | |
| IAS 7 | ✓ | | ✓ | | | | ✓ | | | |
| IAS 8 | | ✓ | ✓ | | | | ✓ | | | |
| IAS 10 | | | | ✓ | | | | ✓ | | |
| IAS 12 | | | ✓ | ✓ | ✓ | ✓ | ✓ | ✓ | ✓ | |

KAPLAN PUBLISHING

| | | | | | | | | | | |
|---|---|---|---|---|---|---|---|---|---|---|
| IAS 16 | ✓ | ✓ | ✓ | ✓ | ✓ | ✓ | ✓ | ✓ | ✓ | |
| IAS 17/IFRS 16 | ✓ | | ✓ | ✓ | | | ✓ | | | |
| IAS 20 | | ✓ | | ✓ | | | ✓ | | | |
| IAS 23 | | | | ✓ | | | | | | |
| IAS 28 | | | | | | | | | ✓ | |
| IAS 32/IAS 39/IFRS 7/IFRS 9 | | | ✓ | ✓ | ✓ | ✓ | ✓ | ✓ | | |
| IAS 33 | | | ✓ | ✓ | | ✓ | ✓ | ✓ | | |
| IAS 36 | | | ✓ | ✓ | | ✓ | ✓ | ✓ | | |
| IAS 37 | ✓ | ✓ | ✓ | ✓ | | | ✓ | | | |
| IAS 38 | | | | ✓ | ✓ | | | ✓ | | |
| IAS 40 | | | | | | | | | | |
| IAS 41 | | | | ✓ | | | | | | |
| IFRS 3 | | | | | | | | | | ✓ |
| IFRS 5 | | | ✓ | | | | | ✓ | ✓ | |
| IFRS 10 | | | | ✓ | | | ✓ | | ✓ | |
| IFRS 13 | | | | | | | | | | |
| IFRS 15 | | | ✓ | ✓ | ✓ | ✓ | | ✓ | | |

# EXAM TECHNIQUE

## Computer-based exams (CBE)

- Do not attempt a CBE until you have **completed all study material** relating to it.

- On the ACCA website there is a specimen Financial Reporting CBE. It is **ESSENTIAL** that you attempt this before your real CBE. You will become familiar with how to move around the screens and the way that questions are formatted, increasing your confidence and speed in the actual exam.

- Be sure you understand how to use the **software** before you start the exam. If in doubt, ask the assessment centre staff to explain it to you.

## Time management

- The examination is 3 hours and 20 minutes long, and incorporates 20 minutes for completion of seeded questions (see Exam Specific Information below).

- This equates to two minutes per mark, so you need to allow 40 minutes per Constructed Response (CR) question and an average of four minutes per objective-test (OT) question.

- Decide whether you want to attempt the OTs first, or after completion of the CR questions. Whichever you choose to do first, ensure that you leave enough time to tackle the remainder.

- Whatever happens, always keep your eye on the clock and **do not over run on any part of any question**!

## Objective-test questions

- **Do not skip any of the material** in the syllabus during revision.

- No credit for workings will be given in these questions. The answer will either be correct (2 marks) or incorrect (0 marks).

- Read each question **very carefully**, as the alternative answer choices will be given based on common mistakes that could be made in attempting the question.

- **Double-check your answer** before committing yourself to it.

- Answer **every** question – if you do not know an answer, you don't lose anything by guessing, but think carefully before you **guess**.

- Remember that there is **only one correct answer to a multiple-choice question**. After you have eliminated the ones that you know to be wrong, if you are still unsure, guess. Only guess after you have **double-checked** that you have only eliminated answers that are **definitely** wrong.

- If you get **completely stuck** with a question, choose your best answer, flag the question for review and **return to it later**.

- The objective –test question types are as follows:
  - **Multiple choice** – choose one answer from a number of given options
  - **Multiple response** – choose more than one an answer from a number of given options
  - **Fill in the blank** – type an answer into a box
  - **Drag and drop** – drag an answer and drop it into place
  - **Drop down list** – choose one answer from a drop down list
  - **Hot spot** – choose one point on an image
  - **Hot area** – choose an area in an image

## Constructed Response questions

- There will be a computational financial statements preparation question and a written analysis question.

- **Computational questions** require the use of a standard format, e.g. statement of profit or loss and other comprehensive income. Be sure that you know all the formats thoroughly before the exam and use the layouts that you see in the answers given in this book and in model answers.

- It is essential to show all your workings in your answer.

- For the **written question** consider how to structure the response and lay it out so as to articulate the answer clearly.

- Stick to the question and **ensure that you explain the reasons** why the numbers have changed.

- Your response should have:
  - a clear structure
  - a brief introduction, a main section and a conclusion.

  It is better to write a little about a lot of different points than a great deal about one or two points.

- You should do everything you can to make things easy for the marker. Cross-reference answers to workings in computational questions and use headings and sub-headings in written answers.

# EXAM SPECIFIC INFORMATION

## THE EXAM

### FORMAT OF THE EXAM

The exam will be in **THREE sections**, and will be a mix of narrative and computational answers. Section A will be 15 objective test questions, each worth 2 marks. Section B will consist of 3 objective case questions, each worth 10 marks and containing 5 questions. Section C will consist of two 20-mark questions

|  |  | Number of marks |
|---|---|---|
| Section A: | Fifteen 2-mark objective test (OT) questions | 30 |
| Section B: | Three 10-mark objective case questions | 30 |
| Section C: | Two 20-mark constructed response questions, covering the interpretation and preparation of financial statements for a single entity or a group | 40 |
|  |  | ——— |
|  |  | 100 |

The exam will contain 110 marks of exam content. Of this, 100 marks contribute to the student result and 10 marks do not. These 10 marks of exam content are referred to as 'seeded questions' and will either be one OT case (five OT questions based around a single scenario) or 5 single OTs distributed randomly within the exam. Of the exam duration of 3 hours and 20 minutes, 3 hours relate to the 100 marks of exam content which contribute to the student result and 20 minutes relate to the seeded content. Seeded questions are included in the exam for quality assurance and security purposes and ensure that a student's mark is fair and reliable.

Note that:

- The FR exam will have both a discursive and computational element. The questions will therefore include a mix of calculation-based and explanations-based questions.

### PASS MARK

The pass mark for all ACCA Qualification examination papers is 50%.

## DETAILED SYLLABUS, STUDY GUIDE AND CBE SPECIMEN EXAM

The detailed syllabus and study guide written by the ACCA, along with the specimen exam, can be found at:

accaglobal.com/financial-reporting

# KAPLAN'S RECOMMENDED REVISION APPROACH

## QUESTION PRACTICE IS THE KEY TO SUCCESS

Success in professional examinations relies upon you acquiring a firm grasp of the required knowledge at the tuition phase. In order to be able to answer the questions, knowledge is essential.

However, the difference between success and failure often hinges on your exam technique on the day and making the most of the revision phase of your studies.

The **Kaplan study text** is the starting point, designed to provide the underpinning knowledge to tackle all questions. However, in the revision phase, poring over text books is not the answer.

**Kaplan Online knowledge check tests** help you consolidate your knowledge and understanding, and are a useful tool to check whether you remember key topic areas.

**Kaplan pocket notes** are designed to help you quickly revise a topic area, but you then need to practise questions. There is a need to progress to full exam standard questions as soon as possible, and to tie your exam technique and technical knowledge together.

**The importance of question practice cannot be over-emphasised.**

The recommended approach below is designed by expert tutors in the field, in conjunction with their knowledge of the examiner.

The approach taken for the Applied Skills exams is to revise by topic area.

**You need to practise as many questions as possible in the time you have left.**

## OUR AIM

Our aim is to get you to the stage where you can attempt exam standard questions confidently, to time, in a closed book environment, with no supplementary help (i.e. to simulate the real examination experience).

Practising your exam technique on exam standard examination questions, in timed conditions, is also vitally important for you to assess your progress and identify areas of weakness that may need more attention in the final run up to the examination.

In order to achieve this we recognise that initially you may feel the need to practise some questions with open book help and exceed the required time.

The approach below shows you which questions you should use to build up to coping with exam standard question practice, and references to the sources of information available should you need to revisit a topic area in more detail.

Remember that in the real examination, all you have to do is:

- attempt all questions required by the exam
- only spend the allotted time on each question, and
- get them at least 50% right!

Try and practise this approach on every question you attempt from now to the real exam.

## EXAMINER COMMENTS

We have included some of the examiner's comments to the examination questions in this kit for you to see the main pitfalls that students fall into with regard to technical content.

However, too many times in the general section of the report, the examiner comments that students had failed due to poor time management where students had shown signs of 'spending too much time on an earlier question and clearly rushing the answer to a subsequent question'.

**Good exam technique is vital.**

# THE KAPLAN FINANCIAL REPORTING REVISION PLAN

## Stage 1: Assess areas of strengths and weaknesses

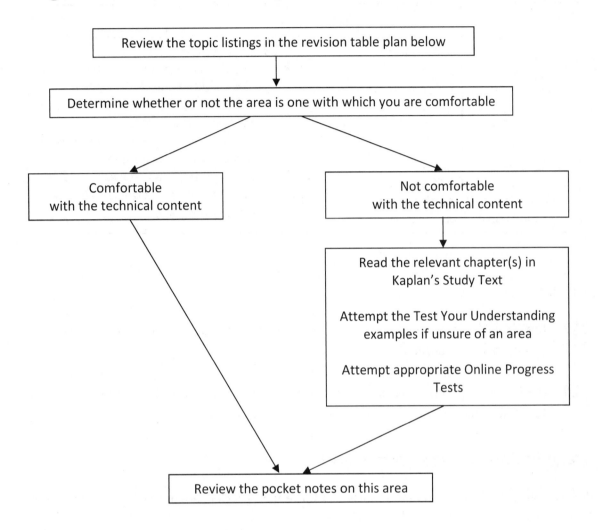

## Stage 2: Practise questions

Follow the order of revision of topics as recommended in the revision table plan below and attempt the questions in the order suggested.

Try to avoid referring to text books, notes or the model answer until you have completed your attempt.

Try to answer the question in the allotted time.

Review your attempt with the model answer and assess how much of the answer you achieved in the allocated exam time.

Fill in the self-assessment box below and decide on your best course of action.

Note that:

  The 'footsteps questions' give guidance on exam techniques and how you should have approached the question.

  The 'clock questions' have an online debrief where a tutor talks you through the exam technique and approach to that question and works the question in full.

## Stage 3: Final pre-exam revision

We recommend that you **attempt at least one three hour mock examination** containing a set of previously unseen exam standard questions.

It is important that you get a feel for the breadth of coverage of a real exam without advanced knowledge of the topic areas covered – just as you will expect to see on the real exam day.

Ideally this mock should be sat in timed, closed book, real exam conditions and could be:

- a mock examination offered by your tuition provider, and/or

- the exam papers in the back of this exam kit, and/or

- the last released examination paper (available shortly afterwards on MyKaplan with 'enhanced walk through answers' and a full 'tutor debrief').

## KAPLAN'S DETAILED REVISION PLAN

| Topic | Study Text Chapter | Pocket note Chapter | Questions to attempt | Tutor guidance | Date attempted | Self assessment |
|---|---|---|---|---|---|---|
| Consolidated statement of financial position | 17/19 | 17/19 | 141–150<br>316–320<br>374, 375<br>379, 384, 389 | Practise the Kaplan 5 working approach. Ensure you get the easy marks available in the question from adding the parent and subsidiary assets and liabilities together. | | |
| Consolidated statement of profit or loss and other comprehensive income | 18/19 | 18/19 | 151–154<br>156–162<br>321–325<br>376, 378, 380<br>383, 386 | Watch the dates carefully – is there a mid-year acquisition? If so you have to time apportion the subsidiary company results when adding the parent and subsidiary together. | | |
| Consolidated statement of profit or loss and other comprehensive income and statement of financial position | | | 373<br>377<br>385<br>387 | Set up your proformas first and get the easy marks by adding the parent and subsidiary results together – then complete the 5 standard statement of financial position workings before moving on to complete the statement of profit or loss. | | |
| Disposal of subsidiaries | 20 | 20 | 182–185<br>330 | Ensure you familiarise yourself with the workings related to calculating a profit/loss on disposal. | | |

| Topic | Study Text Chapter | Pocket note Chapter | Questions to attempt | Tutor guidance | Date attempted | Self assessment |
|---|---|---|---|---|---|---|
| Accounting standards: | | | | | | |
| Non-current assets (IAS 16, IAS 20, IAS 23, IAS 38, IAS 40, IFRS 5) | 2 | 2 | 1–22, 30–36<br>221–230<br>231–235<br>236–245 | Be clear on initial recognition rules and subsequent measurement for PPE, intangible assets and investment properties. Ensure you know the definition of borrowing costs and the 3 recognition and 2 derecognition criteria. Ensure you understand how to deal with assets held for sale. | | |
| IAS 36 | 4 | 4 | 23–29<br>246–250 | Learn the impairment test proforma and the cash generating unit write down rules. | | |
| Framework | 6/7 | 6/7 | 37–58 | Learn the key definitions and be able to apply them to various situations | | |
| IAS 2, IAS 8, IAS 41, IFRS 13 | 8 | 8 | 59–62<br>69–75<br>256–265 | Each standard is relatively small, but it is key that you learn definitions and the specific rules relating to each. | | |
| IFRS 16 | 9 | 9 | 76–86<br>266–275 | Be sure that you are able to construct a liability table. | | |

| Topic | Study Text Chapter | Pocket note Chapter | Questions to attempt | Tutor guidance | Date attempted | Self assessment |
|---|---|---|---|---|---|---|
| IAS 32/IFRS 7/IFRS 9 | 10 | 10 | 87–96 276–285 | Amortised cost is the core area of financial liabilities here. Make sure you can deal with loans issued at a discount & redeemed at a premium. You will also need an awareness of the categories of financial asset in accordance with IFRS 9 and the accounting treatment for them. | | |
| IAS 21 | 11 | 11 | 97–101 286–288 | Examine the initial and subsequent treatment, in addition to the rules for unsettled transactions. | | |
| IFRS 15 | 12 | 12 | 102–114 291–300 | The different revenue scenarios should be looked at, in particular where revenue is recognised over time. | | |
| IAS 12 | 13 | 13 | 115–118 289–290 | Learn the definition of a temporary difference and practise its application. | | |
| IAS 33 | 14 | 14 | 119–128 301–305 | Learn the formula and apply to share issues. | | |
| IAS 37, IAS 10 | 15 | 15 | 129–140 306–312 | For IAS 37 the recognition rules are very clear – learn the 3 recognition rules. Learn the differences between adjusting and non-adjusting events. | | |

| Topic | Study Text Chapter | Pocket note Chapter | Questions to attempt | Tutor guidance | Date attempted | Self assessment |
|---|---|---|---|---|---|---|
| Preparation of individual company financial statements | 1, 23 | 1 | 351–367 | You have to learn the accounting standards examinable first and then apply your knowledge to these recommended questions. | | |
| Ratio interpretation | 21 | 21 | 186–210 331–340 390–400 | Learn the ratio calculations and practise identifying where you pull the information for the formula out of the financial statements. | | |
| Statement of cash flows | 22 | 22 | 211–220 341–350 368–372 | Learn the proforma. Start with calculations in questions 201, 203, and 204 before moving on to analysing cash flows in 221 and 226. | | |

# TECHNICAL UPDATE

There were no additions or amendments to the Financial Reporting syllabus from 2017 to 2018, other than the withdrawal of the direct method for preparation of a statement of cash flows.

# Section 1

# OBJECTIVE TEST QUESTIONS – SECTION A

## CONCEPTUAL FRAMEWORK/INTERNATIONAL FINANCIAL REPORTING STANDARDS

1   IAS 16 *Property, Plant and Equipment* requires an asset to be measured at cost on its original recognition in the financial statements. EW used its own staff, assisted by contractors when required, to construct a new warehouse for its own use.

**Identify whether the costs listed below should be capitalised or expensed.**

|  | Capitalise | Expense |
| --- | --- | --- |
| Clearance of the site prior to commencement of construction |  |  |
| Professional surveyor fees for managing the construction work |  |  |
| EW's own staff wages for time spent working on construction |  |  |
| A proportion of EW's administration costs, based on staff time spent |  |  |

2   On 1 July 20X4, Experimenter opened a chemical reprocessing plant. The plant was due to be active for five years until 30 June 20X9, when it would be decommissioned. At 1 July 20X4, the costs of decommissioning the plant were estimated to be $4 million in 5 years' time. Experimenter considers that a discount rate of 12% is appropriate for the calculation of a present value, and the discount factor at 12% for five years is 0.567.

**What is the total charge to the statement of profit or loss in respect of the decommissioning for the year ended 30 June 20X5?**

A   $453,600

B   $725,760

C   $800,000

D   $2,268,000

**3**    An entity purchased property for $6 million on 1 July 20X3. The land element of the purchase was $1 million. The expected life of the building was 50 years and its residual value nil. On 30 June 20X5 the property was revalued to $7 million, of which the land element was $1.24 million and the buildings $5.76 million.  On 30 June 20X7, the property was sold for $6.8 million.

**What is the gain on disposal of the property that would be reported in the statement of profit or loss for the year to 30 June 20X7?**

A    Gain $40,000

B    Loss $200,000

C    Gain $1,000,000

D    Gain $1,240,000

**4**    A manufacturing entity receives a grant of $1m towards the purchase of a machine on 1 January 20X3. The grant will be repayable if the entity sells the asset within 4 years, which it does not intend to do. The asset has a useful life of 5 years.

**What is the deferred income liability balance at 30 June 20X3?**

$_____ ,000

**5**    On 1 January 20X1 Sty received $1m from the local government on the condition that they employ at least 100 staff each year for the next 4 years. Due to an economic downturn and reduced consumer demand on 1 January 20X2, Sty no longer needed to employ any more staff and the conditions of the grant required full repayment.

**What should be recorded in the financial statements on 1 January 20X2?**

A    Reduce deferred income balance by $750,000

B    Reduce deferred income by $750,000 and recognise a loss of $250,000

C    Reduce deferred income by $1,000,000

D    Reduce deferred income by $1,000,000 and recognise a gain of $250,000

**6**    **Which of the following properties owned by Scoop would be classified as an investment property?**

A    A property that had been leased to a tenant but which is no longer required and is now being held for resale

B    Land purchased for its investment potential.  Planning permission has not been obtained for building construction of any kind

C    A new office building used as Scoop's head office, purchased specifically in order to exploit its capital gains potential

D    A stately home used for executive training

**7**     During the current year an entity had in place $1 million of 6% loan finance and $2 million of 8% loan finance.

It constructed a new factory which cost $600,000 and this was funded out of the existing loan finance. The factory took 8 months to complete.

**To the nearest thousand, what borrowing costs should be capitalised?**

A     $44,000

B     $29,000

C     $28,000

D     $24,000

**8**     **Which of the following statements is correct?**

**Statement 1** If the revaluation model is used for property, plant and equipment, revaluations must subsequently be made with sufficient regularity to ensure that the carrying amount does not differ materially from the fair value at each reporting date.

**Statement 2** When an item of property, plant and equipment is revalued, there is no requirement that the entire class of assets to which the item belongs must be revalued.

|       | Statement 1 | Statement 2 |
|-------|-------------|-------------|
| True  |             |             |
| False |             |             |

**9**     **Which TWO of the following items should be capitalised within the initial carrying amount of an item of plant?**

A     Cost of transporting the plant to the factory

B     Cost of installing a new power supply required to operate the plant

C     A deduction to reflect the estimated realisable value

D     Cost of a three-year maintenance agreement

E     Cost of a three-week training course for staff to operate the plant

**10**    Tibet acquired a new office building on 1 October 20X4.  Its initial carrying amount consisted of:

|                        | $000   |
|------------------------|--------|
| Land                   | 2,000  |
| Building structure     | 10,000 |
| Air conditioning system | 4,000  |
|                        | 16,000 |

The estimated lives of the building structure and air conditioning system are 25 years and 10 years respectively.

When the air conditioning system is due for replacement, it is estimated that the old system will be dismantled and sold for $500,000.

Depreciation is time-apportioned where appropriate.

**At what amount will the office building be shown in Tibet's statement of financial position as at 31 March 20X5?**

A    $15,625,000

B    $15,250,000

C    $15,585,000

D    $15,600,000

11    The following trial balance extract relates to a property which is owned by Veeton as at 1 April 20X4.

|  | Dr | Cr |
|---|---|---|
|  | $000 | $000 |
| Property at cost (20 year original life) | 12,000 | |
| Accumulated depreciation as at 1 April 20X4 | | 3,600 |

On 1 October 20X4, following a sustained increase in property prices, Veeton revalued its property to $10.8 million.

**What will be the depreciation charge in Veeton's statement of profit or loss for the year ended 31 March 20X5?**

A    $540,000

B    $570,000

C    $700,000

D    $800,000

12    **Which TWO of the following statements about IAS 20 *Accounting for Government Grants and Disclosure of Government Assistance* are true?**

A    A government grant related to the purchase of an asset must be deducted from the carrying amount of the asset in the statement of financial position.

B    A government grant related to the purchase of an asset should be recognised in profit or loss over the life of the asset.

C    Free marketing advice provided by a government department is excluded from the definition of government grants.

D    Any required repayment of a government grant received in an earlier reporting period is treated as prior period adjustment.

**13** Smithson Co purchased a new building with a 50-year life for $10 million on 1 January 20X3. On 30 June 20X5, Smithson Co moved out of the building and rented it out to third parties on a short-term lease. Smithson Co uses the fair value model for investment properties. At 30 June 20X5 the fair value of the property was $11 million and at 31 December 20X5 it was $11.5 million.

**What is the total net amount to be recorded in the statement of profit or loss in respect of the office for the year ended 31 December 20X5?**

A    Net income $400,000

B    Net income $500,000

C    Net income $1,900,000

D    Net income $2,000,000

**14** Gilbert took out a $7.5 million 10% loan on 1 January 20X6 to build a new warehouse during the year. Construction of the warehouse began on 1 February 20X6 and was completed on 30 November 20X6. As not all the funds were needed immediately, Gilbert invested $2 million in 4.5% bonds from 1 January to 1 May 20X6.

**What are the total borrowing costs to be capitalised in respect of the warehouse?**

$_____

**15** Croft acquired a building with a 40-year life for its investment potential for $8 million on 1 January 20X3. At 31 December 20X3, the fair value of the property was estimated at $9 million with costs to sell estimated at $200,000.

**If Croft Co uses the fair value model for investment properties, what gain should be recorded in the statement of profit or loss for the year ended 31 December 20X3?**

$_____ ,000

**16** **Which of the following CANNOT be recognised as an intangible non-current asset in GHK's consolidated statement of financial position at 30 September 20X1?**

A    GHK spent $132,000 developing a new type of product. In June 20X1 management worried that it would be too expensive to fund. The finances to complete the project came from a cash injection from a benefactor received in November 20X1.

B    GHK purchased a subsidiary during the year. During the fair value exercise, it was found that the subsidiary had a brand name with an estimated value of $50,000, but had not been recognised by the subsidiary as it was internally generated.

C    GHK purchased a brand name from a competitor on 1 November 20X0, for $65,000.

D    GHK spent $21,000 during the year on the development of a new product, after management concluded it would be viable in November 20X0. The product is being launched on the market on 1 December 20X1 and is expected to be profitable.

**17** Which of the following could be classified as development expenditure in M's statement of financial position as at 31 March 20Y0 according to IAS 38 *Intangible Assets?*

A    $120,000 spent on developing a prototype and testing a new type of propulsion system. The project needs further work on it as the system is currently not viable.

B    A payment of $50,000 to a local university's engineering faculty to research new environmentally friendly building techniques.

C    $35,000 developing an electric bicycle. This is near completion and the product will be launched soon. As this project is first of its kind it is expected to make a loss.

D    $65,000 developing a special type of new packaging for a new energy-efficient light bulb. The packaging is expected to reduce M's distribution costs by $35,000 a year.

**18** Which TWO of the following factors are reasons why key staff cannot be capitalised as an intangible asset by an entity?

A    They do not provide expected future economic benefits

B    They cannot be controlled by an entity

C    Their value cannot be measured reliably

D    They are not separable from the business as a whole

**19** Amco Co carries out research and development. In the year ended 30 June 20X5 Amco Co incurred total costs in relation to project X of $750,000, spending the same amount each month up to 30 April 20X5, when the project was completed. The product produced by the project went on sale from 31 May 20X5.

The project had been confirmed as feasible on 1 January 20X5, and the product produced by the project was expected to have a useful life of five years.

**What is the carrying amount of the development expenditure asset as at 30 June 20X5?**

A    $295,000

B    $725,000

C    $300,000

D    $0

**20** Sybil has acquired a subsidiary Basil in the current year.

Basil has a brand which has been reliably valued by Sybil at $500,000, and a customer list which Sybil has been unable to value.

**Which of these describes how Sybil should treat these intangible assets of Basil in their consolidated Financial Statements?**

A    They should be included in goodwill.

B    The brand should be capitalised as a separate intangible asset, whereas the customer list should be included within goodwill.

C    Both the brand and the customer list should be capitalised as separate intangible assets.

D    The customer list should be capitalised as a separate intangible asset, whereas the brand should be included within goodwill.

21    Dempsey Co owns a pharmaceutical business with a year-end of 30 September 20X4. Dempsey Co commenced the development stage of a new drug on 1 January 20X4. $40,000 per month was incurred until the project was completed on 30 June 20X4, when the drug went into immediate production. The directors became confident of the project's success on 1 March 20X4. The drug has an estimated life span of five years and time-apportionment is used by Dempsey where applicable.

**What amount will Dempsey charge to profit or loss for development costs, including any amortisation, for the year ended 30 September 20X4?**

A    $12,000

B    $98,667

C    $48,000

D    $88,000

22    **Which of the following statements relating to intangible assets is true?**

A    All intangible assets must be carried at amortised cost or at an impaired amount, they cannot be revalued upwards.

B    The development of a new process which is not expected to increase sales revenues may still be recognised as an intangible asset.

C    Expenditure on the prototype of a new engine cannot be classified as an intangible asset because the prototype has physical substance.

D    Impairment losses for a cash generating unit are first applied to goodwill and then to other intangible assets before being applied to tangible assets.

**The following information is to be used for questions 23 and 24.**

A division of an entity has the following balances in its financial statements:

Goodwill            $700,000

Plant               $950,000

Building            $2,300,000

Intangibles         $800,000

Other net assets    $430,000

Following a period of losses, the recoverable amount of the division is deemed to be $4 million. A recent valuation of the building showed that the building has a market value of $2.5 million. The other net assets are at their recoverable amount. The entity uses the cost model for valuing building and plant.

23    **To the nearest thousand, what is the balance on the building following the impairment review?**

A    $2,300,000

B    $2,500,000

C    $2,027,000

D    $1,776,000

**24** **To the nearest thousand, what is the balance on plant following the impairment review?**

A $862,000

B $837,000

C $689,000

D $261,000

**25** A vehicle was involved in an accident exactly halfway through the year. The vehicle cost $10,000 and had a remaining life of 10 years at the start of the year. Following the accident, the expected present value of cash flows associated with the vehicle was $3,400 and the fair value less costs to sell was $6,500.

**What is the recoverable amount of the vehicle following the accident?**

$_____

**26** The net assets of Fyngle, a cash generating unit (CGU), are:

| | $ |
|---|---|
| Property, plant and equipment | 200,000 |
| Allocated goodwill | 50,000 |
| Product patent | 20,000 |
| Net current assets (at net realisable value) | 30,000 |
| | 300,000 |

As a result of adverse publicity, Fyngle has a recoverable amount of only $200,000.

**What would be the value of Fyngle's property, plant and equipment after the allocation of the impairment loss?**

A $154,545

B $170,000

C $160,000

D $133,333

**27** **Which of the following is NOT an indicator of impairment?**

A Advances in the technological environment in which an asset is employed have an adverse impact on its future use.

B An increase in interest rates which increases the discount rate an entity uses.

C The carrying amount of an entity's net assets is higher than the entity's number of shares in issue multiplied by its share price.

D The estimated net realisable value of inventory has been reduced due to fire damage although this value is greater than its carrying amount.

**28**  Riley acquired a non-current asset on 1 October 20X9 at a cost of $100,000 which had a useful life of ten years and a nil residual value. The asset had been correctly depreciated up to 30 September 20Y4. At that date the asset was damaged and an impairment review was performed. On 30 September 20Y4, the fair value of the asset less costs to sell was $30,000 and the expected future cash flows were $8,500 per annum for the next five years. The current cost of capital is 10% and a five year annuity of $1 per annum at 10% would have a present value of $3.79.

**What amount would be charged to profit or loss for the impairment of this asset for the year ended 30 September 20Y4?**

$_____

**29**  Metric owns an item of plant which has a carrying amount of $248,000 as at 1 April 20X3. It is being depreciated at 12.5% per annum on a reducing balance basis.

The plant is used to manufacture a specific product which has been suffering a slow decline in sales.  Metric has estimated that the plant will be retired from use on 31 March 20X7.

The estimated net cash flows from the use of the plant and their present values are:

|                         | Net cash flows | Present values |
|-------------------------|---------------:|---------------:|
|                         | $              | $              |
| Year to 31 March 20X5   | 120,000        | 109,200        |
| Year to 31 March 20X6   | 80,000         | 66,400         |
| Year to 31 March 20X7   | 52,000         | 39,000         |
|                         | ———            | ———            |
|                         | 252,000        | 214,600        |

On 1 April 20X4, Metric had an offer from a rival to purchase the plant for $200,000.

**At what value should the plant appear in Metric's statement of financial position as at 31 March 20X4?**

$_____

**30**  As at 30 September 20X3 the value of Dune's property in its statement of financial position comprised:

| | |
|---|---|
| Cost (useful life 15 years) | $45 million |
| Accumulated depreciation | $6 million |

On 1 April 20X4, Dune decided to sell the property.  The property is being marketed by a property agent at a price of $42 million, which was considered a reasonably achievable price at that date. The expected costs to sell have been agreed at $1 million.  Recent market transactions suggest that actual sale prices achieved for this type of property in the current market conditions are 10% less than the price at which they are marketed.

At 30 September 20X4 the property has not been sold.

**At what value should the property be reported in Dune's statement of financial position as at 30 September 20X4?**

A       $36 million

B       $37.5 million

C       $36.8 million

D       $42 million

31      BN has an asset that was classified as held for sale at 31 March 20X2. The asset had a carrying amount of $900 and a fair value of $800. The cost of disposal was estimated to be $50.

**According to IFRS 5 *Non-current Assets Held for Sale and Discontinued Operations*, which value should be used for the asset as at 31 March 20X2?**

A       $750

B       $800

C       $850

D       $900

32      **According to IFRS 5 *Non-current Assets Held for Sale and Discontinued Operations* which of the following represent criteria for an asset to be classified as held for sale?**

(i)      Available for immediate sale in its present condition.

(ii)     Sale is highly probable.

(iii)    The sale is expected to be completed within the next month.

(iv)    The asset is being marketed at a reasonable price.

A       All of the above

B       (i), (ii) and (iii)

C       (i), (ii) and (iv)

D       (ii), (iii) and (iv)

33      **According to IFRS 5 *Non-current Assets Held for Sale and Discontinued Operations* which of the following amounts in respect of a discontinued operation must be shown on the face of the statement of profit or loss?**

|  | Shown on the face of the statement of profit or loss | Not shown |
|---|---|---|
| Revenue |  |  |
| Gross profit |  |  |
| Profit after tax |  |  |

**34**   Rural has the following two lines of business that have been disposed of in the year:

Sector X operated in Country A.  Rural has no other operations in Country A, and Sector X produced 0.5% of the total revenue of Rural.

Sector Y operated in the same country as the Rural head office.  It sold a different product from the other components of Rural, and contributed 10% of the total revenue of Rural Co.

**Which of these sectors, if either, should be disclosed as a discontinued operation in the current year?**

|  | **Discontinued operation Yes/No** |
|---|---|
| Sector X |  |
| Sector Y |  |

**35**   **What is the primary reason why discontinued operations are presented separately within financial statements?**

   A     To show an accurate valuation of the business

   B     To enhance the predictive nature of financial statements

   C     To make the financial statements easier to understand

   D     So the financial statements are verifiable

**36**   At 1 April 20X4, Tilly owned a property with a carrying amount of $800,000 which had a remaining estimated life of 16 years, and was carried under the cost model.  On 1 October 20X4, Tilly decided to sell the property and correctly classified it as being 'held-for-sale'.  A property agent reported that the property's fair value less costs to sell at 1 October 20X4 was expected to be $790,500 which had not changed at 31 March 20X5.

**What should be the carrying amount of the property in Tilly's statement of financial position as at 31 March 20X5?**

   A     $775,000

   B     $790,500

   C     $765,000

   D     $750,000

**37**   **Which of the following gives the best description of the objectives of financial statements as set out by the International Accounting Standards Board's (The Board's) Conceptual Framework for Financial Reporting?**

   A     To fairly present the financial position and performance of an enterprise.

   B     To fairly present the financial position, performance and changes in financial position of an enterprise.

   C     To provide information about the financial position and performance of an enterprise that is useful to a wide range of users in making economic decisions.

   D     To provide information about the financial position, performance and changes in financial position of an enterprise that is useful to a wide range of users in making economic decisions.

**38** The International Accounting Standards Board's Conceptual Framework for Financial Reporting defines a liability as:

A an amount owed to another entity

B a present obligation arising as a result of past events, the settlement of which is expected to result in an outflow of economic benefits

C expenditure that has been incurred but not yet charged to the statement of profit or loss

D an obligation that may arise in the future

**39** The International Accounting Standards Board's Conceptual Framework for Financial Reporting lists two fundamental qualitative characteristics of financial statements, relevance and faithful representation.

**Place the qualities listed alongside the appropriate qualitative characteristic.**

|  | Faithful representation | Relevance |
|---|---|---|
| Completeness |  |  |
| Predictive value |  |  |
| Neutrality |  |  |

**40** The International Accounting Standards Board's Conceptual Framework for Financial Reporting identifies qualitative characteristics of financial statements.

**Which TWO of the following characteristics are NOT fundamental qualitative characteristics according to the *IASB's The Conceptual Framework for Financial Reporting?***

A Relevance

B Reliability

C Faithful representation

D Comparability

**41** **Match the element to the correct definition according to the International Accounting Standards Board's Conceptual Framework for Financial Reporting?**

| Element | Definition |
|---|---|
| Expense | A resource controlled by the entity as a result of past events and from which future economic benefits are expected to flow to the entity. |
| Liability | The residual interest in the assets of the entity after deducting all its liabilities. |
| Asset | A present obligation of the entity arising from past events, the settlement of which is expected to result in an outflow from the entity of resources embodying economic benefits. |
| Equity | Decrease in economic benefits during the accounting period in the form of outflows or depletions of assets or incurrences of liabilities. |

**42** Which of the following explains the value that relevant information contains?

A    Instructive value

B    Fair value

C    Confirmatory value

D    Approximate value

**43** Which of the following is an example of following the principle of faithful representation?

A    Showing lease payments as a rental expense

B    Being prudent by recording the entire amount of a convertible loan as a liability

C    Creating a provision for staff relocation costs as part of a planned restructuring

D    Recording a sale and repurchase transaction with a bank as a loan rather than a sale

**44** The International Accounting Standards Board's Conceptual Framework for Financial Reporting defines an asset as:

A    A resource controlled by an entity which is capable of generating independent cash flows.

B    A resource controlled by an entity as a result of past events, from which future economic benefits are expected.

C    A resource owned by an entity as a result of past events, from which future economic benefits are expected.

D    A resource capable of generating income for the entity.

**45** Which of the following criteria need to be satisfied in order for an element to be recognised within the financial statements?

(i)    It meets the definition of an element of the financial statements.

(ii)   It is probable that future economic benefits will flow to or from the enterprise.

(iii)  It is certain that future economic benefits will flow to or from the enterprise.

(iv)   The item has a cost or value.

(v)    The item has a cost or value that can be reliably measured.

A    (i), (ii) and (v)

B    (i), (iii) and (v)

C    (i), (ii) and (iv)

D    (i), (iii) and (iv)

**46**   **Which description defines information that is relevant to users of financial information?**

A   Information that is free from error, bias and is a faithful representation of events

B   Information that has been prudently prepared

C   Information that is comparable from one period to the next

D   Information that influences the decisions of users

**47**   **Which description is most representative of the accounting framework used under IFRS Standards?**

|                                   | True | False |
| --------------------------------- | ---- | ----- |
| It is a principles-based framework |      |       |
| It is a legal obligation          |      |       |

**48**   **Which of the advantages below is NOT a likely advantage of the global harmonisation of accounting standards?**

A   Greater comparability between different firms

B   Greater ease for preparing consolidated financial statements

C   Easier for large international accounting firms

D   Greater compatibility with legal systems

**49**   **Which THREE of the following are advantages of applying a principles-based framework of accounting rather than a rules-based framework?**

A   It avoids 'fire-fighting', where standards are developed in responses to specific problems as they arise

B   It allows preparers and auditors to deal with complex transactions which may not be specifically covered by an accounting standard

C   Principles-based standards are thought to be harder to circumvent

D   A set of rules is given which attempts to cover every eventuality

E   It is easier to prove non-compliance

**50**   **Which of the following is NOT a purpose of the International Accounting Standards Board's (the Board's) Conceptual Framework?**

A   To assist the Board in the preparation and review of IFRS Standards.

B   To assist auditors in forming an opinion on whether financial statements comply with IFRS Standards.

C   To assist in determining the treatment of items not covered by an existing IFRS Standards.

D   To be authoritative where a specific IFRS Standard conflicts with the Conceptual Framework.

**51** Financial statements represent transactions in words and numbers. To be useful, financial information must represent faithfully these transactions in terms of how they are reported.

**Which of the following accounting treatments would be an example of faithful representation?**

A   Capitalising development costs as an intangible asset

B   Including a convertible loan note in equity on the basis that the holders are likely to choose the equity option on conversion

C   Continuing to recognise factored trade receivables sold with recourse

D   Treating redeemable preference shares as equity

**52** Faithful representation is a fundamental characteristic of useful information within the International Accounting Standards Board's Conceptual Framework for financial reporting.

**Which of the following treatments applies the principle of faithful representation?**

A   Reporting a transaction based on its legal status rather than its economic substance.

B   Excluding a subsidiary from consolidation because its activities are not compatible with those of the rest of the group.

C   Recording the whole of the net proceeds from the issue of a loan note which is potentially convertible to equity shares as a liability.

D   Allocating part of the sales proceeds of a motor vehicle to interest received even though it was sold with interest-free finance.

**53** The International Accounting Standards Board's Conceptual Framework for Financial Reporting defines recognition as the process of incorporating within the financial statements an item which meets the definition of an element and satisfies certain criteria.

**Which of the following elements should be recognised in the financial statements of an entity in the manner described?**

A   As a non-current liability: a provision for possible hurricane damage to property for an entity located in an area which experiences a high incidence of hurricanes.

B   In equity: irredeemable preference shares.

C   As a trade receivable: an amount of $10,000 due from a customer which has been sold (factored) to a finance company with no recourse to the seller.

D   In revenue: the whole of the proceeds from the sale of an item of manufactured plant which has to be maintained by the seller for three years as part of the sale agreement.

**54** Increasingly the International Accounting Standards Board is requiring or allowing current cost to be used in many areas of financial reporting.

Drexler acquired an item of plant on 1 October 20X2 at a cost of $500,000. It is being depreciated over five years, using straight-line depreciation and an estimated residual value of 10% of its historical cost or current cost as appropriate. As at 30 September 20X4, the manufacturer of the plant still makes the same item of plant and its current price is $600,000.

**What is the correct carrying amount to be shown in the statement of financial position of Drexler as at 30 September 20X4 under historical cost and current cost?**

|   | Historical cost | Current cost |
|---|---|---|
|   | $ | $ |
| A | 320,000 | 600,000 |
| B | 320,000 | 384,000 |
| C | 300,000 | 600,000 |
| D | 300,000 | 384,000 |

**55** Tynan's year end is 30 September 20X4 and a number of potential liabilities have been identified.

**Which TWO of the following should Tynan recognise as liabilities as at 30 September 20X4?**

A The signing of a non-cancellable contract in September 20X4 to supply goods in the following year on which, due to a pricing error, a loss will be made.

B The cost of a reorganisation which was approved by the board in August 20X4 but has not yet been implemented, communicated to interested parties or announced publicly.

C An amount of deferred tax relating to the gain on the revaluation of a property during the current year. Tynan has no intention of selling the property in the foreseeable future.

D The balance on the warranty provision which relates to products for which there are no outstanding claims and whose warranties had expired by 30 September 20X4.

**56 Which of the following items should be recognised as an asset in the statement of financial position of an entity?**

A A skilled and efficient workforce which has been very expensive to train. Some of these staff are still employed by the entity.

B A highly lucrative contract signed during the year which is due to commence shortly after the year-end.

C A government grant relating to the purchase of an item of plant several years ago which has a remaining life of four years.

D A receivable from a customer which has been sold (factored) to a finance company. The finance company has full recourse to the entity for any losses.

**57** Comparability is identified as an enhancing qualitative characteristic in the International Accounting Standards Board's Conceptual Framework for Financial Reporting.

**Which of the following does NOT improve comparability?**

A Restating the financial statements of previous years when there has been a change of accounting policy.

B Prohibiting changes of accounting policy unless required by an IFRS Standard or to give more relevant and reliable information.

C Disclosing discontinued operations separately in financial statements.

D Applying an entity's current accounting policy to a transaction which an entity has not engaged in before.

**58** **Which of the following criticisms does NOT apply to historical cost financial statements during a period of rising prices?**

A They contain mixed values, some items are at current values, some at out-of-date values

B They are difficult to verify as transactions could have happened many years ago

C They understate assets and overstate profit

D They overstate gearing in the statement of financial position

**59** **According to IAS 8 *Accounting Policies, Changes in Accounting Estimates and Errors*, how should a material error in the previous financial reporting period be accounted for in the current period?**

A By making an adjustment in the financial statements of the current period through the statement of profit or loss, and disclosing the nature of the error in a note.

B By making an adjustment in the financial statements of the current period as a movement on reserves, and disclosing the nature of the error in a note.

C By restating the comparative amounts for the previous period at their correct value, and disclosing the nature of the error in a note.

D By restating the comparative amounts for the previous period at their correct value, but without the requirement for a disclosure of the nature of the error in a note.

**60** **Which of the following statements regarding IFRS 13 *Fair Value Measurement* is not true?**

A Level 1 inputs are likely to be used without adjustment.

B Level 3 inputs are based on the best information available to market participants and are therefore regarded as providing the most reliable evidence of fair value.

C Level 2 inputs may include quoted prices for similar (but not identical) assets and liabilities in active markets.

D Level 1 inputs comprise quoted prices in active markets for identical assets and liabilities at the reporting date.

**61** Which of these changes would be classified as 'a change in accounting policy' as determined by IAS 8 *Accounting Policies, Changes in Accounting Estimates and Errors*?

A   Increased the allowance for irrecoverable receivables from 5% to 10% of outstanding debts

B   Changed the method of valuing inventory from FIFO to average cost

C   Changed the depreciation of plant and equipment from straight line depreciation to reducing balance depreciation

D   Changed the useful life of motor vehicles from six years to four years

**62** In which TWO of the following situations can a change in accounting policy be made by an entity?

A   If the change is required by an IFRS Standard

B   If the entity thinks that a new accounting policy would be easier to report

C   If a new accounting policy would show more favourable results

D   If a new accounting policy results in more reliable and relevant presentation of events or transactions

**63** According to the International Accounting Standards Board's Conceptual Framework for Financial Reporting which of the measurement bases below can be used by an entity for measuring assets and liabilities shown in its statement of financial position?

|                 | Can be used | Cannot be used |
|-----------------|-------------|----------------|
| Historical cost |             |                |
| Present value   |             |                |
| Realisable value|             |                |

**64** Which of the following statements is true about historical cost financial statements in times of rising prices?

A   Profits will be overstated and assets will be understated

B   The asset values will be overstated

C   Unrecognised gains will be recorded incorrectly

D   Depreciation will be overstated

**65** Which of the following concepts aims to ensure that excess dividends are not paid in times of changing prices?

A   Going concern

B   Amortised cost

C   Faithful representation

D   Capital maintenance

**66** Which of the following is a change in accounting policy and which a change in accounting estimate in accordance with IAS 8 *Accounting Policies, Changes in Accounting Estimates and Errors*?

| | Change in accounting policy | Change in accounting estimate |
|---|---|---|
| Classifying commission earned as revenue in the statement of profit or loss, having previously classified it as other operating income | | |
| Revising the remaining useful life of a depreciable asset | | |

**67** Which of the following would be a change in accounting policy in accordance with IAS 8 *Accounting Policies, Changes in Accounting Estimates and Errors*?

A   Adjusting the financial statements of a subsidiary prior to consolidation as its accounting policies differ from those of its parent.

B   A change to reporting depreciation charges as cost of sales rather than as administrative expenses.

C   Depreciation method changed to reducing balance method rather than straight line.

D   Reducing the value of inventory from cost to net realisable value due to a valid adjusting event after the reporting period.

**68** Isaac is an entity which buys agricultural produce from wholesale suppliers for retail to the general public. It is preparing its financial statements for the year ending 30 September 20X4 and is considering its closing inventory.

**In addition to IAS 2 *Inventories*, which of the following IFRS Standards may be relevant in determining the figure to be included in its financial statements for closing inventories?**

A   IAS 10 *Events After the Reporting Period*

B   IAS 36 *Impairment*

C   IAS 16 *Property, Plant and Equipment*

D   IAS 41 *Agriculture*

**69** To which of the following items does IAS 41 *Agriculture* apply?

(i)   A change in fair value of a herd of animals relating to the unit price of the animals.

(ii)   Logs held in a wood yard.

(iii)   Farm land which is used for growing vegetables.

(iv)   The cost of developing a new type of crop seed which is resistant to tropical diseases.

A   All four

B   (i) only

C   (i) and (ii) only

D   (ii) and (iii) only

**70**   IAS 2 Inventories specifies expenses that should be included in year-end inventory values. **Which THREE of the expenses below are allowable by IAS 2 as expenses that should be included in the cost of finished goods inventories?**

A   Marketing and selling overhead

B   Variable production overhead

C   General management overhead

D   Factory management overhead allocated to production

E   Cost of delivering raw materials to the factory

F   Abnormal increase in overhead charges caused by unusually low production levels due to the exceptionally hot weather.

**71**   Neville has only two items of inventory on hand at its reporting date.

**Item 1** – Materials costing $24,000 bought for processing and assembly for a customer under a 'one off' order which is expected to produce a high profit margin. Since buying this material, the cost price has fallen to $20,000.

**Item 2** – A machine constructed for another customer for a contracted price of $36,000. This has recently been completed at a cost of $33,600. It has now been discovered that in order to meet certain health and safety regulations modifications at an extra cost of $8,400 will be required. The customer has agreed to meet half of the extra cost.

**What should be the total value of these two items of inventory in the statement of financial position?**

$_____

**72**   Mario has incurred the following costs in relation to a unit of inventory:

|                                    | $    |
| ---------------------------------- | ---- |
| Raw materials cost                 | 1.50 |
| Import duties                      | 0.40 |
| Direct labour                      | 0.50 |
| Subcontracted labour costs         | 0.80 |
| Recoverable sales tax              | 0.20 |
| Storage costs                      | 0.05 |
| Production overheads (per unit)    | 0.25 |

There was a problem with the first batch of items produced, so abnormal wastage costs of $0.10 per unit have also been incurred by Mario.

**At what cost should Mario value this inventory in its financial statements?**

A   $3.50

B   $3.45

C   $3.80

D   $3.70

**73** On 30 September 20X4 Razor's closing inventory was counted and valued at its cost of $1 million.

This included some items of inventory which had cost $210,000 and had been damaged in a flood on 15 September 20X4. These are not expected to achieve their normal selling price which is calculated to achieve a gross profit margin of 30%.

The sale of these goods will be handled by an agent who sells them at 80% of the normal selling price and charges Razor a commission of 25%.

**At what value will the closing inventory of Razor be reported in its statement of financial position as at 30 September 20X4?**

$_____

**74** **Identify whether the following items would be accounted for under IAS 41 *Agriculture* or not.**

| | Accounted for under IAS 41 *Agriculture* | Outside the scope of IAS 41 *Agriculture* |
|---|---|---|
| Dairy cattle | | |
| Milk | | |
| Cheese | | |

**75** Magna owned cattle recorded in the financial statements at $10,500 on 1 January 20X4. At 31 December 20X4 the cattle have a fair value of $13,000. If Magna sold the cattle, commission of 2% would be payable.

**What is the correct accounting treatment for the cattle at 31 December 20X4 according to IAS 41 *Agriculture*?**

A    Hold at cost of $10,500

B    Revalue to $13,000, taking gain of $2,500 to the statement of profit or loss

C    Revalue to $13,000, taking gain of $2,500 to the revaluation surplus

D    Revalue to $12,740, taking gain of $2,240 to the statement of profit or loss

**76** During the year ended 30 September 20X4 Hyper entered into two lease transactions.

On 1 October 20X3, Hyper made a payment of $90,000 being the first of five equal annual payments under a lease for an item of plant. The lease has an implicit interest rate of 10% and the present value of the total lease payments on 1 October 20X3 was $340,000.

On 1 January 20X4, Hyper made a payment of $18,000 for a one-year lease of an item of equipment.

**What amount in total would be charged to Hyper's statement of profit or loss for the year ended 30 September 20X4 in respect of the above transactions?**

A    $108,000

B    $111,000

C    $106,500

D    $115,500

**77**  Z entered into a five year lease agreement on 1 November 20X2, paying $10,975 per annum, commencing on 31 October 20X3. The present value of the lease payments was $45,000 and the interest rate implicit in the lease was 7%.

**What is the amount to be shown within non-current liabilities at 31 October 20X3?**

    A    $26,200

    B    $28,802

    C    $37,175

    D    $36,407

**78**  IFRS 16 *Leases* permits certain assets to be exempt from the recognition treatment for right-of-use assets. Which of the following assets leased to an entity would be permitted to be exempt?

    A    A used motor vehicle with an original cost of $15,000 and a current fair value of $700, leased for 24 months

    B    A new motor vehicle with a cost of $15,000, leased for 24 months

    C    A new motor vehicle with a cost of $15,000, leased for 24 months, to be rented to customers on a daily rental basis

    D    A new motor vehicle with a cost of $15,000, leased for 12 months

**79**  On 1 January 20X3 Rabbit acquires a new machine with an estimated useful life of 6 years under the following agreement:

An initial payment of $13,760 will be payable immediately

5 further annual payments of $20,000 will be due, commencing 1 January 20X3

The interest rate implicit in the lease is 8%

The present value of the lease payments, excluding the initial payment, is $86,240

**What will be recorded in Rabbit's financial statements at 31 December 20X4 in respect of the lease liability?**

| | Finance cost | Non-current liability | Current liability |
|---|---|---|---|
| A | 4,123 | 35,662 | 20,000 |
| B | 5,299 | 51,539 | 20,000 |
| C | 5,312 | 51,712 | 20,000 |
| D | 5,851 | 43,709 | 15,281 |

**80**  **On 1 April 20X7 Pigeon entered into a five-year lease agreement for a machine with an estimated life of 7 years. Which of the following conditions would require the machine to be depreciated over 7 years?**

    A    Pigeon has the option to extend the lease for two years at a market-rate rental

    B    Pigeon has the option to purchase the asset at market value at the end of the lease

    C    Ownership of the asset passes to Pigeon at the end of the lease period

    D    Pigeon's policy for purchased assets is to depreciate over 7 years

**81** On 1 January 20X4 Badger entered into a lease agreement to lease an item of machinery for 4 years with rentals of $210,000 payable annually in arrears. The asset has a useful life of 5 years and at the end of the lease term legal ownership will pass to Badger. The present value of the lease payments at the inception of the lease was $635,000 and the interest rate implicit in the lease is 12.2%. For the year ended 31 December 20X4 Badger accounted for this lease by recording the payment of $210,000 as an operating expense. This treatment was discovered during 20X5, after the financial statements for 20X4 had been finalised.

**In the statement of changes in equity for the year ended 31 December 20X5 what adjustment will be necessary to retained earnings brought forward?**

A   $5,530 credit

B   $132,530 credit

C   $210,000 debit

D   $Nil

**82** Owl leases an asset with an estimated useful life of 6 years for an initial period of 5 years, and an optional secondary period of 2 years during which a nominal rental will be payable. The present value of the initial period lease payments is $87,000.

**What will be the carrying amount of the asset in Owl's statement of financial position at the end of the second year of the lease?**

$_____

**83** On 1 January 20X6, Sideshow sold a property for its fair value of $2 million, transferring title to the property on that date. Sideshow then leased it back under a 5-year lease, paying $150,000 per annum on 31 December each year. The present value of rentals payable was $599,000 and the interest rate implicit in the lease was 8%. The carrying amount of the property on 1 January 20X6 was $1.6 million and it had a remaining useful life of 20 years.

**What entries would be made in Sideshow's statement of profit or loss for the year ended 31 December 20X6?**

A   Profit on disposal of $280,200, depreciation of $95,840, finance cost of $47,920

B   Profit on disposal of $400,000, rental expense of $150,000

C   Profit on disposal of $400,000, depreciation expense of $95,840, finance cost of $47,920

D   Profit on disposal of $280,200, depreciation of $119,800, finance cost of $47,920

**84** On 1 October 20X3, Fresco acquired an item of plant under a five-year lease agreement. The agreement had an implicit interest rate of 10% and required annual rentals of $6 million to be paid on 30 September each year for five years. The present value of the annual rental payments was $23 million.

**What would be the current liability for the leased plant in Fresco's statement of financial position as at 30 September 20X4?**

A    $19,300,000

B    $4,070,000

C    $5,000,000

D    $3,850,000

**85** **Which of the following would not be included within the initial cost of a right-of-use asset?**

A    Installation cost of the asset

B    Estimated cost of dismantling the asset at the end of the lease period

C    Payments made to the lessor before commencement of the lease

D    Total lease rentals payable under the lease agreement

**86** On 1 January 20X4, Stark entered into a sale and leaseback of its property. When it was sold, the asset had a carrying amount of $6 million and a remaining life of 10 years. Stark sold the asset for $7 million and leased it back on a 10 year lease, paying $1 million on 31 December each year. The lease carried an implicit interest rate of 7%.

**What is the total expense that should be recorded in the statement of profit or loss for the year ended 31 December 20X4?**

$_____ ,000

**87** Viking issues $100,000 5% loan notes on 1 January 20X4, incurring issue costs of $3,000. These loan notes are redeemable at a premium, meaning that the effective rate of interest is 8% per annum.

**What is the finance cost to be shown in the statement of profit or loss for the year ended 31 December 20X5?**

A    $8,240

B    $7,981

C    $7,760

D    $8,000

88  An entity issues 3,000 convertible bonds at the start of year 1 at par.  They have a three year term and a face value of $1,000 per bond.  Interest is payable annually in arrears at 7% per annum.  Each bond is convertible at any time up to maturity into 250 common shares.  When the bonds are issued the prevailing market interest rate for similar debt without conversion options is 9%. The relevant discount factors are shown below.

| Discount factors | 7% | 9% |
|---|---|---|
| Year 1 | 0.933 | 0.914 |
| Year 2 | 0.871 | 0.837 |
| Year 3 | 0.813 | 0.766 |

**How is this initially recorded between the debt and equity elements?**

| | Debt element | Equity element |
|---|---|---|
| A | $2,988,570 | $11,430 |
| B | $2,826,570 | $173,430 |
| C | $528,570 | $2,471,430 |
| D | $3,000,000 | $Nil |

89  For a debt investment to be held under amortised cost, it must pass two tests. One of these is the contractual cash flow characteristics test.

**What is the other test which must be passed?**

A    The business model test

B    The amortised cost test

C    The fair value test

D    The purchase agreement test

90  **What is the default classification for an equity investment?**

A    Fair value through profit or loss

B    Fair value through other comprehensive income

C    Amortised cost

D    Net proceeds

91  ABC purchased 10,000 shares on 1 September 20X4, making the election to use the alternative treatment under IFRS 9 *Financial Instruments*. The shares cost $3.50 each. Transaction costs associated with the purchase were $500.

At 31 December 20X4, the shares are trading at $4.50 each.

**What is the gain to be recognised on these shares for the year ended 31 December 20X4?**

$_____

**92** DEF purchased 15,000 shares in KMH Co on 1 August 20X6 at a cost of $6.50 each. Transaction costs on the purchase amounted to $1,500.

At the year-end 30 September 20X6, these shares are now worth $7.75 each.

**Select the correct gain and the place it will be recorded.**

| Gain |
| --- |
| $17,250 |
| $18,750 |

| Where recorded |
| --- |
| Other comprehensive income |
| Statement of profit or loss |

**93** For which category of financial instruments are transaction costs excluded from the initial value, and instead expensed to profit or loss?

A       Financial liabilities at amortised cost

B       Financial assets at fair value through profit or loss

C       Financial assets at fair value through other comprehensive income

D       Financial assets at amortised cost

**94** On 1 October 20X3, Bertrand issued $10 million convertible loan notes which carry a coupon rate of 5% per annum. The loan notes are redeemable on 30 September 20X6 at par for cash or can be exchanged for equity shares. A similar loan note, without the conversion option, would have required Bertrand to pay an interest rate of 8%.

The present value of $1 receivable at the end of each year, based on discount rates of 5% and 8%, can be taken as:

|  | 5% | 8% |
| --- | --- | --- |
| End of year 1 | 0.95 | 0.93 |
| 2 | 0.91 | 0.86 |
| 3 | 0.86 | 0.79 |

**How much would be recorded in equity in relation to the loan notes?**

$_____ ,000

**95** Wonder issued $10 million 5% loan notes on 1 January 20X9, incurring issue costs of $400,000. The loan notes are redeemable at a premium, giving them an effective interest rate of 8%.

**What expense should be recorded in relation to the loan notes for the year ended 31 December 20X9?**

$_____ ,000

**96**     For each of the financial instruments below, match them to the appropriate accounting treatment.

| Instrument |
| --- |
| Convertible loan notes |
| Equity investments where the entity has an intention to hold long-term and has chosen to apply the alternative treatment |
| Financial liability, not held for trading |
| Equity investments (default position) |

| Treatment |
| --- |
| Fair value through profit or loss |
| Amortised cost |
| Split accounting |
| Fair value through other comprehensive income |

**97**     IAS 21 *The Effects of Changes in Foreign Exchange Rates* defines the term 'functional currency'.

**Which of the following is the correct definition of 'functional currency'?**

A      The currency in which the financial statements are presented

B      The currency of the country where the reporting entity is located

C      The currency that mainly influences sales prices and operating costs

D      The currency of the primary economic environment in which an entity operates

**98**     Sunshine is an entity with a reporting date of 31 December 20X1 and a functional currency of dollars ($).  On 30 June 20X1, it purchased land from overseas at a cost of 30 million dinars. The land is an item of property, plant and equipment and is measured using the cost model.

Exchange rates are as follows:

|  | Dinars: $1 |
| --- | --- |
| As at 30 June 20X1 | 3.0 |
| As at 31 December 20X1 | 2.0 |
| Average rate for year-ended 31 December 20X1 | 2.5 |

The fair value of the land at 31 December 20X1 was 32 million dinars.

**What is the carrying amount of the land as at 31 December 20X1?**

A      $10 million

B      $15 million

C      $12 million

D      $16 million

**99** In relation to IAS 21 *The Effects of Changes in Foreign Exchange Rates*, which of the following statements are true?

(i) Exchange gains and losses arising on the retranslation of monetary items are recognised in other comprehensive income in the period.

(ii) Non-monetary items measured at historical cost in a foreign currency are not retranslated at the reporting date.

(iii) An intangible asset is a non-monetary item.

A  All of the above

B  (ii) and (iii) only

C  (i) and (iii) only

D  (i) and (ii) only

**100** An entity took out a bank loan for 12 million dinars on 1 January 20X1. It repaid 3 million dinars to the bank on 30 November 20X1. The entity has a reporting date of 31 December 20X1 and a functional currency of dollars ($). Exchange rates are as follows:

|  | Dinars: $1 |
|---|---|
| 1 January 20X1 | 6.0 |
| 30 November 20X1 | 5.0 |
| 31 December 20X1 | 5.6 |

**What is the total loss arising (to the nearest $000) on the above transactions in the year ended 31 December 20X1?**

$_____,000

**101** A manufacturing entity buys a machine (an item of property, plant and equipment) for 20 million dinars on 1 January 20X1. The machine is held under the cost model and has a useful life of 20 years. The entity has a reporting date of 31 December 20X1 and a functional currency of dollars ($). Exchange rates are as follows:

|  | Dinars: $1 |
|---|---|
| 1 January 20X1 | 2.0 |
| 31 December 20X1 | 3.0 |
| Average rate for year-ended 31 December 20X1 | 2.5 |

**What is the carrying amount of the machine as at 31 December 20X1?**

A  $9.7 million

B  $9.6 million

C  $9.5 million

D  $6.3 million

**102** Mango sold an item of maturing inventory to a bank on 1 January 20X3 for $500,000. At this date the inventory had cost $200,000 to produce but had a fair value of $900,000, which was expected to increase over the next 3 years. At the end of 3 years, Mango have the option to repurchase the inventory at $665,500, giving an effective interest rate of 10%.

**What items should be recorded in the statement of profit or loss for the year ended 31 December 20X3?**

A   Revenue $500,000, cost of sales $200,000

B   Profit on disposal $300,000

C   Deferred income $500,000

D   Finance cost $50,000

**103** Repro has prepared its draft financial statements for the year ended 30 September 20X4. It has included the following transactions in revenue at the amounts stated below.

**Which of these has been correctly included in revenue according to IFRS 15 *Revenue from Contracts with Customers*?**

A   Agency sales of $250,000 on which Repro is entitled to a commission of 10%.

B   Sale proceeds of $20,000 for motor vehicles which were no longer required by Repro.

C   Sales of $150,000 on 30 September 20X4. The amount invoiced to and received from the customer was $180,000, which includes $30,000 for ongoing servicing work to be done by Repro over the next two years.

D   Sales of $200,000 on 1 October 20X3 to an established customer who (with the agreement of Repro) will make full payment on 30 September 20X5. Repro has a cost of capital of 10%.

**104** Yling entered into a contract to construct an asset for a customer on 1 January 20X4 which is expected to last 24 months. The agreed price for the contract is $5 million. At 30 September 20X4, the costs incurred on the contract were $1.6 million and the estimated remaining costs to complete were $2.4 million. On 20 September 20X4, Yling received a payment from the customer of $1.8 million which was equal to the full amount billed. Yling calculates contract progress using the output method, on the basis of amount billed compared to the contract price.

**What amount would be reported as a contract asset in Yling's statement of financial position as at 30 September 20X4?**

$_____

**105** CN started a three-year contract to build a new university campus on 1 April 20X4. The contract had a fixed price of $90 million. CN will satisfy the performance obligation over time. CN incurred costs to 31 March 20X5 of $77 million and estimated that a further $33 million would need to be spent to complete the contract.

CN measures the progress of contracts using work completed compared to contract price. At 31 March 20X5, a surveyor valued the work completed to date at $63 million.

**Select the correct amounts to be shown in revenue and cost of sales in the statement of profit or loss for the year ended 31 March 20X5?**

| Revenue | Cost of sales |
| --- | --- |
| $63 million | $77 million |
| $57 million | $83 million |

**106** Locke sells machines, and also offers installation and technical support services. The individual selling prices of each product are shown below.

Sale price of goods     $75
Installation     $30
One year service     $45

Locke sold a machine on 1 May 20X1, charging a reduced price of $100, including installation and one year's service.

Locke only offers discounts when customers purchase a package of products together.

**According to IFRS 15 *Revenue from Contracts with Customers*, how much should Locke record in revenue for the year ended 31 December 20X1? Workings should be rounded to the nearest $.**

$_____

**107** Place the following steps for recognising revenue in order in accordance with IFRS 15 *Revenue from Contracts with Customers*.

| Step | Correct order |
| --- | --- |
| Identify the separate performance obligations within a contract | |
| Identify the contract | |
| Determine the transaction price | |
| Recognise revenue when (or as) a performance obligation is satisfied | |
| Allocate the transaction price to the performance obligations in the contract | |

**108** BL entered into a contract with a customer on 1 November 20X4. The contract was scheduled to run for two years and has a sales value of $40 million. BL will satisfy the performance obligations over time.

At 31 October 20X5, the following details were obtained from BL's records:

|  | $m |
| --- | --- |
| Costs incurred to date | 16 |
| Estimated costs to completion | 18 |
| Progress at 31 October 20X5 | 45% |

**Applying IFRS 15 *Revenue from Contracts with Customers*, how much revenue and cost of sales should BL recognise in its statement of profit or loss for the year ended 31 October 20X5?**

|  | *Revenue* | *Cost of sales* |
| --- | --- | --- |
| A | $40 million | $15.3 million |
| B | $40 million | $34 million |
| C | $18 million | $16 million |
| D | $18 million | $15.3 million |

**109** Malik is a construction business, recognising progress based on work certified as a proportion of total contract value. Malik will satisfy the performance obligation over time. The following information relates to one of its long-term contracts as at 31 May 20X4, Malik's year-end.

|  | $ |
| --- | --- |
| Contract price | 200,000 |
| Costs incurred to date | 130,000 |
| Estimated cost to complete | 20,000 |
| Invoiced to customer | 120,000 |
| Work certified to date | 180,000 |

In the year to 31 May 20X3 Malik had recognised revenue of $60,000 and profit of $15,000 in respect of this contract.

**What profit should appear in Malik's statement of profit or loss as at 31 May 20X4 in respect of this contract?**

$_____

**110** **Which of the following items has correctly been included in Hatton's revenue for the year to 31 December 20X1?**

A $2 million in relation to a fee negotiated for an advertising contract for Rees, one of Hatton's clients. Hatton acted as an agent during the deal and is entitled to 10% commission.

B $500,000 relating to a sale of specialised equipment on 31 December 20X1. The full sales value was $700,000 but $200,000 relates to servicing that Hatton will provide over the next 2 years, so Hatton has not included that in revenue this year.

C $800,000 relating to a sale of some surplus land owned by Hatton.

D $1 million in relation to a sale to a new customer on 31 December 20X1. Control passed to the customer on 31 December 20X1. The $1 million is payable on 31 December 20X3. Interest rates are 10%.

**111** Sugar has entered into a long-term contract to build an asset for a customer, Hewer. Sugar will satisfy the performance obligation over time and has measured the progress towards satisfying the performance obligation at 45% at the year end.

The price of the contract is $8 million. Sugar has spent $4.5 million to date, but the estimated costs to complete are $5.5 million. To date, Hewer has paid Sugar $3 million.

**What is the net liability that should be recorded in Sugar's statement of financial position?**

$_____ ,000

**112** Ratten commenced a contract to build an asset for a customer in the year ended 30 September 20X4. The contract price was agreed at $1.5m, and the total expected costs of the contract are $800,000. Ratten will satisfy the performance obligation over time.

The following figures were correctly recognised in the profit or loss account for the year ended 30 September 20X4:

|  | $000 |
|---|---|
| Revenue | 450 |
| Cost of sales | (240) |
| Profit | 210 |

The following figures are also relevant in relation to this contract:

|  | 20X4 $000 | 20X5 $000 |
|---|---|---|
| Costs incurred to date | 325 | 575 |
| Work certified to date | 450 | 1,050 |

Ratten recognises progress on the basis of work certified compared to contract price.

**What should Ratten include in its statement of profit or loss for the year ended 30 September 20X5 for cost of sales in respect of the contract?**

A $320,000

B $250,000

C $560,000

D $240,000

113 Sawyer entered into a contract to construct an asset for a customer during the year, and identified the performance obligation as one which is satisfied over time. Sawyer recognises progress towards completion using an output method, based on work certified compared to contract price. The following information is relevant to the contract.

|  | $ |
|---|---|
| Contract price | 1,000,000 |
| Costs incurred to date | 530,000 |
| Estimated cost to complete | 170,000 |
| Work certified to date and invoiced | 600,000 |

**What is the value of the contract asset to be recorded in Sawyer's statement of financial position?**

A    $110,000

B    $100,000

C    $190,000

D    $150,000

114 Hindberg is a car retailer. On 1 April 20X4, Hindberg sold a car to Latterly on the following terms:

The selling price of the car was $25,300. Latterly paid $12,650 (half of the cost) on 1 April 20X4 and will pay the remaining $12,650 on 31 March 20X6 (two years after the sale). Latterly can obtain finance at 10% per annum.

**What is the total amount which Hindberg should credit to profit or loss in respect of this transaction in the year ended 31 March 20X5?**

A    $23,105

B    $23,000

C    $20,909

D    $24,150

115 Tamsin Co's accounting records shown the following:

|  | $ |
|---|---|
| Income tax payable for the year | 60,000 |
| Over provision in relation to the previous year | 4,500 |
| Opening provision for deferred tax | 2,600 |
| Closing provision for deferred tax | 3,200 |

**What is the income tax expense that will be shown in the statement of profit or loss for the year?**

A    $54,900

B    $67,700

C    $65,100

D    $56,100

**116** The following information has been extracted from the accounting records of Clara Co:

|  | $ |
|---|---|
| Estimated income tax for the year ended 30 September 20X0 | $75,000 |
| Income tax paid for the year ended 30 September 20X0 | $80,000 |
| Estimated income tax for the year ended 30 September 20X1 | $83,000 |

**What figures will be shown in the statement of profit or loss for the year ended 30 September 20X1 and the statement of financial position as at that date in respect of income tax?**

| Statement of profit or loss | Statement of financial position |
|---|---|
|  |  |

Options:

| |
|---|
| $75,000 |
| $80,000 |
| $83,000 |
| $88,000 |

**117** Hudson has the following balances included on its trial balance at 30 June 20X4.

|  | $ | |
|---|---|---|
| Taxation | 4,000 | Credit |
| Deferred taxation | 12,000 | Credit |

The taxation balance relates to an overprovision from 30 June 20X3.

At 30 June 20X4, the directors estimate that the provision necessary for taxation on current year profits is $15,000.

The carrying amount of Hudson's non-current assets exceeds the tax written-down value by $30,000. The rate of tax is 30%.

**What is the charge for taxation that will appear in the statement of profit or loss for the year to 30 June 20X4?**

A    $23,000

B    $28,000

C    $8,000

D    $12,000

**118** Holmes has the following balances included on its trial balance at 30 June 20X4:

|  | $ |  |
|---|---|---|
| Taxation | 7,000 | Credit |
| Deferred taxation | 16,000 | Credit |

The taxation balance relates to an overprovision from 30 June 20X3.

At 30 June 20X4, the directors estimate that the provision necessary for taxation on current year profits is $12,000. The balance on the deferred tax account needs to be increased to $23,000, which includes the impact of the increase in property valuation below.

During the year Holmes revalued its property for the first time, resulting in a gain of $10,000. The rate of tax is 30%.

**What is the charge for taxation that will appear in the statement of profit or loss for the year to 30 June 20X4?**

A    $9,000

B    $12,000

C    $23,000

D    $1,000

**119** Garfish had profits after tax of $3 million in the year ended 31 December 20X7. On 1 January 20X7, Garfish had 2.4 million ordinary shares in issue. On 1 April 20X7 Garfish made a one for two rights issue at a price of $1.40 when the market price of Garfish's shares was $2.00.

**What is the basic earnings per share (to one decimal place) for the year ended 31 December 20X7, according to IAS 33 *Earnings Per Share*?**

_____ cents.

**120** On 1 January 20X4, Sam Co had 3 million ordinary shares in issue. On 1 June 20X4, Sam Co made a 1 for 3 bonus issue. On 30 September 20X4, Sam Co issued a further 1 million shares at full market price. Sam Co had profits attributable to ordinary equity holders of $2 million for the year ended 31 December 20X4.

**What is the basic earnings per share figure for the year ended 31 December 20X4, according to IAS 33 *Earnings Per Share*?**

A    47.1¢

B    52.2¢

C    56.8¢

D    50.0¢

**121** During the year, Mac made a 1 for 3 rights issue at $1.60 when the market price was $2.20. Last year's EPS was 81 cents. There were no other issues of shares during the year.

**What is the restated earnings per share figure for comparative purposes?**

_____ cents.

**122** Coral Co has net profit for the year ended 30 September 20X5 of $10,500,000. Coral has had 6 million shares in issue for many years. On 1 October 20X4 Coral issued a convertible bond. It had an initial liability element of $2,500,000, and the market interest rate for non-convertible instruments is 8%. The bond is convertible in five years, with 50 shares issued for every $100 nominal of convertible bond held. Coral Co pays tax at a rate of 28%

**What is the Diluted Earnings per Share figure?**

A    177.4¢

B    175.0¢

C    147.6¢

D    146.8¢

**123** Isco's financial statements show a profit for the year to 31 December 20X5 of $2 million. On 1 January 20X5 Isco had 4 million shares in issue and made no further issues of shares during the year. At 31 December 20X5 there were 1 million outstanding options to buy shares at $3 each. For the year to 31 December 20X5, the average market value of Isco's shares was $5.

**What is Isco's diluted earnings per share for the year ended 31 December 20X5?**

A    50.0¢

B    28.6¢

C    45.5¢

D    43.4¢

**124** Gromit Co has the following extract from its consolidated profit or loss account:

|  | $000 |
|---|---|
| Profit for the period | 2,800 |
| Other comprehensive income: revaluation gain | 500 |
| Total comprehensive income | 3,300 |
| Profit for the period attributable to: | |
| Parent | 2,250 |
| Non-controlling Interest | 550 |
|  | 2,800 |
| Total comprehensive income attributable to: | |
| Parent | 2,600 |
| Non-controlling interest | 700 |
|  | 3,300 |

**What figure should be used as earnings by Gromit in its earnings per share (EPS) calculation?**

$_____ ,000

**125** **Which TWO of the following do NOT need to be removed from an entity's net profit in a statement of profit or loss in order to calculate the earnings figure to be used in the earnings per share calculation?**

A    Redeemable preference share dividends

B    Irredeemable preference share dividends

C    Profit attributable to the non-controlling interest

D    An error in expenses discovered after the financial statements have been authorised for issue

E    Ordinary dividends

**126** Aqua has correctly calculated its basic earnings per share (EPS) for the current year.

**Allocate the items to the appropriate category.**

| Included within Diluted EPS calculation | Included within Basic EPS calculation |
|---|---|
| | |
| | |

Options:

| |
|---|
| A 1 for 5 rights issue of equity shares during the year at $1.20 when the market price of the equity shares was $2.00 |
| The issue during the year of a loan note, convertible into ordinary shares |
| The granting of directors' share options during the year, exercisable in three years' time |
| Equity shares issued during the year as the purchase consideration for the acquisition of a new subsidiary |

**127** Many commentators believe that the trend of earnings per share (EPS) is a more reliable indicator of underlying performance than the trend of the net profit for the year.

**Which of the following statements supports this view?**

A    Net profit can be manipulated by the choice of accounting policies but EPS cannot be manipulated in this way.

B    EPS takes into account the additional resources made available to earn profit when new shares are issued for cash, whereas net profit does not.

C    The disclosure of a diluted EPS figure is a forecast of the trend of profit for future periods.

D    The comparative EPS is restated where a change in accounting policy affects the previous year's profits.

**128** On 1 October 20X3, Hoy had $2.5 million of equity shares of 50 cents each in issue.

No new shares were issued during the year ended 30 September 20X4, but on that date there were outstanding share options to purchase 2 million equity shares at $1.20 each. The average market value of Hoy's equity shares during the year was $3 per share.

Hoy's profit after tax for the year ended 30 September 20X4 was $1,550,000.

**What is Hoy's diluted earnings per share for the year ended 30 September 20X4?**

A    25.0¢

B    31.0¢

C    26.7¢

D    22.1¢

**129** AP has the following two legal claims outstanding:

- A legal action claiming compensation of $500,000 filed against AP in March 20X4.

- A legal action taken by AP against a third party, claiming damages of $200,000, which was started in January 20X3 and is nearing completion.

In both cases, it is more likely than not that the amount claimed will have to be paid.

**How should AP report these legal actions in its financial statements for the year ended 31 March 20X5?**

**Allocate the correct treatment against each of the cases.**

| Legal action against AP | Legal action by AP |
|---|---|
|  |  |

Options:

| |
|---|
| Contingent Liability |
| Contingent Asset |
| Provision |
| Asset |

**130** **Which of the following would require a provision for a liability to be created by BW at its reporting date of 31 October 20X5?**

A    The government introduced new laws on data protection which come into force on 1 January 20X6. BW's directors have agreed that this will require a large number of staff to be retrained. At 31 October 20X5, the directors were waiting on a report they had commissioned that would identify the actual training requirements.

B    At the year-end BW is negotiating with its insurance provider about an outstanding insurance claim. On 20 November 20X5, the provider agreed to pay $200,000.

C    BW makes refunds to customers for any goods returned within 30 days of sale, and has done so for many years.

D    A customer is suing BW for damages alleged to have been caused by BW's product. BW is contesting the claim and at 31 October 20X5 the directors have been advised by BW's legal advisers that it is very unlikely to lose the case.

**131** Using the requirements set out in IAS 10 *Events after the Reporting Period*, which of the following would be classified as an adjusting event after the reporting period in financial statements ended 31 March 20X4 that were approved by the directors on 31 August 20X4?

    A    A reorganisation of the enterprise, proposed by a director on 31 January 20X4 and agreed by the Board on 10 July 20X4.

    B    A strike by the workforce which started on 1 May 20X4 and stopped all production for 10 weeks before being settled.

    C    The receipt of cash from a claim on an insurance policy for damage caused by a fire in a warehouse on 1 January 20X4. The claim was made in January 20X4 and the amount of the claim had not been recognised at 31 March 20X4 as it was uncertain that any money would be paid. The insurance enterprise settled with a payment of $1.5 million on 1 June 20X4.

    D    The enterprise had made large export sales to the USA during the year. The year-end receivables included $2 million for amounts outstanding that were due to be paid in US dollars between 1 April 20X4 and 1 July 20X4. By the time these amounts were received, the exchange rate had moved in favour of the enterprise.

**132** Target is preparing its financial statements for the year ended 30 September 20X7. Target is facing a number of legal claims from its customers with regards to a faulty product sold. The total amount being claimed is $3.5 million. Target's lawyers say that the customers have an 80% chance of being successful.

**According to IAS 37 *Provisions, Contingent Liabilities and Contingent Assets*, what amount, if any, should be recognised in respect of the above in Target's statement of financial position as at 30 September 20X7?**

$_____,000

**133** ABC has a year end of 31 December 20X4. On 15 December 20X4 the directors publicly announced their decision to close an operating unit and make a number of employees redundant. Some of the employees currently working in the unit will be transferred to other operating units within ABC.

The estimated costs of the closure are as follows:

|  | $000 |
| --- | --- |
| Redundancy costs | 800 |
| Lease termination costs | 200 |
| Relocation of continuing employees to new locations | 400 |
| Retraining of continuing employees | 300 |
|  | 1,700 |

**What is the closure provision that should be recognised?**

    A    $800,000

    B    $1,000,000

    C    $1,400,000

    D    $1,700,000

**134** On 1 October 20X3, Xplorer commenced drilling for oil in an undersea oilfield. The extraction of oil causes damage to the seabed which has a restorative cost (ignore discounting) of $10,000 per million barrels of oil extracted. Xplorer extracted 250 million barrels of oil in the year ended 30 September 20X4.

Xplorer is also required to dismantle the drilling equipment at the end of its five-year licence.  This has an estimated cost of $30 million on 30 September 20X8. Xplorer's cost of capital is 8% per annum and $1 has a present value of 68 cents in five years' time.

**What is the total provision (extraction plus dismantling) which Xplorer would report in its statement of financial position as at 30 September 20X4 in respect of its oil operations?**

A $34,900,000

B $24,532,000

C $22,900,000

D $4,132,000

**135** **Which TWO of the following events which occur after the reporting date of an entity but before the financial statements are authorised for issue are classified as ADJUSTING events in accordance with IAS 10** *Events after the Reporting Period***?**

A A change in tax rate announced after the reporting date, but affecting the current tax liability

B The discovery of a fraud which had occurred during the year

C The determination of the sale proceeds of an item of plant sold before the year end

D The destruction of a factory by fire

**136** Each of the following events occurred after the reporting date of 31 March 20X5, but before the financial statements were authorised for issue.

**Identify whether the events would represent adjusting or non-adjusting events.**

| | Adjusting | Non-adjusting |
|---|---|---|
| A public announcement in April 20X5 of a formal plan to discontinue an operation which had been approved by the board in February 20X5. | | |
| The settlement of an insurance claim for a loss sustained in December 20X4. | | |

**137** In a review of its provisions for the year ended 31 March 20X5, Cumla's assistant accountant has suggested the following accounting treatments:

(i) Based on past experience, a $200,000 provision for unforeseen liabilities arising after the year end.

(ii) The partial reversal (as a credit to the statement of profit or loss) of the accumulated depreciation provision on an item of plant because the estimate of its remaining useful life has been increased by three years.

(iii) Providing $1 million for deferred tax at 25% relating to a $4 million revaluation of property during March 20X5 even though Cumla has no intention of selling the property in the near future.

**Which of the above suggested treatments of provisions is/are permitted by IFRS Standards?**

A (i) only

B (i) and (ii)

C (ii) and (iii)

D (iii) only

**138** **Identify whether the statements below are true or false:**

| | True | False |
|---|---|---|
| IAS 10 *Events After the Reporting Period* covers the period from the reporting date to the annual general meeting | | |
| According to IAS 10 *Events After the Reporting Period*, any non-adjusting event should be disclosed as a note in the financial statements | | |

**139** Fauberg owns a number of offices in country Y and is in the process of finishing its financial statements for the year ended 31 December 20X4. In December 20X4, country Y announced changes to health and safety regulations, meaning that Fauberg's air conditioning units will have to be replaced by 30 June 20X5.

This is estimated to cost Fauberg $500,000. Fauberg has a history of compliance with regulations and intends to do the work by June 20X5.

**Which of the conditions for a provision will be met at 31 December 20X4?**

| | Yes/No |
|---|---|
| There is a present obligation from a past event | |
| A reliable estimate can be made | |
| There is a probable outflow of economic benefits | |

**140** Which TWO of the following statements about provisions are true?

A Future operating losses cannot be provided for

B Changes in provisions should be applied retrospectively, adjusting the prior year financial statements

C Provisions should be accounted for prudently, reflecting the maximum that could possibly be paid out

D Provisions should be discounted to present value if the effect of the time value of money is material

# CONSOLIDATED FINANCIAL STATEMENTS

**141** Petre owns 100% of the share capital of the following companies. The directors are unsure of whether the investments should be consolidated into the group financial statements of not.

**Identify whether the following companies should be consolidated or not.**

| | Consolidated | Not to be consolidated |
|---|---|---|
| Beta is a bank and its activity is so different from the engineering activities of the rest of the group that it would be meaningless to consolidate it. | | |
| Delta is located in a country where local accounting standards are compulsory and these are not compatible with IFRS Standards used by the rest of the group. | | |
| Gamma is located in a country where a military coup has taken place and Petre has lost control of the investment for the foreseeable future. | | |

**142** Tazer acquired Lowdown, an unincorporated entity, for $2.8 million. A fair value exercise performed on Lowdown's net assets at the date of purchase showed:

| | $000 |
|---|---|
| Property, plant and equipment | 3,000 |
| Identifiable intangible asset | 500 |
| Inventory | 300 |
| Trade receivables less payables | 200 |
| | ——— |
| | 4,000 |
| | ——— |

**How would the purchase be reflected in the consolidated statement of financial position?**

A    Record the net assets at their above values and credit profit or loss with $1.2 million

B    Record the net assets at their above values and credit goodwill with $1.2 million

C    Ignore the intangible asset ($500,000), recording the remaining net assets at their values shown above and crediting profit or loss with $700,000

D    Record the purchase as a financial asset investment at $2.8 million

**143   Which of the following definitions is not included within the definition of control per IFRS 10 *Consolidated Financial Statements*?**

A    Having power over the investee

B    Having exposure, or rights, to variable returns from its investment with the investee

C    Having the majority of shares in the investee

D    Having the ability to use its power over the investee to affect the amount of the investor's returns

**144   Pamela acquired 80% of the share capital of Samantha on 1 January 20X1. Part of the purchase consideration was $200,000 cash to be paid on 1 January 20X4. The applicable cost of capital is 10%.**

**What will the deferred consideration liability be at 31 December 20X2?**

A    $150,262

B    $165,288

C    $200,000

D    $181,818

**145   Philip acquired 85% of the share capital of Stanley on 1 October 20X1. The profit for the year ended 31 December 20X1 for Stanley was $36,000. Profits are deemed to accrue evenly over the year. At 31 December 20X1 Stanley's statement of financial position showed:**

Equity share capital                $200,000

Retained earnings                  $180,000

**What were the net assets of Stanley on acquisition?**

$_____ ,000

**146**   On 30 June 20X4 GHI acquired 800,000 of JKL's 1 million shares.

GHI issued 3 shares for every 4 shares acquired in JKL. On 30 June 20X4 the market price of a GHI share was $3.80 and the market price of a JKL share was $3.

GHI agreed to pay $550,000 in cash to the existing shareholders on 30 June 20X5. GHI's borrowing rate was 10% per annum.

GHI paid professional fees of $100,000 for advice on the acquisition.

**What is the cost of investment that will be used in the goodwill calculation in the consolidated financial statements of GHI?**

$_____ ,000

**147**   MNO has a 75% owned subsidiary PQR. During the year MNO sold inventory to PQR for an invoiced price of $800,000. PQR have since sold 75% of that inventory on to third parties. The sale was at a mark-up of 25% on cost to MNO. PQR is the only subsidiary of MNO.

**What is the adjustment to inventory that would be included in the consolidated statement of financial position of MNO at the year-end resulting from this sale?**

A   $120,000

B   $40,000

C   $160,000

D   $50,000

**148**   West has a 75% subsidiary Life, and is preparing its consolidated statement of financial position as at 31 December 20X6. The carrying amount of property, plant and equipment in the two companies at that date is as follows:

West $300,000

Life   $60,000

On 1 January 20X6 Life had transferred some property to West for $40,000. At the date of transfer the property, which had cost $42,000, had a carrying amount of $30,000 and a remaining useful life of five years.

**What is the carrying amount of property, plant and equipment in the consolidated statement of financial position of West as at 31 December 20X6?**

$_____ ,000

**149**   **Which TWO of the following situations are unlikely to represent control over an investee?**

A   Owning 55% and being able to elect 4 of the 7 directors

B   Owning 51%, but the constitution requires that decisions need the unanimous consent of shareholders

C   Having currently exercisable options which would take the shareholding in the investee to 55%

D   Owning 40% of the shares but having majority of voting rights within the investee

E   Owning 35% of the ordinary shares and 80% of the preference shares of the investee

**150** Identify if the following will be recognised as part of the cost of an investment in a subsidiary.

| | Include in cost of investment | Do not include in the cost of investment |
|---|---|---|
| An agreement to pay a further $30,000 if the subsidiary achieves an operating profit of over $100,000 in the first 3 years after acquisition | | |
| Professional fees of $10,000 in connection with the investment | | |

**151** Peter acquires 80% of the share capital of Paul on 1 August 20X6 and is preparing its group financial statements for the year ended 31 December 20X6.

**How will Paul's results be included in the group statement of profit or loss?**

A    80% of Paul's revenue and expenses for the year ended 31 December 20X6

B    100% of Paul's revenue and expenses for the year ended 31 December 20X6

C    80% of Paul's revenue and expenses for the period 1 August 20X6 to 31 December 20X6

D    100% of Paul's revenue and expenses for the period ended 1 August 20X6 to 31 December 20X6

**152** Which of the following would result in an unrealised profit within a group scenario?

A    A parent sells a building originally costing $800,000 to its subsidiary for $900,000. The subsidiary still holds this asset at the date of consolidation.

B    A parent sells a building originally costing $800,000 to its subsidiary for $900,000. The subsidiary has sold this asset before the date of consolidation.

C    A parent sells goods which originally cost $14,000 to its subsidiary for $18,000. The subsidiary has sold all of these goods at the date of consolidation.

D    A parent sells goods which originally cost $14,000 to an associate for $18,000. The associate has sold all of these goods at the date of consolidation.

**153** Identify whether the following facts about impairment are true or false.

| | True | False |
|---|---|---|
| Impairment will always be deducted in full from the parent's retained earnings | | |
| Impairment will be apportioned between the parent and the non-controlling interest (NCI) when the NCI is valued at fair value | | |

**154** **Which of the following is not a condition which must be met for the parent to be exempt from producing consolidated financial statements?**

A    The activities of the subsidiary are significantly different to the rest of the group and to consolidate them would prejudice the overall group position

B    The ultimate parent produces consolidated financial statements that comply with IFRS Standards and are publicly available

C    The parent's debt or equity instruments are not traded in a public market

D    The parent itself is a wholly owned subsidiary or a partially owned subsidiary whose owners do not object to the parent not producing consolidated financial statements

**155** On 1 January 20X1, Branch purchased 75% of Leaf's 80 million shares. At this date, Leaf's retained earnings were $60 million. The consideration paid for Leaf was 2 Branch shares for every 3 Leaf shares purchased, plus a cash payment of $1 per purchased share.  At the date of acquisition, the value of a Branch share was $2.50.

**What is the consideration paid for Branch on 1 January 20X1?**

$_____

**156** STU has an 80% subsidiary VWX, which has been a subsidiary of STU for the whole of the current year.  VWX reported a profit after tax of $600,000 in its own financial statements. You ascertain that at the year-end there was unrealised profit of $60,000 on sales by VWX to STU.

**What is the non-controlling interest in VWX that would be reported in the consolidated statement of profit or loss and other comprehensive income of STU for the year?**

$_____

**157** Harry acquired an 80% holding in Style on 1 April 20X6. From 1 April 20X6 to 31 December 20X6 Style sold goods to Harry for $4.3m at a mark-up of 10%.  Harry's inventory at 31 December 20X6 included $2.2m of such inventory. The statements of profit or loss for each entity for the year to 31 December 20X6 showed the following in respect of cost of sales:

Harry $14.7m

Style  $11.6m

**What is the cost of sales figure to be shown in the consolidated statement of profit or loss for the year to 31 December 20X6?**

A    $18,900,000

B    $20,200,000

C    $19,100,000

D    $19,300,000

**158** Heel acquired a 60% holding in Sock on 1 January 20X6. At this date Sock owned a building with a fair value $200,000 in excess of its carrying amount, and a remaining life of 10 years. All depreciation is charged to operating expenses. Goodwill had been impaired by $55,000 in the year to 31 December 20X6. The balances on operating expenses for the year to 31 December 20X7 are shown below:

Heel $600,000

Sock $350,000

**What are consolidated operating expenses for the year to 31 December 20X7?**

$_____ ,000

**159** A acquired a 60% holding in B on 1 July 20X6. At this date, A gave B a $500,000 8% loan. The interest on the loan has been accounted for correctly in the individual financial statements. The totals for finance costs for the year to 31 December 20X6 in the individual financial statements are shown below.

A $200,000

B $70,000

**What are consolidated finance costs for the year to 31 December 20X6?**

A $215,000

B $225,000

C $230,000

D $250,000

**160** **Identify whether the following would affect the profit attributable to the non-controlling interest in the consolidated statement of profit or loss if the non-controlling interest is measured at fair value**

| | Affects the NCI share of profit | Does not affect the NCI share |
|---|---|---|
| Goodwill impairment | | |
| The parent selling inventory to the subsidiary at a profit of $10,000, all of which remains in the subsidiary's inventory at the year end | | |
| The subsidiary having an item of plant with a fair value of $500,000 above its carrying amount at acquisition, and a remaining life of 10 years | | |

**161** AB has owned 80% of CD for many years. In the current year ended 30 June 20X3, AB has reported total revenues of $5.5 million, and CD of $2.1 million. AB has sold goods to CD during the year with a total value of $1 million, earning a margin of 20%. Half of these goods remain in year-end inventories.

**What is the consolidated revenue figure for the AB group for the year ended 30 June 20X3?**

$_____ ,000

**162** Burridge bought 30% of Allen on 1 July 20X4. Allen's statement of profit or loss for the year shows a profit of $400,000. Allen paid a dividend to Burridge of $50,000 on 1 December 20X4. At the year end, the investment in Allen was judged to have been impaired by $10,000.

**What will be the share of profit from associate shown in the consolidated statement of profit or loss for the year ended 31 December 20X4?**

A    $57,000

B    $50,000

C    $60,000

D    $110,000

**163** Beasant bought 30% of Arnie on 1 January 20X8, when Arnie had share capital of 100,000 $1 shares and $400,000 retained earnings. The consideration comprised one Beasant share for every 3 shares bought in Arnie. At the date of acquisition, Beasant's shares had a market value of $4.50 and Arnie's had a market value of $2. At 31 December 20X8, Arnie's net assets were $460,000.

**What is the value of investment in associate shown in the consolidated statement of financial position as at 31 December 20X8?**

A    $8,000

B    $33,000

C    $63,000

D    $123,000

**164** **Identify which concept each of the following transactions is applying**

|  | Single entity concept | Going concern concept |
|---|---|---|
| Removing unrealised profits on group sales |  |  |
| Removing intra-group balances |  |  |

**165** **Identify the correct treatments for the following investments in the consolidated financial statements of the Nicol group.**

| | |
|---|---|
| 30% of the share capital of Hansen. The other 70% is owned by Lawro, another listed entity, whose directors make up Hansen's board. | Subsidiary |
| 80% of the share capital of Kennedy, whose activities are significantly different from the rest of the Nicol group. | Associate |
| 30% of the share capital of Bruce. The Nicol group have appointed 2 of the 5 board members of Bruce, with the other board members coming from three other entities. | Investment |

**166** Badger acquired 30% of Eagle on 1 July 20X3 at a cost of $5.5 million. Badger has classified Eagle as an associate undertaking. For the year ended 30 September 20X3, Eagle has reported a net profit of $625,000.

**What is the value of the associate investment in the group statement of financial position of Badger as at 30 September 20X3?**

A    $5,546,875

B    $5,500,000

C    $6,125,000

D    $5,968,750

**167** Green is an associate undertaking of Purple. Purple owns 30% of the shares in Green, and has done so for many years.

During the year ended 31 December 20X4, Green made a net profit of $1.5 million. Green sold goods to Purple during the year with a value of $2 million, and half are still in Purple's inventories at year end. All the goods were sold at a margin of 30%.

Purple has recognised previous impairments in relation to its investment in Green of $225,000. In the current year, Purple wishes to recognise an additional impairment charge of $35,000.

**What is the share of profit of associate to be shown in Purple's consolidated statement of profit or loss?**

$_____ ,000

**168** **Which of the following statements regarding consolidated financial statements is correct?**

A    For consolidation, it may be acceptable to use financial statements of the subsidiary where the year-end differs from the parent by 2 months.

B    For consolidation, all companies within the group must have the same year end.

C    All companies within a group must have the same accounting policy in their individual financial statements.

D    The profit made on all intra-group sales in the year must be removed from the consolidated financial statements.

**169** 'An associate is an entity over which the investor has significant influence' (IAS28, para 3).

**Which TWO of the following indicate the presence of significant influence?**

A    The investor owns 330,000 of the 1,500,000 equity voting shares of the investee

B    The investor has representation on the board of directors of the investee

C    The investor is able to insist that all of the sales of the investee are made to a subsidiary of the investor

D    The investor controls the votes of a majority of the board members

**170** Consolidated financial statements are presented on the basis that the companies within the group are treated as if they are a single economic entity.

**Which TWO of the following are requirements of preparing consolidated financial statements?**

A   All subsidiaries must adopt the accounting policies of the parent in their individual financial statements

B   Subsidiaries with activities which are substantially different to the activities of other members of the group should not be consolidated

C   All assets and liabilities of subsidiaries should be included at fair value

D   Unrealised profits within the group must be eliminated from the consolidated financial statements

**171** The Caddy group acquired 240,000 of August's 800,000 equity shares for $6 per share on 1 April 20X4. August's profit after tax for the year ended 30 September 20X4 was $400,000.

**On the assumption that August is an associate of Caddy, what would be the carrying amount of the investment in August in the consolidated statement of financial position of Caddy as at 30 September 20X4?**

A   $1,455,000

B   $1,500,000

C   $1,515,000

D   $1,395,000

**172** On 1 January 20X4, Viagem acquired 80% of the equity share capital of Greca.

Extracts of their statements of profit or loss for the year ended 30 September 20X4 are:

|               | Viagem   | Greca    |
|---------------|----------|----------|
|               | $000     | $000     |
| Revenue       | 64,600   | 38,000   |
| Cost of sales | (51,200) | (26,000) |

Sales from Viagem to Greca throughout the year to 30 September 20X4 had consistently been $800,000 per month.

Viagem made a mark-up on cost of 25% on these sales.

Greca had $1.5 million of these goods in inventory as at 30 September 20X4.

**What would be the cost of sales in Viagem's consolidated statement of profit or loss for the year ended 30 September 20X4?**

$_____ ,000

**173** Pact acquired 80% of the equity shares of Sact on 1 July 20X4, paying $3 for each share acquired. This represented a premium of 20% over the market price of Sact's shares at that date.

Sact's equity at 31 March 20X5 comprised:

|  | $ | $ |
|---|---|---|
| Equity shares of $1 each |  | 100,000 |
| Retained earnings at 1 April 20X4 | 80,000 |  |
| Profit for the year ended 31 March 20X5 | 40,000 |  |
|  | ——— | 120,000 |
|  |  | 220,000 |

The only fair value adjustment required to Sact's net assets on consolidation was a $20,000 increase in the value of its land.

Pact's policy is to value non-controlling interests at fair value at the date of acquisition.

For this purpose the market price of Sact's shares at that date can be deemed to be representative of the fair value of the shares held by the non-controlling interest.

**What would be the carrying amount of the non-controlling interest of Sact in the consolidated statement of financial position of Pact as at 31 March 20X5?**

A    $54,000

B    $50,000

C    $56,000

D    $58,000

**174** Germane has a number of relationships with other companies.

**In which of the following relationships is Germane necessarily the parent?**

(i)    Foll has 50,000 non-voting and 100,000 voting equity shares in issue with each share receiving the same dividend. Germane owns all of Foll's non-voting shares and 40,000 of its voting shares.

(ii)    Kipp has 1 million equity shares in issue of which Germane owns 40%. Germane also owns $800,000 out of $1 million 8% convertible loan notes issued by Kipp. These loan notes may be converted on the basis of 40 equity shares for each $100 of loan note, or they may be redeemed in cash at the option of the holder.

(iii)    Germane owns 49% of the equity shares in Polly and 52% of its non-redeemable preference shares. As a result of these investments, Germane receives variable returns from Polly and has the ability to affect these returns through its power over Polly.

A    (i) only

B    (i) and (ii) only

C    (ii) and (iii) only

D    All three

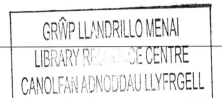

236079

**175** Wilmslow acquired 80% of the equity shares of Zeta on 1 April 20X4 when Zeta's retained earnings were $200,000. During the year ended 31 March 20X5, Zeta purchased goods from Wilmslow totalling $320,000. At 31 March 20X5, one quarter of these goods were still in the inventory of Zeta. Wilmslow applies a mark-up on cost of 25% to all of its sales.

At 31 March 20X5, the retained earnings of Wilmslow and Zeta were $450,000 and $340,000 respectively.

**What would be the amount of retained earnings in Wilmslow's consolidated statement of financial position as at 31 March 20X5?**

$_____ ,000

**176** IFRS Standards require extensive use of fair values when recording the acquisition of a subsidiary.

**Which TWO of the following comments, regarding the use of fair values on the acquisition of a subsidiary, are correct?**

A    The use of fair value to record a subsidiary's acquired assets does not comply with the historical cost principle.

B    The use of fair values to record the acquisition of plant always increases consolidated post-acquisition depreciation charges compared to the corresponding charge in the subsidiary's own financial statements.

C    Cash consideration payable one year after the date of acquisition needs to be discounted to reflect its fair value.

D    When acquiring a subsidiary, the fair value of liabilities and contingent liabilities must also be considered.

E    Patents must be included as part of goodwill because it is impossible to determine the fair value of an acquired patent, as, by definition, patents are unique.

**177    Identify whether the following statements are true or false**

|  | True | False |
|---|---|---|
| The profit made by a parent on the sale of goods to a subsidiary is only realised when the subsidiary sells the goods to a third party |  |  |
| Eliminating intra-group unrealised profits never affects non-controlling interests |  |  |
| The profit element of goods supplied by the parent to an associate and held in year-end inventory must be eliminated in full |  |  |

**178** Johnson paid $1.2 million for a 30% investment in Treem's equity shares on 1 August 20X4.

Treem's profit after tax for the year ended 31 March 20X5 was $750,000. On 31 March 20X5, Treem had $300,000 goods in its inventory which it had bought from Johnson in March 20X5. These had been sold by Johnson at a mark-up on cost of 20%.

Treem has not paid any dividends.

**On the assumption that Treem is an associate of Johnson, what would be the carrying amount of the investment in Treem in the consolidated statement of financial position of Johnson as at 31 March 20X5?**

$_____ ,000

**179** On 1 January 20X4, Pigagem acquired 80% of the equity share capital of Streca.

Extracts of their statements of financial position for the year ended 31 December 20X4 are:

|  | Pigagem | Streca |
| --- | --- | --- |
|  | $000 | $000 |
| Receivables | 64,600 | 38,000 |

At 31 December 20X4, Streca recorded a payable to Pigagem of $3 million which did not agree to Pigagem's receivable balance due to $1 million cash in transit.

**What is the value of receivables in the consolidated statement of financial position as at 31 December 20X4?**

$_____ ,000

**180** **Identify whether the following statements are true or false.**

|  | True | False |
| --- | --- | --- |
| If a subsidiary is disposed of on the last day of the reporting period then its assets and liabilities must still be included in the consolidated statement of financial position. |  |  |
| The gain or loss arising on the disposal of a subsidiary in the consolidated financial statements is recorded in other comprehensive income. |  |  |

181 Johanna acquired 100% of Sidney on 1 January 20X4, paying $5 million cash, including $200,000 professional fees. Johanna also agreed to pay $10 million on 1 January 20X6. Johanna Co has a cost of capital of 10%

**Identify the components to be included within the calculation of goodwill for the acquisition of Sidney Co for the year ended 31 December 20X4.**

| Consideration | | To be included in goodwill |
|---|---|---|
| Cash consideration of $5 million | | |
| Cash consideration of $4.8 million | | |
| Deferred cash consideration of $8.3 million | | |
| Deferred cash consideration of $9.1 million | | |

182 The Garden group has a reporting date of 31 December 20X3. On 30 September 20X3, the group disposed of its 80% holding in the ordinary shares of Shed for $10 million in cash. The disposal of Shed constitutes a discontinued operation. The following information relates to Shed:

|  | $m |
|---|---|
| Goodwill at disposal | 2 |
| Net assets at disposal | 9 |
| Non-controlling interest at disposal | 3 |

**What should be recorded as the profit (or loss) on disposal in the consolidated statement of profit or loss for the year ended 31 December 20X3?**

A   Loss of $2 million

B   Profit of $2 million

C   Profit of $4 million

D   Loss of $4 million

183 Wind purchased 80% of the ordinary shares of Snow for $4 million many years ago and holds the investment in its individual statement of financial position at cost. On 30 September 20X3, Wind disposed of its shares in Snow for $10 million in cash

**What is the profit arising on the disposal of the shares that will be reported in Wind's individual statement of profit or loss for the year ended 30 September 20X3?**

$_____

**184** On 30 June 20X4, the Winter group disposed of its 70% holding in the ordinary shares of Spring for $9 million in cash. Winter originally purchased the shares for $6 million. At the acquisition date, the goodwill was $4.6 million, and has not been impaired. Spring's net assets at the disposal date were $5 million. The non-controlling interest in Spring at the disposal date was $3.1 million.

**What is the profit arising on the disposal of Spring that will be recorded in the consolidated statement of profit or loss for the year ended 31 December 20X4?**

$_____ ,000

**185** On 30 June 20X4, the Tea group disposed of its 60% holding in the ordinary shares of Coffee for $15 million in cash. The non-controlling interest at the acquisition date was measured at its fair value of $2.2 million.

Coffee's net assets at the acquisition and the disposal date were $5 million and $8 million respectively. Goodwill arising on the acquisition of Coffee of $1 million had been fully impaired by the disposal date.

**What is the profit arising on the disposal of Coffee that will be recorded in the consolidated statement of profit or loss for the year ended 31 December 20X4?**

A   Profit of $10.0 million

B   Profit of $9.2 million

C   Profit of $10.4 million

D   Profit of $10.2 million

# INTERPRETATION OF FINANCIAL STATEMENTS

**186   Which of the following statements about a not-for-profit entity is valid?**

A   There is no requirement to calculate an earnings per share figure as it is not likely to have shareholders who need to assess its earnings performance.

B   The current value of its property is not relevant as it is not a commercial entity.

C   Interpretation of its financial performance using ratio analysis is meaningless.

D   Its financial statements will not be closely scrutinised as it does not have investors.

**187   Which of the following ratios is likely to be most relevant for a local charity?**

A   Operating profit margin

B   Current ratio

C   Earnings per share

D   Return on capital employed

**188** Identify whether each of the following is a limitation of applying ratio analysis to published financial statements or not.

| | Limitation | Not a limitation |
|---|---|---|
| Different ways of calculating certain ratios exist | | |
| Accounting policy choices can limit comparability between different companies | | |

**189** The following information has been taken from Preston's financial statements:

Preston has inventory turnover of six times.

The year-end receivables collection period is 42 days.

Cost of sales for the year was $1,690,000. Credit purchases for the year were $2,150,000.

Preston's cash cycle at 31 December 20X7 was 68 days

All calculations should be made to the nearest full day, and the trading year has 365 days.

**What is Preston's trade payables collection period as at 31 December 20X7?**

_____ days

**190** **Which TWO of the following explanations are unlikely to lead to an increase in receivables collection period?**

A   A new contract with a large customer has been won following a competitive tender

B   A large one-off credit sale has been completed just before the year end

C   The entity has recently expanded into a number of high street retail units

D   Difficult economic conditions have led to some customers struggling to pay on time

E   A website has been opened in the year for trade direct to the public

**191** The following extracts of the financial statements of Wiggo have been obtained:

| | |
|---|---|
| Revenue | $980,000 |
| Cost of sales | ($530,000) |
| Operating expenses | ($210,000) |
| | |
| Equity | $600,000 |
| Loan | $300,000 |
| Deferred tax | $44,000 |
| Payables | $46,000 |

**What is the return on capital employed of Wiggo?**

A   24.2%

B   25.4%

C   26.7%

D   50%

**192** The following extracts of the financial statements of Wiggo have been obtained:

|                      | *20X5*     |
|----------------------|-----------|
| Inventories          | $130,000  |
| Receivables          | $80,000   |
| Cash                 | $10,000   |
| Loan repayable 20X8  | $90,000   |
| Deferred tax         | $14,000   |
| Payables             | $70,000   |
| Overdraft            | $34,000   |

**What is the quick ratio of Wiggo?**

_____:1

**193** **Which of the following items is unlikely to be considered a 'one-off' item which would impact the comparability of ratios?**

A    A new website selling direct to the public has meant that deliveries are now made to more diverse geographical areas, increasing delivery costs

B    A closure of a department has led to redundancies

C    Sale of surplus property leading to a profit on disposal

D    A storm in the year led to significant damage to the warehouse

**194** **Which of the following is not a valid reason for a decrease in gross profit margin?**

A    A major customer renewed their contract during the year following a competitive tender process

B    New plant and equipment used in the manufacturing process has been purchased in the year, which has increased the depreciation expense

C    Delivery costs to customers have risen following an increase in the rates charged by couriers

D    A national recession has led to sales prices being cut in response

**195** KRL manufactures pharmaceuticals, and is investigating a proposed takeover of another entity which is based overseas.

**Identify which sources of information will be available for KRL to use in relation to the acquisition.**

|                                                                      | **Available to KRL to use** | **Not available to KRL to use** |
|----------------------------------------------------------------------|------------------------------|---------------------------------|
| Details of the overseas country in which the target entity operates  |                              |                                 |
| Recent financial statements of the entity                            |                              |                                 |
| Internal business plans of the takeover target                       |                              |                                 |

**196**   Marcel has calculated that its current year Price Earnings (P/E) ratio is 12.6.

The sector average P/E ratio is 10.5

**Which of the following would be an explanation of the difference between Marcel's P/E ratio and the sector average?**

A   Marcel is seen as a less risky investment than the sector average, and there is higher confidence about the future prospects of Marcel.

B   Marcel is seen as a more risky investment than the sector average, however there is higher confidence about the future prospects of Marcel.

C   Marcel is seen as a less risky investment than the sector average, however there is low confidence about the future prospects of Marcel.

D   Marcel is seen as a more risky investment than the sector average, and there is low confidence about the future prospects of Marcel.

**197**   **Identify whether the statements about diluted earnings per share below are true or false.**

|  | True | False |
|---|---|---|
| It acts as a prediction of the future Earnings Per Share figure |  |  |
| It discloses that Earnings Per Share could have been higher |  |  |

**198**   Apollo took out a new loan on 1 January 20X6. This loan carries an effective interest rate of 8%. The initial proceeds of the loan are $2.5m, which is after paying issue costs of $250k. The coupon rate on the loan is 6%. Apollo must keep to an interest cover ratio of 9 times under the arrangements made with the bank.

**What operating profit must be maintained by Apollo in the year ended 31 December 20X6, in order to meet the minimum interest cover ratio specified by the bank?**

A   $1,350,000

B   $1,800,000

C   $450,000

D   $1,980,000

---

**The following information is to be used for questions 199 and 200:**

Rogers has just completed their financial statements for the year ended 30 June 20X6. They are reporting a net profit of $1,250,000 for the current year, and they have $1 million 50 cent shares in issue.  The current market price of Rogers' shares is $3.50.

Rogers has paid total dividends during the year ended 30 June 20X6 of $1,500,000.

---

**199**   **What is the Price Earnings (P/E) ratio of Rogers for the year ended 30 June 20X6?**

_____ times

**200**   **What is the dividend yield (to one decimal place) for the year ended 30 June 20X6?**

_____ %

---

**201** Alco and Saleco are both food retailers. They are both showing a return on capital employed (ROCE) figure of 10% for the current year. Both companies have the same financial year end. Alco has reported a net profit (based on profit before interest and tax) of 25% and Saleco has reported a net profit of 2%.

**What, if any, is the difference between these two companies, even though they are showing the same ROCE calculation?**

A    The companies are identical

B    Alco operates at the high end of the market, and Saleco at the lower end

C    Alco operates at the lower end of the market, and Saleco at the high end

D    There is not enough information in the question to determine the difference

**202** **Identify whether each of the following is a limitation of applying ratio analysis to published financial statements or not.**

|  | Limitation | Not a limitation |
|---|---|---|
| Financial statements often use historic cost, meaning that inflation is not taken into account |  |  |
| Complex items may not fit into any accounting standards and therefore may be omitted from the financial statements |  |  |

**203** Lepchem is a pharmaceutical business which was launched in September 20X1. Lepchem have been funded through bank loans and equity investment. Lepchem's aim is to develop new pharmaceuticals which could then be sold for a high margin. So far, Lepchem have not managed to successfully develop or sell any pharmaceuticals.

**Which ratio is likely to be the most relevant for Lepchem for the year to 31 December 20X1?**

A    Current ratio

B    Gross profit margin

C    Operating profit margin

D    Receivables collection period

**204** **Identify whether the following criteria could be used to assess the performance of a not-for-profit entity.**

|  | Could be used to assess | Will not be used |
|---|---|---|
| The return given to investors |  |  |
| The success in achieving the organisation's stated aims |  |  |
| How well costs are being managed |  |  |

**205** Which of the following measures is likely to be the least relevant to a property management business which rents out commercial properties?

A    Non-current asset turnover

B    Return on capital employed

C    Average rent earned

D    Inventory turnover period

**206** Quartile is in the jewellery retail business which can be assumed to be highly seasonal. For the year ended 30 September 20X4, Quartile assessed its operating performance by comparing selected accounting ratios with those of its business sector average as provided by an agency. You may assume that the business sector used by the agency is an accurate representation of Quartile's business.

**Which TWO of the following circumstances may invalidate the comparison of Quartile's ratios with those of the sector average?**

A    In the current year, Quartile has experienced significant rising costs for its purchases

B    The sector average figures are compiled from companies whose year-end is between 1 July 20X4 and 30 September 20X4

C    Quartile does not revalue its properties, but is aware that others in this sector do

D    During the year, Quartile discovered an error relating to the inventory count at 30 September 20X3. This error was correctly accounted for in the financial statements for the current year ended 30 September 20X4

**207** The following information has been taken or calculated from Fowler's financial statements for the year ended 30 September 20X4.

Fowler's cash cycle at 30 September 20X4 is 70 days. Its inventory turnover is six times.

Year-end trade payables are $230,000.

Purchases on credit for the year were $2 million.

Cost of sales for the year was $1.8 million.

**What is Fowler's trade receivables collection period as at 30 September 20X4?**

$_____ days

**208** Trent uses the formula (year-end trade receivables/credit sales for the year) × 365 to calculate how many days on average its customers take to pay.

**Which TWO of the following would NOT affect the correctness of the above calculation of the average number of days a customer takes to pay?**

A    Trent experiences considerable seasonal trading

B    Trent makes a number of cash sales through retail outlets

C    Revenue does not include a 15% sales tax whereas the receivables do include the tax

D    Trent factors with recourse the receivable of its largest customer

**209** At 31 March 20X5 Jasim had equity of $200,000 and debt of $100,000.

**Which of the following transactions, considered separately, would increase Jasim's gearing?**

A    During the year a property was revalued upwards by $20,000

B    A bonus issue of equity shares of 1 for 4 was made during the year using other components of equity

C    A provision for estimated damages was reduced during the year from $21,000 to $15,000 based on the most recent legal advice

D    An asset was acquired under a lease with a present value of lease payments of $23,000

**210** **Which of the following current year events would explain a fall in an entity's operating profit margin compared to the previous year?**

A    An increase in gearing leading to higher interest costs

B    A reduction in the allowance for uncollectable receivables

C    A decision to value inventory on the average cost basis from the first in first out (FIFO) basis. Unit prices of inventory had risen during the current year

D    A change from the amortisation of development costs being included in cost of sales to being included in administrative expenses

## STATEMENT OF CASH FLOWS

**211** The following information is available for the property, plant and equipment of Fry as at 30 September:

|  | 20X4 | 20X3 |
| --- | --- | --- |
|  | $000 | $000 |
| Carrying amounts | 23,400 | 14,400 |

The following items were recorded during the year ended 30 September 20X4:

(i)    Depreciation charge of $2.5 million

(ii)   An item of plant, with a carrying amount of $3 million, was sold for $1.8 million

(iii)  A property was revalued upwards by $2 million

(iv)   Environmental provisions of $4 million relating to property, plant and equipment were capitalised during the year

**What amount would be shown in Fry's statement of cash flows for purchase of property, plant and equipment for the year ended 30 September 20X4?**

$_____ '000

**212** At 1 October 20X4, BK had accrued interest payable of $12,000.

During the year ended 30 September 20X5, BK charged finance costs of $41,000 to its statement of profit or loss, including unwinding a discount relating to a provision stated at its present value of $150,000 at 1 October 20X4. The closing balance on accrued interest payable account at 30 September 20X5 was $15,000, and BK has a discount rate of 6%.

**How much interest paid should BK show on its statement of cash flows for the year ended 30 September 20X5?**

A     $38,000

B     $29,000

C     $35,000

D     $41,000

**213** The following balances were extracted from N's statement of financial position as at 31 December.

| | 20X9 | 20X8 |
| --- | --- | --- |
| | $000 | $000 |
| Deferred taxation | 38 | 27 |
| Current tax payable | 119 | 106 |

Extract from statement of profit or loss for the year ended 31 December 20X9.

| | $000 |
| --- | --- |
| Income tax expense | 122 |

**The amount of tax paid that should be included in N's statement of cash flows for the year ended 31 December 20X9 is:**

$_____ ,000

**214** **Which item would be NOT be shown in a statement of cash flow using the direct method?**

A     Cash payments to employees

B     Cash paid to suppliers

C     Cash sales

D     Finance costs

**215** IAS 7 *Statement of Cash Flows* sets out the three main headings to be used in a statement of cash flows.

**Which TWO of the items below would be included under the heading 'Cash flows from operating activities' according to IAS 7?**

A     Tax paid

B     Purchase of investments

C     Loss on disposal of machinery

D     Purchase of equipment

**216** During the year to 31 July 20X7 Smartypants made a profit of $37,500 after accounting for depreciation of $2,500.

During the year non-current assets were purchased for $16,000, receivables increased by $2,000, inventories decreased by $3,600 and trade payables increased by $700.

**What was the increase in cash and bank balances during the year?**

A  $21,300

B  $30,300

C  $24,900

D  $26,300

**217** **Identify the correct treatment in the calculation of net cash from operating activities under the indirect method.**

| | Add to profit before tax | Deduct from profit before tax |
|---|---|---|
| Decrease in trade receivables | | |
| Increase in inventories | | |
| Profit on sale of non-current assets | | |
| Depreciation | | |

**218** Butcher had the following balances in its statement of financial position as at 30 June 20X0 and 20X1:

| | 20X1 | 20X0 |
|---|---|---|
| Share capital | $170,000 | $150,000 |
| Share premium | $105,000 | $95,000 |
| 10% debentures | $170,000 | $190,000 |

**How much will appear in the statement of cash flows for the year ended 30 June 20X1 under the heading 'cash flows from financing activities'?**

$_____ ,000

**219** At 1 January 20X0 Casey had property, plant and equipment with a carrying amount of $180,000. In the year ended 31 December 20X0 Casey disposed of assets with a carrying amount of $60,000 for $50,000. Casey revalued a building from $75,000 to $100,000 and charged depreciation for the year of $20,000. At the end of the year, the carrying amount of property, plant and equipment was $250,000.

**How much will be reported in the statement of cash flows for the year ended 31 December 20X0 under the heading 'cash flows from investing activities'?**

A  $75,000 outflow

B  $125,000 outflow

C  $135,000 outflow

D  $50,000 inflow

**220** At 1 January 20X0 Casey had government grants held in deferred income of $900,000. During the year, Casey released $100,000 to the statement of profit or loss. At 31 December 20X0, the remaining deferred income balance was $1,100,000.

**Select the TWO amounts to be included in the statement of cash flows for Casey.**

| Amortisation of government grant | Receipt of grant |
|---|---|
| Increase of 100,000 to cash generated from operations | Cash received from grant $300,000 in investing activities |
| Decrease of 100,000 to cash generated from operations | Cash received from grant $100,000 in investing activities |

# Section 2

# OBJECTIVE CASE QUESTIONS – SECTION B

## CONCEPTUAL FRAMEWORK/INTERNATIONAL FINANCIAL REPORTING STANDARDS

**The following scenario relates to questions 221–225**

Flightline is an airline which treats its aircraft as complex non-current assets, accounted for under the historical cost model. The cost and other details of an aircraft are:

|  | $000 | Estimated life |
|---|---|---|
| Interior cabin fittings – installed 1 April 20X5 | 25,000 | 5 years |
| Engine - installed 1 April 20X5 | 9,000 | 36,000 flying hours |

In the year ended 31 March 20X9, the aircraft flew for 1,200 hours for the six months to 30 September 20X8.

On 1 October 20X8 the aircraft suffered a 'bird strike' accident which damaged the engine beyond repair. This was replaced by a new engine with a life of 36,000 hours at cost of $10.8 million.

Flightline's year end is 31 March 20X9.

221 What is the depreciation to be charged in respect of the engine for the 6 month period to 1 October 20X8?

$_____ ,000

222 Which of the following explains the correct accounting treatment of the engine?

    A    Write off the damaged engine, capitalise the new engine and depreciate over 24,000 hours

    B    Treat the $10.8 million as a repair to the damaged engine and continue to depreciate the engine as in the first 6 months

    C    Capitalise $6 million to replace the damaged engine, expense the other $4.8 million

    D    Write off the damaged engine, capitalise the new engine and depreciate over 36,000 hours

**223** A wing was also damaged, but was repaired at a cost of $3 million. The accident also caused cosmetic damage to the exterior of the aircraft which required repainting at a cost of $2 million.

**Identify the correct treatment for the $3 million repair costs to the wing and the $2 million repainting of the aircraft**

|  | Capitalise | Expense |
|---|---|---|
| $3 million repair of the wing |  |  |
| $2 million repainting of the exterior |  |  |

**224** As the aircraft was out of service for some weeks due to the accident, Flightline took the opportunity to upgrade its cabin facilities at a cost of $4.5 million. This did not increase the estimated remaining life of the cabin fittings, but the improved facilities enabled Flightline to substantially increase the air fares on this aircraft.

**What is the carrying amount of the cabin fittings as at 31 March 20X9?**

A    $8,600,000

B    $8,000,000

C    $5,000,000

D    $7,250,000

**225** The 'bird strike' accident represents an indication of impairment.

**Complete the following sentence from the choice below.**

The aircraft will be impaired if its _____ exceeds its recoverable amount.

Options: Replacement cost, Fair value less costs to sell, Carrying amount, Value in use

---

**The following scenario relates to questions 226–230**

Speculate owns two properties and uses fair value accounting where possible.

Property A: An office building used by Speculate for administrative purposes. At 1 April 20X2 it had a carrying amount of $2 million and a remaining life of 20 years. On 1 October 20X2, the property was let to a third party and reclassified as an investment property. The property had a fair value of $2.3 million at 1 October 20X2, and $2.34 million at 31 March 20X3.

Property B: Another office building let on a 12-month lease to a subsidiary of Speculate. At 1 April 20X2, it had a fair value of $1.5 million which had risen to $1.65 million at 31 March 20X3.

---

**226** **What is the correct treatment when Property A is reclassified as an investment property?**

A    Take $350,000 gain to other comprehensive income

B    Take $350,000 gain to the statement of profit or loss

C    Take $400,000 gain to other comprehensive income

D    Take $400,000 gain to the statement of profit or loss

227    Which of the following models can Speculate use to account for investment properties in its individual financial statements?

(i)     Cost model

(ii)    Revaluation model

(iii)   Fair value model

A      (i) and (ii) only

B      (i) and (iii) only

C      (ii) and (iii) only

D      All three

228    What is the total gain for investment properties to be included in Speculate's individual statement of profit or loss for the year ended 31 March 20X3? Enter your answer to the nearest dollar ($).

$ _____

229    In the individual and consolidated financial statements of Speculate, how would Property B be accounted for?

| Individual | ✓ | Consolidated | ✓ |
|---|---|---|---|
| Investment property | | Investment property | |
| Property, plant & equipment | | Property, plant & equipment | |
| Within goodwill | | Cancelled as an intra-group item | |

230    What would the carrying amount of Property A be at 31 March 20X3 if Speculate used the cost model for investment properties?

A      $1,950,000

B      $1,900,000

C      $2,185,000

D      $2,182,051

**The following scenario relates to questions 231–235**

Apex received a $10 million 6% loan on 1 April 20X7. The loan will be redeemable at a premium which means the loan has an effective finance cost of 7.5% per annum. The loan was specifically issued to finance the building of a new store.

Construction of the store commenced on 1 May 20X7 and it was completed and ready for use on 28 February 20X8, but did not open for trading until 1 April 20X8.

**231** **How should the loan be treated in the financial statements of Apex for the year ended 31 March 20X8?**

A     Present value

B     Fair value through other comprehensive income

C     Fair value through profit or loss

D     Amortised cost

**232** **Which TWO of the statements below regarding IAS 23 *Borrowing Costs* are correct?**

A     Borrowing costs must be capitalised if they are directly attributable to qualifying assets

B     Borrowing costs should cease to be capitalised once the related asset is substantially complete

C     Borrowing costs must be capitalised if they are directly attributable to non-current assets

D     Borrowing costs may be capitalised if they are directly attributable to qualifying assets

E     Borrowing costs should commence to be capitalised once expenditure is being incurred on the construction of the asset

**233** **How much should be recorded as finance costs in the statement of profit or loss for the year ended 31 March 20X8?**

$_____ ,000

**234** **How much interest should be capitalised as part of property, plant and equipment as at 31 March 20X8?**

$_____ ,000

**235** Apex decided that not all of the funds raised were needed immediately and temporarily invested some of the funds in April 20X7, earning $40,000 interest.

**How should the $40,000 be accounted for in the financial statements of Apex?**

A     Net off the amount capitalised in property, plant and equipment

B     Taken to the statement of profit or loss as investment income

C     Taken as other comprehensive income

D     Deducted from the outstanding loan amount in the statement of financial position

**The following scenario relates to questions 236–240**

Shawler constructed a furnace on 1 April 20X3, causing significant environmental damage which must be repaired at the end of the asset's useful life of ten years. The present value of this is estimated to be $4 million. Shawler has a cost of capital of 8%.

On 1 October 20X3, Shawler received a government grant of $1.2 million relating to the cost of plant with a five year life. Shawler accounts for grants using the deferred credit method.

On 1 October 20X3, Shawler also acquired land for 12 million dinars. The land was used to construct a factory during the year. Shawler's functional currency is the dollar ($).

On 1 October 20X3 the exchange rate was 4 Dinars: $1. At 31 March 20X4 the exchange rate was 2 Dinars:$1 and the average rate for the year was 3 Dinars:$1.

236    What is the total finance cost (to the nearest thousand) to be recorded in the statement of profit or loss in respect of the environmental damage caused by the furnace for the year ended 31 March 20X4?

    A    $400,000

    B    $320,000

    C    $4,000,000

    D    $185,000

237    What is the non-current liability in respect of the government grant to be shown in Shawler's statement of financial position as at 31 March 20X4?

    A    $840,000

    B    $1,080,000

    C    $960,000

    D    $720,000

238    What is the carrying amount of the land to be shown in the statement of financial position of Shawler as at 31 March 20X4? Give your answer to the nearest $000.

    $_____ ,000

239    The costs below are the costs associated with the construction of the factory.

    **Which of the following can NOT be capitalised?**

    A    Legal fees relating to the site purchase

    B    Health and safety training for new construction workers

    C    Direct labour costs associated with the construction

    D    Costs of site preparation

**240** In the following year it was discovered that Shawler had breached the conditions relating to the government grant and therefore the grant had to be repaid.

**Which TWO of the following describe the correct accounting treatment to record the repayment of the grant?**

A Remove all deferred income balances

B Record an expense in the statement of profit or loss

C Increase the cost of plant

D Make an adjustment to the prior year financial statements

---

**The following scenario relates to questions 241–245**

During the year Darby started research work on a new processor chip. Darby has a past history of being particularly successful in bringing similar projects to a profitable conclusion. In addition to this, Darby spent $200,000 training staff to use new equipment.

Darby also developed a new online platform during the year, spending $100,000 a month evenly from 1 February 20X5 to 31 October 20X5. Darby was unsure of the outcome of the project, but doubts were resolved on 1 May, following successful testing. The platform launched on 1 November 20X5 and was expected to last 5 years.

---

**241** Darby's accounting assistant has read something which states that intangible assets are identifiable, non-monetary items without physical substance.

**Which TWO of the following relate to items being classed as identifiable?**

A Items must have probable future economic benefits

B Items must arise from legal or contractual rights

C Items must have a measurable cost

D Items must be separable

**242** Identify the correct accounting treatment for items below.

|  | Capitalise | Expense |
|---|---|---|
| Training for staff |  |  |
| Expenditure on processor chip |  |  |

**243** How much should be recorded in Darby's statement of profit or loss for the year ended 31 December 20X5 in relation to the development of the online platform?

$_____ ,000

**244** **Which of the facts relating to the online platform is correct?**

(i)  The online platform will be subject to annual impairment review due to the judgemental nature of the project.

(ii)  Once capitalised, the development costs should be held at fair value at each year-end.

(iii)  Depreciation on any plant used to develop the platform would be capitalised as part of the development costs.

A  (i) only

B  (ii) and (iii) only

C  (iii) only

D  (i) and (ii) only

**245** Darby acquired a patent with a 10 year life for $500,000 on 1 January 20X5. On 31 December 20X5, management believed that the patent was less fully utilised than expected and determined the following information as part of their impairment review:

|  | $000 |
|---|---|
| Potential sale proceeds of the patent | 400 |
| Estimated disposal costs | 20 |
| Value in use of the asset | 480 |

**What is the value of the impairment loss in the year ended 31 December 20X5?**

A  $70,000

B  $30,000

C  $20,000

D  Nil

**The following scenario relates to questions 246–250**

Aphrodite has a year end of 31 December and operates a factory which makes computer chips for mobile phones. It purchased a machine on 1 July 20X3 for $80,000 which had a useful life of ten years and is depreciated on the straight-line basis, time apportioned in the years of acquisition and disposal. The machine was revalued to $81,000 on 1 July 20X4. There was no change to its useful life at that date.

A fire at the factory on 1 October 20X6 damaged the machine, leaving it with a lower operating capacity. The accountant considers that Aphrodite will need to recognise an impairment loss in relation to this damage. The accountant has ascertained the following information at 1 October 20X6:

(1)     The carrying amount of the machine is $60,750.

(2)     An equivalent new machine would cost $90,000.

(3)     The machine could be sold in its current condition for a gross amount of $45,000. Dismantling costs would amount to $2,000.

(4)     In its current condition, the machine could operate for three more years which gives it a value in use figure of $38,685.

246     **In accordance with IAS 16 *Property, Plant and Equipment*, what is the depreciation charged to Aphrodite's statement of profit or loss in respect of the machine for the year ended 31 December 20X4?**

    A    $9,000

    B    $8,000

    C    $8,263

    D    $8,500

247     IAS 36 *Impairment of Assets* contains a number of examples of internal and external events which may indicate the impairment of an asset.

    **In accordance with IAS 36, which of the following would definitely NOT be an indicator of the potential impairment of an asset (or group of assets)?**

    A    An unexpected fall in the market value of one or more assets

    B    Adverse changes in the economic performance of one or more assets

    C    A significant change in the technological environment in which an asset is employed making its software effectively obsolete

    D    The carrying amount of an entity's net assets being below the entity's market capitalisation

248     **What is the total impairment loss associated with Aphrodite's machine at 1 October 20X6?**

    A    $nil

    B    $17,750

    C    $22,065

    D    $15,750

**249** The accountant has decided that it is too difficult to reliably attribute cash flows to this one machine and that it would be more accurate to calculate the impairment on the basis of the factory as a cash-generating unit.

**In accordance with IAS 36 *Impairment of Assets*, which TWO of the following are TRUE regarding cash generating units?**

A   A cash-generating unit to which goodwill has been allocated should be tested for impairment every five years.

B   A cash-generating unit must be a subsidiary of the parent.

C   There is no need to consistently identify cash-generating units based on the same types of asset from period to period.

D   A cash-generating unit is the smallest identifiable group of assets for which independent cash flows can be identified.

E   Assets in a cash-generating unit should never be impaired below their recoverable amount.

**250** On 1 July 20X7, it is discovered that the damage to the machine is worse than originally thought. The machine is now considered to be worthless and the recoverable amount of the factory as a cash-generating unit is estimated to be $950,000.

At 1 July 20X7, the cash-generating unit comprises the following assets:

|  | $000 |
|---|---|
| Building | 500 |
| Plant and equipment (including the damaged machine at a carrying amount of $35,000) | 335 |
| Goodwill | 85 |
| Net current assets (at recoverable amount) | 250 |
|  | 1,170 |

**In accordance with IAS 36 *Impairment of Assets*, what will be the carrying amount of Aphrodite's plant and equipment when the impairment loss has been allocated to the cash-generating unit?**

$_____

**The following scenario relates to questions 251–255**

Radar's directors made the following decisions during the year ended 31 March 20X3:

- it disposed of all of its outlets in country A

- it rebranded all of its outlets in country B to target the tourism market. The previous target market in country B had been aimed at business clients.

At a board meeting on 1 January 20X3, Pulsar's directors decided sell an item of plant, which had a carrying value of $4 million at 1 April 20X2 and a remaining life of 20 years. The plant is expected to sell for $3.9 million within 12 months.

A decision was also made to close down a regional office, which was communicated to the employees before the year-end. 50 employees would be retrained and kept within Radar at a cost of $100,000, the others took redundancy and will be paid $300,000.

$75,000 is to be spent on marketing materials directing customers of the existing factory to other production facilities operated by Radar.

251 **Which of the following statements regarding discontinued operations is correct?**

    A      Profit from discontinued operations is shown under other comprehensive income

    B      Profit from discontinued operations includes any gain or loss on disposal

    C      Profit or loss from discontinued operations only relates to items that have already been sold or disposed by the year-end

    D      Profit or loss from discontinued operations excludes any closure costs

252 **Identify whether the change in operations in countries A and B represent a discontinued operation in accordance with IFRS 5 *Non-Current Assets Held for Sale and Discontinued Operations*.**

    A      Only country A represents a discontinued operation

    B      Only country B represents a discontinued operation

    C      Both countries will be regarded as discontinued operations

    D      Neither country will be regarded as a discontinued operation

253 **At what value should the plant be held at 31 March 20X3 according to IFRS 5 *Non-Current Assets Held for Sale and Discontinued Operations*?**

    A      $3,800,000

    B      $3,900,000

    C      $4,000,000

    D      $3,850,000

**254**   **What provision should be recorded in relation to the office closure?**

  A   $300,000

  B   $475,000

  C   $375,000

  D   $400,000

**255**   On 30 June 20X3, before the financial statements were authorised for issue, the plant was sold at a loss of $100,000 and the redundancies were settled at $50,000 more than expected.

  **Identify whether each item represents an adjusting or non-adjusting event according to IAS 10 Events After the Reporting Period**

| | Adjusting event | Non-adjusting event |
|---|---|---|
| Disposal of plant | | |
| Redundancy settlement | | |

---

**The following scenario relates to questions 256–260**

Tunshill has an item of plant with an estimated five-year life. The plant is wearing well and at 1 October 20X8 the production manager believed that the plant was likely to last 5 more years.

Tunshill wishes to change its method of inventory valuation from first-in/first-out (FIFO) to average cost (AVCO). The value of Tunshill's inventory at 30 September 20X9 (on the FIFO basis) is $20 million.  However, on the AVCO basis it would be valued at $18 million. Tunshill's inventory at 30 September 20X8 was $15 million, but on the AVCO basis it would have been reported as $13.4 million.

Tunshill also has two items of inventory that require review.  Item A cost $50 per unit. Tunshill has struggled to sell the item and has 2,000 units still in inventory.  Tunshill has agreed a contract with a distributor to sell the items for $55 each, but will charge commission of 20%.

Item B relates to a one-off purchase of rare metal for a profitable contract costing $80,000.  No work has yet been done, but after further costs of $20,000 it will be converted into a product and sold for an agreed price of $150,000. Since buying the metal, the cost price has fallen to $50,000.

---

**256**   **Which TWO circumstances are outlined in IAS 8 *Accounting Policies, Changes in Accounting Estimates and Errors* as acceptable reasons to change accounting policy?**

  A   To provide greater comparison with competitors

  B   If a change results in providing more reliable and relevant information to users

  C   If required by an International Financial Reporting Standard

  D   If tax law in a country changes

  E   To show the best possible results for the investors

**257** **Fill in the blanks in the sentence below with the correct option.**

The change in useful life of the plant will be a change in accounting _____ and should be applied _____.

Options: Policy, Estimate, Error, Retrospectively, Prospectively, Prudently

**258** **Which of the options below outline the correct treatment for the change in valuation method from FIFO to AVCO?**

A       Profit would be reduced by $400,000

B       Profit would be reduced by $2,000,000

C       Opening retained earnings would increase by $1,600,000

D       Opening retained earnings would decrease by $400,000

**259** **At what value should item A be included in Tunshill's statement of financial position as at 30 September 20X9?**

$_____ ,000

**260** **At what value should item B be included in Tunshill's statement of financial position as at 30 September 20X9?**

A       $50,000

B       $80,000

C       $130,000

D       $100,000

**The following scenario relates to questions 261–265**

Schrute owns a herd of cattle, which produce milk. Schrute then turns this into cheese.

On 1 April 20X5, Schrute purchased a flock of sheep for $100,000, which included transaction costs of $5,000. At 31 March 20X6, the flock was valued at $120,000. Every time animals are sold there is a 5% commission fee payable to the national farming agency.

Shrute uses the historical cost model and charges all depreciation as an operating expense.

In addition to this, Schrute uses a number of items of specialised farm machinery. This machinery cost Schrute $200,000 on 1 April 20X2 and has a 10-year useful life. At 31 March 20X6, there is only one supplier who still sells this machinery and the current price of new machinery is $300,000.

261 **Which of the following items held by Schrute will be accounted for under the provisions of IAS 41 *Agriculture*?**

   (i)     Herd of cattle

   (ii)    Milk

   (iii)   Cheese

   A     (i) only

   B     (ii) and (iii) only

   C     (i) and (ii) only

   D     All three items

262 **What gain should be taken to Shrute's statement of profit or loss for the year ended 31 March 20X6 in respect of the flock of sheep?**

   $_____

263 **Using current cost accounting, what is the value of the machinery at 31 March 20X6?**

   A     $120,000

   B     $180,000

   C     $200,000

   D     $300,000

264 At 31 March 20X6, a valuations expert informed the directors of Schrute that the property owned and used by Shrute for farming had significantly increased in value. This had been decided by looking at the price per square metre at similar properties in the area and concluded that this could be used to value Schrute's farm with no adjustments necessary.

   **Which of the following bases describes the fair value method used to value the farm?**

   A     Level 1 input

   B     Level 2 input

   C     Level 3 input

   D     Level 4 input

**265** If Schrute chooses to value the farm at the market value, which TWO of the following ratios will NOT be affected?

A    Current ratio

B    Return on capital employed

C    Gross profit margin

D    Gearing

E    Net profit (before tax) margin

---

**The following scenario relates to questions 266–270**

On 1 October 20X6 Fino entered into an agreement to lease twenty telephones for its team of sales staff. The telephones are to be leased for a period of 24 months at a cost of $240 per telephone per annum, payable annually in advance. The present value of the lease payments at 1 October 20X6 is $9,164.

On 1 April 20X7, Fino entered into an agreement to lease an item of plant from the manufacturer. The lease required four annual payments in advance of $100,000 each commencing on 1 April 20X7. The plant would have a useful life of four years and would be scrapped at the end of this period. The present value of the total lease payments is $350,000.

Fino has a cost of capital of 10%.

---

**266** Which of the following applies the principle of faithful representation to the above plant lease agreement?

A    Recording an annual rent expense in Fino's statement of profit or loss

B    Expensing any interest on a straight-line basis over 4 years

C    Recording an asset in Fino's statement of financial position to reflect control

D    Record the $100,000 paid as a prepayment to be released over 4 years

**267** How much would be charged to Fino's statement of profit or loss for the year ended 30 September 20X7 in respect of the telephones?

A    $4,800

B    $4,582

C    $4,364

D    $5,498

**268** What would be the carrying amount of the leased plant as at 30 September 20X7?

$_____

**269** What interest would be charged to Fino's statement of profit or loss for the year ended 30 September 20X7 in respect of the plant lease?

A    $12,500

B    $25,000

C    $17,500

D    $35,000

270 Applying the principles of IFRS 16 *Leases* to capitalise the plant and recognise the lease liability would have what impact upon the following ratios?

| | Increase | Decrease |
|---|---|---|
| Return on Capital Employed | | |
| Gearing | | |
| Interest cover | | |

---

**The following scenario relates to questions 271–275**

On 1 January 20X6 Lotso entered into an agreement to lease new machinery under a 5 year lease, with $300,000 payable on 31 December each year. The asset has a useful life of 6 years, and ownership transfers to Lotso at the end of the lease. The interest rate implicit in the lease is 6% and the present value of the lease payments is $1,263,000.

On 1 January 20X6 Lotso sold its head office to a finance company, but continued to use the head office for the remainder of its 20-year estimated useful life under a lease agreement. The carrying amount of the head office on 1 January 20X6 was $10 million and the fair value of the asset and sale proceeds received on 1 January 20X6 were $11.5 million.

271 What would be the finance cost in respect of the machinery lease for the year ended 31 December 20X6?

    A    $62,327

    B    $90,000

    C    $75,780

    D    $63,150

272 What current liability (to the nearest thousand) will be recorded in Lotso's statement of financial position as at 31 December 20X6 in relation to the machinery lease?

    A    $300,000

    B    $238,000

    C    $1,039,000

    D    $801,000

273 What is the carrying amount of the machinery as at 31 December 20X6?

    A    $1,039,000

    B    $1,263,000

    C    $1,052,500

    D    $1,010,400

**274** **What would be the carrying amount of the head office at 31 December 20X6?**

A    Nil

B    $9,500,000

C    $8,075,000

D    $10,925,000

**275** **Identify if the statements below are true or false**

Statement 1: In a sale and leaseback transaction, no profit will be recognised by the lessee.

Statement 2: In a sale and leaseback transaction, the sale proceeds will usually be treated as a loan to the lessee.

|             | True | False |
|-------------|------|-------|
| Statement 1 |      |       |
| Statement 2 |      |       |

---

**The following scenario relates to questions 276–280**

On 1 September 20X3, Laidlaw factored (sold) $2 million of trade receivables to Finease. Laidlaw received an immediate payment of $1.8 million. Under the factoring agreement any receivables not collected after four months will be sold back to Laidlaw.

On 1 October 20X2, Laidlaw sold some maturing inventory which had a cost of $4.5 million to a bank for its fair value of $5 million. Under the terms of the sale agreement Laidlaw has the option to repurchase the inventory after a period of ten years at a price of $7.4 million. At this date the fair value of the inventory is expected to be $11 million, and the repurchase price reflects an equivalent annual rate of interest of 4%

Laidlaw issued $10 million convertible loan notes on 1 October 20X2 that carry a nominal (coupon) interest rate of 5% per annum, and are redeemable on 1 October 20X5. A similar loan note, without the conversion option, would have required Laidlaw to pay an interest rate of 8%.

Relevant discount rates are shown below:

|             |   | 5%   | 8%   |
|-------------|---|------|------|
| End of year | 1 | 0.95 | 0.93 |
|             | 2 | 0.91 | 0.86 |
|             | 3 | 0.86 | 0.79 |

---

**276** **Which of the following is correct regarding Laidlaw's factoring of trade receivables for the year ended 30 September 20X3?**

A    $200,000 should be recorded as an administrative expense for the disposal of the receivables

B    The receivables should be removed from the statement of financial position

C    This represents a 'without recourse' factoring agreement

D    The receipt of $1.8 million should be treated as a loan

277 **What amount should be recorded in equity (to the nearest thousand) in respect of the convertible loan notes issued by Laidlaw?**

$_____000

278 **Which TWO of the following items should be recorded in Laidlaw's financial statements for the year ended 30 September 20X3 in respect of the maturing inventory sale?**

A    $200,000 finance cost

B    $50,000 release of deferred income

C    $5 million revenue

D    $5.2 million loan

E    $450,000 deferred income liability

F    $500,000 gross profit

279 **Which of the following statements regarding the convertible loan notes is NOT true?**

A    The convertible loan notes will affect gearing due to the liability component being different to the equity component

B    The equity amount will remain fixed until the date of conversion

C    The liability at 30 September 20X5 will be $10 million

D    5% interest will be charged to the statement of profit or loss as a finance cost

280 **Applying the principle of split accounting to convertible loan notes is important to satisfy which of the following qualitative characteristics?**

A    Faithful representation

B    Timeliness

C    Verifiability

D    Relevance

**The following scenario relates to questions 281–285**

The following trial balance extract relates to Howard at 30 September 20X5:

|  | $000 | $000 |
|---|---|---|
| Convertible loan notes – Liability component at 1 Oct X4 (note (i)) |  | 28,508 |
| 5% loan notes (note (ii)) |  | 10,000 |
| Equity investments (note (iii)) | 6,000 |  |

The following notes are relevant:

(i)     The convertible loan notes are 8% $30 million convertible loan notes issued on 1 October 20X4 at par. An equivalent loan without the conversion would carry an interest rate of 10%. Howard's finance director correctly split the instrument into its equity and liability components at 1 October 20X4, but has done nothing else.

(ii)    The 5% loan notes were issued at par of $10 million, but Howard incurred $400,000 issue costs. The loan notes have an effective interest rate of 8%.

(iii)   The equity investments relate to 1 million shares in Kapoor, an unrelated entity. During the year, Kapoor paid a dividend of 10 cents per share. At 30 September 20X5 the fair value of each Kapoor share was $7.

**281    Which of the items included in the trial balance extract will be classified as financial instruments?**

A       Convertible loan notes and equity investments only

B       Loan notes and equity investments only

C       Convertible loan notes and loan notes only

D       All three items

**282    What should the value of the liability element of the convertible loan note be at 30 September 20X5, to the nearest thousand?**

A       $28,508,000

B       $28,389,000

C       $28,959,000

D       $30,000,000

**283    What finance cost should be shown in the statement of profit or loss in respect of the loan notes?**

$_____

**284    What income should be recorded in the statement of profit or loss in relation to the equity investments?**

A       $600,000

B       $1,100,000

C       $1,600,000

D       $1,000,000

285 Howard is uncertain of how to treat professional fees. For which of the following investments should professional fees be capitalised as part of initial value of the asset?

| | Capitalised | Not capitalised |
|---|---|---|
| Fair value through other comprehensive income investments | | |
| Fair value through profit or loss investments | | |
| Amortised cost investments | | |

---

**The following scenario relates to questions 286–290**

Vance buys and sells goods in Kromits (Kr), but has a functional currency of dollars ($).

Vance purchased goods for Kr 10,000 on 1 September 20X1. At Vance's year-end of 31 December 20X1 this amount remains unpaid.

Vance sold goods on 1 September 20X1 for Kr 60,000. On 1 October 20X1 Vance received Kr 30,000. The remaining Kr 30,000 is unpaid at 31 December 20X1.

Vance's assistant accountant estimated the tax expense for the year ended 31 December 20X1 at $43,000. However, he had ignored deferred tax. At 1 January 20X1 Vance had a deferred tax liability of $130,000. At 31 December 20X1 Vance had temporary taxable differences of $360,000. Vance pays tax at 25%. All movements in deferred tax are taken to the statement of profit or loss.

Relevant exchange rates are:

| | |
|---|---|
| 1 September | Kr10:$1 |
| 1 October | Kr10.5:$1 |
| 31 December | Kr8:$1 |
| Average rate | Kr9:$1 |

---

286 What gain or loss should be recorded in the statement of profit or loss for the year ended 31 December 20X1 in relation to the payable recorded for the purchase of goods?

    A     Loss of $111

    B     Gain of $111

    C     Loss of $250

    D     Gain of $250

287 What gain or loss should be recorded in the statement of profit or loss for the year ended 31 December 20X1 in relation to the sale of goods?

    A     Loss of $607

    B     Gain of $607

    C     Loss of $893

    D     Gain of $893

**288** **Which of the statements below is/are true?**

Statement 1: The inventory purchased on 1 October 20X1 should be retranslated at the closing rate if the goods remain in inventory at 31 December 20X1.

Statement 2: The foreign exchange gains will be added to the revenue for the year.

| | True | False |
|---|---|---|
| Statement 1 | | |
| Statement 2 | | |

**289** **What will be recorded as the tax expense in the statement of profit or loss for the year ended 31 December 20X7?**

$_____

**290** Vance's assistant accountant has discovered that there is a debit balance on the trial balance of $3,000 relating to the over/under-provision of tax from the prior year.

**What impact will this have on Vance's current year financial statements?**

A    Increase the tax liability by $3,000 in the statement of financial position

B    Decrease the tax liability by $3,000 in the statement of financial position

C    Increase the tax expense by $3,000 in the statement of profit or loss

D    Decrease the tax expense by $3,000 in the statement of profit or loss

---

**The following scenario relates to questions 291–295**

Bailey constructs buildings for customers which can take many years to complete. Bailey has three contracts in progress at 30 September 20X7, which are detailed below. All of the contracts below began in the current year.

| | Contract 1 $000 | Contract 2 $000 | Contract 3 $000 |
|---|---|---|---|
| Price | 10,000 | 8,000 | 4,000 |
| Costs incurred to date | (6,000) | (4,000) | (500) |
| Costs to complete | (1,000) | (6,000) | (2,000) |
| Progress | 80% | 60% | 25% |
| Amount billed to date | 7,000 | 3,000 | 1,000 |

---

**291** **What revenue should be recorded (to the nearest thousand) in relation to contract 1?**

A    $8,000,000

B    $8,571,000

C    $7,000,000

D    $2,400,000

---

**292   What cost of sales should be recorded (to the nearest thousand) in relation to contract 2?**

A    $4,200,000

B    $9,400,000

C    $5,640,000

D    $6,800,000

**293   What should be recorded in the statement of financial position (to the nearest thousand) in relation to contract 3?**

A    Nil

B    $500,000 contract liability

C    $125,000 contract liability

D    $3,000,000 contract asset

**294**   Bailey's assistant accountant is unsure about how to deal with a brand new contract where the progress and overall profit cannot yet be ascertained.

**Identify which of the following statements, if any, are true.**

Statement 1 – Where the progress and overall profit are unknown, no contract asset or liability can be recognised.

Statement 2 – Where the progress and overall profit are unknown, revenue should be recognised to the level of recoverable costs.

A    Statement 1 is true

B    Statement 2 is true

C    Both statements are true

D    Neither statement is true

**295**   Bailey's assistant has also enquired about changing the way of measuring the progress of contracts.

**Complete the following to show how the change should be applied.**

As a change in accounting _____ , applied _____ .

Options: prospectively, retrospectively, estimate, policy

**The following scenario relates to questions 296–300**

Creg sold and installed a large item of machinery for $800,000 on 1 November 20X7. Included within the price was a 2 year servicing contract which has a value of $240,000 and a fee for installation of $50,000.

Creg works as an agent for a number of smaller contractors, earning commission of 10%. Creg's revenue includes $6 million received from clients under these agreements with $5.4 million in cost of sales representing the amount paid to the contractors.

Creg sold a large number of vehicles to a new customer for $10 million on 1 July 20X7. The customer paid $990,000 up front and agreed to pay the remaining balance on 1 July 20X8. Creg has a cost of capital of 6%.

296 **How much should be recorded in Creg's revenue in its statement of profit or loss for the year ended 31 December 20X7 in relation to the large machinery sale?**

    A    $530,000

    B    $680,000

    C    $560,000

    D    $580,000

297 Creg's sales director is close to selling another large machine, offering free service, therefore selling the entire machine for $560,000. Creg never sells servicing separately.

**How should this discount be applied in relation to the sale of the machinery?**

| Sales element | Discount applied | Discount not applied |
|---|---|---|
| Machine | | |
| Installation | | |
| Service | | |

298 **What adjustment needs to be made to revenue in respect of the commission sales?**

    A    Reduce revenue by $6 million

    B    Reduce revenue by $5.4 million

    C    Increase revenue by $600,000

    D    No adjustment is required

**299** **How much should initially be recorded in revenue in respect of the sale of vehicles in the statement of profit or loss for the year ended 31 December 20X7? Answer to the nearest $000.**

$_____,000

**300** On 31 December 20X7 Creg sold some maturing goods to a bank for $3 million. The estimated value of the goods at that date was $5 million, which is expected to keep rising. Creg keeps the goods on its premises and has the option to repurchase the goods on 31 December 20X9 for $3.63 million.

**Which of the following outlines the correct treatment for the maturing inventory?**

   A    Record a loss on disposal of $2 million in the statement of profit or loss

   B    Take $3 million to revenue, disclosing the repurchase option

   C    Leave the inventory in current assets, increasing in value as the goods mature

   D    Treat the $3 million as a loan with 10% compound interest accruing over the 2 years

---

**The following scenario relates to questions 301–305**

The profit after tax for Barstead for the year ended 30 September 20X7 was $15 million. At 1 October 20X6 Barstead had in issue 36 million equity shares. On 1 January 20X7 Barstead made a fully subscribed rights issue of one new share for every four shares held at a price of $2.80 each. The market price of the equity shares of Barstead immediately before the issue was $3.80.

The profit after tax for Cabott for the year ended 30 September 20X7 was $15 million. At 1 October 20X6 Cabott had in issue 43.25 million equity shares and a $10 million convertible loan note which has an effective interest rate of 8%. The loan note will mature in 20X8 and will be redeemed at par or converted to equity shares on the basis of 25 shares for each $100 of loan note at the loan-note holders' option. The loan interest is tax deductible. Cabott's tax rate is 25%.

The profit after tax for Dunstan for the year ended 30 September 20X7 was $12 million. On 1 October 20X6 Dunstan had 34 million shares in issue. On 1 February 20X7 Dunstan made a market issue of 3 million shares at full price. On 1 July 20X7 Dunstan made a bonus issue of one new share for every five shares held.

---

**301** **What is the basic earnings per share for Barstead for the year ended 30 September 20X7?**

   A    42¢

   B    35¢

   C    33¢

   D    35¢

**302** **What is the diluted earnings per share for Cabott for the year ended 30 September 20X7?**

  A   34¢

  B   35¢

  C   36¢

  D   33¢

**303** **What is the basic earnings per share for Dunstan for the year ended 30 September 20X7?**

  A   26¢

  B   32¢

  C   28¢

  D   31¢

**304** **Which of the three companies will have to restate the prior year comparative earnings per share figure?**

| Company | Comparative restated | No restatement |
|---------|---------------------|----------------|
| Barstead |  |  |
| Cabott |  |  |
| Dunstan |  |  |

**305** **Which, if any, of the statements below regarding diluted earnings per share is/are correct?**

Statement 1: Diluted earnings per share is a forecast of a future trend in profit, showing the expected earnings in the next period to improve the relevance of information for users.

Statement 2: Diluted earnings per share acts as a warning to shareholders and shows how the current earnings per share could fall based on items currently in existence.

|  | Correct | Incorrect |
|--|---------|-----------|
| Statement 1 |  |  |
| Statement 2 |  |  |

**The following scenario relates to questions 306–310**

On 7 January 20X5, Hermione was informed that it was being sued by an employee in respect of a workplace accident that took place in October 20X4. Legal advisors advise that Hermione is certain to lose the case. They have provided the following information:

| Estimated pay-out | Probability of payment occurring |
|---|---|
| $1 million | 30% |
| $2 million | 60% |
| $3 million | 10% |

Hermione has sold 100,000 machines that are covered by a warranty agreement as at 31 December 20X4. If a machine develops a major fault then the average cost to Hermione of repairing it is $100. If a machine develops a minor fault then the average cost to Hermione of repairing it is $30. It is believed that 6% of the machines under warranty will develop major faults and that 8% will develop minor faults. The time value of money can be ignored.

On 15 December 20X4, the directors of Hermione decided to restructure the business and created a detailed and formal plan. On that date, an announcement was made to the employees who were informed that they would be made redundant in March 20X5. The directors estimate that the restructuring exercise will involve the following costs:

| Type of cost | $m |
|---|---|
| Redundancy payments | 1.2 |
| Staff relocation | 0.8 |
| Investment in new systems | 2.0 |

**306** **Which of the following are outlined in IAS 37** *Provisions, Contingent Liabilities and Contingent Assets* **as criteria required for recognising a provision?**

(i)     An entity has a present obligation from a past event.

(ii)    It is possible that an outflow of resources will be required.

(iii)   A reliable estimate can be made of the amount of the obligation.

A     (i), (ii) and (iii)

B     (i) and (ii) only

C     (i) and (iii) only

D     (ii) and (iii) only

**307** **What amount should be recognised as a provision in respect of the workplace accident claim in the year ended 31 December 20X4?**

A     Nil

B     $1.8 million

C     $2 million

D     $3 million

**308** **What amount should be recognised as a warranty provision in the year ended 31 December 20X4?**

$_____ ,000

**309** **What amount should be recognised as a restructuring provision in the year ended 31 December 20X4?**

    A    $1.2 million

    B    $2.0 million

    C    $3.2 million

    D    $4.0 million

**310** The following situations have arisen in the year ended 31 December 20X4:

Situation 1: A law was introduced in November 20X4 requiring Hermione to fit new smoke filters in its factory by February 20X5 at an estimated cost of $500,000. By the reporting date, Hermione had not fitted the smoke filters.

Situation 2: The management accountant of Hermione has reliably forecast an operating loss of $4 million for the year ended 31 December 20X5.

**Which, if any, of the situations require a provision to be recognised?**

|  | Provision | No provision |
|---|---|---|
| Situation 1 |  |  |
| Situation 2 |  |  |

**The following scenario relates to questions 311–315**

Promoil's financial statements for the year ended 30 September 20X8 were authorised for issue by its directors on 6 November 20X8 and the Annual General Meeting will be held on 6 December 20X8.

On 1 October 20X7, Promoil acquired an oil platform at a cost of $30 million. The estimated cost of removing the platform at the end of the asset's life on 30 September 20Y7 will be $15 million. The present value of $1 in 10 years using Promoil's cost of capital of 8% is $0.46.

On 12 October 20X8 a fire destroyed Promoil's largest warehouse. The carrying amount of the warehouse was $10 million. Promoil expects to be able to recover $9 million from its insurers and its going concern is not in doubt.

A single class of inventory held at another warehouse was valued at its cost of $460,000 and sold for $280,000 on 10 October 20X8.

**311** There is no legal obligation for Promoil to remove the oil platform, but Promoil has a published environmental policy which it has a history of honouring.

**Which of the following is correct regarding Promoil's proposed accounting treatment?**

    A    No provision should be recorded as there is no legal obligation

    B    Promoil should recognise a provision as there is a constructive obligation

    C    No provision should be made but a contingent liability should be recorded

    D    If Promoil make a provision, the present value of the costs will be expensed in the statement of profit or loss for the year to 30 September 20X8

**312** If Promoil makes the provision, what liability (to the nearest thousand) will be shown in its statement of financial position as at 30 September 20X8?

$_____ ,000

**313** Select the correct category for the events listed below in relation to IAS 10 *Events After the Reporting Period.*

|  | Adjusting | Non-adjusting |
|---|---|---|
| Fire in the warehouse |  |  |
| Sale of inventory |  |  |

**314** On 18 November 20X8 the government announced tax changes which have the effect of increasing Promoil's deferred tax liability by $650,000 as at 30 September 20X8.

**Which of the following is correct in respect of IAS 10 *Events After the Reporting Period* regarding the tax changes?**

A    This is a non-adjusting event and no disclosure is required

B    This is an adjusting event

C    This is neither an adjusting or non-adjusting event

D    This is an adjusting event and the financial statements should be reissued

**315** Promoil owns the whole of the equity share capital of its subsidiary Hamlet. Hamlet's statement of financial position includes a loan of $25 million that is repayable in five years' time. $15 million of this loan is secured on Hamlet's property and the remaining $10 million is guaranteed by Promoil in the event of a default by Hamlet. It is possible that Hamlet will be unable to repay the loan, but not likely.

**How should this be treated in the financial statements of Promoil?**

A    A contingent liability

B    A provision

C    Not included in Promoil's financial statements

D    A reduction to property, plant and equipment

# CONSOLIDATED FINANCIAL STATEMENTS

**The following scenario relates to questions 316–320**

On 1 April 20X4 Penfold acquired 80% of Superted's equity shares in a share for share exchange. Penfold issued 2 shares for every 5 acquired in Superted. Penfold's share price on 1 April 20X4 was $5.30. The share exchange has not yet been recorded.

Extracts from the individual financial statements of Penfold and Superted as at 30 September 20X4 are shown below.

|  | Penfold | Superted |
|---|---|---|
|  | $000 | $000 |
| Property, plant and equipment | 345,000 | 141,000 |
| Trade receivables | 32,400 | 38,000 |
| Equity shares of $1 each | 170,000 | 15,000 |
| Other components of equity (share premium) | 6,000 | 2,000 |

(i) During the year, Penfold traded with Superted, and had a payable of $6 million at 30 September 20X4. Superted's receivable balance differed from this due to a $2 million payment from Penfold not being received until October 20X4.

(ii) Penfold measures the non-controlling interest at fair value. At the date of acquisition this was $7.2 million.

(iii) Superted made a profit of $24 million for the year ended 30 September 20X4.

(iv) Penfold sold an item of plant to Superted on 1 April 20X4 for $25 million when its carrying amount was $20 million. It had a remaining useful life of 5 years at this date.

(v) Penfold also owns 30% of Arnold, an unrelated entity. Penfold are not able to appoint any members of the board of Arnold as the other 70% is held by another investor who is able to appoint all members of the board.

316 **What will be reported as other components of equity on the consolidated statement of financial position as at 30 September 20X4?**

    A    $31,440,000

    B    $26,640,000

    C    $28,640,000

    D    $33,440,000

317 **What will be reported as receivables on the consolidated statement of financial position as at 30 September 20X4?**

    $_____,000

318 **What will be reported as non-controlling interest on the consolidated statement of financial position as at 30 September 20X4?**

    A    $9,700,000

    B    $9,500,000

    C    $7,200,000

    D    $9,600,000

**319** **What will be reported as property, plant and equipment on the consolidated statement of financial position as at 30 September 20X4?**

$_____,000

**320** **How should the investment in Arnold be recorded in the consolidated statement of financial position of Penfold?**

A    A subsidiary

B    An associate

C    A financial instrument

D    A contingent asset

**The following scenario relates to questions 321–325**

On 1 October 20X4, Popper purchased 70% of the share capital of Stopper. Popper agreed to pay $6 million on 30 September 20X6. Popper has a cost of capital of 8%.

Extracts from the statements of profit or loss for the year ended 31 March 20X5 for both Popper and Stopper are shown below.

|  | Popper | Stopper |
|---|---|---|
|  | $000 | $000 |
| Cost of sales | (319,200) | (176,400) |
| Operating expenses | (50,610) | (33,120) |

The following notes are relevant:

(i)    Since acquisition, Popper sold goods to Stopper totalling $1 million per month, making a margin of 20%. At the year end, Stopper held 30% of these goods.

(ii)   On acquisition, Stopper's net assets were equal to their carrying amount, with the exception of Stopper's head office, which had a fair value of $4 million in excess of its carrying amount and a remaining life at acquisition of 20 years. All depreciation is charged to operating expenses.

(iii)  At 31 March 20X5, goodwill is impaired by $600,000. Goodwill impairment is included within operating expenses. Popper measures the non-controlling interest using the fair value method.

**321** **What liability (to the nearest thousand) should be recorded in respect of the deferred consideration in Popper's consolidated statement of financial position as at 31 March 20X5?**

A    $5,144,000

B    $5,350,000

C    $5,556,000

D    $6,000,000

**322** **What is the cost of sales figure to be included in the consolidated statement of profit or loss for the year ended 31 March 20X5?**

A  $402,600,000

B  $401,760,000

C  $395,760,000

D  $396,400,000

**323** **What is the operating expenses figure to be included in the consolidated statement of profit or loss for the year ended 31 March 20X5?**

A  $67,970,000

B  $67,670,000

C  $67,570,000

D  $67,870,000

**324** **Which of the items in the scenario would affect the profit attributable to the non-controlling interest?**

A  Notes (i) and (ii) only

B  Notes (i) and (iii) only

C  Notes (ii) and (iii) only

D  Notes (i), (ii) and (iii)

**325** **Which, if any, of the following statements about fair values is/are correct?**

Statement 1: Popper must include all of Stopper's assets, liabilities and contingent liabilities at fair value in the consolidated financial statements.

Statement 2: Professional fees associated with the acquisition of Stopper can be included within the goodwill because the non-controlling interest is measured at fair value.

|  | Correct | Incorrect |
|---|---|---|
| Statement 1 |  |  |
| Statement 2 |  |  |

**The following scenario relates to questions 326–330**

On 1 January 20X5, Prunier acquired 80% of Sheringham's two million $1 ordinary shares. At this date, Sheringham had retained earnings of $4 million and a revaluation surplus of $2 million. Prunier had retained earnings of $10 million and a revaluation surplus of $5 million.

The fair value of Sheringham's net assets at acquisition were equal to their carrying amounts with the exception of Sheringham's property which had a fair value of $800,000 in excess of its carrying amount and a remaining life of 20 years.

At 31 December 20X5, Prunier and Sheringham both revalued their assets. Prunier's assets increased by a further $2 million while Sheringham's increased by $500,000. At this date, Prunier's retained earnings were $11 million and Sheringham's were $3.5 million.

326 **What will the consolidated retained earnings be at 31 December 20X5?**

    A    $11,432,000

    B    $10,560,000

    C    $11,368,000

    D    $10,568,000

327 **What will be the other comprehensive income attributable to the parent for the year ended 31 December 20X5?**

    $_____ ,000

328 **Identify whether or not the following items should be recognised as assets in the consolidated financial statements of Prunier.**

| | Recognised | Not to be recognised |
|---|---|---|
| Prunier's brand name, which was internally generated so not shown in Prunier's financial statements but has a fair value of $3 million | | |
| A research project in progress, which was one of the main reasons Prunier purchased Sheringham and has a fair value of $2 million | | |
| An intangible asset related to an encryption process which has now been deemed illegal. This is included within intangibles at $1.5 million | | |

**329** Prunier has also owned 30% of Anderson for many years, and uses equity accounting to account for the investment. During the year Prunier sold $3 million of goods to Anderson at a mark-up of 20%. Anderson has a quarter of the goods left in inventory at the year end.

**What is the value of the unrealised profit adjustment as at 31 December 20X5?**

A    $150,000

B    $37,500

C    $125,000

D    $45,000

**330** On 31 December 20X9, Prunier disposed of its entire holding of Sheringham for $9 million. At this date, the remaining goodwill was $1 million. The fair value of the non-controlling interest was $2.5 million and the fair value of the net assets (including the fair value adjustment) was $10.6 million.

**What is the profit/loss on the disposal of Sheringham to be shown in the consolidated financial statements of Prunier?**

A    $100,000 loss on disposal

B    $1,900,000 gain on disposal

C    $5,100,000 loss on disposal

D    $2,020,000 gain on disposal

# INTERPRETATION OF FINANCIAL STATEMENTS

**The following scenario relates to questions 331–335**

LOP is looking to expand overseas by acquiring a new subsidiary.

Two geographical areas have been targeted, Frontland and Sideland.

Entity A operates in Frontland and entity B operates in Sideland. Both entities are listed on their local exchanges.

Figures for entities A, B and LOP are provided below for the last trading period.

|  | A | B | LOP |
|---|---|---|---|
| Revenue | $160m | $300m | $500m |
| Gross profit margin | 26% | 17% | 28% |
| Profit from operations margin | 9% | 11% | 16% |
| Gearing | 65% | 30% | 38% |
| Average rate of interest expensed in profit or loss | 4% | 9% | 8% |
| Price/Earnings (P/E) ratio | 11.6 | 15.9 | 16.3 |

**331** Which of the following statements is a realistic conclusion that could be drawn from the above information?

   A    A appears to be benefiting from economies of scale.

   B    B has lower operating expenses than A.

   C    A has attracted a lower rate of interest on its borrowings than B because it's gearing level would suggest that is a lower risk to lenders than B.

   D    Acquisition of either entity would lead to an improvement in LOP's gross margin due to the increased revenue that would be achieved.

**332** Which TWO of the following statements are true, based on the information provided?

   A    A would be a riskier investment than B because it has higher gearing.

   B    A would give LOP greater benefit in terms of additional borrowing capacity.

   C    The market is more confident about the future performance of B than LOP.

   D    The market is more confident about the future performance of LOP than A or B.

   E    LOP's P/E ratio would definitely fall if it acquired either A or B.

**333** Which of the following statements concerning the use of ratio analysis to make a decision about investing in A or B is FALSE?

   A    A and B may use different accounting standards when preparing their financial statements and this would reduce the comparability of their profit margins.

   B    A and B may target different types of customer, meaning that comparison between the two is difficult.

   C    A and B may apply different accounting policies, such as cost model v revaluation model for property, plant and equipment. This would reduce comparability of their gearing ratios.

   D    A and B are listed on different stock exchanges which reduces comparability of their P/E ratios.

**334** If LOP acquired B, it has assessed that combining the two companies would lead to an overall saving in cost of sales of $5 million.

**If this was taken into account, what would be the gross margin of LOP combined with B to one decimal place?**

_____%

**335** Your assistant has raised concerns about B, having heard that they may have treated lease payments as operating expenses instead of capitalising the right-of-use assets as required by IFRS 16 *Leases*.

**Which, if any, of the following statements is/are true in relation to this?**

Statement 1: If B has incorrectly treated the leases, gearing will be overstated.

Statement 2: If B has incorrectly treated the leases, the average rate of interest calculated could be inaccurate.

|  | Correct | Incorrect |
|---|---|---|
| Statement 1 |  |  |
| Statement 2 |  |  |

---

**The following scenario relates to questions 336–340**

Key figures from Franck's financial statements for the year ended 30 September 20X2 are shown below.

|  | $000 |
|---|---|
| Revenue | 9,400 |
| Profit from operations | 1,500 |
| Share capital | 15,000 |
| Retained earnings | 3,000 |
| Loans | 2,000 |

Franck has operated in the computer software industry for many years, gaining a reputation for steady growth. It is interested in acquiring Duik, which has recently been put up for sale. Extracts from Duik's financial statements can be seen below.

|  | $000 |
|---|---|
| Revenue | 1,200 |
| Loss from operations | (600) |
| Share capital | 24,000 |
| Retained losses | (1,200) |
| Loans | 4,000 |

---

**336 Calculate Franck's return on capital employed (based on profit from operations) without the acquisition of Duik to one decimal place.**

_____%

337 **What is the combined operating margin if Franck and Duik are combined?**

A    9.6%

B    19.8%

C    14.2%

D    8.5%

338 **Which, if any, of the following statements is/are correct?**

Statement 1: If Duik is acquired, gearing will increase.

Statement 2: If Duik is acquired, return on capital employed will decrease.

|                | Correct | Incorrect |
|----------------|---------|-----------|
| Statement 1    |         |           |
| Statement 2    |         |           |

339 **Which of the following is NOT a factor to consider in respect of Duik being a subsidiary of another entity?**

A    Sales or purchases between the parent and Duik may not be at market rates

B    Duik may get the benefit of shared assets with the parent

C    Duik's individual financial statements may contain errors

D    Loans made from Duik's parent may carry lower interest than market rates

340 **What other information is NOT likely to be available to Franck before entering into negotiations for the acquisition of Duik?**

A    A breakdown of dividends paid by Duik historically

B    Duik's statement of cash flows

C    A breakdown of Duik's upcoming projects which are in progress

D    The directors' report outlining the performance for the year

# STATEMENT OF CASH FLOWS

**The following scenario relates to questions 341–345**

The assistant accountant of Cooper has started work on the statement of cash flows for the year ended 31 December 20X8, completing a draft of the cash generated from operations as shown below.

|  | $000 |
|---|---|
| Profit from operations | 3,500 |
| Depreciation | 4,600 |
| Release of government grant | 1,400 |
| Profit on disposal of property | (3,700) |
| Increase in inventories | (400) |
| Decrease in trade and other receivables | (300) |
| Increase in trade and other payables | 900 |
| **Cash generated from operations** | **13,400** |

In addition to this, the assistant has seen that the balance of property was $39.5 million at 1 January 20X8 and $29 million at 31 December 20X8. There were no additions of property in the year.

There was also a deferred income balance relating to government grants of $6 million at 1 January 20X8. The closing deferred income balance was $8 million.

341 **What method has Cooper's assistant accountant used to calculate the cash generated from operations?**

 A    Classification by function

 B    Classification by nature

 C    Indirect method

 D    Direct method

**342** In relation to the calculation of cash generated from operations, select the TWO cells which contain errors made by the assistant.

|  | $000 |
|---|---|
| Profit from operations | 3,500 |
| Depreciation | 4,600 |
| Release of government grant | 1,400 |
| Profit on disposal of property | (3,700) |
| Increase in inventories | (400) |
| Decrease in trade and other receivables | (300) |
| Increase in trade and other payables | 900 |
| Cash generated from operations | 6,000 |

**343** How much would be recorded in Cooper's statement of cash flows in relation to the sale of property?

A    $9,600,000

B    $2,200,000

C    $3,700,000

D    $5,900,000

**344** What will be recorded as the receipt of government grants in the year?

$_____ ,000

**345** Cooper's assistant accountant has been studying statements of cash flows and is unsure whether the information contained in the study material is true.

**Which, if any, of the following statements is/are true?**

Statement 1: Intangible assets will have no impact on the statement of cash flow as they have no physical substance.

Statement 2: A rights issue of shares will increase the cash flows from financing activities.

A    Statement 1 is correct

B    Statement 2 is correct

C    Both statements are correct

D    Neither statement is correct

**The following scenario relates to questions 346–350**

Extracts from Depay's financial statements for the year ended 30 September 20X2 are shown below.

| Statement of profit or loss extract: | $000 |
|---|---|
| Finance costs | (60) |
| | |
| Profit before tax | 142 |
| Income tax expense | (57) |
| | |
| Profit for the year | 85 |

| Statement of financial position extract: | 20X2 | 20X1 |
|---|---|---|
| | $000 | $000 |
| Retained earnings | 900 | 940 |
| 5% loan notes | 515 | 500 |
| Deferred tax liability | 150 | 125 |
| Tax payable | 30 | 40 |
| Lease liabilities | 300 | 310 |

The following information is relevant:

(i)     Depay disposed of some land during the year, which had a remaining revaluation surplus at disposal of $20,000.

(ii)    $40,000 of the finance costs relate to the loan notes which are repayable at a premium, making the effective rate of interest 8%. The remaining interest relates to the lease liabilities.

(iii)   During the year, Depay received a dividend from a subsidiary.

(iv)    Depay acquired $70,000 of new assets under lease agreements during the year. Depay makes annual payments under leases on 30 September each year.

**346   What will be recorded in Depay's statement of cash flows under dividends paid?**

    A     $145,000

    B     $105,000

    C     $40,000

    D     $125,000

**347   What will be recorded in Depay's statement of cash flows under interest paid?**

    A     $20,000

    B     $25,000

    C     $45,000

    D     $60,000

**348**   **What will be recorded in Depay's statement of cash flows under tax paid?**

$_____

**349**   **Where should the dividend received be shown in Depay's statement of cash flows?**

A       Operating activities

B       Investing activities

C       Financing activities

D       It should not be recorded

**350**   **How much should be shown within financing activities in respect of lease liabilities repaid?**

$_____

# Section 3

# CONSTRUCTED RESPONSE QUESTIONS – SECTION C

**Please note that the following icons will be used in this section**

🖥 = word processing

⊞ = spreadsheet

## PREPARATION OF SINGLE ENTITY FINANCIAL STATEMENTS

**351 CANDEL**  *Walk in the footsteps of a top tutor*

The following trial balance relates to Candel at 30 September 20X8:

| | $000 | $000 |
|---|---|---|
| Leasehold property – at valuation 1 October 20X7 (note (i)) | 50,000 | |
| Plant and equipment – at cost (note (i)) | 76,600 | |
| Plant and equipment – accumulated depreciation at 1 October 20X7 | | 24,600 |
| Capitalised development expenditure – at 1 October 20X7 (note (ii)) | 20,000 | |
| Development expenditure – accumulated amortisation at 1 October 20X7 | | 6,000 |
| Closing inventory at 30 September 20X8 | 20,000 | |
| Trade receivables | 43,100 | |
| Bank | | 1,300 |
| Trade payables and provisions (note (iii)) | | 23,800 |
| Draft profit before tax | | 59,100 |
| Preference dividend paid (note (iv)) | 800 | |
| Research and development costs (note (ii)) | 8,600 | |
| Equity shares of 25 cents each | | 50,000 |
| 8% redeemable preference shares of $1 each (note (iv)) | | 20,000 |
| Retained earnings at 1 October 20X7 | | 18,500 |
| Deferred tax (note (v)) | | 5,800 |
| Leasehold property revaluation surplus at 1 October 20X7 | | 10,000 |
| | ——— | ——— |
| | 219,100 | 219,100 |
| | ——— | ——— |

The following notes are relevant:

(i)     **Non-current assets – tangible:**

The leasehold property had a remaining life of 20 years at 1 October 20X7. Candel's policy is to revalue its property at each year-end and at 30 September 20X8 it was valued at $43 million. Ignore deferred tax on the revaluation.

On 1 October 20X7 an item of plant was disposed of for $2.5 million cash. The proceeds have been treated as sales revenue by Candel. The plant is still included in the above trial balance figures at its cost of $8 million and accumulated depreciation of $4 million (to the date of disposal).

All plant is depreciated at 20% per annum using the reducing balance method.

Depreciation and amortisation of all non-current assets is charged to cost of sales.

(ii)    **Non-current assets – intangible:**

In addition to the capitalised development expenditure of $20 million, further research and development costs were incurred on a new project which commenced on 1 October 20X7. The research stage of the new project lasted until 31 December 20X7 and incurred $1.4 million of costs. From that date the project incurred development costs of $800,000 per month. On 1 April 20X8 the directors became confident that the project would be successful and yield a profit well in excess of its costs. The project is still in development at 30 September 20X8.

Capitalised development expenditure is amortised at 20% per annum using the straight-line method. All expensed research and development is charged to cost of sales.

(iii)   Candel is being sued by a customer for $2 million for breach of contract over a cancelled order. Candel has obtained legal opinion that there is a 20% chance that Candel will lose the case. Accordingly Candel has provided $400,000 ($2 million × 20%) included in administrative expenses in respect of the claim. The unrecoverable legal costs of defending the action are estimated at $100,000. These have not been provided for as the legal action will not go to court until next year.

(iv)    The preference shares were issued on 1 April 20X8 at par. They are redeemable at a large premium which gives them an effective finance cost of 12% per annum. The finance assistant in Candel was uncertain how to deal with these. The dividend paid in the trial balance represents the debit side of the cash payment made during the year.

(v)     The directors have estimated the provision for income tax for the year ended 30 September 20X8 at $11.4 million. The required deferred tax provision at 30 September 20X8 is $6 million.

**Required:**

(a)     **Calculate the revised profit for the year, taking into account the items from notes (i) to (v).** ⊞                                                                    **(8 marks)**

(b)     **Prepare the statement of financial position as at 30 September 20X8.** ⊞

**(12 marks)**

**Notes to the financial statements and a statement of changes in equity are not required.**

**(Total: 20 marks)**

## 352   PRICEWELL

 **Question debrief**

The following trial balance relates to Pricewell at 31 March 20X9:

|  | $000 | $000 |
|---|---|---|
| Leasehold property – at valuation 31 March 20X8 (note (i)) | 25,200 | |
| Plant and equipment (owned) – at cost (note (i)) | 46,800 | |
| Right-of-use assets – at cost (note (i)) | 20,000 | |
| Accumulated depreciation at 31 March 20X8: | | |
| Owned plant and equipment | | 12,800 |
| Right-of-use plant | | 5,000 |
| Lease payment (paid on 31 March 20X9) (note (i)) | 6,000 | |
| Lease liability at 1 April 20X8 (note (i)) | | 15,600 |
| Contract with customer (note (ii)) | 14,300 | |
| Inventory at 31 March 20X9 | 28,200 | |
| Trade receivables | 33,100 | |
| Bank | 5,500 | |
| Trade payables | | 33,400 |
| Revenue (note (iii)) | | 310,000 |
| Cost of sales (note (iii)) | 234,500 | |
| Distribution costs | 19,500 | |
| Administrative expenses | 27,500 | |
| Equity dividend paid | 8,000 | |
| Equity shares of 50 cents each | | 40,000 |
| Retained earnings at 31 March 20X8 | | 44,100 |
| Current tax (note (iv)) | 700 | |
| Deferred tax (note (iv)) | | 8,400 |
| | 469,300 | 469,300 |

The following notes are relevant:

(i)   **Non-current assets:**

The 15 year leasehold property was acquired on 1 April 20X7 at a cost of $30 million. The accounting policy is to revalue the property at fair value at each year end. The valuation in the trial balance of $25.2 million as at 31 March 20X8 led to an impairment charge of $2.8 million which was reported in the statement of profit or loss and other comprehensive income in the year ended 31 March 20X8.  At 31 March 20X9 the property was valued at $24.9 million.

Owned plant is depreciated at 25% per annum using the reducing balance method.

The right-of-use plant was acquired on 1 April 20X7. The rentals are $6 million per annum for four years payable in arrears on 31 March each year. The interest rate implicit in the lease is 8% per annum. Right-of-use plant is depreciated over the lease period.

No depreciation has yet been charged on any non-current assets for the year ended 31 March 20X9. All depreciation is charged to cost of sales.

(ii)  On 1 October 20X8 Pricewell entered into a contract to construct a bridge over a river. The performance obligation will be satisfied over time. The agreed price of the bridge is $50 million and construction was expected to be completed on 30 September 20Y0.  The $14.3 million in the trial balance is:

|  | $000 |
|---|---|
| Materials, labour and overheads | 12,000 |
| Specialist plant acquired 1 October 20X8 | 8,000 |
| Payment from customer | (5,700) |
|  | 14,300 |

The sales value of the work done at 31 March 20X9 has been agreed at $22 million and the estimated cost to complete (excluding plant depreciation) is $10 million. The specialist plant will have no residual value at the end of the contract and should be depreciated on a monthly basis.  Pricewell recognises progress towards satisfaction of the performance obligation on the outputs basis as determined by the agreed work to date compared to the total contract price.

(iii)  Pricewell's revenue includes $8 million for goods it sold acting as an agent for Trilby. Pricewell earned a commission of 20% on these sales and remitted the difference of $6.4 million (included in cost of sales) to Trilby.

(iv)  The directors have estimated the provision for income tax for the year ended 31 March 20X9 at $4.5 million. The required deferred tax provision at 31 March 20X9 is $5.6 million.  All adjustments to deferred tax should be taken to the statement of profit or loss. The balance of current tax in the trial balance represents the under/over provision of the income tax liability for the year ended 31 March 20X8.

**Required:**

**(a)  Prepare the statement of profit or loss and other comprehensive income for the year ended 31 March 20X9.**                                      **(10 marks)**

**(b)  Prepare the statement of financial position as at 31 March 20X9.**       **(10 marks)**

**Note:  A statement of changes in equity and notes to the financial statements are not required.**

**(Total: 20 marks)**

*Calculate your allowed time, allocate the time to the separate parts*

## 353 HIGHWOOD

The following trial balance relates to Highwood at 31 March 20X1:

|  | $000 | $000 |
|---|---|---|
| Equity shares of 50 cents each | | 6,000 |
| Retained earnings at 1 April 20X0 | | 1,400 |
| 8% convertible loan note (note (i)) | | 30,000 |
| Property – at cost 1 April 20W5 (land element $25m (note (ii))) | 75,000 | |
| Accumulated depreciation – 1 April 20X0 – building | | 10,000 |
| Current tax (note (iii)) | | 800 |
| Deferred tax (note (iii)) | | 2,600 |
| Inventory – 4 April 20X1 (note (iv)) | 36,000 | |
| Trade receivables | 47,100 | |
| Bank | | 11,500 |
| Trade payables | | 24,500 |
| Revenue | | 339,650 |
| Cost of sales | 207,750 | |
| Distribution costs | 27,500 | |
| Administrative expenses (note (v)) | 30,700 | |
| Loan interest paid (note (i)) | 2,400 | |
|  | ——— | ——— |
|  | 426,450 | 426,450 |
|  | ——— | ——— |

The following notes are relevant:

(i) The 8% $30 million convertible loan note was issued on 1 April 20X0 at par. Interest is payable in arrears on 31 March each year. The loan note is redeemable at par on 31 March 20X3 or convertible into equity shares at the option of the loan note holders on the basis of 30 equity shares for each $100 of loan note. Highwood's finance director has calculated that to issue an equivalent loan note without the conversion rights it would have to pay an interest rate of 10% per annum to attract investors.

Applicable discount rates are:

|  | 8% | 10% |
|---|---|---|
| End of year 1 | 0.93 | 0.91 |
| 2 | 0.86 | 0.83 |
| 3 | 0.79 | 0.75 |

(ii) On 1 April 20X0 Highwood decided to revalue its property. The market value of the property on this date was $80 million, of which $30 million related to the land. At this date the remaining estimated life of the property was 20 years. Highwood does not make a transfer to retained earnings in respect of excess depreciation on the revaluation of its assets. All depreciation is charged to cost of sales.

(iii) Current tax represents the under/over provision of the tax liability for the year ended 31 March 20X0. The required provision for income tax for the year ended 31 March 20X1 is $19.4 million. The difference between the carrying amounts of the assets of Highwood (including the property revaluation in note (ii) above) and their (lower) tax base at 31 March 20X1 is $27 million. Highwood's rate of income tax is 25%.

(iv) The inventory of Highwood was not counted until 4 April 20X1 due to operational reasons. At this date its value at cost was $36 million and this figure has been used in the cost of sales calculation above. Between the year end of 31 March 20X1 and 4 April 20X1, Highwood received a delivery of goods at a cost of $2.7 million and made sales of $7.8 million at a mark-up on cost of 30%. Neither the goods delivered nor the sales made in this period were included in Highwood's purchases (as part of cost of sales) or revenue in the above trial balance.

(v) On 31 March 20X1 Highwood factored (sold) trade receivables with a book value of $10 million to Easyfinance. Highwood received an immediate payment of $8.7 million and will pay Easyfinance 2% per month on any uncollected balances. Any of the factored receivables outstanding after six months will be refunded to Easyfinance. Highwood has derecognised the receivables and charged $1.3 million to administrative expenses. If Highwood had not factored these receivables it would have made an allowance of $600,000 against them.

**Required:**

(a) **Prepare the statement of profit or loss and other comprehensive income for Highwood for the year ended 31 March 20X1.** ▦ **(9 marks)**

(b) **Prepare the statement of changes in equity for year ended 31 March 20X1.** ▦

**(3 marks)**

(c) **Prepare the statement of financial position as at 31 March 20X1.** ▦ **(8 marks)**

**Note: your answers and workings should be presented to the nearest $000.**

**(Total: 20 marks)**

## 354 KEYSTONE

The following trial balance relates to Keystone at 30 September 20X1:

|  | $000 | $000 |
|---|---|---|
| Revenue |  | 377,600 |
| Material purchases (note (i)) | 64,000 |  |
| Production labour (note (i)) | 124,000 |  |
| Factory overheads (note (i)) | 80,000 |  |
| Distribution costs | 14,200 |  |
| Administrative expenses (note (ii)) | 46,400 |  |
| Finance costs | 350 |  |
| Investment income |  | 800 |
| Property – at cost (note (i)) | 50,000 |  |
| Plant and equipment – at cost (note (i)) | 44,500 |  |
| Accumulated amortisation/depreciation at 1 October 20X0 |  |  |
| – property |  | 10,000 |
| – plant and equipment |  | 14,500 |
| Inventory at 1 October 20X0 | 46,700 |  |
| Trade receivables | 31,150 |  |
| Trade payables |  | 27,800 |
| Bank |  | 2,300 |
| Equity shares of 20 cents each |  | 50,000 |
| Retained earnings at 1 October 20X0 |  | 15,600 |
| Deferred tax (note (iv)) |  | 2,700 |
|  | ——— | ——— |
|  | 501,300 | 501,300 |
|  | ——— | ——— |

The following notes are relevant:

(i)     During the year Keystone manufactured an item of plant for its own use. The direct materials and labour were $3 million and $4 million respectively. Production overheads are 75% of direct labour cost and Keystone determines the final selling price for goods by adding a mark-up on total cost of 40%. These manufacturing costs are included in the relevant expense items in the trial balance. The plant was completed and put into immediate use on 1 April 20X1.

All plant and equipment is depreciated at 20% per annum using the reducing balance method with time apportionment in the year of acquisition.

The directors decided to revalue the property in line with recent increases in market values. On 1 October 20X0 an independent surveyor valued the property at $48 million, which the directors have accepted. The property was being amortised over an original life of 20 years which has not changed. Keystone does not make a transfer to retained earnings in respect of excess amortisation. The revaluation gain will create a deferred tax liability (see note (iv)).

All depreciation and amortisation is charged to cost of sales. No depreciation or amortisation has yet been charged on any non-current asset for the year ended 30 September 20X1.

(ii) On 15 August 20X1, Keystone's share price stood at $2.40 per share. On this date Keystone paid a dividend (included in administrative expenses) that was calculated to give a dividend yield of 4%.

(iii) The inventory at 30 September 20X1 was valued at $56.6 million.

(iv) A provision for income tax for the year ended 30 September 20X1 of $24.3 million is required. At 30 September 20X1, the tax base of Keystone's net assets was $15 million less than their carrying amounts. This excludes the effects of the revaluation of the leased property. The income tax rate of Keystone is 30%.

**Required:**

(a) **Prepare the statement of profit or loss and other comprehensive income for Keystone for the year ended 30 September 20X1.** ▦ **(12 marks)**

(b) **Prepare the statement of financial position for Keystone as at 30 September 20X1.** ▦ **(8 marks)**

**A statement of changes in equity is not required.**

**(Total: 20 marks)**

## 355 FRESCO

The following trial balance relates to Fresco at 31 March 20X2:

|  | $000 | $000 |
|---|---|---|
| Equity shares of 50 cents each (note (i)) |  | 45,000 |
| Share premium (note (i)) |  | 5,000 |
| Retained earnings at 1 April 20X1 |  | 5,100 |
| Leased property (12 years) – at cost (note (ii)) | 48,000 |  |
| Plant and equipment – at cost (note (ii)) | 47,500 |  |
| Accumulated amortisation of leased property at 1 April 20X1 |  | 16,000 |
| Accumulated depreciation of plant and equipment at 1 April 20X1 |  | 33,500 |
| Inventory at 31 March 20X2 | 25,200 |  |
| Trade receivables (note (iii)) | 28,500 |  |
| Bank |  | 1,400 |
| Deferred tax (note (iv)) |  | 3,200 |
| Trade payables |  | 27,300 |
| Revenue |  | 350,000 |
| Cost of sales | 298,700 |  |
| Lease payments (note (ii)) | 8,000 |  |
| Distribution costs | 16,100 |  |
| Administrative expenses | 26,900 |  |
| Bank interest | 300 |  |
| Current tax (note (iv)) | 800 |  |
| Suspense account (note (i)) |  | 13,500 |
|  | ――――― | ――――― |
|  | 500,000 | 500,000 |
|  | ――――― | ――――― |

The following notes are relevant:

(i)   The suspense account represents the corresponding credit for cash received for a fully subscribed rights issue of equity shares made on 1 January 20X2. The terms of the share issue were one new share for every five held at a price of 75 cents each.

(ii)  Non-current assets:

To reflect a marked increase in property prices, Fresco decided to revalue its leased property on 1 April 20X1. The directors accepted the report of an independent surveyor who valued the leased property at $36 million on that date. Fresco has not yet recorded the revaluation. The remaining life of the leased property is eight years at the date of the revaluation. Fresco makes an annual transfer to retained profits to reflect the realisation of the revaluation surplus. In Fresco's tax jurisdiction the revaluation does not give rise to a deferred tax liability.

On 1 April 20X1, Fresco acquired an item of plant under a lease agreement that had an implicit finance cost of 10% per annum. The lease payments in the trial balance represent an initial deposit of $2 million paid on 1 April 20X1 and the first annual rental of $6 million paid on 31 March 20X2. The lease agreement requires further annual payments of $6 million on 31 March each year for the next four years. The present value of the lease payments, excluding the initial deposit, was $23 million.

Plant and equipment (other than the leased plant) is depreciated at 20% per annum using the reducing balance method.

No depreciation or amortisation has yet been charged on any non-current asset for the year ended 31 March 20X2. Depreciation and amortisation are charged to cost of sales.

(iii) In March 20X2, Fresco's internal audit department discovered a fraud committed by the credit controller who did not return from a foreign business trip. The outcome of the fraud is that $4 million of the trade receivables have been stolen by the credit controller and are not recoverable. Of this amount, $1 million relates to the year ended 31 March 20X1 and the remainder to the current year. Fresco is not insured against this fraud.

(iv)  Fresco's income tax calculation for the year ended 31 March 20X2 shows a tax refund of $2.4 million. The balance on current tax in the trial balance represents the under/over provision of the tax liability for the year ended 31 March 20X1. At 31 March 20X2, Fresco had taxable temporary differences of $12 million requiring a deferred tax liability. The income tax rate of Fresco is 25%.

**Required:**

(a)  **Prepare the statement of profit or loss for Fresco for the year ended 31 March 20X2.** ▦                                                                   **(8 marks)**

(b)  **Prepare the statement of changes in equity for Fresco for the year ended 31 March 20X2.** ▦                                                           **(4 marks)**

(c)  **Prepare the statement of financial position of Fresco as at 31 March 20X2.** ▦

**(8 marks)**

**(Total: 20 marks)**

## 356 QUINCY

The following trial balance relates to Quincy as at 30 September 20X2:

|  | $000 | $000 |
|---|---|---|
| Revenue (note (i)) |  | 213,500 |
| Cost of sales | 136,800 |  |
| Distribution costs | 12,500 |  |
| Administrative expenses (note (ii)) | 19,000 |  |
| Loan note interest and dividend paid (notes (ii) and (iii)) | 20,700 |  |
| Investment income |  | 400 |
| Equity shares of 25 cents each |  | 60,000 |
| 6% loan note (note (ii)) |  | 25,000 |
| Retained earnings at 1 October 20X1 |  | 6,500 |
| Plant and equipment at cost (note (iv)) | 83,700 |  |
| Accumulated depreciation at 1 October 20X1: plant and equipment |  | 33,700 |
| Equity financial asset investments (note (v)) | 17,000 |  |
| Inventory at 30 September 20X2 | 24,800 |  |
| Trade receivables | 28,500 |  |
| Bank | 2,900 |  |
| Current tax (note (vi)) | 1,100 |  |
| Deferred tax (note (vi)) |  | 1,200 |
| Trade payables |  | 6,700 |
|  | ———— | ———— |
|  | 347,000 | 347,000 |
|  | ———— | ———— |

The following notes are relevant:

(i) On 1 October 20X1, Quincy sold one of its products for $10 million (included in revenue in the trial balance). As part of the sale agreement, Quincy is committed to the ongoing servicing of this product until 30 September 20X4 (i.e. three years from the date of sale). The value of this service has been included in the selling price of $10 million. The estimated cost to Quincy of the servicing is $600,000 per annum and Quincy's normal gross profit margin on this type of servicing is 25%. The service performance obligation will be satisfied over time. Ignore discounting.

(ii) Quincy issued a $25 million 6% loan note on 1 October 20X1. Issue costs were $1 million and these have been charged to administrative expenses. The loan will be redeemed on 30 September 20X4 at a premium which gives an effective interest rate on the loan of 8%.

(iii) Quincy paid an equity dividend of 8 cents per share during the year ended 30 September 20X2.

(iv) Plant and equipment is depreciated at 15% per annum using the reducing balance method.

No depreciation has yet been charged for the year ended 30 September 20X2. All depreciation is charged to cost of sales.

(v)  The investments had a fair value of $15.7 million as at 30 September 20X2. There were no acquisitions or disposals of these investments during the year ended 30 September 20X2.

(vi)  The balance on current tax represents the under/over provision of the tax liability for the year ended 30 September 20X1. A provision for income tax for the year ended 30 September 20X2 of $7.4 million is required. At 30 September 20X2, Quincy had taxable temporary differences of $5 million, requiring a provision for deferred tax. Any deferred tax adjustment should be reported in the statement of profit or loss. The income tax rate of Quincy is 20%.

**Required:**

(a)  **Prepare the statement of profit or loss and other comprehensive income for Quincy for the year ended 30 September 20X2.** ▦                       **(10 marks)**

(b)  **Prepare the statement of changes in equity for Quincy for the year ended 30 September 20X2.** ▦                       **(2 marks)**

(c)  **Prepare the statement of financial position for Quincy as at 30 September 20X2.** ▦                       **(8 marks)**

**Notes to the financial statements are not required.**

**(Total: 20 marks)**

## 357  ATLAS

The following trial balance relates to Atlas at 31 March 20X3:

|  | $000 | $000 |
|---|---|---|
| Equity shares of 50 cents each |  | 50,000 |
| Retained earnings at 1 April 20X2 |  | 11,200 |
| Land and buildings – at cost (land $10 million) (note (ii)) | 60,000 |  |
| Plant and equipment – at cost (note (ii)) | 94,500 |  |
| Accumulated depreciation at 1 April 20X2: – buildings |  | 20,000 |
| – plant and equipment |  | 24,500 |
| Inventory at 31 March 20X3 | 43,700 |  |
| Trade receivables | 42,200 |  |
| Bank |  | 6,800 |
| Deferred tax (note (iv)) |  | 6,200 |
| Trade payables |  | 35,100 |
| Revenue (note (i)) |  | 550,000 |
| Cost of sales | 411,500 |  |
| Distribution costs | 21,500 |  |
| Administrative expenses | 30,900 |  |
| Bank interest | 700 |  |
| Current tax (note (iv)) |  | 1,200 |
|  | ——— | ——— |
|  | 705,000 | 705,000 |
|  | ——— | ——— |

The following notes are relevant:

(i)     Revenue includes the sale of $10 million of maturing inventory made to Xpede on 1 October 20X2. The cost of the goods at the date of sale was $7 million and Atlas has an option to repurchase these goods at any time within three years of the sale at a price of $10 million plus accrued interest from the date of sale at 10% per annum. At 31 March 20X3 the option had not been exercised, but it is highly likely that it will be before the date it lapses.

(ii)    Non-current assets:

On 1 October 20X2, Atlas terminated the production of one of its product lines. From this date, the plant used to manufacture the product has been actively marketed at an advertised price of $4.2 million which is considered realistic. It is included in the trial balance at a cost of $9 million with accumulated depreciation (at 1 April 20X2) of $5 million.

On 1 April 20X2, the directors of Atlas decided that the financial statements would show an improved position if the land and buildings were revalued to market value. At that date, an independent valuer valued the land at $12 million and the buildings at $35 million and these valuations were accepted by the directors. The remaining life of the buildings at that date was 14 years. Atlas does not make a transfer to retained earnings for excess depreciation. Ignore deferred tax on the revaluation surplus.

Plant and equipment is depreciated at 20% per annum using the reducing balance method and time apportioned as appropriate.

All depreciation is charged to cost of sales, but none has yet been charged on any non-current asset for the year ended 31 March 20X3.

(iii)   At 31 March 20X3, a provision is required for directors' bonuses equal to 1% of revenue for the year.

(iv)    Atlas estimates that an income tax provision of $27.2 million is required for the year ended 31 March 20X3 and at that date the liability to deferred tax is $9.4 million. The movement on deferred tax should be taken to profit or loss. The balance on current tax in the trial balance represents the under/over provision of the tax liability for the year ended 31 March 20X2.

**Required:**

**(i)     Prepare the statement of profit or loss and other comprehensive income for Atlas for the year ended 31 March 20X3.** ▦                                                    **(9 marks)**

**(ii)    Prepare the statement of financial position of Atlas as at 31 March 20X3.** ▦

**(11 marks)**

**Notes to the financial statements and a statement of changes in equity are not required.**

**(Total: 20 marks)**

## 358 MOBY

> 🕐 **Question debrief**

The following trial balance relates to Moby as at 30 September 20X3:

|  | $000 | $000 |
|---|---|---|
| Revenue |  | 227,800 |
| Cost of sales | 164,500 |  |
| Contract to construct asset (note (i)) | 4,000 |  |
| Operating expenses | 29,850 |  |
| Lease rental paid on 30 September 20X3 (note (ii)) | 9,200 |  |
| Land ($12 million) and building ($48 million) at cost (note (ii)) | 60,000 |  |
| Leased plant at initial carrying amount (note (ii)) | 35,000 |  |
| Accumulated depreciation at 1 October 20X2: |  |  |
| building |  | 10,000 |
| leased plant |  | 7,000 |
| Inventory at 30 September 20X3 | 56,600 |  |
| Trade receivables | 38,500 |  |
| Bank |  | 7,300 |
| Insurance provision (note (iii)) |  | 150 |
| Deferred tax (note (iv)) |  | 8,000 |
| Lease liability at 1 October 20X2 (note (ii)) |  | 29,300 |
| Trade payables |  | 21,300 |
| Equity shares of 20 cents each |  | 27,000 |
| Loan note (note (v)) |  | 40,000 |
| Retained earnings at 1 October 20X2 |  | 19,800 |
|  | ——— | ——— |
|  | 397,650 | 397,650 |
|  | ——— | ——— |

The following notes are relevant:

(i)  During the year, Moby entered into a contract to construct an asset for a customer. The performance obligation is satisfied over time. The balance in the trial balance represents:

| Cost incurred to date | $14 million |
|---|---|
| Value of contract billed (work certified) and cash received | $10 million |

The contract commenced on 1 October 20X2 and is for a fixed price of $25 million. The costs to complete the contract at 30 September 20X3 are estimated at $6 million. Moby's policy is to measure progress based on the work certified as a percentage of the contract price.

(ii)    Non-current assets:

Moby decided to revalue its land and building, for the first time, on 1 October 20X2. A qualified valuer determined the relevant revalued amounts to be $16 million for the land and $38.4 million for the building. The building's remaining life at the date of the revaluation was 16 years. This revaluation has not yet been reflected in the trial balance figures. Moby does not make a transfer from the revaluation surplus to retained earnings in respect of the realisation of the revaluation surplus. Deferred tax is applicable to the revaluation surplus at 25%.

The leased plant was acquired on 1 October 20X1 under a five-year lease which has an implicit interest rate of 10% per annum. The rentals are $9.2 million per annum payable on 30 September each year.

No depreciation has yet been charged on any non-current asset for the year ended 30 September 20X3. All depreciation is charged to cost of sales.

(iii)    On 1 October 20X2, Moby received a renewal quote of $400,000 from their property insurer. The directors were surprised at how much it had increased and believed it would be less expensive to 'self-insure'. Accordingly, they charged $400,000 to operating expenses and credited the same amount to the insurance provision. During the year expenses of $250,000 were incurred, relating to previously insured property damage which Moby has debited to the provision.

(iv)    A provision for income tax for the year ended 30 September 20X3 of $3.4 million is required. At 30 September 20X3, the tax base of Moby's net assets was $24 million less than their carrying amounts. This does not include the effect of the revaluation in note (ii) above. The income tax rate of Moby is 25%.

(v)    The $40 million loan note was issued at par on 1 October 20X2. No interest will be paid on the loan. However, it will be redeemed on 30 September 20X5 for $53,240,000 which gives an effective finance cost of 10% per annum.

**Required:**

(a)    **Prepare the statement of profit or loss and other comprehensive income for Moby for the year ended 30 September 20X3.** ▦                    **(10 marks)**

(b)    **Prepare the statement of financial position for Moby as at 30 September 20X3.** ▦
                                **(10 marks)**

Note:    **A statement of changes in equity and notes to the financial statements are not required.**

                                **(Total: 20 marks)**

 *Calculate your allowed time, allocate the time to the separate parts*

## 359 XTOL

The following trial balance relates to Xtol at 31 March 20X4:

|  | $000 | $000 |
|---|---|---|
| Revenue (note (i)) |  | 490,000 |
| Cost of sales | 290,600 |  |
| Distribution costs | 33,500 |  |
| Administrative expenses | 36,800 |  |
| Loan note interest (note (iv)) | 2,500 |  |
| Bank interest | 900 |  |
| Land at cost (note (ii)) | 75,000 |  |
| Plant and equipment at cost (note (ii)) | 155,500 |  |
| Accumulated depreciation at 1 April 20X3: |  |  |
| plant and equipment |  | 43,500 |
| Inventory at 31 March 20X4 | 61,000 |  |
| Trade receivables | 63,000 |  |
| Trade payables |  | 32,200 |
| Bank |  | 5,500 |
| Equity shares of $1 each (note (iii)) |  | 66,000 |
| Share premium |  | 15,000 |
| Retained earnings at 1 April 20X3 |  | 15,200 |
| 5% convertible loan note (note (iii)) |  | 50,000 |
| Current tax (note (iv)) | 3,200 |  |
| Deferred tax (note (iv)) |  | 4,600 |
|  | ——— | ——— |
|  | 722,000 | 722,000 |
|  | ——— | ——— |

The following notes are relevant:

(i)     Revenue includes $20 million cash sales made through Xtol's retail outlets during the year on behalf of Francais. Xtol, acting as agent, is entitled to a commission of 10% of the selling price of these goods. By 31 March 20X4, Xtol had remitted to Francais $15 million (of the $20 million sales) and recorded this amount in cost of sales.

(ii)    Plant and equipment is depreciated at 12½% per annum on the reducing balance basis. All amortisation/depreciation of non-current assets is charged to cost of sales.

(iii)   On 1 April 20X3, Xtol issued a 5% $50 million convertible loan note at par. Interest is payable annually in arrears on 31 March each year. The loan note is redeemable at par or convertible into equity shares at the option of the loan note holders on 31 March 20X6. The interest on an equivalent loan note without the conversion rights would be 8% per annum.

The present values of $1 receivable at the end of each year, based on discount rates of 5% and 8%, are:

|  | 5% | 8% |
|---|---|---|
| End of year 1 | 0.95 | 0.93 |
| 2 | 0.91 | 0.86 |
| 3 | 0.86 | 0.79 |

(iv)   The balance on current tax represents the under/over provision of the tax liability for the year ended 31 March 20X3. A provision of $28 million is required for current tax for the year ended 31 March 20X4 and at this date the deferred tax liability was assessed at $8.3 million.

(v)   The equity shares and share premium balances in the trial balance above include a fully subscribed 1 for 5 rights issue at $1.60 per share which was made by Xtol on 1 October 20X3. The market value of Xtol's shares was $2.50 on 1 October 20X3.

**Required:**

**(a)   Prepare the Xtol's statement of profit or loss for the year ended 31 March 20X4.** ▦

**(b)   Prepare the statement of financial position for Xtol as at 31 March 20X4.** ▦

**(c)   Calculate the basic earnings per share of Xtol for the year ended 31 March 20X4.** ▦

**Note:   Answers and workings (for parts (a) to (b)) should be presented to the nearest $1,000.  A statement of changes in equity is not required.**

**The following mark allocation is provided as guidance for this question:**

**(a)   7 marks**

**(b)   8 marks**

**(c)   5 marks**

**(Total: 20 marks)**

## 360 DUNE

The following trial balance relates to Dune at 31 March 20X4:

| | $000 | $000 |
|---|---|---|
| Equity shares of $1 each | | 40,000 |
| Other components of equity | | 20,000 |
| 5% loan note (note (i)) | | 20,000 |
| Retained earnings at 1 April 20X3 | | 38,400 |
| Leasehold (15 years) property – at cost (note (ii)) | 45,000 | |
| Plant and equipment – at cost (note (ii)) | 67,500 | |
| Accumulated depreciation – 1 April 20X3 – leasehold property | | 6,000 |
| – plant and equipment | | 23,500 |
| Investments at fair value through profit or loss (note (iii)) | 26,500 | |
| Inventory at 31 March 20X4 | 48,000 | |
| Trade receivables | 40,700 | |
| Bank | 15,500 | |
| Deferred tax (note (iv)) | | 6,000 |
| Trade payables | | 52,000 |
| Revenue (note (iv)) | | 400,000 |
| Cost of sales | 294,000 | |
| Distribution costs | 26,400 | |
| Administrative expenses (note (i)) | 34,200 | |
| Dividend paid | 10,000 | |
| Loan note interest paid (six months) | 500 | |
| Bank interest | 200 | |
| Investment income | | 1,200 |
| Current tax (note (iv)) | | 1,400 |
| | ——— | ——— |
| | 608,500 | 608,500 |
| | ——— | ——— |

The following notes are relevant:

(i)     The 5% loan note was issued on 1 April 20X3 at its nominal (face) value of $20 million. The direct costs of the issue were $500,000 and these have been charged to administrative expenses. The loan note will be redeemed on 31 March 20X6 at a substantial premium. The effective finance cost of the loan note is 10% per annum.

(ii)    Non-current assets:

In order to fund a new project, on 1 October 20X3 Dune decided to sell its leasehold property. From that date it commenced a short-term rental of an equivalent property. The leasehold property is being marketed by a property agent at a price of $40 million, which was considered a reasonably achievable price at that date. The expected costs to sell have been agreed at $500,000. Recent market transactions suggest that actual selling prices achieved for this type of property in the current market conditions are 15% less than the value at which they are marketed. At 31 March 20X4 the property had not been sold.

Plant and equipment is depreciated at 15% per annum using the reducing balance method.

No depreciation/amortisation has yet been charged on any non-current asset for the year ended 31 March 20X4. Depreciation, amortisation and impairment charges are all charged to cost of sales.

(iii) The investments at fair value through profit or loss had a fair value of $28 million on 31 March 20X4. There were no purchases or disposals of any of these investments during the year.

(iv) A provision for income tax for the year ended 31 March 20X4 of $12 million is required. The balance on current tax represents the under/over provision of the tax liability for the year ended 31 March 20X3. At 31 March 20X4 the tax base of Dune's net assets was $14 million less than their carrying amounts. The income tax rate of Dune is 30%.

(v) Dune has accounted for a fully subscribed rights issue of equity shares made on 1 January 20X4 of one new share for every four in issue at 42 cents each, when the market value of a Dune share was 82 cents.

**Required:**

(a) **Prepare the statement of profit or loss for Dune for the year ended 31 March 20X4, and the statement of financial position for Dune as at 31 March 20X4.** ▦

**Notes to the financial statements and a statement of changes in equity are not required.** **(15 marks)**

(b) **Using the information in note (v), calculate earnings per share for Dune for the year ended 31 March 20X4. Also, calculate the re-stated figure for 20X3 if the EPS figure in the original 20X3 financial statements was 68¢ per share.** ▦ **(5 marks)**

**(Total: 20 marks)**

## 361 KANDY

After preparing a draft statement of profit or loss for the year ended 30 September 20X4 and adding the year's profit (before any adjustments required by notes (i) to (iii) below) to retained earnings, the summarised trial balance of Kandy as at 30 September 20X4 is:

|  | $000 | $000 |
|---|---|---|
| Equity shares of $1 each |  | 40,000 |
| Retained earnings as at 30 September 20X4 |  | 19,500 |
| Proceeds of 6% loan (note (i)) |  | 30,000 |
| Land ($5 million) and buildings – at cost (note (ii)) | 55,000 |  |
| Plant and equipment – at cost (note (ii)) | 58,500 |  |
| Accumulated depreciation at 1 October 20X3: buildings |  | 20,000 |
| plant and equipment |  | 34,500 |
| Current assets | 68,700 |  |
| Current liabilities |  | 38,400 |
| Deferred tax (note (iii)) |  | 2,500 |
| Interest payment (note (i)) | 1,800 |  |
| Investments (note (iv)) | 2,000 |  |
| Current tax (note (iii)) |  | 1,100 |
|  | ——— | ——— |
|  | 184,000 | 184,000 |
|  | ——— | ——— |

The following notes are relevant:

(i) The loan note was issued on 1 October 20X3 and incurred issue costs of $1 million which were charged to profit or loss. Interest of $1.8 million ($30 million at 6%) was paid on 30 September 20X4. The loan is redeemable on 30 September 20X8 at a substantial premium which gives an effective interest rate of 9% per annum. No other repayments are due until 30 September 20X8.

(ii) Non-current assets:

The price of property has increased significantly in recent years and on 1 October 20X3, the directors decided to revalue the land and buildings. The directors accepted the report of an independent surveyor who valued the land at $8 million and the buildings at $39 million on that date. The remaining life of the buildings at 1 October 20X3 was 15 years. Kandy does not make an annual transfer to retained earnings to reflect the realisation of the revaluation gain. However the revaluation will give rise to a deferred tax liability. The income tax rate of Kandy is 20%.

Plant and equipment is depreciated at 12½% per annum using the reducing balance method.

No depreciation has been charged for the year ended 30 September 20X4.

(iii) A provision of $2.4 million is required for current income tax on the profit of the year to 30 September 20X4. The balance on current tax in the trial balance is the under/over provision of tax for the previous year. In addition to the temporary differences relating to the information in note (ii), Kandy has further taxable temporary differences of $10 million as at 30 September 20X4.

(iv) The investments in the trial balance are held at their fair value at 1 October 20X3. At 30 September 20X4 the value had risen to $2.6 million.

**Required:**

(a)     Prepare a schedule of adjustments required to the retained earnings of Kandy as at 30 September 20X4 as a result of the information in notes (i) to (iv) above. ⊞

**(9 marks)**

(b)     Prepare the statement of financial position of Kandy as at 30 September 20X4. ⊞

**(11 marks)**

Note:    The notes to the statement of financial position are not required.

**(Total: 20 marks)**

## 362   CLARION

The following trial balance relates to Clarion as at 31 March 20X5.

|  | $000 | $000 |
|---|---:|---:|
| Equity shares of $1 each | | 35,000 |
| Retained earnings – 1 April 20X4 | | 4,700 |
| 8% loan notes (note (i)) | | 20,000 |
| Plant and equipment at cost (note (ii)) | 77,000 | |
| Right-of-use plant (note (iii)) | 8,000 | |
| Accumulated depreciation plant and equipment – 1 April 20X4 | | 19,000 |
| Investments through profit or loss – value at 1 April 20X4 (note (iv)) | 6,000 | |
| Inventory at 31 March 20X5 | 11,700 | |
| Trade receivables | 20,500 | |
| Bank | | 1,900 |
| Deferred tax (note (v)) | | 2,700 |
| Trade payables | | 9,400 |
| Environmental provision (note (ii)) | | 4,000 |
| Lease liability (note (iii)) | | 4,200 |
| Revenue | | 132,000 |
| Cost of sales | 88,300 | |
| Administrative expenses | 8,000 | |
| Distribution costs | 7,400 | |
| Loan note interest paid | 800 | |
| Suspense account (note (i)) | 5,800 | |
| Bank interest | 300 | |
| Investment income (note (iii)) | | 500 |
| Current tax (note (v)) | | 400 |
|  | ——— | ——— |
|  | 233,800 | 233,800 |
|  | ——— | ——— |

The following notes are also relevant.

(i)     On 31 March 20X5, one quarter of the 8% loan notes were redeemed at par and six months' outstanding loan interest was paid. The suspense account represents the debit entry corresponding to the cash payment for the capital redemption and the outstanding interest.

(ii)    Property, plant and equipment

Included in property, plant and equipment is an item of plant with a cost of $14 million. However, the plant will cause environmental damage which will have to be rectified when it is dismantled at the end of its five year life. The present value (discounting at 8%) on 1 April 20X4 of the rectification is $4 million. The environmental provision has been correctly accounted for, however, no finance cost has yet been charged on the provision.

No depreciation has yet been charged on plant and equipment which should be charged to cost of sales on a straight-line basis over a five-year life. No plant is more than four years old.

(iii)   The right-of-use plant was acquired on 1 April 20X4 under a five-year lease with an initial deposit of $2.3 million and annual payments of $1.5 million on 31 March each year. The present value of the annual payments under the lease (**excluding the initial deposit**) at 1 April 20X4 was $5.7 million, the lease has an implicit rate of interest of 10%, and the right-of-use plant has been correctly capitalised. The lease liability in the trial balance above represents the initial liability less the first annual payment.

(iv)    The investments through profit or loss are those held at 31 March 20X5 (after the sale below). They are carried at their fair value as at 1 April 20X4, however, they had a fair value of $6.5 million on 31 March 20X5. During the year an investment which had a carrying amount of $1.4 million was sold for $1.6 million. Investment income in the trial balance above includes the profit on the sale of the investment and dividends received during the year.

(v)     A provision for current tax for the year ended 31 March 20X5 of $3.5 million is required. The balance on current tax in the trial balance above represents the under/over provision of the tax liability for the year ended 31 March 20X4. At 31 March 20X5, the tax base of Clarion's net assets was $12 million less than their carrying amounts. The income tax rate of Clarion is 25%.

**Required:**

(a)    **Prepare the statement of profit or loss for Clarion for the year ended 31 March 20X5.** ⊞                                                                          **(8 marks)**

(b)    **Prepare Clarion's statement of financial position as at 31 March 20X5.** ⊞  **(9 marks)**

(c)    **Prepare extracts from the statement of cash flows for Clarion for the year ended 31 March 20X5 in respect of cash flows from investing (ignore investment income) and financing activities.** ⊞                                                                          **(3 marks)**

**Notes to the financial statements are not required.**

**(Total: 20 marks)**

**363   MOSTON**  *Walk in the footsteps of a top tutor*

The following trial balance **extracts** (i.e. it is not a complete trial balance) relate to Moston as at 30 June 20X5:

|  | $000 | $000 |
|---|---|---|
| Revenue (note (i)) | | 113,500 |
| Cost of sales | 88,500 | |
| Research and development costs (note (ii)) | 7,800 | |
| Distribution costs | 3,600 | |
| Administrative expenses (note (iv)) | 6,800 | |
| Loan note interest and dividends paid (notes (iv) and (vii)) | 5,000 | |
| Investment income | | 300 |
| Equity shares of $1 each (note (vii)) | | 30,000 |
| 5% loan note (note (iv)) | | 20,000 |
| Retained earnings as at 1 July 20X4 | | 6,200 |
| Revaluation surplus as at 1 July 20X4 | | 3,000 |
| Other components of equity | | 9,300 |
| Property at valuation 1 July 20X4 (note (iii)) | 28,500 | |
| Plant and equipment at cost (note (iii)) | 27,100 | |
| Accumulated depreciation plant and equipment 1 July 20X4 | | 9,100 |
| Financial asset equity investments at fair value 1 July 20X4 (note (v)) | 8,800 | |

The following notes are relevant:

(i)     Revenue includes a $3 million sale made on 1 January 20X5 of maturing goods which are not biological assets. The carrying amount of these goods at the date of sale was $2 million. Moston is still in possession of the goods (but they have not been included in the inventory count) and has an unexercised option to repurchase them at any time in the next three years. In three years' time the goods are expected to be worth $5 million. The repurchase price will be the original selling price plus interest at 10% per annum from the date of sale to the date of repurchase.

(ii)    Moston commenced a research and development project on 1 January 20X5. It spent $1 million per month on research until 31 March 20X5, at which date the project passed into the development stage. From this date it spent $1.6 million per month until the year end (30 June 20X5), at which date development was completed. However, it was not until 1 May 20X5 that the directors of Moston were confident that the new product would be a commercial success.

Expensed research and development costs should be charged to cost of sales.

(iii)   Non-current assets:

Moston's property is carried at fair value which at 30 June 20X5 was $29 million. The remaining life of the property at the beginning of the year (1 July 20X4) was 15 years. Moston does not make an annual transfer to retained earnings in respect of the revaluation surplus. Ignore deferred tax on the revaluation.

Plant and equipment is depreciated at 15% per annum using the reducing balance method.

No depreciation has yet been charged on any non-current asset for the year ended 30 June 20X5. All depreciation is charged to cost of sales.

(iv)   The 5% loan note was issued on 1 July 20X4 at its nominal value of $20 million incurring direct issue costs of $500,000 which have been charged to administrative expenses. The loan note will be redeemed after three years at a premium which gives the loan note an effective finance cost of 8% per annum. Annual interest was paid on 30 June 20X5.

(v)   At 30 June 20X5, the financial asset equity investments had a fair value of $9.6 million. There were no acquisitions or disposals of these investments during the year.

(vi)   A provision for current tax for the year ended 30 June 20X5 of $1.2 million is required, together with an increase to the deferred tax provision to be charged to profit or loss of $800,000.

(vii)   Moston paid a dividend of 20 cents per share on 30 March 20X5, which was followed the day after by an issue of 10 million equity shares at their full market value of $1.70. The share premium on the issue was recorded in other components of equity.

**Required:**

**(a)   Prepare the statement of profit or loss and other comprehensive income for Moston for the year ended 30 June 20X5.** ⊞                               **(11 marks)**

**(b)   Prepare the statement of changes in equity for Moston for the year ended 30 June 20X5.** ⊞                                                          **(4 marks)**

**(c)   Prepare extracts from the statement of cash flows for Moston for the year ended 30 June 20X5 in respect of cash flows from investing and financing activities.** ⊞

**(5 marks)**

**Note: The statement of financial position and notes to the financial statements are NOT required.**

**(Total: 20 marks)**

## 364 TRIAGE

After preparing a draft statement of profit or loss (before interest and tax) for the year ended 31 March 20X6 (before any adjustments which may be required by notes (i) to (iv) below), the summarised trial balance of Triage Co as at 31 March 20X6 is:

|  | $000 | $000 |
|---|---|---|
| Equity shares of $1 each |  | 50,000 |
| Retained earnings as at 1 April 20X5 |  | 3,500 |
| Draft profit before interest and tax for year ended 31 March 20X6 |  | 30,000 |
| 6% convertible loan notes (note (i)) |  | 40,000 |
| Leased property (original life 25 years) – at cost (note (ii)) | 75,000 |  |
| Plant and equipment – at cost (note (ii)) | 72,100 |  |
| Accumulated amortisation/depreciation at 1 April 20X5: |  |  |
| leased property |  | 15,000 |
| plant and equipment |  | 28,100 |
| Trade receivables (note (iii)) | 28,000 |  |
| Other current assets | 9,300 |  |
| Current liabilities |  | 17,700 |
| Deferred tax (note (iv)) |  | 3,200 |
| Interest payment (note (i)) | 2,400 |  |
| Current tax (note (iv) | 700 |  |
|  | ——— | ——— |
|  | 187,500 | 187,500 |
|  | ——— | ——— |

The following notes are relevant:

(i)   Triage Co issued 400,000 $100 6% convertible loan notes on 1 April 20X5. Interest is payable annually in arrears on 31 March each year. The loans can be converted to equity shares on the basis of 20 shares for each $100 loan note on 31 March 20X8 or redeemed at par for cash on the same date. An equivalent loan without the conversion rights would have required an interest rate of 8%.

The present value of $1 receivable at the end of each year, based on discount rates of 6% and 8%, are:

|  |  | 6% | 8% |
|---|---|---|---|
| End of year | 1 | 0.94 | 0.93 |
|  | 2 | 0.89 | 0.86 |
|  | 3 | 0.84 | 0.79 |

(ii)    Non-current assets:

The directors decided to revalue the leased property at $66.3m on 1 October 20X5. Triage Co does not make an annual transfer from the revaluation surplus to retained earnings to reflect the realisation of the revaluation gain; however, the revaluation will give rise to a deferred tax liability at a tax rate of 20%.

The leased property is depreciated on a straight-line basis and plant and equipment at 15% per annum using the reducing balance method.

No depreciation has yet been charged on any non-current assets for the year ended 31 March 20X6.

(iii)   In September 20X5, the directors of Triage Co discovered a fraud. In total, $700,000 which had been included as receivables in the above trial balance had been stolen by an employee. $450,000 of this related to the year ended 31 March 20X5, the rest to the current year. The directors are hopeful that 50% of the losses can be recovered from their insurers.

(iv)    A provision of $2.7m is required for current income tax on the profit of the year to 31 March 20X6. The balance on current tax in the trial balance is the under/over provision of tax for the previous year. In addition to the temporary differences relating to the information in note (ii), at 31 March 20X6 the carrying amounts of Triage Co's net assets are $12m more than their tax base.

**Required:**

**(a)    Prepare a schedule of adjustments required to the draft profit before interest and tax (in the above trial balance) to give the profit or loss of Triage Co for the year ended 31 March 20X6 as a result of the information in notes (i) to (iv) above.**
                                                                                              **(5 marks)**

**(b)    Prepare the statement of financial position of Triage Co as at 31 March 20X6.**
                                                                                              **(12 marks)**

**(c)**    The issue of convertible loan notes can potentially dilute the basic earnings per share (EPS).

**Calculate the diluted earnings per share for Triage Co for the year ended 31 March 20X6 (there is no need to calculate the basic EPS).**                              **(3 marks)**

**Note:    A statement of changes in equity and the notes to the statement of financial position are not required.**

                                                                                              **(Total: 20 marks)**

# STATEMENT OF CASH FLOWS

These questions include the preparation of a full statement of cashflows (SCF). This skill is tested in FA and, as such, FR is unlikely to test the preparation of a full SCF. FR is more likely to test the elements not covered in FA (for example leases and loan notes), an SCF extract or the analysis of an SCF. In order to answer the above questions, candidates need to know how to prepare a full SCF, and the questions below are therefore included for revision purposes only.

**365 TABBA**  *Walk in the footsteps of a top tutor*

The following draft financial statements relate to Tabba, a privately owned entity.

| Statements of financial position as at: | 30 September 20X5 | | 30 September 20X4 | |
|---|---|---|---|---|
| | $000 | $000 | $000 | $000 |
| Tangible non-current assets (note (ii)) | | 10,600 | | 15,800 |
| Current assets | | | | |
| Inventories | 2,550 | | 1,850 | |
| Trade receivables | 3,100 | | 2,600 | |
| Insurance claim (note (iii)) | 1,500 | | 1,200 | |
| Cash and bank | 850 | | Nil | |
| | ——— | 8,000 | ——— | 5,650 |
| Total assets | | 18,600 | | 21,450 |
| | | | | |
| Equity and liabilities | | | | |
| Share capital ($1 each) | | 6,000 | | 6,000 |
| Reserves: | | | | |
| Revaluation (note (ii)) | nil | | 1,600 | |
| Retained earnings | 2,550 | | 850 | |
| | ——— | 2,550 | ——— | 2,450 |
| | | 8,550 | | 8,450 |
| Non-current liabilities | | | | |
| Lease liability (note (ii)) | 2,000 | | 1,700 | |
| 6% loan notes | 800 | | Nil | |
| 10% loan notes | nil | | 4,000 | |
| Deferred tax | 200 | | 500 | |
| Government grants (note (ii)) | 1,400 | | 900 | |
| | ——— | 4,400 | ——— | 7,100 |

| Current liabilities | | | | |
|---|---|---|---|---|
| Bank overdraft | nil | | 550 | |
| Trade payables | 4,050 | | 2,950 | |
| Government grants (note (ii)) | 600 | | 400 | |
| Lease liability (note (ii)) | 900 | | 800 | |
| Current tax payable | 100 | | 1,200 | |
| | ——— | 5,650 | ——— | 5,900 |
| Total equity and liabilities | | 18,600 | | 21,450 |

The following information is relevant:

(i)     Statement of profit or loss extract for the year ended 30 September 20X5:

| | $000 |
|---|---|
| Profit from operations | 270 |
| Finance cost | (260) |
| Interest income | 40 |
| Profit before tax | 50 |
| Net tax credit | 50 |
| Profit for the period | 100 |

**Note:**   The finance cost includes lease interest.

(ii)    The details of the tangible non-current assets are:

| | Cost | Accumulated depreciation | Carrying amount |
|---|---|---|---|
| | $000 | $000 | $000 |
| At 30 September 20X4 | 20,200 | 4,400 | 15,800 |
| At 30 September 20X5 | 16,000 | 5,400 | 10,600 |

During the year Tabba sold its factory for its fair value of $12 million.  At the date of sale it had a carrying amount of $7.4 million based on a previous revaluation of $8.6 million less depreciation of $1.2 million since the revaluation.  The profit on the sale of the factory has been included in operating profit. The surplus on the revaluation surplus related entirely to the factory. No other disposals of non-current assets were made during the year.

Plant acquired under leases during the year was $1.5 million and has been included within tangible non-current assets.   Other purchases of plant during the year qualified for government grants of $950,000 received in the year.   Release of government grants has been credited to cost of sales.

(iii)   The insurance claim relates to flood damage to Tabba's inventories which occurred in September 20X4. The original estimate has been revised during the year. The claim is expected to be settled in the near future.

**Required:**

(a)    **Prepare a statement of cash flows using the indirect method for Tabba for the year ended 30 September 20X5.** ⊞                                                    **(17 marks)**

(b)    **Comment on the cash generated from operations for Tabba for the year ended 30 September 20X5.** ⊞                                                                **(3 marks)**

**(Total: 20 marks)**

## 366 COALTOWN  *Walk in the footsteps of a top tutor*

 **Question debrief**

Coaltown is a wholesaler and retailer of office furniture. Extracts from their financial statements are set out below.

**Statement of profit or loss and other comprehensive income for the year ended:**

|  |  | 31 March 20X9 | |
| --- | --- | ---: | ---: |
|  |  | $000 | $000 |
| Revenue | – cash | 12,800 | |
|  | – credit | 53,000 | 65,800 |
| Cost of sales |  |  | (43,800) |
| Gross profit |  |  | 22,000 |
| Operating expenses |  |  | (11,200) |
| Finance costs – loan notes |  | (380) | |
|  | – overdraft | (220) | (600) |
| Profit before tax |  |  | 10,200 |
| Income tax expense |  |  | (3,200) |
| Profit for period |  |  | 7,000 |
| Other comprehensive income |  |  | |
| Gain on property revaluation |  |  | 5,000 |
| Total comprehensive income for the year |  |  | 12,000 |

**Statements of financial position as at 31 March:**

| | 20X9 | | 20X8 | |
|---|---|---|---|---|
| | $000 | $000 | $000 | $000 |
| **Assets** | | | | |
| Non-current assets (notes (i), (ii)) | | | | |
| Cost | | 93,500 | | 80,000 |
| Accumulated depreciation | | (43,000) | | (48,000) |
| | | 50,500 | | 32,000 |
| **Current assets** | | | | |
| Inventory | 5,200 | | 4,400 | |
| Trade receivables | 7,800 | | 2,800 | |
| Bank | nil | 13,000 | 700 | 7,900 |
| **Total assets** | | 63,500 | | 39,900 |
| **Equity and liabilities** | | | | |
| Equity shares of $1 each | | 16,600 | | 6,000 |
| Other components of equity | | 4,800 | | 500 |
| Revaluation surplus (note (ii)) | | 6,500 | | 2,500 |
| Retained earnings (note (ii)) | | 19,800 | | 15,800 |
| | | 47,700 | | 24,800 |
| **Non-current liabilities** | | | | |
| 10% loan notes | 4,000 | | 3,000 | |
| Convertible loan (note (v)) | Nil | | 2,000 | |
| | | 4,000 | | 5,000 |
| **Current liabilities** | | | | |
| Bank overdraft | 3,600 | | Nil | |
| Trade payables | 4,200 | | 4,500 | |
| Taxation | 3,000 | | 5,300 | |
| Negligence claim (note (iii)) | Nil | | 120 | |
| Warranty provision | 1,000 | 11,800 | 180 | 10,100 |
| **Total equity and liabilities** | | 63,500 | | 39,900 |

(i) During the year Coaltown redesigned its display areas in all of its outlets. The previous displays had cost $10 million and had been written down by $9 million. There was an unexpected cost of $500,000 for the removal and disposal of the old display areas.

(ii) Also during the year Coaltown revalued the carrying amount of its property upwards by $5 million, the accumulated depreciation on these properties of $2 million was reset to zero. All depreciation is charged to operating expenses. Coaltown makes annual reserves transfer from the revaluation surplus in respect of excess depreciation.

(iii) In June 20X9 Coaltown made an out of court settlement of a negligence claim brought about by a former employee. The dispute had been in progress for two years and Coaltown had made provisions for the potential liability in each of the two previous years. The unprovided amount of the claim at the time of settlement was $30,000 and this was charged to operating expenses.

(iv) The warranty provision relates to the future repair of goods and is charged to operating expenses.

(v) During the year 20% of the convertible loan holders exercised their right to convert to ordinary shares. The terms of conversion were 25 ordinary shares of $1 each for each $100 of convertible loan. The remainder were repaid in cash. Ignore any transfer from other components of equity to retained earnings in respect of the redemption of the loan notes.

**Required:**

**Prepare a statement of cash flows for Coaltown for the year ended 31 March 20X9 in accordance with IAS 7 *Statement of Cash Flows* by the indirect method.** ▦

**(Total: 20 marks)**

---

 **Calculate your allowed time, allocate the time to the separate parts**

---

### 367 MONTY

Monty is a publicly listed entity. Its financial statements for the year ended 31 March 20X3 including comparatives are shown below:

**Statement of profit or loss and other comprehensive income for the year ended 31 March 20X3**

|  | $000 |
|---|---|
| Revenue | 31,000 |
| Cost of sales | (21,800) |
| | ――――― |
| Gross profit | 9,200 |
| Distribution costs | (3,450) |
| Administrative expenses | (2,200) |
| Finance costs – loan interest | (400) |
| – lease interest | (150) |
| | ――――― |
| Profit before tax | 3,000 |
| Income tax expense | (1,000) |
| | ――――― |
| Profit for the year | 2,000 |
| Other comprehensive income (note (i)) | 1,350 |
| | ――――― |
| | 3,350 |
| | ――――― |

**Statements of financial position as at:**

|  | 31 March 20X3 | | 31 March 20X2 | |
|---|---|---|---|---|
|  | $000 | $000 | $000 | $000 |
| **Assets** | | | | |
| Non-current assets | | | | |
| Property, plant and equipment | | 14,000 | | 10,700 |
| Deferred development expenditure | | 1,000 | | nil |
|  | | ––––– | | ––––– |
|  | | 15,000 | | 10,700 |
| Current assets | | | | |
| Inventory | 3,300 | | 3,800 | |
| Trade receivables | 2,950 | | 2,200 | |
| Bank | 1,980 | 8,230 | 1,300 | 7,300 |
|  | ––––– | ––––– | ––––– | ––––– |
| Total assets | | 23,230 | | 18,000 |
|  | | ––––– | | ––––– |
| **Equity and liabilities** | | | | |
| Equity | | | | |
| Equity shares of $1 each | | 7,000 | | 7,000 |
| Revaluation surplus | | 1,350 | | nil |
| Retained earnings | | 3,200 | | 1,750 |
|  | | ––––– | | ––––– |
|  | | 11,550 | | 8,750 |
| Non-current liabilities | | | | |
| 8% loan notes (note(iii)) | 4,080 | | 4,000 | |
| Deferred tax | 1,500 | | 800 | |
| Lease liability | 1,200 | | 900 | |
| Government grant | 200 | | 100 | |
|  | ––––– | 6,980 | ––––– | 5,800 |
| Current liabilities | | | | |
| Lease liability | 750 | | 600 | |
| Trade payables | 2,650 | | 2,100 | |
| Current tax payable | 1,250 | | 725 | |
| Government grant | 50 | 4,700 | 25 | 3,450 |
|  | ––––– | ––––– | ––––– | ––––– |
| Total equity and liabilities | | 23,230 | | 18,000 |
|  | | ––––– | | ––––– |

**Notes:**

(i) On 1 July 20X2, Monty acquired additional plant under a lease with an initial value of $1.5 million. The right-of-use asset is included within property, plant and equipment. On this date it also revalued its property upwards by $2 million and transferred $650,000 of the resulting revaluation surplus this created to deferred tax. There were no disposals of non-current assets during the period.

(ii)    Depreciation of property, plant and equipment was $900,000 and amortisation of the deferred development expenditure was $200,000 for the year ended 31 March 20X3.

(iii)   The 8% loan notes are repayable at a premium, giving them an effective rate of 10%. No loan notes were issued or redeemed during the year.

(iv)   $25,000 was credited to administrative expenses in respect of government grants during the year.

**Required:**

**Prepare a statement of cash flows for Monty for the year ended 31 March 20X3, in accordance with IAS 7 *Statement of Cash Flows*, using the indirect method.** ⊞

(Total: 20 marks)

**368   KINGDOM**

 **Question debrief**

Kingdom is a publicly listed manufacturing entity. Its draft summarised financial statements for the year ended 30 September 20X3 (and 20X2 comparatives) are:

**Statements of profit or loss and other comprehensive income for the year ended 30 September:**

|  | 20X3 | 20X2 |
|---|---|---|
|  | $000 | $000 |
| Revenue | 44,900 | 44,000 |
| Cost of sales | (31,300) | (29,000) |
| Gross profit | 13,600 | 15,000 |
| Distribution costs | (2,400) | (2,100) |
| Administrative expenses | (7,850) | (5,900) |
| Investment properties  – rentals received | 350 | 400 |
|                                – fair value changes | (700) | 500 |
| Finance costs | (600) | (600) |
| Profit before taxation | 2,400 | 7,300 |
| Income tax | (600) | (1,700) |
| Profit for the year | 1,800 | 5,600 |
| Other comprehensive income | (1,300) | 1,000 |
| Total comprehensive income | 500 | 6,600 |

**Statements of financial position as at 30 September:**

|  | 20X3 | | 20X2 | |
|---|---|---|---|---|
|  | $000 | $000 | $000 | $000 |
| **Assets** | | | | |
| Non-current assets | | | | |
| Property, plant and equipment | | 26,700 | | 25,200 |
| Investment properties | | 4,100 | | 5,000 |
| | | ——— | | ——— |
| | | 30,800 | | 30,200 |
| Current assets | | | | |
| Inventory | 2,300 | | 3,100 | |
| Trade receivables | 3,000 | | 3,400 | |
| Bank | nil | 5,300 | 300 | 6,800 |
| | ——— | ——— | ——— | ——— |
| Total assets | | 36,100 | | 37,000 |
| | | ——— | | ——— |
| **Equity and liabilities** | | | | |
| Equity | | | | |
| Equity shares of $1 each | | 17,200 | | 15,000 |
| Revaluation surplus | | 1,200 | | 2,500 |
| Retained earnings | | 7,700 | | 8,700 |
| | | ——— | | ——— |
| | | 26,100 | | 26,200 |
| Non-current liabilities | | | | |
| 12% loan notes | | 5,000 | | 5,000 |
| Current liabilities | | | | |
| Trade payables | 4,200 | | 3,900 | |
| Accrued finance costs | 100 | | 50 | |
| Bank | 200 | | nil | |
| Current tax payable | 500 | 5,000 | 1,850 | 5,800 |
| | ——— | ——— | ——— | ——— |
| Total equity and liabilities | | 36,100 | | 37,000 |
| | | ——— | | ——— |

On 1 July 20X3, Kingdom acquired a new investment property at a cost of $1.4 million. On this date, it also transferred one of its other investment properties to property, plant and equipment at its fair value of $1.6 million as it became owner-occupied on that date. Kingdom adopts the fair value model for its investment properties.

Kingdom also has a policy of revaluing its other properties (included as property, plant and equipment) to market value at the end of each year. Other comprehensive income and the revaluation surplus both relate to these properties.

Depreciation of property, plant and equipment during the year was $1.5 million. An item of plant with a carrying amount of $2.3 million was sold for $1.8 million during September 20X3.

**Required:**

(a)   Prepare the statement of cash flows for Kingdom for the year ended 30 September 20X3 in accordance with IAS 7 *Statement of Cash Flows* using the indirect method.                                                       **(15 marks)**

(b)   At a board meeting to consider the results shown by the draft financial statements, concern was expressed that, although there had been a slight increase in revenue during the current year, the profit before tax had fallen dramatically. The purchasing director commented that he was concerned about the impact of rising prices. During the year to 30 September 20X3, most of Kingdom's manufacturing and operating costs have risen by an estimated 8% per annum.

**Required:**

Explain the causes of the fall in Kingdom's profit before tax.           **(5 marks)**

**(Total: 20 marks)**

---

> Calculate your allowed time, allocate the time to the separate parts

---

# BUSINESS COMBINATIONS

**369   PREMIER** *Walk in the footsteps of a top tutor*

On 1 June 20X0, Premier acquired 80% of the equity share capital of Sanford. The consideration consisted of two elements: a share exchange of three shares in Premier for every five acquired shares in Sanford and $800,000 cash. The share issue has not yet been recorded by Premier. At the date of acquisition shares in Premier had a market value of $5 each. Below are the summarised draft financial statements of both entities.

**Extracts from statements of profit or loss for the year ended 30 September 20X0**

|  | Premier | Sanford |
|---|---|---|
|  | $000 | $000 |
| Revenue | 92,500 | 45,000 |
| Cost of sales | (70,500) | (36,000) |
| Gross profit | 22,000 | 9,000 |
| Other expenses | (12,000) | (5,100) |
| Profit for the year | 10,000 | 3,900 |
| Other comprehensive income: |  |  |
| Gains on revaluation | nil | nil |
| Total comprehensive income | 10,000 | 3,900 |

---

**Statements of financial position as at 30 September 20X0**

| Assets | | |
|---|---|---|
| Non-current assets | | |
| Property, plant and equipment | 25,500 | 13,900 |
| Investments | 1,800 | nil |
| | 27,300 | 13,900 |
| Current assets | 12,500 | 2,400 |
| Total assets | 39,800 | 16,300 |
| | | |
| Equity and liabilities | | |
| Equity | | |
| Equity shares of $1 each | 12,000 | 5,000 |
| Other equity reserve – 30 September 20W9 (note (iv)) | 500 | nil |
| Retained earnings | 12,300 | 4,500 |
| | 24,800 | 9,500 |
| Liabilities | | |
| Current liabilities | 15,000 | 6,800 |
| Total equity and liabilities | 39,800 | 16,300 |

The following information is relevant:

(i)    At the date of acquisition, the fair values of Sanford's assets were equal to their carrying amounts with the exception of its property. This had a fair value of $1.2 million **below** its carrying amount, and had a remaining useful life of 8 years at the date of acquisition. Sanford has not incorporated this in its financial statements.

(ii)    Sales from Sanford to Premier throughout the year ended 30 September 20X0 had consistently been $1 million per month. Sanford made a mark-up on cost of 25% on these sales. Premier had $2 million (at cost to Premier) of inventory that had been supplied in the post-acquisition period by Sanford as at 30 September 20X0.

(iii)    Premier had a trade payable balance owing to Sanford of $350,000 as at 30 September 20X0. This did not agree with the corresponding receivable in Sanford's books due to a $130,000 payment made to Sanford, which Sanford has not yet recorded.

(iv)    Premier's investments include investments in shares which at the date of acquisition were classified as fair value through other comprehensive income (FVTOCI). The investments have increased in value by $300,000 during the year. The other equity reserve relates to these investments and is based on their value as at 30 September 20W9. There were no acquisitions or disposals of any of these investments during the year ended 30 September 20X0.

(v) Premier's policy is to value the non-controlling interest at fair value at the date of acquisition, deemed to be $3.5 million.

(vi) There has been no impairment of consolidated goodwill.

**Required:**

(a) **Prepare the consolidated statement of profit or loss and other comprehensive income for Premier for the year ended 30 September 20X0.** ▦ **(6 marks)**

(b) **Prepare the consolidated statement of financial position for Premier as at 30 September 20X0.** ▦ **(14 marks)**

**(Total: 20 marks)**

## 370 PATRONIC  *Walk in the footsteps of a top tutor*

On 1 August 20X7 Patronic purchased 18 million of a total of 24 million equity shares in Sardonic. The acquisition was through a share exchange of two shares in Patronic for every three shares in Sardonic. Both entities have shares with a par value of $1 each.

The market price of Patronic's shares at 1 August 20X7 was $5.75 per share.

Patronic will also pay in cash on 31 July 20X9 (two years after acquisition) $2.42 per acquired share of Sardonic. Patronic's cost of capital is 10% per annum.

The reserves of Sardonic on 1 April 20X7 were $69 million.

Patronic has held an investment of 30% of the equity shares in Acerbic for many years. Acerbic made a profit of $6 million in the year.

The summarised statement of profit or loss for the two entities for the year ended 31 March 20X8 are:

|  | Patronic | Sardonic |
|---|---|---|
|  | $000 | $000 |
| Revenue | 150,000 | 78,000 |
| Cost of sales | (94,000) | (51,000) |
| Gross profit | 56,000 | 27,000 |
| Distribution costs | (7,400) | (3,000) |
| Administrative expenses | (12,500) | (6,000) |
| Finance costs (note (ii)) | (2,000) | (900) |
| Profit before tax | 34,100 | 17,100 |
| Income tax expense | (10,400) | (3,600) |
| Profit for the period | 23,700 | 13,500 |

The following information is relevant:

(i) The fair values of the net assets of Sardonic at the date of acquisition were equal to their carrying amounts with the exception of property and plant. Property and plant had fair values of $4.1 million and $2.4 million respectively in excess of their carrying amounts. The increase in the fair value of the property would create additional depreciation of $200,000 in the consolidated financial statements in the post-acquisition period to 31 March 20X8 and the plant had a remaining life of four years (straight-line depreciation) at the date of acquisition of Sardonic. All depreciation is treated as part of cost of sales.

The fair values have not been reflected in Sardonic's financial statements.

No fair value adjustments were required on the acquisition of Acerbic.

(ii) The finance costs of Patronic do not include the finance cost on the deferred consideration.

(iii) Prior to its acquisition, Sardonic had been a good customer of Patronic. In the year to 31 March 20X8, Patronic sold goods at a selling price of $1.25 million per month to Sardonic both before and after its acquisition. Patronic made a profit of 20% on the cost of these sales. At 31 March 20X8 Sardonic still held inventory of $3 million (at cost to Sardonic) of goods purchased in the post-acquisition period from Patronic.

(iv) Patronic has a policy of valuing non-controlling interests using fair value. An impairment test on the goodwill of Sardonic conducted on 31 March 20X8 concluded that it should be written down by $2 million. The value of the investment in Acerbic was not impaired.

(v) All items are deemed to accrue evenly over the year.

**Required:**

(a) **Calculate the consideration paid on the acquisition of Sardonic at 1 August 20X7.** ▦

(3 marks)

(b) **Prepare the consolidated statement of profit or loss for the Patronic Group for the year ended 31 March 20X8.** ▦                                                                 **(17 marks)**

**(Total: 20 marks)**

## 371 PEDANTIC

On 1 April 20X8, Pedantic acquired 60% of the equity share capital of Sophistic in a share exchange of two shares in Pedantic for three shares in Sophistic. The issue of shares has not yet been recorded by Pedantic. At the date of acquisition shares in Pedantic had a market value of $6 each. Below are the summarised draft financial statements of both entities.

**Statement of profit or loss for the year ended 30 September 20X8**

|  | Pedantic | Sophistic |
|---|---|---|
|  | $000 | $000 |
| Revenue | 85,000 | 42,000 |
| Cost of sales | (63,000) | (32,000) |
| Gross profit | 22,000 | 10,000 |
| Operating expenses | (8,300) | (5,600) |
| Profit before tax | 13,700 | 4,400 |
| Income tax expense | (4,700) | (1,400) |
| Profit for the year | 9,000 | 3,000 |

**Statements of financial position as at 30 September 20X8**

Assets

Non-current assets

| | | |
|---|---:|---:|
| Property, plant and equipment | 40,600 | 12,600 |
| Current assets | 16,000 | 6,600 |
| Total assets | 56,600 | 19,200 |

Equity and liabilities

| | | |
|---|---:|---:|
| Equity shares of $1 each | 10,000 | 4,000 |
| Retained earnings | 35,400 | 6,500 |
| | 45,400 | 10,500 |
| Non-current liabilities | | |
| 10% loan notes | 3,000 | 4,000 |
| Current liabilities | 8,200 | 4,700 |
| Total equity and liabilities | 56,600 | 19,200 |

The following information is relevant:

(i) At the date of acquisition, the fair values of Sophistic's assets were equal to their carrying amounts with the exception of an item of plant, which had a fair value of $2 million in excess of its carrying amount. It had a remaining life of five years at that date [straight-line depreciation is used]. Sophistic has not adjusted the carrying amount of its plant as a result of the fair value exercise.

(ii) Sales from Sophistic to Pedantic in the post-acquisition period were $8 million. Sophistic made a mark-up on cost of 40% on these sales. Pedantic had sold $5.2 million (at cost to Pedantic) of these goods by 30 September 20X8.

(iii) Other than where indicated, statement of profit or loss items are deemed to accrue evenly on a time basis.

(iv) Sophistic's trade receivables at 30 September 20X8 include $600,000 due from Pedantic which did not agree with Pedantic's corresponding trade payable. This was due to cash in transit of $200,000 from Pedantic to Sophistic. Both entities have positive bank balances.

(v) Pedantic has a policy of accounting for any non-controlling interest at fair value. The fair value of the non-controlling interest at the acquisition date was $5.9 million. Consolidated goodwill was impaired by $1 million at 30 September 20X8.

**Required:**

(a) **Prepare the consolidated statement of profit or loss for Pedantic for the year ended 30 September 20X8.** ▦ **(7 marks)**

(b) **Prepare the consolidated statement of financial position for Pedantic as at 30 September 20X8.** ▦ **(13 marks)**

**(Total: 20 marks)**

**372 PANDAR**  *Walk in the footsteps of a top tutor*

On 1 April 20X9 Pandar purchased 80% of the equity shares in Salva. On the same date Pandar acquired 40% of the 40 million equity shares in Ambra paying $2 per share.

The statement of profit or loss for the year ended 30 September 20X9 are:

|  | Pandar | Salva | Ambra |
|---|---|---|---|
|  | $000 | $000 | $000 |
| Revenue | 210,000 | 150,000 | 50,000 |
| Cost of sales | (126,000) | (100,000) | (40,000) |
| Gross profit | 84,000 | 50,000 | 10,000 |
| Distribution costs | (11,200) | (7,000) | (5,000) |
| Administrative expenses | (18,300) | (9,000) | (11,000) |
| Investment income (interest and dividends) | 9,500 |  |  |
| Finance costs | (1,800) | (3,000) | Nil |
| Profit (loss) before tax | 62,200 | 31,000 | (6,000) |
| Income tax (expense) relief | (15,000) | (10,000) | 1,000 |
| Profit (loss) for the year | 47,200 | 21,000 | (5,000) |

The following information is relevant:

(i)　The fair values of the net assets of Salva at the date of acquisition were equal to their carrying amounts with the exception of an item of plant which had a carrying amount of $12 million and a fair value of $17 million. This plant had a remaining life of five years (straight-line depreciation) at the date of acquisition of Salva. All depreciation is charged to cost of sales.

　　The fair value of the plant has not been reflected in Salva's financial statements.

　　No fair value adjustments were required on the acquisition of the investment in Ambra.

(ii)　Immediately after its acquisition of Salva, Pandar invested $50 million in an 8% loan note from Salva. All interest accruing to 30 September 20X9 has been accounted for by both entities. Salva also has other loans in issue at 30 September 20X9.

(iii)　Salva paid a dividend of $8 million during the year.

(iv)　After the acquisition, Pandar sold goods to Salva for $15 million on which Pandar made a gross profit of 20%. Salva had one third of these goods still in its inventory at 30 September 20X9. Pandar also sold goods to Ambra for $6 million, making the same margin. Ambra had half of these goods still in inventory at 30 September 20X9.

(v)　The non-controlling interest in Salva is to be valued at its (full) fair value at the date of acquisition.

(vi)  The goodwill of Salva has been impaired by $2 million at 30 September 20X9. Due to its losses, the value of Pandar's investment in Ambra has been impaired by $3 million at 30 September 20X9.

(vii)  All items in the above statement of profit or loss are deemed to accrue evenly over the year unless otherwise indicated.

**Required:**

(a)  **Calculate the carrying amount of the investment in Ambra to be included within the consolidated statement of financial position as at 30 September 20X9.** ▦

**(4 marks)**

(b)  **Prepare the consolidated statement of profit or loss for the Pandar Group for the year ended 30 September 20X9.** ▦  **(16 marks)**

**(Total: 20 marks)**

## 373  PICANT

On 1 April 20X3 Picant acquired 75% of Sander's equity shares in a share exchange of three shares in Picant for every two shares in Sander. The market prices of Picant's and Sander's shares at the date of acquisition were $3.20 and $4.50 respectively.

In addition to this Picant agreed to pay a further amount on 1 April 20X4 that was contingent upon the post-acquisition performance of Sander. At the date of acquisition Picant assessed the fair value of this contingent consideration at $4.2 million, but by 31 March 20X4 it was clear that the actual amount to be paid would be only $2.7 million (ignore discounting). Picant has recorded the share exchange and provided for the initial estimate of $4.2 million for the contingent consideration.

On 1 October 20X3 Picant also acquired 40% of the equity shares of Adler paying $4 in cash per acquired share and issuing at par one $100 7% loan note for every 50 shares acquired in Adler. This consideration has also been recorded by Picant.

Picant has no other investments.

The summarised statements of financial position of the three entities at 31 March 20X4 are:

|  | Picant | Sander | Adler |
|---|---|---|---|
| Assets | $000 | $000 | $000 |
| Non-current assets |  |  |  |
| Property, plant and equipment | 37,500 | 24,500 | 21,000 |
| Investments | 45,000 | nil | nil |
|  | 82,500 | 24,500 | 21,000 |
| Current assets |  |  |  |
| Inventory | 10,000 | 9,000 | 5,000 |
| Trade receivables | 6,500 | 1,500 | 3,000 |
| Total assets | 99,000 | 35,000 | 29,000 |

| | Picant $000 | Sander $000 | Adler $000 |
|---|---|---|---|
| **Equity** | | | |
| Equity shares of $1 each | 25,000 | 8,000 | 5,000 |
| Share premium | 19,800 | nil | nil |
| Retained earnings  – at 1 April 20X3 | 16,200 | 16,500 | 15,000 |
| – for the year ended 31 March 20X4 | 11,000 | 1,000 | 6,000 |
| | 72,000 | 25,500 | 26,000 |
| **Non-current liabilities** | | | |
| 7% loan notes | 14,500 | 2,000 | nil |
| **Current liabilities** | | | |
| Contingent consideration | 4,200 | nil | nil |
| Other current liabilities | 8,300 | 7,500 | 3,000 |
| Total equity and liabilities | 99,000 | 35,000 | 29,000 |

The following information is relevant:

(i) At the date of acquisition the fair values of Sander's property, plant and equipment was equal to its carrying amount with the exception of Sander's factory which had a fair value of $2 million above its carrying amount. Sander has not adjusted the carrying amount of the factory as a result of the fair value exercise. This requires additional annual depreciation of $100,000 in the consolidated financial statements in the post-acquisition period.

Also at the date of acquisition, Sander had an intangible asset of $500,000 for software in its statement of financial position. Picant's directors believed the software to have no recoverable value at the date of acquisition and Sander wrote it off shortly after its acquisition.

(ii) At 31 March 20X4 Picant's current account with Sander was $3.4 million (debit). This did not agree with the equivalent balance in Sander's books due to some goods-in-transit invoiced at $1.8 million that were sent by Picant on 28 March 20X4, but had not been received by Sander until after the year end. Picant sold all these goods at cost plus 50%.

(iii) Picant's policy is to value the non-controlling interest at fair value at the date of acquisition. For this purpose Sander's share price at that date can be deemed to be representative of the fair value of the shares held by the non-controlling interest.

(iv) Impairment tests were carried out on 31 March 20X4 which concluded that the value of the investment in Adler was not impaired but, due to poor trading performance, consolidated goodwill was impaired by $3.8 million.

(v) Assume all profits accrue evenly through the year.

**Required:**

(a)  **Prepare the consolidated statement of financial position for Picant as at 31 March 20X4.** ⊞                                                              **(15 marks)**

(b)  At 31 March 20X4 the other equity shares (60%) in Adler were owned by many separate investors. Shortly after this date Spekulate (an entity unrelated to Picant) accumulated a 60% interest in Adler by buying shares from the other shareholders. In May 20X4 a meeting of the board of directors of Adler was held at which Picant lost its seat on Adler's board.

**Required:**

**Explain, with reasons, the accounting treatment Picant should adopt for its investment in Adler when it prepares its financial statements for the year ending 31 March 20X5.** 🖥                                                              **(5 marks)**

**(Total: 20 marks)**

**374  PRODIGAL**

On 1 October 20X0 Prodigal purchased 75% of the equity shares in Sentinel. The summarised statements of profit or loss and other comprehensive income for the two entities for the year ended 31 March 20X1 are:

|  | Prodigal $000 | Sentinel $000 |
|---|---|---|
| Revenue | 450,000 | 240,000 |
| Cost of sales | (260,000) | (110,000) |
| Gross profit | 190,000 | 130,000 |
| Distribution costs | (23,600) | (12,000) |
| Administrative expenses | (27,000) | (23,000) |
| Finance costs | (1,500) | (1,200) |
| Profit before tax | 137,900 | 93,800 |
| Income tax expense | (48,000) | (27,800) |
| Profit for the year | 89,900 | 66,000 |
| Other comprehensive income | | |
| Gain on revaluation of land (note (i)) | 2,500 | 1,000 |
| Total comprehensive income | 92,400 | 67,000 |

The following extracts for the equity of the entities at 1 April 20X0 (before acquisition) is available:

|  | $000 | $000 |
|---|---|---|
| Revaluation surplus (land) | 8,400 | nil |
| Retained earnings | 90,000 | 125,000 |

The following information is relevant:

(i)    Prodigal's policy is to revalue the group's land to market value at the end of each accounting period. Prior to its acquisition by Prodigal, Sentinel's land had been valued at historical cost. During the post-acquisition period Sentinel's land had increased in value over its value at the date of acquisition by $1 million. Sentinel has recognised the revaluation within its own financial statements.

(ii)   Immediately after the acquisition of Sentinel on 1 October 20X0, Prodigal transferred an item of plant with a carrying amount of $4 million to Sentinel at an agreed value of $5 million. At this date the plant had a remaining life of two and half years. Prodigal had included the profit on this transfer as a reduction in its depreciation costs. All depreciation is charged to cost of sales.

(iii)  After the acquisition Sentinel sold goods to Prodigal for $40 million. These goods had cost Sentinel $30 million. $12 million of the goods sold remained in Prodigal's closing inventory.

(iv)   Prodigal's policy is to value the non-controlling interest of Sentinel at the date of acquisition at its fair value which the directors determined to be $100 million.

(v)    The goodwill of Sentinel has not suffered any impairment.

(vi)   All items in the above statements of comprehensive income are deemed to accrue evenly over the year unless otherwise indicated.

**Required:**

(a)   **Prepare the consolidated statement of profit or loss and other comprehensive income of Prodigal for the year ended 31 March 20X1.** ▦                    **(15 marks)**

(b)   **Prepare extracts of the equity section (including the non-controlling interest) of the consolidated statement of financial position of Prodigal as at 31 March 20X1.** ▦
                                                                            **(5 marks)**

**Note: you are NOT required to calculate consolidated goodwill or produce the statement of changes in equity.**

**(Total: 20 marks)**

## 375 PALADIN

On 1 October 20X0, Paladin secured a majority equity shareholding in Saracen on the following terms:

– an immediate payment of $4 per share on 1 October 20X0.

– and a further amount deferred until 1 October 20X1 of $5.4 million.

The immediate payment has been recorded in Paladin's financial statements, but the deferred payment has not been recorded. Paladin's cost of capital is 8% per annum.

On 1 February 20X1, Paladin also acquired 25% of the equity shares of Augusta paying $10 million in cash. Augusta made a profit of $1.2 million for the year ended 30 September 20X1.

The summarised statements of financial position of the three entities at 30 September 20X1 are:

|  | Paladin | Saracen |
|---|---|---|
| Assets | $000 | $000 |
| Non-current assets | | |
| Property, plant and equipment | 40,000 | 31,000 |
| Intangible assets | 7,500 | |
| Investments  – Saracen (8 million shares at $4 each) | 32,000 | |
|               – Augusta | 10,000 | nil |
|  | ——— | ——— |
|  | 89,500 | 31,000 |
|  | | |
| Current assets | 22,000 | 13,700 |
|  | ——— | ——— |
| Total assets | 111,500 | 44,700 |
|  | ——— | ——— |
| Equity and liabilities | | |
| Equity | | |
| Equity shares of $1 each | 50,000 | 10,000 |
| Retained earnings – at 1 October 20X0 | 25,700 | 12,000 |
|                       – for year ended 30 September 20X1 | 9,200 | 6,000 |
|  | ——— | ——— |
|  | 84,900 | 28,000 |
| Non-current liabilities | | |
| Deferred tax | 15,000 | 8,000 |
|  | | |
| Current liabilities | 11,600 | 8,700 |
|  | ——— | ——— |
| Total equity and liabilities | 111,500 | 44,700 |
|  | ——— | ——— |

The following information is relevant:

(i)     Paladin's policy is to value the non-controlling interest at fair value at the date of acquisition. For this purpose the directors of Paladin considered a share price for Saracen of $3.50 per share to be appropriate.

(ii)    At the date of acquisition, the fair values of Saracen's property, plant and equipment was equal to its carrying amount with the exception of Saracen's plant which had a fair value of $4 million above its carrying amount. At that date the plant had a remaining life of four years. Saracen uses straight-line depreciation for plant assuming a nil residual value.

Also at the date of acquisition, Paladin valued Saracen's customer relationships as an intangible asset at fair value of $3 million. Saracen has not accounted for this asset. Trading relationships with Saracen's customers last on average for six years.

(iii)   At 30 September 20X1, Saracen's inventory included goods bought from Paladin (at cost to Saracen) of $2.6 million. Paladin had marked up these goods by 30% on cost.

(iv)    Impairment tests were carried out on 30 September 20X1 which concluded that consolidated goodwill was not impaired, but, due to disappointing earnings, the value of the investment in Augusta was impaired by $2.5 million.

(v)     Assume all profits accrue evenly through the year.

**Required:**

**Prepare the consolidated statement of financial position for Paladin as at 30 September 20X1.** ⊞

(Total: 20 marks)

## 376  PYRAMID

On 1 April 20X1, Pyramid acquired 80% of Square's equity shares by means of an immediate share exchange and a cash payment of 88 cents per acquired share, deferred until 1 April 20X2. Pyramid has recorded the share exchange, but not the cash consideration. Pyramid's cost of capital is 10% per annum.

The summarised statements of financial position of the two entities as at 31 March 20X2 are:

|  | Pyramid | Square |
|---|---|---|
| Assets | $000 | $000 |
| Non-current assets |  |  |
| Property, plant and equipment | 38,100 | 28,500 |
| Investments  – Square | 24,000 |  |
|              – Other equity (note (iii)) | 2,000 | nil |
|  | ——— | ——— |
|  | 64,100 | 28,500 |
| Current assets |  |  |
| Inventory (note (ii)) | 13,900 | 10,400 |
| Trade receivables (note (ii)) | 11,400 | 5,500 |
| Bank (note (ii)) | 9,400 | 600 |
|  | ——— | ——— |
| Total assets | 98,800 | 45,000 |
|  | ——— | ——— |

| | | |
|---|---|---|
| Equity shares of $1 each | 25,000 | 10,000 |
| Share premium | 17,600 | nil |
| Retained earnings – at 1 April 20X1 | 16,200 | 18,000 |
| – for year ended 31 March 20X2 | 14,000 | 8,000 |
| | | |
| | 72,800 | 36,000 |
| Non-current liabilities (note (i)) | 16,500 | 4,000 |
| Current liabilities (note (ii)) | 9,500 | 5,000 |
| | | |
| Total equity and liabilities | 98,800 | 45,000 |

The following information is relevant:

(i)    At the date of acquisition, Pyramid conducted a fair value exercise on Square's net assets which were equal to their carrying amounts with the following exceptions:

- An item of plant had a fair value of $3 million above its carrying amount. At the date of acquisition it had a remaining life of five years. Ignore deferred tax relating to this fair value.

- Square had an unrecorded deferred tax liability of $1 million, which was unchanged as at 31 March 20X2.

Pyramid's policy is to value the non-controlling interest at fair value at the date of acquisition. For this purpose a share price for Square of $3.50 each is representative of the fair value of the shares held by the non-controlling interest.

(ii)   Pyramid sells goods to Square at cost plus 50%. Below is a summary of the recorded activities for the year ended 31 March 20X2 and balances as at 31 March 20X2:

| | Pyramid | Square |
|---|---|---|
| | $000 | $000 |
| Sales to Square | 16,000 | |
| Purchases from Pyramid | | 14,500 |
| Included in Pyramid's receivables | 4,400 | |
| Included in Square's payables | | 1,700 |

On 26 March 20X2, Pyramid sold and despatched goods to Square, which Square did not record until they were received on 2 April 20X2. Square's inventory was counted on 31 March 20X2 and does not include any goods purchased from Pyramid.

On 27 March 20X2, Square remitted to Pyramid a cash payment which was not received by Pyramid until 4 April 20X2. This payment accounted for the remaining difference on the current accounts.

(iii)  The other equity investments of Pyramid are carried at their fair values on 1 April 20X1. At 31 March 20X2, these had increased to $2.8 million.

**Required:**

**Prepare the consolidated statement of financial position for Pyramid as at 31 March 20X2.** ▦

(Total: 20 marks)

## 377 VIAGEM

 **Question debrief**

On 1 January 20X2, Viagem acquired 90% of the equity share capital of Greca in a share exchange in which Viagem issued two new shares for every three shares it acquired in Greca. Additionally, on 31 December 20X2, Viagem will pay the shareholders of Greca $1.76 per share acquired. Viagem's cost of capital is 10% per annum. The deferred consideration has not yet been recorded by Viagem.

At the date of acquisition, shares in Viagem and Greca had a stock market value of $6.50 and $2.50 each, respectively.

**Statements of profit or loss for the year ended 30 September 20X2**

|  | Viagem | Greca |
|---|---|---|
|  | $000 | $000 |
| Revenue | 64,600 | 38,000 |
| Cost of sales | (51,200) | (26,000) |
| Gross profit | 13,400 | 12,000 |
| Distribution costs | (1,600) | (1,800) |
| Administrative expenses | (3,800) | (2,400) |
| Investment income | 500 | nil |
| Finance costs | (420) | nil |
| Profit before tax | 8,080 | 7,800 |
| Income tax expense | (2,800) | (1,600) |
| Profit for the year | 5,280 | 6,200 |
| Equity as at 1 October 20X1 |  |  |
| Equity shares of $1 each | 30,000 | 10,000 |
| Retained earnings | 54,000 | 35,000 |

The following information is relevant:

(i)    At the date of acquisition, the fair values of Greca's assets were equal to their carrying amounts with the exception of two items:

• An item of plant had a fair value of $1.8 million above its carrying amount. The remaining life of the plant at the date of acquisition was three years. Depreciation is charged to cost of sales.

• Greca had a contingent liability which Viagem estimated to have a fair value of $450,000. This has not changed as at 30 September 20X2.

Greca has not incorporated these fair value changes into its financial statements.

(ii)   Viagem's policy is to value the non-controlling interest at fair value at the date of acquisition. For this purpose, Greca's share price at that date can be deemed to be representative of the fair value of the shares held by the non-controlling interest.

(iii) Sales from Viagem to Greca throughout the year ended 30 September 20X2 had consistently been $800,000 per month. Viagem made a mark-up on cost of 25% on these sales. Greca had $1.5 million of these goods in inventory as at 30 September 20X2.

(iv) Viagem's investment income is a dividend received from its investment in a 40% owned associate which it has held for several years. The underlying earnings for the associate for the year ended 30 September 20X2 were $2 million.

(v) Although Greca has been profitable since its acquisition by Viagem, the market for Greca's products has been badly hit in recent months and Viagem has calculated that the goodwill has been impaired by $2 million as at 30 September 20X2.

**Required:**

(a) Calculate the consolidated goodwill at the date of acquisition of Greca. ▦

(7 marks)

(b) Prepare the consolidated statement of profit or loss for Viagem for the year ended 30 September 20X2. ▦ (13 marks)

(Total: 20 marks)

---

 **Calculate your allowed time, allocate the time to the separate parts**

---

## 378 PARADIGM

On 1 October 20X2, Paradigm acquired 75% of Strata's equity shares by means of a share exchange of two new shares in Paradigm for every five acquired shares in Strata. In addition, Paradigm issued to the shareholders of Strata a $100 10% loan note for every 1,000 shares it acquired in Strata. Paradigm has not recorded any of the purchase consideration, although it does have other 10% loan notes already in issue.

The market value of Paradigm's shares at 1 October 20X2 was $2 each.

The summarised statements of financial position of the two entities as at 31 March 20X3 are:

|  | Paradigm | Strata |
|---|---|---|
| **Assets** | $000 | $000 |
| Non-current assets |  |  |
| Property, plant and equipment | 47,400 | 25,500 |
| Financial asset: equity investments (notes (i) and (iii)) | 7,500 | 3,200 |
|  | 54,900 | 28,700 |
| Current assets |  |  |
| Inventory (note (ii)) | 20,400 | 8,400 |
| Trade receivables | 14,800 | 9,000 |
| Bank | 2,100 | nil |
| Total assets | 92,200 | 46,100 |

---

**Equity and liabilities**

Equity

| | | |
|---|---:|---:|
| Equity shares of $1 each | 40,000 | 20,000 |
| Retained earnings/(losses) – at 1 April 20X2 | 19,200 | (4,000) |
| – for year ended 31 March 20X3 | 7,400 | 8,000 |
| | 66,600 | 24,000 |
| Non-current liabilities | | |
| 10% loan notes | 8,000 | nil |
| Current liabilities | | |
| Trade payables | 17,600 | 13,000 |
| Bank overdraft | nil | 9,100 |
| Total equity and liabilities | 92,200 | 46,100 |

The following information is relevant:

(i)   At the date of acquisition, Strata produced a draft statement of profit or loss which showed it had made a net loss after tax of $2 million at that date. Paradigm accepted this figure as the basis for calculating the pre- and post-acquisition split of Strata's profit for the year ended 31 March 20X3.

Also at the date of acquisition, Paradigm conducted a fair value exercise on Strata's net assets which were equal to their carrying amounts (including Strata's financial asset equity investments) with the exception of an item of plant which had a fair value of $3 million **below** its carrying amount. The plant had a remaining useful life of three years at 1 October 20X2.

Paradigm's policy is to value the non-controlling interest at fair value at the date of acquisition. For this purpose, a share price for Strata of $1.20 each is representative of the fair value of the shares held by the non-controlling interest.

(ii)   Each month since acquisition, Paradigm's sales to Strata were consistently $4.6 million. Paradigm had marked these up by 15% on cost. Strata had one month's supply ($4.6 million) of these goods in inventory at 31 March 20X3. Paradigm's normal mark-up (to third party customers) is 40%.

(iii)   The financial asset equity investments of Paradigm and Strata are carried at their fair values as at 1 April 20X2. As at 31 March 20X3, these had fair values of $7.1 million and $3.9 million respectively.

(iv)   There were no impairment losses within the group during the year ended 31 March 20X3.

**Required:**

(a)    Prepare the consolidated statement of financial position for Paradigm as at 31 March 20X3. ▦                                                          **(15 marks)**

(b)    A financial assistant has observed that the fair value exercise means that a subsidiary's net assets are included at acquisition at their fair (current) values in the consolidated statement of financial position. The assistant believes that it is inconsistent to aggregate the subsidiary's net assets with those of the parent because most of the parent's assets are carried at historical cost.

**Required:**

**Comment on the assistant's observation and explain why the net assets of acquired subsidiaries are consolidated at acquisition at their fair values.** ▭          **(5 marks)**

**(Total: 20 marks)**

## 379   POLESTAR

On 1 April 20X3, Polestar acquired 75% of Southstar. Southstar had been experiencing difficult trading conditions and making significant losses. In allowing for Southstar's difficulties, Polestar made an immediate cash payment of only $1.50 per share. In addition, Polestar will pay a further amount in cash on 30 September 20X4 if Southstar returns to profitability by that date. The fair value of this contingent consideration at the date of acquisition was estimated to be $1.8 million, but at 30 September 20X3 in the light of continuing losses, its value was estimated at only $1.5 million. The contingent consideration has not been recorded by Polestar. Overall, the directors of Polestar expect the acquisition to be a bargain purchase leading to negative goodwill.

Below are the summarised draft financial statements of both entities.

**Statements of profit or loss for the year ended 30 September 20X3**

|  | Polestar | Southstar |
|---|---|---|
|  | $000 | $000 |
| Revenue | 110,000 | 66,000 |
| Cost of sales | (88,000) | (67,200) |
| Gross profit (loss) | 22,000 | (1,200) |
| Operating expenses | (8,500) | (4,400) |
| Profit (loss) before tax | 13,500 | (5,600) |
| Income tax (expense)/relief | (3,500) | 1,000 |
| Profit (loss) for the year | 10,000 | (4,600) |

**Statements of financial position as at 30 September 20X3**

| | Polestar | Southstar |
|---|---|---|
| **Assets** | $000 | $000 |
| Non-current assets | | |
| Property, plant and equipment | 41,000 | 21,000 |
| Investments | 13,500 | |
| | | |
| Current assets | 19,000 | 4,800 |
| | | |
| Total assets | 73,500 | 25,800 |
| | | |
| **Equity and liabilities** | | |
| Equity shares of 50 cents each | 30,000 | 6,000 |
| Retained earnings | 28,500 | 12,000 |
| | | |
| | 58,500 | 18,000 |
| Current liabilities | 15,000 | 7,800 |
| | | |
| Total equity and liabilities | 73,500 | 25,800 |

The following information is relevant:

(i)   At the date of acquisition, the fair values of Southstar's assets were equal to their carrying amounts with the exception of a property. This had a fair value of $2 million above its carrying amount and a remaining useful life of 10 years at that date. All depreciation is included in cost of sales.

(ii)  Polestar transferred raw materials at their cost of $4 million to Southstar in June 20X3. Southstar processed all of these materials incurring additional direct costs of $1.4 million and sold them back to Polestar in August 20X3 for $9 million. At 30 September 20X3 Polestar had $1.5 million of these goods still in inventory. There were no other intra-group sales.

(iii) Polestar's policy is to value the non-controlling interest at fair value at the date of acquisition. This was deemed to be $3.6 million.

(iv)  All items in the above statements of profit or loss are deemed to accrue evenly over the year unless otherwise indicated.

**Required:**

(a)   **Prepare the consolidated statement of profit or loss for Polestar for the year ended 30 September 20X3.** ▦                                           **(11 marks)**

(b)   **Prepare the consolidated statement of financial position for Polestar as at 30 September 20X3.** ▦                                           **(9 marks)**

**(Total: 20 marks)**

## 380 PENKETH

On 1 October 20X3, Penketh acquired 90 million of Sphere's 150 million $0.50 equity shares. Penketh will pay $1.54 cash on 30 September 20X4 for each share acquired. Penketh's finance cost is 10% per annum. Sphere's share price as at 1 October 20X3 was $1.25. The statements of profit or loss and other comprehensive income for the year ended 31 March 20X4 are:

|  | Penketh | Sphere |
|  | $000 | $000 |
|---|---|---|
| Revenue | 620,000 | 310,000 |
| Cost of sales | (400,000) | (150,000) |
| Gross profit | 220,000 | 160,000 |
| Distribution costs | (40,000) | (20,000) |
| Administrative expenses | (36,000) | (25,000) |
| Investment income | 5,000 | 1,600 |
| Finance costs | (2,000) | (5,600) |
| Profit before tax | 147,000 | 111,000 |
| Income tax expense | (45,000) | (31,000) |
| Profit for the year | 102,000 | 80,000 |
| Other comprehensive income |  |  |
| Gain/(loss) on revaluation of land (note (ii)) | (2,200) | 1,000 |
| Total comprehensive income for the year | 99,800 | 81,000 |

The following information is relevant:

(i) A fair value exercise on 1 October 20X3 concluded that the carrying amounts of Sphere's net assets were equal to their fair values with the following exceptions:

- Plant with a remaining life of two years had a fair value of $6 million in excess of its carrying amount. Plant depreciation is charged to cost of sales.

- Penketh placed a value of $5 million on Sphere's good relationships with its customers. Penketh expected, on average, a customer relationship to last for a further five years. Amortisation is charged to administrative expenses.

(ii) Sphere's land, valued using the revaluation model, increased by $1 million since the acquisition.

(iii) After the acquisition Penketh sold goods to Sphere for $20 million at a 25% mark-up. Sphere had one fifth of these goods still in inventory at 31 March 20X4.

(iv)  All items accrue evenly over the year unless otherwise indicated. Sphere had retained earnings of $70 million at 1 April 20X3. There were no other components of equity at this date.

(v)  Penketh measures the non-controlling interest at fair value at the date of acquisition. To calculate fair value, the share price of Sphere should be used.

**Required:**

(a)  Calculate goodwill arising on the acquisition of Sphere as at 1 October 20X3. ▦

(5 marks)

(b)  Prepare the consolidated statement of profit or loss and other comprehensive income of Penketh for the year ended 31 March 20X4. ▦ (15 marks)

(Total: 20 marks)

## 381  PLASTIK

 **Question debrief**

On 1 January 20X4, Plastik acquired 80% of the equity share capital of Subtrak. The consideration was satisfied by a share exchange of two shares in Plastik for every three acquired shares in Subtrak. At the date of acquisition, shares in Plastik and Subtrak had a market value of $3 and $2.50 each respectively. Plastik will also pay cash consideration of 27.5 cents on 1 January 20X5 for each acquired share in Subtrak. Plastik has a cost of capital of 10% per annum. None of the consideration has been recorded by Plastik.

Below are the extracts from the draft financial statements of both entities.

**Extracts from the statements of profit or loss and other comprehensive income for the year ended 30 September 20X4**

|  | Plastik | Subtrak |
|---|---|---|
|  | $000 | $000 |
| Revenue | 62,600 | 30,000 |
| Cost of sales | (45,800) | (24,000) |
| Finance costs | (200) | (nil) |

**Statements of financial position as at 30 September 20X4**

| Assets | Plastik | Subtrak |
|---|---|---|
| Non-current assets | $000 | $000 |
| Property, plant and equipment | 18,700 | 13,900 |
| Investments: 10% loan note from Subtrak (note (ii)) | 1,000 | nil |
|  | 19,700 | 13,900 |
| Current assets | 9,000 | 4,000 |
| Total assets | 28,700 | 17,900 |

|  | Plastik $000 | Subtrak $000 |
|---|---|---|
| **Equity and liabilities** |  |  |
| Equity |  |  |
| Equity shares of $1 each | 10,000 | 9,000 |
| Revaluation surplus (note (i)) | 2,000 | nil |
| Retained earnings | 6,300 | 3,500 |
|  | 18,300 | 12,500 |
| Non-current liabilities |  |  |
| 10% loan notes (note (ii)) | 2,500 | 1,000 |
| Current liabilities |  |  |
| Trade payables (note (iv)) | 7,900 | 4,400 |
| Total equity and liabilities | 28,700 | 17,900 |

The following information is relevant:

(i)   At the date of acquisition, the fair values of Subtrak's assets and liabilities were equal to their carrying amounts with the exception of Subtrak's property which had a fair value of $4 million above its carrying amount. For consolidation purposes, this led to an increase in depreciation charges (in cost of sales) of $100,000 in the post-acquisition period to 30 September 20X4. Subtrak has not incorporated the fair value property increase into its entity financial statements.

The policy of the Plastik group is to revalue all properties to fair value at each year end. On 30 September 20X4, the increase in Plastik's property has already been recorded, however, a further increase of $600,000 in the value of Subtrak's property since its value at acquisition and 30 September 20X4 has not been recorded.

(ii)   On 30 September 20X4, Plastik accepted a $1 million 10% loan note from Subtrak.

(iii)   Sales from Plastik to Subtrak throughout the year ended 30 September 20X4 had consistently been $300,000 per month. Plastik made a mark-up on cost of 25% on all these sales. $600,000 (at cost to Subtrak) of Subtrak's inventory at 30 September 20X4 had been supplied by Plastik in the post-acquisition period.

(iv)   Plastik had a trade receivable balance owing from Subtrak of $1.2 million as at 30 September 20X4. This differed to the equivalent trade payable of Subtrak due to a payment by Subtrak of $400,000 made in September 20X4 which did not clear Plastik's bank account until 4 October 20X4. Both entities have overdrafts rather than positive cash balances.

(v)   Plastik's policy is to value the non-controlling interest at fair value at the date of acquisition. For this purpose Subtrak's share price at that date can be deemed to be representative of the fair value of the shares held by the non-controlling interest.

(vi)   Assume, except where indicated otherwise, that all items of income and expenditure accrue evenly throughout the year. Subtrak's profit for the year ended 30 September 20X4 was $2 million.

**Required:**

(a) **Prepare extracts from Plastik's consolidated statement of profit or loss for the year ended 30 September 20X4 for:**

    (i)    **revenue** ▦

    (ii)   **cost of sales** ▦

    (iii)  **finance costs.** ▦                         **(5 marks)**

(b) **Prepare the consolidated statement of financial position for Plastik as at 30 September 20X4.** ▦               **(15 marks)**

                                               **(Total: 20 marks)**

---

 Calculate your allowed time, allocate the time to the separate parts

---

## 382 BYCOMB

On 1 July 20X4 Bycomb acquired 80% of Cyclip's equity shares on the following terms:

- a share exchange of two shares in Bycomb for every three shares acquired in Cyclip; and

- a cash payment due on 30 June 20X5 of $1.54 per share acquired (Bycomb's cost of capital is 10% per annum).

At the date of acquisition, shares in Bycomb and Cyclip had a stock market value of $3.00 and $2.50 each respectively.

**Statements of profit or loss for the year ended 31 March 20X5:**

|  | Bycomb | Cyclip |
|---|---|---|
|  | $000 | $000 |
| Revenue | 24,200 | 10,800 |
| Cost of sales | (17,800) | (6,800) |
|  | ———— | ———— |
| Gross profit | 6,400 | 4,000 |
| Distribution costs | (500) | (340) |
| Administrative expenses | (800) | (360) |
| Finance costs | (400) | (300) |
|  | ———— | ———— |
| Profit before tax | 4,700 | 3,000 |
| Income tax expense | (1,700) | (600) |
|  | ———— | ———— |
| Profit for the year | 3,000 | 2,400 |
|  | ———— | ———— |

**Equity in the separate financial statements of Cyclip as at 1 April 20X4:**

|  | $000 |
|---|---|
| **Equity** | |
| Equity shares of $1 each | 12,000 |
| Retained earnings | 13,500 |

The following information is also relevant:

(i) At the date of acquisition, the fair values of Cyclip's assets were equal to their carrying amounts with the exception of an item of plant which had a fair value of $720,000 above its carrying amount. The remaining life of the plant at the date of acquisition was 18 months. Depreciation is charged to cost of sales.

(ii) On 1 April 20X4, Cyclip commenced the construction of a new production facility, financing this by a bank loan. Cyclip has followed the local GAAP in the country where it operates which prohibits the capitalisation of interest. Bycomb has calculated that, in accordance with IAS 23 *Borrowing Costs*, interest of $100,000 (which accrued evenly throughout the year) would have been capitalised at 31 March 20X5. The production facility is still under construction as at 31 March 20X5.

(iii) Sales from Bycomb to Cyclip in the post-acquisition period were $3 million at a mark-up on cost of 20%. Cyclip had $420,000 of these goods in inventory as at 31 March 20X5.

(iv) Bycomb's policy is to value the non-controlling interest at fair value at the date of acquisition. For this purpose Cyclip's share price at that date can be deemed to be representative of the fair value of the shares held by the non-controlling interest.

(v) On 31 March 20X5, Bycomb carried out an impairment review which identified that the goodwill on the acquisition of Cyclip was impaired by $500,000. Impaired goodwill is charged to cost of sales.

**Required:**

(a) Calculate the consolidated goodwill at the date of acquisition of Cyclip. 🔳

(6 marks)

(b) Prepare extracts from Bycomb's consolidated statement of profit or loss for the year ended 31 March 20X5, for:

(i) revenue 🔳 (1 mark)

(ii) cost of sales 🔳 (3 marks)

(iii) finance costs 🔳 (2½ marks)

(iv) profit or loss attributable to the non-controlling interest 🔳 (2½ marks)

(Total for (b) 9 marks)

(c) IFRS 3 *Business combinations* permits a non-controlling interest at the date of acquisition to be valued by one of two methods:

(i) at its proportionate share of the subsidiary's identifiable net assets; or

(ii) at its fair value (usually determined by the directors of the parent).

**Required: Explain the difference that the accounting treatment of these alternative methods could have on the consolidated financial statements, including where consolidated goodwill may be impaired.** 💻 (5 marks)

(Total: 20 marks)

### 383   PALISTAR

On 1 January 20X5, Palistar acquired 75% of Stretcher's equity shares by means of an immediate share exchange of two shares in Palistar for five shares in Stretcher. The fair value of Palistar and Stretcher's shares on 1 January 20X5 were $4 and $3 respectively. In addition to the share exchange, Palistar will make a cash payment of $1.32 per acquired share, deferred until 1 January 20X6. Palistar has not recorded any of the consideration for Stretcher in its financial statements. Palistar's cost of capital is 10% per annum.

The summarised statements of financial position of the two entities as at 30 June 20X5 are:

|  | Palistar $000 | Stretcher $000 |
|---|---|---|
| **Assets** | | |
| **Non-current assets (note (ii))** | | |
| Property, plant and equipment | 55,000 | 28,600 |
| Financial asset equity investments (note (v)) | 11,500 | 6,000 |
| | 66,500 | 34,600 |
| **Current assets** | | |
| Inventory (note (iv)) | 17,000 | 15,400 |
| Trade receivables (note (iv)) | 14,300 | 10,500 |
| Bank | 2,200 | 1,600 |
| | 33,500 | 27,500 |
| **Total assets** | 100,000 | 62,100 |
| **Equity and liabilities** | | |
| **Equity** | | |
| Equity shares of $1 each | 20,000 | 20,000 |
| Other component of equity | 4,000 | nil |
| Retained earnings – at 1 July 20X4 | 26,200 | 14,000 |
| – for year ended 30 June 20X5 | 24,000 | 10,000 |
| | 74,200 | 44,000 |
| Current liabilities (note (iv)) | 25,800 | 18,100 |
| **Total equity and liabilities** | 100,000 | 62,100 |

The following information is relevant:

(i)     Stretcher's business is seasonal and 60% of its annual profit is made in the period 1 January to 30 June each year.

(ii)    At the date of acquisition, the fair value of Stretcher's net assets was equal to their carrying amounts with the following exceptions:

The fair value of Stretcher's financial asset equity investments, carried at a value of $6 million, was $7 million (see also note (v)).

Stretcher owned the rights to a popular mobile (cell) phone game. At the date of acquisition, a specialist valuer estimated that the rights were worth $12 million and had an estimated remaining life of five years.

(iii)   Following an impairment review, consolidated goodwill is to be written down by $3 million as at 30 June 20X5.

(iv)    Palistar sells goods to Stretcher at cost plus 30%. Stretcher had $1.8 million of goods in its inventory at 30 June 20X5 which had been supplied by Palistar. In addition, on 28 June 20X5, Palistar processed the sale of $800,000 of goods to Stretcher, which Stretcher did not account for until their receipt on 2 July 20X5. The in-transit reconciliation should be achieved by assuming the transaction had been recorded in the books of Stretcher before the year end. At 30 June 20X5, Palistar had a trade receivable balance of $2.4 million due from Stretcher which differed to the equivalent balance in Stretcher's books due to the sale made on 28 June 20X5.

(v)     At 30 June 20X5, the fair values of the financial asset equity investments of Palistar and Stretcher were $13.2 million and $7.9 million respectively.

(vi)    Palistar's policy is to value the non-controlling interest at fair value at the date of acquisition. At 1 January 20X5, this was valued at $15 million.

**Required:**

**Prepare the consolidated statement of financial position for Palistar as at 30 June 20X5.** ⊞

**(Total: 20 marks)**

## 384 LAUREL

On 1 January 20X6, Laurel acquired 60% of the equity share capital of Rakewood in a share exchange in which Laurel issued three new shares for every five shares it acquired in Rakewood. The share issue has not yet been recorded by Laurel. Additionally, on 31 December 20X6, Laurel will pay to the shareholders of Rakewood $1.62 per share acquired. Laurel's cost of capital is 8% per annum.

At the date of acquisition, shares in Laurel and Rakewood had a market value of $7 and $2 each respectively.

### Statements of profit or loss for the year ended 30 September 20X6

|                                | Laurel | Rakewood |
|--------------------------------|--------|----------|
|                                | $000   | $000     |
| Revenue                        | 84,500 | 52,000   |
| Cost of sales                  | (58,200) | (34,000) |
|                                |        |          |
| Gross profit                   | 26,300 | 18,000   |
| Distribution costs             | (2,000) | (1,600) |
| Administrative expenses        | (4,100) | (2,800) |
| Investment income (note (iv))  | 500    | 400      |
| Finance costs                  | (300)  | nil      |
|                                |        |          |
| Profit before tax              | 20,400 | 14,000   |
| Income tax expense             | (4,800) | (3,600) |
|                                |        |          |
| Profit for the year            | 15,600 | 10,400   |

### Equity as at 1 October 20X5

|                          | $000   | $000   |
|--------------------------|--------|--------|
| Equity shares of $1 each | 20,000 | 15,000 |
| Retained earnings        | 72,000 | 25,000 |

The following information is relevant:

(i)     At the date of acquisition, Laurel conducted a fair value exercise on Rakewood's net assets which were equal to their carrying amounts with the following exceptions:

– an item of plant had a fair value of $4m above its carrying amount. At the date of acquisition it had a remaining life of two years.

– inventory of $800,000 had a fair value of $1m. All of this inventory had been sold by 30 September 20X6.

(ii) Laurel's policy is to value the non-controlling interest at fair value at the date of acquisition. For this purpose Rakewood's share price at 1 January 20X6 can be deemed to be representative of the fair value of the shares held by the non-controlling interest.

(iii) Laurel had traded with Rakewood for many years before the acquisition. Sales from Rakewood to Laurel throughout the year ended 30 September 20X6 were consistently $1.2m per month. Rakewood made a mark-up on cost of 20% on these sales. Laurel had $1.8m of these goods in inventory as at 30 September 20X6.

(iv) Laurel's investment income consists of:

   – its share of a dividend of $500,000 paid by Rakewood in August 20X6.

   – a dividend of $200,000 received from Artic, a 25% owned associate which it has held for several years. The profit after tax of Artic for the year ended 30 September 20X6 was $2.4m.

(v) Assume, except where indicated otherwise, that all items of income and expense accrue evenly throughout the year.

(vi) There were no impairment losses within the group during the year ended 30 September 20X6.

**Required:**

**(a) Calculate the consolidated goodwill at the date of acquisition of Rakewood Co.** ▦

**(7 marks)**

**(b) Prepare the consolidated statement of profit or loss for Laurel Co for the year ended 30 September 20X6.** ▦  **(13 marks)**

**(Total: 20 marks)**

## 385 DARGENT CO

On 1 January 20X6 Dargent Co acquired 75% of Latree Co's equity shares by means of a share exchange of two shares in Dargent Co for every three Latree Co shares acquired. On that date, further consideration was also issued to the shareholders of Latree Co in the form of a $100 8% loan note for every 100 shares acquired in Latree Co. None of the purchase consideration, nor the outstanding interest on the loan notes at 31 March 20X6, has yet been recorded by Dargent Co. At the date of acquisition, the share prices of Dargent Co and Latree Co are $3.20 and $1.80 respectively.

The summarised statements of financial position of the two companies as at 31 March 20X6 are:

|  | Dargent Co $000 | Latree Co $000 |
|---|---|---|
| **Assets** | | |
| **Non-current assets** | | |
| Property, plant and equipment (note (i)) | 75,200 | 31,500 |
| Investment in Amery Co at 1 April 20X5 (note (iv)) | 4,500 | nil |
| | 79,700 | 31,500 |
| **Current assets** | | |
| Inventory (note (iii)) | 19,400 | 18,800 |
| Trade receivables (note (iii)) | 14,700 | 12,500 |
| Bank | 1,200 | 600 |
| | 35,300 | 31,900 |
| **Total assets** | 115,000 | 63,400 |
| **Equity and liabilities** | | |
| Equity shares of $1 each | 50,000 | 20,000 |
| Retained earnings    – at 1 April 20X5 | 20,000 | 19,000 |
|                             – for year ended 31 March 20X6 | 16,000 | 8,000 |
| | 86,000 | 47,000 |
| **Non-current liabilities** | | |
| 8% loan notes | 5,000 | nil |
| Current liabilities (note (iii)) | 24,000 | 16,400 |
| **Total equity and liabilities** | 115,000 | 63,400 |

The following information is relevant:

(i) At the date of acquisition, the fair values of Latree Co's assets were equal to their carrying amounts. However, Latree Co operates a mine which requires to be decommissioned in five years' time. No provision has been made for these decommissioning costs by Latree Co. The present value (discounted at 8%) of the decommissioning is estimated at $4m and will be paid five years from the date of acquisition (the end of the mine's life).

(ii) Dargent Co's policy is to value the non-controlling interest at fair value at the date of acquisition. Latree Co's share price at that date can be deemed to be representative of the fair value of the shares held by the non-controlling interest.

(iii) The inventory of Latree Co includes goods bought from Dargent Co for $2.1m. Dargent Co applies a consistent mark-up on cost of 40% when arriving at its selling prices.

On 28 March 20X6, Dargent Co despatched goods to Latree Co with a selling price of $700,000. These were not received by Latree Co until after the year-end, and so have not been included in the above inventory at 31 March 20X6.

At 31 March 20X6, Dargent Co's records showed a receivable due from Latree Co of $3m. This differed to the equivalent payable in Latree Co's records due to the goods in transit.

The intra-group reconciliation should be achieved by assuming that Latree Co had received the goods in transit before the year-end.

(iv) The investment in Amery Co represents 30% of its voting share capital and Dargent Co uses equity accounting to account for this investment. Amery Co's profit for the year ended 31 March 20X6 was $6m and Amery Co paid total dividends during the year ended 31 March 20X6 of $2m. Dargent Co has recorded its share of the dividend received from Amery Co in investment income (and cash).

(v) All profits and losses accrued evenly throughout the year.

(vi) There were no impairment losses within the group for the year ended 31 March 20X6.

**Required:**

**Prepare the consolidated statement of financial position for Dargent Co as at 31 March 20X6.** ▦

**(Total: 20 marks)**

# ANALYSING FINANCIAL STATEMENTS

**386 HARDY**  *Walk in the footsteps of a top tutor*

Hardy is a public listed manufacturing entity. Its summarised financial statements are shown below.

**Statements of profit or loss for the year ended 30 September:**

|  | 20X6 | 20X5 |
|---|---|---|
|  | $000 | $000 |
| Revenue | 29,500 | 36,000 |
| Cost of sales | (25,500) | (26,000) |
| Gross profit | 4,000 | 10,000 |
| Distribution costs | (1,050) | (800) |
| Administrative expenses | (4,900) | (3,900) |
| Investment income | 50 | 200 |
| Finance costs | (600) | (500) |
| Profit (loss) before taxation | (2,500) | 5,000 |
| Income tax (expense) relief | 400 | (1,500) |
| Profit (loss) for the year | (2,100) | 3,500 |

**Statements of financial position as at 30 September:**

|  | 20X6 | | 20X5 | |
|---|---|---|---|---|
|  | $000 | $000 | $000 | $000 |
| Assets |  |  |  |  |
| Non-current assets |  |  |  |  |
| Property, plant and equipment |  | 17,600 |  | 24,500 |
| Investments at fair value through profit or loss |  | 2,400 |  | 4,000 |
|  |  | 20,000 |  | 28,500 |
| Current assets |  |  |  |  |
| Inventory and work-in-progress | 2,200 |  | 1,900 |  |
| Trade receivables | 2,200 |  | 2,800 |  |
| Tax asset | 600 |  | nil |  |
| Bank | 1,200 |  | 100 |  |
|  |  | 6,200 |  | 4,800 |
| Total assets |  | 26,200 |  | 33,300 |

| Equity and liabilities | | | | |
|---|---|---|---|---|
| Equity | | | | |
| Equity shares of $1 each | | 13,000 | | 12,000 |
| Share premium | | 1,000 | | nil |
| Revaluation surplus | | nil | | 4,500 |
| Retained earnings | | 3,600 | | 6,500 |
| | | ------ | | ------ |
| | | 17,600 | | 23,000 |
| Non-current liabilities | | | | |
| Bank loan | | 4,000 | | 5,000 |
| Deferred tax | | 1,200 | | 700 |
| Current liabilities | | | | |
| Trade payables | 3,400 | | 2,800 | |
| Current tax payable | nil | | 1,800 | |
| | ------ | 3,400 | ------ | 4,600 |
| Total equity and liabilities | | 26,200 | | 33,300 |

The following information has been obtained from the Chairman's Statement and the notes to the financial statements:

'Market conditions during the year ended 30 September 20X6 proved very challenging due largely to difficulties in the global economy as a result of a sharp recession which has led to steep falls in share prices and property values. Hardy has not been immune from these effects and our properties have suffered impairment losses of $6 million in the year.'

The excess of these losses over previous surpluses has led to a charge to cost of sales of $1.5 million in addition to the normal depreciation charge.

'Our portfolio of investments at fair value through profit or loss has been 'marked to market' (fair valued) resulting in a loss of $1.6 million (included in administrative expenses).'

There were no additions to or disposals of non-current assets during the year.

'In response to the downturn we have unfortunately had to make a number of employees redundant incurring severance costs of $1.3 million (included in cost of sales) and undertaken cost savings in advertising and other administrative expenses.'

'The difficulty in the credit markets has meant that the finance cost of our variable rate bank loan has increased from 4.5% to 8%. In order to help cash flows, we made a rights issue during the year and reduced the dividend per share by 50%.'

'Despite the above events and associated costs, the Board believes our underlying performance has been quite resilient in these difficult times.'

**Required:**

**Analyse and discuss the financial performance and position of Hardy as portrayed by the above financial statements and the additional information provided.**

**Your analysis should be supported by any SEVEN profitability, liquidity and gearing and other appropriate ratios (up to 7 marks available).** 🖥

**(Total: 20 marks)**

## 387  PINTO

Pinto is a publicly listed entity. The statement of cash flows of Pinto is available:

**Statement of cash flows of Pinto for the year to 31 March 20X8:**

| Cash flows from operating activities | $000 | $000 |
|---|---|---|
| Profit before tax | | 440 |
| Depreciation | | 280 |
| Loss on disposal of plant and machinery | | 90 |
| Increase in warranty provision | | 100 |
| Investment income | | (60) |
| Finance costs | | 50 |
| Redemption penalty costs included in administrative expenses | | 20 |
| | | 920 |
| Increase in inventories | (400) | |
| Decrease in trade receivables | 60 | |
| Increase in trade payables | 360 | |
| | | 20 |
| Cash generated from operations | | 940 |
| Interest paid | | (50) |
| Tax refund received | | 60 |
| Net cash from operating activities | | 950 |
| Cash flows from investing activities | | |
| Purchase of property, plant and equipment | (1,440) | |
| Sale of property, plant and equipment | 150 | |
| Rental income received from investment property | 40 | |
| Net cash used in investing activities | | (1,250) |
| Cash flows from financing activities | | |
| Proceeds from issue of shares | 1,000 | |
| Repayment of loan notes | (420) | |
| Dividends paid | (150) | |
| Net cash from financing activities | | 430 |
| Net increase in cash and cash equivalents | | 130 |
| Cash and cash equivalents at beginning of period | | (120) |
| Cash and cash equivalents at end of period | | 10 |

The following supporting information is available:

(i)  An item of plant with a carrying amount of $240,000 was sold at a loss of $90,000 during the year. Depreciation of $280,000 was charged (to cost of sales) for property, plant and equipment in the year ended 31 March 20X8.

Pinto uses the fair value model in IAS 40 *Investment Property*. There were no purchases or sales of investment property during the year.

(ii) The 6% loan notes were redeemed early incurring a penalty payment of $20,000 which has been charged as an administrative expense in the statement of profit or loss and other comprehensive income.

(iii) There was an issue of shares for cash on 1 October 20X7.

(iv) Pinto gives a 12 month warranty on some of the products it sells. The amounts shown in current liabilities as warranty provision are an accurate assessment, based on past experience, of the amount of claims likely to be made in respect of warranties outstanding at each year end. Warranty costs are included in cost of sales.

**Required:**

**(a)** **Comment on the cash flow management of Pinto as revealed by the statement of cash flows and the information provided by the above financial statements.** ⌨

Note:   **Ratio analysis is not required, and will not be awarded any marks.**      **(15 marks)**

**(b)** In recent years many analysts have commented on a growing disillusionment with the usefulness and reliability of the information contained in some entities' statements of profit or loss and other comprehensive income.

**Required:**

**Discuss the extent to which an entity's statement of cash flows may be more useful and reliable than its statement of profit or loss.** ⌨      **(5 marks)**

**(Total: 20 marks)**

## 388 HARBIN  *Walk in the footsteps of a top tutor*

Shown below are the recently issued summarised financial statements of Harbin, a listed entity, for the year ended 30 September 20X7, together with comparatives for 20X6 and extracts from the Chief Executive's report that accompanied their issue.

**Consolidated statements of profit or loss**

|  | 20X7 | 20X6 |
|---|---|---|
|  | $000 | $000 |
| Revenue | 250,000 | 180,000 |
| Cost of sales | (200,000) | (150,000) |
| Gross profit | 50,000 | 30,000 |
| Operating expenses | (26,000) | (22,000) |
| Finance costs | (8,000) | (Nil) |
| Profit before tax | 16,000 | 8,000 |
| Income tax expense (at 25%) | (4,000) | (2,000) |
| Profit for the period | 12,000 | 6,000 |

**Consolidated statement of financial position**

| | 20X7 | 20X6 |
|---|---:|---:|
| | $000 | $000 |
| **Non-current assets** | | |
| Property, plant and equipment | 210,000 | 90,000 |
| Goodwill | 10,000 | Nil |
| | 220,000 | 90,000 |
| **Current assets** | | |
| Inventory | 25,000 | 15,000 |
| Trade receivables | 13,000 | 8,000 |
| Bank | nil | 14,000 |
| | 38,000 | 37,000 |
| **Total assets** | 258,000 | 127,000 |
| **Equity and liabilities** | | |
| Equity shares of $1 each | 100,000 | 100,000 |
| Retained earnings | 14,000 | 12,000 |
| | 114,000 | 112,000 |
| **Non-current liabilities** | | |
| 8% loan notes | 100,000 | Nil |
| **Current liabilities** | | |
| Bank overdraft | 17,000 | Nil |
| Trade payables | 23,000 | 13,000 |
| Current tax payable | 4,000 | 2,000 |
| | 44,000 | 15,000 |
| **Total equity and liabilities** | 258,000 | 127,000 |

**Extracts from the Chief Executive's report:**

'Highlights of Harbin's performance for the year ended 30 September 20X7:

- an increase in sales revenue of 39%

- gross profit margin up from 16.7% to 20%

- a doubling of the profit for the period.

In response to the improved position the Board paid a dividend of 10 cents per share in September 20X7 an increase of 25% on the previous year.'

You have also been provided with the following further information.

On 1 October 20X6 Harbin purchased the whole of the net assets of Fatima (previously a privately owned entity) for $100 million. The contribution of the purchase to Harbin's results for the year ended 30 September 20X7 was:

|  | $000 |
|---|---|
| Revenue | 70,000 |
| Cost of sales | (40,000) |
| | |
| Gross profit | 30,000 |
| Operating expenses | (8,000) |
| | |
| Profit before tax | 22,000 |

There were no disposals of non-current assets during the year.

The following ratios have been calculated for the year ended 30 September 20X6 and 20X7:

|  | 20X7 | 20X6 |
|---|---|---|
| Return on year-end capital employed | | 7.1% |
| (profit before interest and tax over total assets less current liabilities) | | |
| Net asset (equal to capital employed) turnover | 1.2 | 1.6 |
| Net profit (before tax) margin | 6.4% | 4.4% |
| Current ratio | | 2.5 |
| Closing inventory holding period (in days) | | 37 |
| Trade receivables' collection period (in days) | | 16 |
| Trade payables' payment period (based on cost of sales) (in days) | 42 | 32 |
| Gearing (debt over debt plus equity) | | Nil |

**Required:**

(a) Calculate the missing ratios for 20X7. 🖳 **(5 marks)**

(b) Assess the financial performance and position of Harbin for the year ended 30 September 20X7 compared to the previous year. Your answer should refer to the information in the Chief Executive's report and the impact of the purchase of the net assets of Fatima. 🖳 **(15 marks)**

**(Total: 20 marks)**

**389 VICTULAR**  *Walk in the footsteps of a top tutor*

Victular would like to acquire 100% of a suitable private entity. It has obtained the following draft financial statements for two entities, Grappa and Merlot. They operate in the same industry and their managements have indicated that they would be receptive to a takeover.

**Statements of profit or loss for the year ended 30 September 20X8**

|  | Grappa | Merlot |
|---|---|---|
|  | $000 | $000 |
| Revenue | 12,000 | 20,500 |
| Cost of sales | (10,500) | (18,000) |
| Gross profit | 1,500 | 2,500 |
| Operating expenses | (240) | (500) |
| Finance costs   – loan | (210) | (300) |
|                 – overdraft | Nil | (10) |
|                 – lease | Nil | (290) |
| Profit before tax | 1,050 | 1,400 |
| Income tax expense | (150) | (400) |
| Profit for the year | 900 | 1,000 |
| **Note:** Dividends paid during the year | 250 | 700 |

**Statements of financial position as at 30 September 20X8**

Assets
Non-current assets

| | | | | |
|---|---|---|---|---|
| Freehold factory (note (i)) | | 4,400 | | Nil |
| Owned plant (note (ii)) | | 5,000 | | 2,200 |
| Right-of-use asset (note (ii)) | | Nil | | 5,300 |
| | | 9,400 | | 7,500 |
| Current assets | | | | |
| Inventory | 2,000 | | 3,600 | |
| Trade receivables | 2,400 | | 3,700 | |
| Bank | 600 | 5,000 | Nil | 7,300 |
| Total assets | | 14,400 | | 14,800 |

| | $000 | $000 | $000 | $000 |
|---|---|---|---|---|
| Equity and liabilities | | | | |
| Equity shares of $1 each | | 2,000 | | 2,000 |
| Property revaluation surplus | 900 | | Nil | |
| Retained earnings | 2,600 | | 800 | |
| | | 3,500 | | 800 |
| | | 5,500 | | 2,800 |
| Non-current liabilities | | | | |
| Lease liabilities (note (iii)) | Nil | | 3,200 | |
| 7% loan notes | 3,000 | | Nil | |
| 10% loan notes | Nil | | 3,000 | |
| Deferred tax | 600 | | 100 | |
| Government grants | 1,200 | | Nil | |
| | | 4,800 | | 6,300 |
| Current liabilities | | | | |
| Bank overdraft | Nil | | 1,200 | |
| Trade payables | 3,100 | | 3,800 | |
| Government grants | 400 | | Nil | |
| Lease liabilities (note (iii)) | Nil | | 500 | |
| Taxation | 600 | | 200 | |
| | | 4,100 | | 5,700 |
| Total equity and liabilities | | 14,400 | | 14,800 |

**Notes**

(i)    Both entities operate from similar premises.

(ii)   Additional details of the two entities' plant are:

| | Grappa $000 | Merlot $000 |
|---|---|---|
| Owned plant – cost | 8,000 | 10,000 |
| Right-of-use plant – initial value | Nil | 7,500 |

There were no disposals of plant during the year by either entity.

(iii)  The interest rate implicit within Merlot's leases is 7.5% per annum. For the purpose of calculating ROCE and gearing, **all** lease obligations are treated as long-term interest bearing borrowings.

(iv) The following ratios have been calculated for Grappa and can be taken to be correct:

| | |
|---|---|
| Return on year end capital employed (ROCE) | 14.8% |

(capital employed taken as shareholders' funds plus long-term interest bearing borrowings – see note (iii) above)

| | |
|---|---|
| Gross profit margin | 12.5% |
| Operating profit margin | 10.5% |
| Current ratio | 1.2:1 |
| Closing inventory holding period | 70 days |
| Trade receivables' collection period | 73 days |
| Trade payables' payment period (using cost of sales) | 108 days |
| Gearing (see note (iii) above) | 35.3% |

**Required:**

(a) **Calculate for Merlot the ratios equivalent to all those given for Grappa above.** 🖥

**(4 marks)**

(b) **Assess the relative performance and financial position of Grappa and Merlot for the year ended 30 September 20X8 to inform the directors of Victular in their acquisition decision.** 🖥 **(11 marks)**

(c) **Outline the problems in using ratios for comparison purposes between entities, and suggest what additional information would be useful for Victular in reaching its decision.** 🖥 **(5 marks)**

**(Total: 20 marks)**

## 390 QUARTILE

Quartile sells jewellery through stores in retail shopping centres throughout the country. Over the last two years it has experienced declining profitability and is wondering if this is related to the sector as whole. It has recently subscribed to an agency that produces average ratios across many businesses. Below are the ratios that have been provided by the agency for Quartile's business sector based on a year end of 30 June 20X2.

| | Sector |
|---|---|
| Return on year-end capital employed (ROCE) | 16.8% |
| Net asset (total assets less current liabilities) turnover | 1.4 times |
| Gross profit margin | 35% |
| Operating profit margin | 12% |
| Current ratio | 1.25:1 |
| Average inventory turnover | 3 times |
| Trade payables payment period | 64 days |
| Debt to equity | 38% |

The financial statements of Quartile for the year ended 30 September 20X2 are shown below.

**Statement of profit or loss**

|  | $000 | $000 |
|---|---:|---:|
| Revenue | | 56,000 |
| Opening inventory | 8,300 | |
| Purchases | 43,900 | |
| | 52,200 | |
| Closing inventory | (10,200) | |
| | | (42,000) |
| Gross profit | | 14,000 |
| Operating costs | | (9,800) |
| Finance costs | | (800) |
| Profit before tax | | 3,400 |
| Income tax expense | | (1,000) |
| Profit for the year | | 2,400 |

**Statement of financial position**

|  | $000 | $000 |
|---|---:|---:|
| **Assets** | | |
| Non-current assets | | |
| Property and shop fittings | | 25,600 |
| Deferred development expenditure | | 5,000 |
| | | 30,600 |
| Current assets | | |
| Inventory | 10,200 | |
| Bank | 1,000 | |
| | | 11,200 |
| Total assets | | 41,800 |

**Equity and liabilities**

Equity

| | |
|---|---:|
| Equity shares of $1 each | 15,000 |
| Property revaluation surplus | 3,000 |
| Retained earnings | 8,600 |
| | 26,600 |

| | | |
|---|---:|---:|
| Non-current liabilities | | |
| 10% loan notes | | 8,000 |
| Current liabilities | | |
| Trade payables | 5,400 | |
| Current tax payable | 1,800 | 7,200 |
| Total equity and liabilities | | 41,800 |

**Note:** The deferred development expenditure relates to an investment in a process to manufacture artificial precious gems for future sale by Quartile in the retail jewellery market.

**Required:**

(a) **Prepare the ratios for Quartile equivalent to those of the sector.** 🖳 **(7 marks)**

(b) **Assess the financial and operating performance of Quartile in comparison to its sector averages.** 🖳 **(13 marks)**

**(Total: 20 marks)**

## 391 BENGAL

Bengal is a public entity. Its most recent financial statements are shown below:

**Statements of profit or loss for the year ended 31 March**

| | 20X1 | 20X0 |
|---|---:|---:|
| | $000 | $000 |
| Revenue | 25,500 | 17,250 |
| Cost of sales | (14,800) | (10,350) |
| Gross profit | 10,700 | 6,900 |
| Distribution costs | (4,800) | (3,300) |
| Finance costs | (650) | (100) |
| Profit before taxation | 5,250 | 3,500 |
| Income tax expense | (2,250) | (1,000) |
| Profit for the year | 3,000 | 2,500 |

**Statement of cash flows for the year ended 31 March 20X1:**

|  | $000 | $000 |
|---|---|---|
| Cash flows from operating activities: |  |  |
| Profit from operations |  | 5,900 |
| Adjustments for: |  |  |
| depreciation of non-current assets |  | 640 |
| increase in inventories |  | (1,800) |
| increase in receivables |  | (1,000) |
| increase in payables |  | 650 |
|  |  | ——— |
| Cash generated from operations |  | 4,390 |
| Finance costs paid |  | (650) |
| Income tax paid |  | (1,250) |
|  |  | ——— |
| Net cash from operating activities |  | 2,490 |
| Cash flows from investing activities: |  |  |
| Purchase of property, plant and equipment | (6,740) |  |
| Purchase of intangibles | (6,200) |  |
|  | ——— |  |
| Net cash used in investing activities |  | (12,940) |
| Cash flows from financing activities: |  |  |
| Issue of 8% loan note | 7,000 |  |
| Equity dividends paid | (750) |  |
|  | ——— |  |
| Net cash from financing activities |  | 6,250 |
|  |  | ——— |
| Net decrease in cash and cash equivalents |  | (4,200) |
| Cash and cash equivalents at beginning of period |  | 4,000 |
|  |  | ——— |
| Cash and cash equivalents at end of period |  | (200) |
|  |  | ——— |

**Notes**

(i)    There were no disposals of non-current assets during the period; however Bengal does have some non-current assets classified as 'held for sale' at 31 March 20X1.

(ii)   Depreciation of property, plant and equipment for the year ended 31 March 20X1 was $640,000.

A disappointed shareholder has observed that although revenue during the year has increased by 48% (8,250/17,250 × 100), profit for the year has only increased by 20% (500/2,500 × 100).

**Required:**

**Comment on the performance (including addressing the shareholder's observation) and cash flow of Bengal for the year ended 31 March 20X1.** 🖳

**Note:   up to 5 marks are available for the calculation of appropriate ratios.**

**(Total: 20 marks)**

## 392 WOODBANK

Shown below are the financial statements of Woodbank for its most recent two years.

**Consolidated statements of profit or loss for the year ended 31 March:**

|  | 20X4 | 20X3 |
|---|---|---|
|  | $000 | $000 |
| Revenue | 150,000 | 110,000 |
| Cost of sales | (117,000) | (85,800) |
|  |  |  |
| Gross profit | 33,000 | 24,200 |
| Distribution costs | (6,000) | (5,000) |
| Administrative expenses | (9,000) | (9,200) |
| Finance costs – loan note interest | (1,750) | (500) |
|  |  |  |
| Profit before tax | 16,250 | 9,500 |
| Income tax expense | (5,750) | (3,000) |
|  |  |  |
| Profit for the year | 10,500 | 6,500 |

**Statements of financial position as at 31 March:**

|  | 20X4 | 20X3 |
|---|---|---|
|  | $000 | $000 |
| **Assets** |  |  |
| Non-current assets |  |  |
| Property, plant and equipment | 118,000 | 85,000 |
| Goodwill | 30,000 | nil |
|  |  |  |
|  | 148,000 | 85,000 |
|  |  |  |
| Current assets |  |  |
| Inventory | 15,500 | 12,000 |
| Trade receivables | 11,000 | 8,000 |
| Bank | 500 | 5,000 |
|  |  |  |
|  | 27,000 | 25,000 |
|  |  |  |
| Total assets | 175,000 | 110,000 |

**Equity and liabilities**

Equity

| | | |
|---|---:|---:|
| Equity shares of $1 each | 80,000 | 80,000 |
| Retained earnings | 15,000 | 10,000 |
| | 95,000 | 90,000 |
| Non-current liabilities | | |
| 10% loan notes | 55,000 | 5,000 |
| Current liabilities | | |
| Trade payables | 21,000 | 13,000 |
| Current tax payable | 4,000 | 2,000 |
| | 25,000 | 15,000 |
| Total equity and liabilities | 175,000 | 110,000 |

The following information is available:

(i)   On 1 January 20X4, Woodbank purchased the trading assets and operations of Shaw for $50 million and, on the same date, issued additional 10% loan notes to finance the purchase. Shaw was an unincorporated entity and its results (for three months from 1 January 20X4 to 31 March 20X4) and net assets (including goodwill not subject to any impairment) are included in Woodbank's financial statements for the year ended 31 March 20X4.  There were no other purchases or sales of non-current assets during the year ended 31 March 20X4.

(ii)  Extracts of the results (for three months) of the previously separate business of Shaw, which are included in Woodbank's statement of profit or loss for the year ended 31 March 20X4, are:

| | $000 |
|---|---:|
| Revenue | 30,000 |
| Cost of sales | (21,000) |
| Gross profit | 9,000 |
| Distribution costs | (2,000) |
| Administrative expenses | (2,000) |

(iii) The following six ratios have been correctly calculated for Woodbank for the year ended 31 March:

| | 20X3 | 20X4 |
|---|---:|---:|
| Return on capital employed (ROCE) | 10.5% | 12.0% |
| (profit before interest and tax/year-end total assets less current liabilities) | | |
| Net asset (equal to capital employed) turnover | 1.16 times | 1.0 times |
| Gross profit margin | 22.0% | 22.0% |
| Profit before interest and tax margin | 9.1% | 12.0% |
| Current ratio | 1.7:1 | 1.08:1 |
| Gearing (debt/(debt + equity)) | 5.3% | 36.7% |

**Required:**

(a) Calculate for the year ended 31 March 20X4 equivalent ratios to the first FOUR only for Woodbank excluding the effects of the purchase of Shaw.

Note: Assume the capital employed for Shaw is equal to its purchase price of $50 million.
(4 marks)

(b) Assess the comparative financial performance and position of Woodbank for the year ended 31 March 20X4. Your answer should refer to the effects of the purchase of Shaw. 
(12 marks)

(c) Discuss what further information specific to the acquisition of Shaw that would allow you to make a more informed assessment of Woodbank's performance and position. 
(4 marks)

(Total: 20 marks)

## 393 HYDAN

> 🕐 **Question debrief**

Xpand is a publicly listed entity which has experienced rapid growth in recent years through the acquisition and integration of other entities. Xpand is interested in acquiring Hydan, a retailing business, which is one of several entities owned and managed by the same family, of which Lodan is the ultimate parent.

The summarised financial statements of Hydan for the year ended 30 September 20X4 are:

**Statement of profit or loss**

|  | $000 |
|---|---|
| Revenue | 70,000 |
| Cost of sales | (45,000) |
| Gross profit | 25,000 |
| Operating costs | (7,000) |
| Directors' salaries | (1,000) |
| Profit before tax | 17,000 |
| Income tax expense | (3,000) |
| Profit for the year | 14,000 |

**Statement of financial position**

|  | $000 | $000 |
|---|---|---|
| **Assets** | | |
| Non-current assets | | |
| Property, plant and equipment | | 32,400 |
| Current assets | | |
| Inventory | 7,500 | |
| Bank | 100 | |
| | ——— | 7,600 |
| Total assets | | 40,000 |
| | | |
| **Equity and liabilities** | | |
| Equity | | |
| Equity shares of $1 each | | 1,000 |
| Retained earnings | | 18,700 |
| | | ——— |
| | | 19,700 |
| Non-current liabilities | | |
| Directors' loan accounts (interest free) | | 10,000 |
| Current liabilities | | |
| Trade payables | 7,500 | |
| Current tax payable | 2,800 | |
| | ——— | 10,300 |
| | | |
| Total equity and liabilities | | 40,000 |

From the above financial statements, Xpand has calculated for Hydan the ratios below for the year ended 30 September 20X4. It has also obtained the equivalent ratios for the retail sector average which can be taken to represent Hydan's sector.

|  | Hydan | Sector average |
|---|---|---|
| Return on equity (ROE) (including directors' loan accounts) | 47.1% | 22.0% |
| Net asset turnover | 2.36 times | 1.67 times |
| Gross profit margin | 35.7% | 30.0% |
| Net profit margin | 20.0% | 12.0% |

From enquiries made, Xpand has learned the following information:

(i) Hydan buys all of its trading inventory from another of the family entities at a price which is 10% less than the market price for such goods.

(ii) After the acquisition, Xpand would replace the existing board of directors and need to pay remuneration of $2.5 million per annum.

(iii) The directors' loan accounts would be repaid by obtaining a loan of the same amount with interest at 10% per annum.

(iv) Xpand expects the purchase price of Hydan to be $30 million.

**Required:**

(a)   Recalculate the ratios for Hydan after making appropriate adjustments to the financial statements for notes (i) to (iv) above. For this purpose, the expected purchase price of $30 million should be taken as Hydan's equity and net assets are equal to this equity plus the loan. You may assume the changes will have no effect on taxation.                                                 (6 marks)

(b)   In relation to the ratios calculated in (a) above, and the ratios for Hydan given in the question, comment on the performance of Hydan compared to its retail sector average.                                                                                              (9 marks)

(c)   One of Xpand's directors has suggested that it would be wise to look at the Lodan group's consolidated financial statements rather than Hydan's individual financial statements.

As an adviser to Xpand, explain any concerns you would raise about basing an investment decision on the information available in Lodan's consolidated financial statements and Hydan's entity financial statements.                            (5 marks)

(Total: 20 marks)

> *Calculate your allowed time, allocate the time to the separate parts*

**394   YOGI**

Yogi is a public entity and extracts from its most recent financial statements are provided below:

**Statements of profit or loss for the year ended 31 March**

|  | 20X5 | 20X4 |
| --- | --- | --- |
|  | $000 | $000 |
| Revenue | 36,000 | 50,000 |
| Cost of sales | (24,000) | (30,000) |
| Gross profit | 12,000 | 20,000 |
| Profit from sale of division (see note (i)) | 1,000 | nil |
| Distribution costs | (3,500) | (5,300) |
| Administrative expenses | (4,800) | (2,900) |
| Finance costs | (400) | (800) |
| Profit before taxation | 4,300 | 11,000 |
| Income tax expense | (1,300) | (3,300) |
| Profit for the year | 3,000 | 7,700 |

**Statements of financial position as at 31 March**

| | 20X5 | | 20X4 | |
| --- | --- | --- | --- | --- |
| | $000 | $000 | $000 | $000 |
| Non-current assets | | | | |
| Property, plant and equipment | | 16,300 | | 19,000 |
| Intangible – goodwill | | nil | | 2,000 |
| | | 16,300 | | 21,000 |
| Current assets | | | | |
| Inventory | 3,400 | | 5,800 | |
| Trade receivables | 1,300 | | 2,400 | |
| Bank | 1,500 | 6,200 | nil | 8,200 |
| Total assets | | 22,500 | | 29,200 |
| Equity and liabilities | | | | |
| Equity | | | | |
| Equity shares of $1 each | | 10,000 | | 10,000 |
| Retained earnings | | 3,000 | | 4,000 |
| | | 13,000 | | 14,000 |
| Non-current liabilities | | | | |
| 10% loan notes | | 4,000 | | 8,000 |
| Current liabilities | | | | |
| Bank overdraft | nil | | 1,400 | |
| Trade payables | 4,300 | | 3,100 | |
| Current tax payable | 1,200 | 5,500 | 2,700 | 7,200 |
| Total equity and liabilities | | 22,500 | | 29,200 |

**Notes**

(i)  On 1 April 20X4, Yogi sold the net assets (including goodwill) of a separately operated division of its business for $8 million cash on which it made a profit of $1 million. This transaction required shareholder approval and, in order to secure this, the management of Yogi offered shareholders a dividend of 40 cents for each share in issue out of the proceeds of the sale. The trading results of the division which are included in the statement of profit or loss for the year ended 31 March 20X4 above are:

| | $000 |
| --- | --- |
| Revenue | 18,000 |
| Cost of sales | (10,000) |
| Gross profit | 8,000 |
| Distribution costs | (1,000) |
| Administrative expenses | (1,200) |
| Profit before interest and tax | 5,800 |

(ii) The following selected ratios for Yogi have been calculated for the year ended 31 March 20X4 (as reported above):

| | |
|---|---|
| Gross profit margin | 40.0% |
| Operating profit margin | 23.6% |
| Return on capital employed | |
| (profit before interest and tax/(total assets – current liabilities)) | 53.6% |
| Net asset turnover | 2.27 times |

**Required:**

**(a)** **Calculate the equivalent ratios for Yogi:**

(i) **for the year ended 31 March 20X4, after excluding the contribution made by the division that has been sold; ⌨ and**

(ii) **for the year ended 31 March 20X5, excluding the profit on the sale of the division. ⌨** **(5 marks)**

**(b)** **Comment on the comparative financial performance and position of Yogi for the year ended 31 March 20X5. ⌨** **(10 marks)**

**(c)** On a separate matter, you have been asked to advise on an application for a loan to build an extension to a sports club which is a not-for-profit organisation. You have been provided with the audited financial statements of the sports club for the last four years.

**Required:**

**Identify and explain the ratios that you would calculate to assist in determining whether you would advise that the loan should be granted. ⌨** **(5 marks)**

**(Total: 20 marks)**

## 395 XPAND

Xpand is a public entity which has grown in recent years by acquiring established businesses. The following financial statements for two potential target entities are shown below. They operate in the same industry sector and Xpand believes their shareholders would be receptive to a takeover. An indicative price for 100% acquisition of the entities is $12 million each.

**Statements of profit or loss for the year ended 30 September 20X5**

| | Kandid | Kovert |
|---|---|---|
| | $000 | $000 |
| Revenue | 25,000 | 40,000 |
| Cost of sales | (19,000) | (32,800) |
| | | |
| Gross profit | 6,000 | 7,200 |
| Distribution and administrative expenses | (1,250) | (2,300) |
| Finance costs | (250) | (900) |
| | | |
| Profit before tax | 4,500 | 4,000 |
| Income tax expense | (900) | (1,000) |
| | | |
| Profit for the year | 3,600 | 3,000 |

**Statements of financial position as at 30 September 20X5**

|  | $000 | $000 |
|---|---|---|
| Non-current assets |  |  |
| Property | nil | 3,000 |
| Owned plant | 4,800 | 2,000 |
| Right-of-use asset | nil | 5,300 |
|  | 4,800 | 10,300 |
| Current assets |  |  |
| Inventory | 1,600 | 3,400 |
| Trade receivables | 2,100 | 5,100 |
| Bank | 1,100 | 200 |
|  | 4,800 | 8,700 |
| Total assets | 9,600 | 19,000 |
| Equity and liabilities |  |  |
| Equity |  |  |
| Equity shares of $1 each | 1,000 | 2,000 |
| Property revaluation surplus | nil | 900 |
| Retained earnings | 1,600 | 2,700 |
|  | 2,600 | 5,600 |
| Non-current liabilities |  |  |
| Lease liability | nil | 4,200 |
| 5% loan notes (31 December 20X6) | 5,000 | nil |
| 10% loan notes (31 December 20X6) | nil | 5,000 |
|  | 5,000 | 9,200 |
| Current liabilities |  |  |
| Trade payables | 1,250 | 2,100 |
| Lease liability | nil | 1,000 |
| Taxation | 750 | 1,100 |
|  | 2,000 | 4,200 |
| Total equity and liabilities | 9,600 | 19,000 |

**Notes**

(i)     Carrying value of plant:

|  | Kandid | Kovert |
|---|---|---|
|  | $000 | $000 |
| Owned plant – cost | 8,000 | 10,000 |
| Less government grant | (2,000) |  |
|  | ───── |  |
|  | 6,000 |  |
| Accumulated depreciation | (1,200) | (8,000) |
|  | ───── | ───── |
|  | 4,800 | 2,000 |
| Right-of-use asset – initial value | nil | 8,000 |

(ii)    The following ratios have been calculated:

|  | Kandid | Kovert |
|---|---|---|
| Return on year-end capital employed (ROCE) | 62.5% |  |
| Net asset (taken as same figure as capital employed) turnover | 3.3 times | 2.5 times |
| Gross profit margin | 24.0% | 18.0% |
| Profit margin (before interest and tax) | 19.0% |  |
| Current ratio | 2.4:1 | 2.1:1 |
| Closing inventory holding period | 31 days | 38 days |
| Trade receivables collection period | 31 days | 47 days |
| Trade payables payment period (using cost of sales) | 24 days |  |
| Gearing (debt/(debt + equity)) | 65.8% |  |

**Required:**

(a)     **Calculate the missing ratios for Kovert. All lease liabilities are treated as debt, and profit before interest and tax should be used for the calculation of return on capital employed.**                                                                              **(4 marks)**

(b)     **Using the above information, assess the relative performance and financial position of Kandid and Kovert for the year ended 30 September 20X5 in order to assist the directors of Xpand to make an acquisition decision.**                                        **(12 marks)**

(c)     **Describe what further information may be useful to Xpand when making an acquisition decision.**                                                                              **(4 marks)**

**(Total: 20 marks)**

## 396 SCHRUTE

Schrute is a group in the farming industry and owns a number of 100% owned farming subsidiaries. Its financial statements for the last two years are shown below.

**Consolidated statement of profit or loss for the year ended 30 September:**

|  | 20X3 | 20X2 |
| --- | --- | --- |
|  | $000 | $000 |
| Revenue | 94,000 | 68,500 |
| Cost of sales | (46,000) | (28,000) |
| Gross profit | 48,000 | 40,500 |
| Distribution costs | (21,200) | (19,300) |
| Administrative expenses | (25,600) | (15,400) |
| Profit from operations | 1,200 | 5,800 |
| Investment income | 0 | 600 |
| Finance costs | (120) | 0 |
| Profit before tax | 1,080 | 6,400 |
| Taxation | (300) | (1,920) |
| Profit for the year | 780 | 4,480 |
| Attributable to: |  |  |
| Shareholders of Schrute | 1,580 | 4,480 |
| Non-controlling interest | (800) | – |
|  | 780 | 4,480 |

**Extracts from the consolidated statement of financial position as at 30 September:**

|  | 20X3 | 20X2 |
| --- | --- | --- |
|  | $000 | $000 |
| Inventories | 6,500 | 4,570 |
| Trade receivables | 17,000 | 15,600 |
| Bank | 610 | 6,000 |
| **Equity:** |  |  |
| Equity shares of $1 each | 25,000 | 6,000 |
| Retained earnings | 73,500 | 72,500 |
| Non-controlling interest | 510 | – |
| **Non-current liabilities:** |  |  |
| Loan | 20,000 | – |
| Current liabilities | 9,100 | 5,690 |

The following information is relevant:

(i)     Schrute has become increasingly worried about two major areas in its business environment. Firstly, there are concerns that reliance on large supermarkets is putting pressure on cash flow, as the supermarkets demand long payment terms. Secondly, the consistent increases in fuel prices mean that delivering the produce nationally is becoming extremely expensive.

(ii)    To manage this, Schrute acquired 80% of Howard on 1 October 20X2, which operates a small number of hotels. It was hoped that this would improve cash flow, as customers pay up front, and reduce the impact of further fuel price rises.

(iii)   To fund this, Schrute disposed of $11 million held in investments, making a $4.5 million profit on disposal. This profit is included within administrative expenses.

(iv)   Howard opened a new hotel in March 20X3. After poor reviews, Schrute Farms recruited a new marketing director in May. Following an extensive marketing campaign, online feedback improved.

(v)    The following ratios have been calculated for the year ended 30 September 20X2:

| | |
|---|---|
| Gross profit margin | 59.1% |
| Operating profit margin | 8.5% |
| Return on Capital Employed | 7.4% |
| Current ratio | 4.6:1 |
| Inventory turnover period | 60 days |
| Receivables collection period | 83 days |

**Required:**

**(a)    For the ratios provided above, prepare the equivalent figures for the year ended 30 September 20X3.** 🖥      **(5 marks)**

**(b)    Analyse the performance and position of Schrute for the year ended 30 September 20X3, making specific reference to any concerns or expectations regarding future periods.** 🖥      **(15 marks)**

**(Total: 20 marks)**

## 397 PITCARN

The Pitcarn group owns a number of subsidiaries. On 31 March 20X6, the Pitcarn group sold its entire holding in Sitor. The consolidated statement of profit or loss of the Pitcarn group for 20X6 has been produced **without** the results of Sitor due to its disposal. No profit or loss on disposal has been included in the 20X6 consolidated statement of profit or loss.

Extracts from the consolidated statements of profit or loss for the Pitcarn group are below:

**Statements of profit or loss (extracts) for the year ended 31 March**

|  | 20X6 | 20X5 |
| --- | --- | --- |
|  | $000 | $000 |
| Revenue | 86,000 | 99,000 |
| Cost of sales (note (ii)) | (63,400) | (67,200) |
| Gross profit | 22,600 | 31,800 |
| Other income (notes (i) and (iii)) | 3,400 | 1,500 |
| Operating expenses | (21,300) | (23,200) |
| Profit from operations | 4,700 | 10,100 |
| Finance costs | (1,500) | (1,900) |

The following notes are relevant:

(i) Sitor was based in the Pitcarn head offices, for which it pays annual rent to Pitcarn of $300,000, significantly below the cost of equivalent office space in Sitor's local area. As Sitor is no longer in the group, Pitcarn has included this income within other income. Sitor expenses rent payments in operating expenses.

(ii) Sitor sold goods totalling $8 million to Pitcarn (included in Pitcarn's cost of sales above) during the year. Pitcarn held none of these goods in inventory at 31 March 20X6. Sitor made a margin of 40% on all goods sold to Pitcarn.

(iii) Pitcarn received a dividend of $1 million from Sitor during the year, as well as recording interest of $500,000 on a loan given to Sitor in 20X3. Both of these amounts are included within Pitcarn's other income.

The following selected ratios for the Pitcarn group have been calculated for the years ended 31 March 20X5 and 31 March 20X6 from the information above.

|  | 20X6 | 20X5 |
| --- | --- | --- |
| Gross profit margin | 26.3% | 32.1% |
| Operating margin | 5.5% | 10.2% |
| Interest cover | 3.1 times | 5.3 times |

(iv)   Sitor's individual statement of profit or loss for the year ended shows the following:

|  | $000 |
|---|---|
| Revenue | 16,000 |
| Cost of sales | (10,400) |
|  | ———— |
| Gross profit | 5,600 |
| Operating expenses | (3,200) |
|  | ———— |
| Profit from operations | 2,400 |
| Finance costs | (900) |

**Required:**

(a)   **Calculate the equivalent ratios for the consolidated statement of profit or loss for the year ended 31 March 20X6 if Sitor had been consolidated.** ▦            **(7 marks)**

(b)   **Analyse the performance of the Pitcarn group for the year ended 31 March 20X6. This should also include a discussion of Sitor.** ▦            **(8 marks)**

(c)   Pitcarn acquired 80% of Sitor's 10 million $1 shares on 1 April 20X1 for $17 million when Sitor had retained earnings of $3 million. Pitcarn uses the fair value method for valuing the non-controlling interest. At acquisition the fair value of the non-controlling interest was $1 million.

On 31 March 20X6, Pitcarn sold its entire shareholding in Sitor for $25 million when Sitor had retained earnings of $7 million. Goodwill had suffered no impairment since acquisition.

**Calculate the gain/loss on disposal to be shown in the consolidated statement of profit or loss for the year ended 31 March 20X6.** ▦            **(5 marks)**

**(Total: 20 marks)**

## 398   GREGORY

Gregory is a listed entity and, until 1 October 20X5, it had no subsidiaries. On that date, it acquired 75% of Tamsin's equity shares by means of a share exchange of two new shares in Gregory for every five acquired shares in Tamsin. These shares were recorded at the market price on the day of the acquisition and were the only shares issued by Gregory during the year ended 31 March 20X6.

The summarised financial statements of Gregory as a group at 31 March 20X6 and as a single entity at 31 March 20X5 are:

| | Gregory group | Gregory single entity |
|---|---|---|
| **Statements of profit or loss for the year ended** | 31 March 20X6 | 31 March 20X5 |
| | $000 | $000 |
| Revenue | 46,500 | 28,000 |
| Cost of sales | (37,200) | (20,800) |
| | | |
| Gross profit | 9,300 | 7,200 |
| Operating expenses | (1,800) | (1,200) |
| | | |
| Profit before tax (operating profit) | 7,500 | 6,000 |
| Income tax expense | (1,500) | (1,000) |
| | | |
| Profit for the year | 6,000 | 5,000 |
| | | |
| Profit for year attributable to: | | |
| Equity holders of the parent | 5,700 | |
| Non-controlling interest | 300 | |
| | | |
| | 6,000 | |

| | | |
|---|---|---|
| **Statements of financial position as at** | 31 March 20X6 | 31 March 20X5 |
| Assets | $000 | $000 |
| Non-current assets | | |
| Property, plant and equipment | 54,600 | 41,500 |
| Goodwill | 3,000 | nil |
| | | |
| | 57,600 | 41,500 |
| Current assets | 44,000 | 36,000 |
| | | |
| Total assets | 101,600 | 77,500 |

|  | 31 March 20X6 | 31 March 20X5 |
|---|---|---|
| Equity and liabilities | $000 | $000 |
| Equity |  |  |
| Equity shares of $1 each | 46,000 | 40,000 |
| Other component of equity (share premium) | 6,000 | nil |
| Retained earnings | 18,700 | 13,000 |
| Equity attributable to owners of the parent | 70,700 | 53,000 |
| Non-controlling interest | 3,600 | nil |
|  | 74,300 | 53,000 |
| Current liabilities | 27,300 | 24,500 |
| Total equity and liabilities | 101,600 | 77,500 |

Other information:

(i) Each month since the acquisition, Gregory's sales to Tamsin were consistently $2m. Gregory had chosen to only make a gross profit margin of 10% on these sales as Tamsin is part of the group.

(ii) The values of property, plant and equipment held by both entities have been rising for several years.

(iii) On reviewing the above financial statements, Gregory's chief executive officer (CEO) made the following observations:

(1) I see the profit for the year has increased by $1m which is up 20% on last year, but I thought it would be more as Tamsin was supposed to be very profitable.

(2) I have calculated the earnings per share (EPS) for 20X6 at 13 cents (6,000/46,000 × 100) and for 20X5 at 12.5 cents (5,000/40,000 × 100) and, although the profit has increased 20%, our EPS has barely changed.

(3) I am worried that the low price at which we are selling goods to Tamsin is undermining our group's overall profitability.

(4) I note that our share price is now $2.30, how does this compare with our share price immediately before we bought Tamsin?

**Required:**

(a) **Reply to the four observations of the CEO.** 🖥 **(8 marks)**

(b) **Using the above financial statements, calculate the following ratios for Gregory for the years ended 31 March 20X6 and 20X5 and comment on the comparative performance:** ▦ / 🖥

(i) **Return on capital employed (ROCE)**

(ii) **Net asset turnover**

(iii) **Gross profit margin**

(iv) **Operating profit margin.**

**Note:** Four marks are available for the ratio calculations. **(12 marks)**

**Note:** Your answers to (a) and (b) should reflect the impact of the consolidation of Tamsin during the year ended 31 March 20X6.

**(Total: 20 marks)**

## 399   LANDING

Landing is considering the acquisition of Archway, a retail entity. The summarised financial statements of Archway for the year ended 30 September 20X6 are:

### Statement of profit or loss

|  | $000 |
|---|---|
| Revenue | 94,000 |
| Cost of sales | (73,000) |
| Gross profit | 21,000 |
| Distribution costs | (4,000) |
| Administrative expenses | (6,000) |
| Finance costs | (400) |
| Profit before tax | 10,600 |
| Income tax expense (at 20%) | (2,120) |
| Profit for the year | 8,480 |

### Statement of financial position

|  | $000 | $000 |
|---|---|---|
| Non-current assets | | |
| Property, plant and equipment | | 29,400 |
| Current assets | | |
| Inventory | 10,500 | |
| Bank | 100 | 10,600 |
| Total assets | | 40,000 |
| Equity and liabilities | | |
| Equity shares of $1 each | | 10,000 |
| Retained earnings | | 8,800 |
| | | 18,800 |
| Current liabilities | | |
| 4% loan notes (redeemable 1 November 20X6) | 10,000 | |
| Trade payables | 9,200 | |
| Current tax payable | 2,000 | 21,200 |
| Total equity and liabilities | | 40,000 |

From enquiries made, Landing has obtained the following information:

(i)   Archway pays an annual licence fee of $1m to Cardol (included in cost of sales) for the right to package and sell some goods under a well-known brand name owned by Cardol. If Archway is acquired, this arrangement would be discontinued. Landing estimates that this would not affect Archway's volume of sales, but without the use of the brand name packaging, overall sales revenue would be 5% lower than currently.

(ii)    Archway buys 50% of its purchases for resale from Cardol, one of Landing's rivals, and receives a bulk buying discount of 10% off normal prices (this discount does not apply to the annual licence fee referred to in note (i) above). This discount would not be available if Archway is acquired by Landing.

(iii)   The 4% loan notes have been classified as a current liability due to their imminent redemption. As such, they should not be treated as long-term funding. However, they will be replaced immediately after redemption by 8% loan notes with the same nominal value, repayable in ten years' time.

(iv)    Landing has obtained some of Archway's retail sector average ratios for the year ended 30 September 20X6. It has then calculated the equivalent ratios for Archway as shown below:

|  | Sector average | Archway |
|---|---|---|
| Annual sales per square metre of floor space | $8,000 | $7,833 |
| Return on capital employed (ROCE) | 18.0% | 58.5% |
| Net asset (total assets less current liabilities) turnover | 2.7 times | 5.0 times |
| Gross profit margin | 22.0% | 22.3% |
| Operating profit (profit before interest and tax) margin | 6.7% | 11.7% |
| Gearing (debt/equity) | 30.0% | nil |

A note accompanying the sector average ratios explains that it is the practice of the sector to carry retail property at market value. The market value of Archway's retail property is $3m more than its carrying amount (ignore the effect of any consequent additional depreciation) and gives 12,000 square metres of floor space.

**Required:**

(a)    **After making adjustments to the financial statements of Archway which you think may be appropriate for comparability purposes, restate:**

(i)     **Revenue** ⊞

(ii)    **Cost of sales** ⊞

(iii)   **Finance costs** ⊞

(iv)    **Equity (assume that your adjustments to profit or loss result in retained earnings of $2.3 million at 30 September 20X6)** ⊞ **and**

(v)     **Non-current liabilities.** ⊞                                               **(5 marks)**

(b)    **Recalculate comparable sector average ratios for Archway based on your restated figures in (a) above.** ⊞                                              **(6 marks)**

(c)    **Comment on the performance and gearing of Archway compared to the retail sector average as a basis for advising Landing regarding the possible acquisition of Archway.** ⊞                                                          **(9 marks)**

**(Total: 20 marks)**

## 400  FUNJECT CO

Funject Co has identified Aspect Co as a possible acquisition within the same industry. Aspect Co is currently owned by the Gamilton Group and the following are extracts from the financial statements of Aspect Co:

**Extract from the statement of profit or loss for the year ended 31 December 20X4**

|  | $000 |
|---|---|
| Revenue | 54,200 |
| Cost of sales | (21,500) |
| Gross profit | 32,700 |
| Operating expenses | (11,700) |
| Operating profit | 21,000 |

**Statement of financial position as at 31 December 20X4**

|  | $000 | $000 |
|---|---|---|
| Non-current assets | | 24,400 |
| Current assets | | |
| Inventory | 4,900 | |
| Receivables | 5,700 | |
| Cash at bank | 2,300 | |
| | | 12,900 |
| Total assets | | 37,300 |
| Equity and liabilities | | |
| Equity shares | | 1,000 |
| Retained earnings | | 8,000 |
| | | 9,000 |
| Non-current liabilities: Loan | | 16,700 |
| Current liabilities | | |
| Trade payables | 5,400 | |
| Current tax payable | 6,200 | |
| | | 11,600 |
| Total equity and liabilities | | 37,300 |

Additional information:

(i)     On 1 April 20X4, Aspect Co decided to focus on its core business, and so disposed of a non-core division. The disposal generated a loss of $1.5m which is included within operating expenses for the year. The following extracts show the results of the non-core division for the period prior to disposal which were included in Aspect Co's results for 20X4:

|  | $000 |
|---|---|
| Revenue | 2,100 |
| Cost of sales | (1,200) |
| Gross profit | 900 |
| Operating expenses | (700) |
| Operating profit | 200 |

(ii)    At present Aspect Co pays a management charge of 1% of revenue to the Gamilton Group, which is included in operating expenses. Funject Co imposes a management charge of 10% of gross profit on all of its subsidiaries.

(iii)   Aspect Co's administration offices are currently located within a building owned by the Gamilton Group. If Aspect Co were acquired, the company would need to seek alternative premises. Aspect Co paid rent of $46,000 in 20X4. Commercial rents for equivalent office space would cost $120,000.

(iv)    The following is a list of comparable industry average key performance indicators (KPIs) for 20X4:

| KPI |  |
|---|---|
| Gross profit margin | 45% |
| Operating profit margin | 28% |
| Receivables collection period | 41 days |
| Current ratio | 1.6:1 |
| Acid test (quick) ratio | 1.4:1 |
| Gearing (debt/equity) | 240% |

**Required:**

**(a)    Redraft Aspect Co's statement of profit or loss for 20X4 to adjust for the disposal of the non-core division in note (i) and the management and rent charges which would be imposed per notes (ii) and (iii) if Aspect Co was acquired by Funject Co.** ⊞

(5 marks)

**(b)    Calculate the 20X4 ratios for Aspect Co equivalent to those shown in note (iv) based on the restated financial information calculated in part (a).**

**Note: You should assume that any increase or decrease in profit as a result of your adjustments in part (a) will also increase or decrease cash.** ⊞     (5 marks)

**(c)    Using the ratios calculated in part (b), comment on Aspect Co's 20X4 performance and financial position compared to the industry average KPIs provided in note (iv).** ⊞                                              (10 marks)

(Total: 20 marks)

# Section 4

# ANSWERS TO OBJECTIVE TEST QUESTIONS – SECTION A

## CONCEPTUAL FRAMEWORK/INTERNATIONAL FINANCIAL REPORTING STANDARDS

**1**

|  | Capitalise | Expense |
|---|:---:|:---:|
| Clearance of the site prior to commencement of construction | ✓ | |
| Professional surveyor fees for managing the construction work | ✓ | |
| EW's own staff wages for time spent working on construction | ✓ | |
| A proportion of EW's administration costs, based on staff time spent | | ✓ |

The allocation of EW's administration costs would not be included as these costs are not directly incurred as a result of carrying out the construction. All of the others are costs which would not have been incurred without the related asset being built.

**2** **B**

The cost of the decommissioning is assumed to be an obligation for the entity. An amount should be included in the cost of the asset when it is first recognised (1 July 20X4).

The amount to include in the cost of the asset for decommissioning costs is the present value of the expected future decommissioning costs. The present value is calculated by multiplying the expected future cost by a discount factor, which in this case is the discount factor for Year 5 (20X9) at 12%. $4 million × 0.567 = $2.268 million.

Therefore:

| Debit: | Cost of asset | $2.268 million |
|---|---|---|
| Credit: | Provision for decommissioning costs | $2.268 million |

The asset is depreciated on a straight-line basis over five years.

In addition, the decommissioning cost should be increased to $4 million by the end of Year 5. This is done by charging a finance cost each year. This is charged at the cost of capital (12%) and applied to the balance on the provision account. The finance charge for the year to 30 June 20X5 is 12% × $2.268 million = $272,160.

| Debit: | Finance cost | $272,160 |
|---|---|---|
| Credit: | Provision for decommissioning costs | $272,160 |

| | $ |
|---|---|
| Depreciation charge ($2.268 million/5 years) | 453,600 |
| Finance charge | 272,160 |
| Total charge | 725,760 |

If you selected A, you have included the depreciation without the finance cost. If you selected C, you have just spread the present value of the dismantling over 5 years. If you selected D, you have expensed the whole asset value.

**3    A**

| | Land $ million | Buildings $ million | Total $ million |
|---|---|---|---|
| Cost 1 July 20X3 | 1.00 | 5.00 | 6.00 |
| Building depreciation | | | |
| = $5 million/50 years = $0.1m per year × 2 | | (0.2) | (0.2) |
| Carrying amount 30 June 20X5 | 1.00 | 4.80 | 5.80 |
| Revaluation gain | 0.24 | 1.96 | 1.20 |
| Revalued amount | 1.24 | 5.76 | 7.00 |
| Building depreciation | | | |
| = $5.76 million/48 years = $0.12m per year × 2 | | (0.24) | (0.24) |
| Carrying amount 30 June 20X7 | 1.24 | 5.52 | 6.76 |
| Disposal proceeds | | | 6.80 |
| Gain on disposal | | | 0.04 |

The gain on disposal is $40,000. The $1.2 million balance on the revaluation reserve is transferred from the revaluation reserve to another reserve account (probably retained earnings) but is not reported through the statement of profit or loss for the year.

If you selected answer B, you have forgotten to record depreciation between 30 June 20X5 and 30 June 20X7. If you selected answer C, you have based the profit on the original depreciation. If you selected D, you have incorrectly transferred the remaining revaluation reserve into the statement of profit or loss.

**4    $900,000**

The grant should be released over the useful life, not based on the possibility of the item being repaid. Therefore the $1m should be released over 5 years, being a release of $200,000 a year. At 30 June 20X1, 6 months should be released, meaning $100,000 has been released ($6/12 × $200,000). This leaves $900,000 in deferred income.

**5    B**

This is a revenue grant, and would therefore be released to the statement of profit or loss over the 4 year life. By the end of year one, $250,000 would have been credited to the statement of profit or loss, leaving $750,000 held in deferred income.  At this point the amount is repaid, meaning that the deferred income is removed, as well as the $250,000 income previously recorded.

If you selected A, you have not removed the income that was released in the prior year. If you selected C, you have missed that $250,000 would have been released in the previous year. If you have chosen D, you have made errors over the deferring of the grant and that the repayment would be treated as an expense.

**6    B**

Asset A would be classed as a non-current asset held for sale under IFRS 5 *Non-current Assets Held for Sale and Discontinued Operations*.  Assets C and D would both be classified as property, plant and equipment per IAS 16 *Property, Plant and Equipment*.

**7    B**

The weighted average cost of borrowing is 7.33% (($1m × 6%) + ($2m × 8%))/$3m.

Therefore the amount to be capitalised = 7.33% × $600,000 × $^8/_{12}$ = $29,333.

If you selected A, you forgot to time apportion the borrowing costs for the construction period. If you selected D you have used 6% rather than the weighted average. If you selected C you have just used 7% as the average rather than calculating the weighted average.

**8**

|  | Statement 1 | Statement 2 |
|---|---|---|
| True | ✓ | |
| False | | ✓ |

IAS 16 (para 31) states that when the revaluation model is used, revaluations should be made with sufficient regularity to ensure that the carrying value of the assets remains close to fair value. IAS 16 also states (para 36) that, if one item in a class of assets is revalued, all the assets in that class must be revalued.

**9    A, B**

The maintenance and training costs should be expensed as incurred. The residual value should be taken into account for the purposes of calculating depreciation, but not for the amount to be capitalised.

**10    A**

Six months' depreciation is required on the building structure and air conditioning system.

|  | $000 |
|---|---|
| Land (not depreciated) | 2,000 |
| Building structure (10,000 – (10,000/25 × $^6/_{12}$)) | 9,800 |
| Air conditioning system (4,000 – (3,500/10 × $^6/_{12}$)) | 3,825 |
|  | ——— |
|  | 15,625 |
|  | ——— |

**11    C**

Six months' depreciation to the date of the revaluation will be $300,000 (12,000/20 years × $^6/_{12}$). Six months' depreciation from the date of revaluation to 31 March 20X5 would be $400,000 (10,800/13.5 years remaining life × $^6/_{12}$). Total depreciation is $700,000.

**12    B, C**

Item A is incorrect as the deferred income method can be used. Item D is incorrect as any repayment is corrected in the current period, not retrospectively.

**13    A**

Six months' depreciation should be accounted for up to 30 June 20X5, which is $100,000 expense ($10 million/50 years × $^6/_{12}$).

When the asset is transferred to investment property it should be revalued to the fair value of $11 million. At the date that the asset's use is changed, this gain should be recorded in other comprehensive income and in a revaluation surplus, not in the statement of profit or loss.

From this date, the fair value model is used. No depreciation is accounted for, but the asset will be revalued to fair value with gains or losses going through the statement of profit or loss. As there is a gain of $500,000 from June 20X5 to December 20X5, this would be included in the statement of profit or loss.

Therefore the total net income will be **$400,000**, being the $500,000 fair value gain less the depreciation expense of $100,000 for the first 6 months of the year.

**14    $602,500**

The interest can only be capitalised during the period of construction, which is from 1 February 20X6. Therefore the interest can be capitalised for 10 months, being from 1 February to 30 November 20X6. This gives $625,000 ($7.5 million × 10% × $^{10}/_{12}$).

Any temporary investment income earned during this period should be netted off the amount capitalised. The amount earned from 1 February to 1 May 20X6 is $22,500 ($2 million × 4.5% × $^3/_{12}$).

Therefore the amount to be capitalised is $625,000 – $22,500 = **$602,500**.

Note that all interest incurred and earned in January 20X6 is before the construction period and therefore is recorded in the statement of profit or loss.

**15**   **$1,000,000**

The fair value gain of $1 million ($9m – $8m) should be taken to the statement of profit or loss. Costs to sell are ignored and, since Croft uses the fair value model, no depreciation will be charged on the building.

**16**   **A**

The finance was only available after the year end. Therefore the criteria of recognising an asset were not met, as the resources were not available to complete the project.

Even though the brand is internally generated in the subsidiary's accounts, it can be recognised at fair value for the group. Item C can be recognised as a purchased intangible and item D meets the criteria for being capitalised as development costs.

**17**   **D**

Item A cannot be capitalised because it does not meet all the criteria as it is not viable.

Item B is research and cannot be capitalised.

Item C cannot be capitalised because it does not meet all the criteria as it is making a loss.

**18**   **B, C**

Key staff cannot be capitalised as firstly they are not controlled by an entity. Secondly, the value that one member of key staff contributes to an entity cannot be measured reliably.

**19**   **A**

The costs of $750,000 relate to ten months of the year (up to April 20X5). Therefore the costs per month were $75,000. As the project was confirmed as feasible on 1 January 20X5, the costs can be capitalised from this date. So four months of these costs can be capitalised = $75,000 × 4 = $300,000.

The asset should be amortised from when the products go on sale, so one month's amortisation should be charged to 30 June 20X5. Amortisation is ($300,000/5) × $1/12$ = $5,000. The carrying amount of the asset at 30 June 20X5 is $300,000 – $5,000 = $295,000.

If you chose C you have forgotten to amortise the development costs. If you chose B or D you have either capitalised the full amount or capitalised none of the costs.

**20**   **B**

The brand can be measured reliably, so this should be accounted for as a separate intangible asset on consolidation. The customer list cannot be valued reliably, and so will form part of the overall goodwill calculation. It will be subsumed within the goodwill value.

**21**   **D**

| | |
|---|---:|
| Write off to 1 January 20X4 to 28 February 20X4 (2 × $40,000) | $80,000 |
| Capitalise March to June = 4 × 40,000 = $160,000 | |
| Amortisation 160,000/5 years × $3/12$ (July to September) | 8,000 |
| | ——— |
| | 88,000 |
| | ——— |

**22    B**

A new process may produce benefits (and therefore be recognised as an asset) other than increased revenues, e.g. it may reduce costs.

**23    A**

In a cash generating unit, no asset should be impaired below its recoverable amount. The valuation of $2.5 million is an indication that the property is not impaired and should therefore be left at $2.3 million.

$2.5 million cannot be chosen as the entity uses the cost model. If you chose item C or D then you have impaired the asset.

**24    C**

The cash generating unit is impaired by $1,180,000, being the difference between the recoverable amount of $4 million and the total carrying values of the assets of $5,180,000. In a cash generating unit, no asset should be impaired below its recoverable amount, meaning that the property and other net assets are not impaired. The impairment is allocated to goodwill first, resulting in the entire $700,000 being written off. This leaves a remaining impairment of $480,000 to be allocated across plant and intangible assets.

This should be allocated on a pro-rata basis according to their carrying value. The plant and intangible assets have a total carrying value of $1,750,000 ($950,000 plant and $800,000 intangible assets). Therefore the impairment should be allocated to plant as follows:

$950,000/$1,750,000 × $480,000 = $261,000.

The carrying value of plant is therefore $950,000 – $261,000 = $689,000

If you selected D you have chosen the impairment rather than the carrying amount. If you selected A or B you have pro-rated the impairment over the property or other net assets as well as the plant and intangible assets.

**25    $6,500**

The recoverable amount of an asset is the higher of its value in use (being the present value of future cash flows) and fair value less costs to sell. Therefore the recoverable amount is $6,500.

**26    A**

Goodwill should be written off in full and the remaining loss is allocated pro rata to property plant and equipment and the product patent.

|  | Carrying amount $ | Impairment $ | Recoverable amount $ |
|---|---|---|---|
| Property, plant and equipment | 200,000 | (45,455) | 154,545 |
| Goodwill | 50,000 | (50,000) | nil |
| Product patent | 20,000 | (4,545) | 15,455 |
| Net current assets (at NRV) | 30,000 | nil | 30,000 |
|  | 300,000 | (100,000) | 200,000 |

**27   D**

Although the estimated net realisable value is lower than it was (due to fire damage), the entity will still make a profit on the inventory and thus it is not an indicator of impairment.

**28   $17,785**

|  | $ |
|---|---|
| Cost 1 October 20X9 | 100,000 |
| Depreciation 1 October 20X9 to 30 September 20Y4 ($100,000 \times {}^5/_{10}$) | (50,000) |
| Carrying amount | 50,000 |

The recoverable amount is the higher of fair value less costs to sell ($30,000) and the value in use ($8,500 \times 3.79 = $32,215$). Recoverable amount is therefore $32,215.

|  | $ |
|---|---|
| Carrying amount | 50,000 |
| Recoverable amount | (32,215) |
| Impairment to statement of profit or loss | 17,785 |

**29   $214,600**

Is the lower of its carrying amount ($217,000) and recoverable amount ($214,600) at 31 March 20X5.

Recoverable amount is the higher of value in use ($214,600) and fair value less costs to ($200,000).

Carrying amount = $217,000 (248,000 – (248,000 × 12.5%))

Value in use is based on present values = $214,600

**30   C**

Asset held for sale will be measured at lower of carrying amount and fair value less cost to sell. Once reclassified, the asset held for sale is not depreciated.

|  | $m |
|---|---|
| Cost | 45.0 |
| Depreciation to 30 September 20X3 | (6.0) |
| Depreciation to 1 April 20X4 ($45 \times {}^1/_{15} \times {}^6/_{12}$) | (1.5) |
| Carrying amount 1 April 20X4 | 37.5 |

Fair value less cost to sell = $36.8 million ((42,000 × 90%) – 1,000).

Therefore the asset is reported at $36.8 million.

**31    A**

Assets held for sale should be held at the lower of carrying value and fair value less costs to sell. Therefore the asset should be held at $750.

Item B is just the fair value. Item C is the fair value plus the costs to sell, which is incorrect. Item D is the carrying value.

**32    C**

A sale has to be expected within 12 months, not one month. The others are all criteria which must be met to classify an asset as held for sale.

**33**

|  | Shown on the face of the statement of profit or loss | Not shown |
|---|---|---|
| Revenue |  | ✓ |
| Gross profit |  | ✓ |
| Profit after tax | ✓ |  |

One line should be shown regarding profit from discontinued operations. This line is the profit after tax from the discontinued operation, with a full breakdown of the amount in the notes to the accounts.

**34**

|  | Discontinued operation Yes/No |
|---|---|
| Sector X | No |
| Sector Y | Yes |

Although Sector X is the only operation of Rural in Country A, it is not a separate major line of geographical operations, as it only contributes 0.5% of total revenue. Therefore Rural would not report this as a discontinued operation.

Sector Y is a separate major line of business operations, as it contributes a significant amount of Rural revenue, and produces a different item from the other parts of Rural. Therefore Rural would report Sector Y as a discontinued operation.

**35    B**

Although disclosing discontinued operations separately may help with business valuation, and understanding the business, the primary reason discontinued operations are separately presented is to enhance the predictive nature of the financial statements. Financial statements are historic, and this is a major limitation of them. Separating information about discontinued operations means that the users of the financial statements can use information about just the continuing operations when predicting the future performance of an entity.

**36    A**

The property would be depreciated by $25,000 (800,000/16 × $^6/_{12}$) for six months giving a carrying amount of $775,000 (800,000 − 25,000) before being classified as held-for-sale. This would also be the value at 31 March 20X5 as the property is no longer depreciated and is lower than its fair value less cost to sell.

**37    D**

The objectives of financial statements are set out in the IASB Framework. Note that providing information about changes in the financial position, as well as information about financial position and financial performance, is included within these objectives.

**38    B**

You should learn the IASB definitions of both assets and liabilities.  The definition in the question is in two parts: (1) a liability is a present obligation that has arisen out of a past event, and (2) it is certain or probable that settlement of this obligation will result in an outflow of economic benefits, such as a payment of money. It is also necessary for the amount of the liability to be measured reliably.

**39**

|  | **Faithful representation** | **Relevance** |
|---|:---:|:---:|
| Completeness | ✓ | |
| Predictive value | | ✓ |
| Neutrality | ✓ | |

Information that is relevant has predictive or confirmatory value. For information to have faithful representation, it must be complete, neutral and free from error.

**40    B, D**

It is important to learn that the two fundamental characteristics are relevance and faithful representation.

**41**

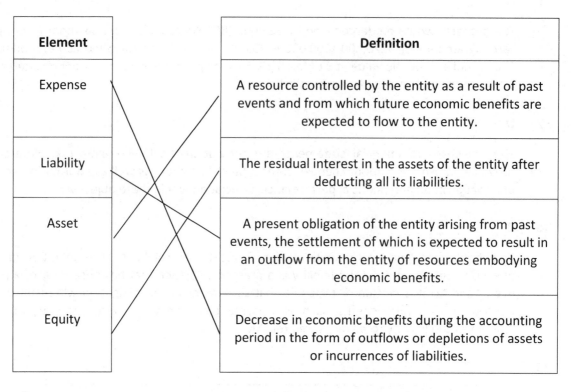

| Element | Definition |
|---|---|
| Expense | A resource controlled by the entity as a result of past events and from which future economic benefits are expected to flow to the entity. |
| Liability | The residual interest in the assets of the entity after deducting all its liabilities. |
| Asset | A present obligation of the entity arising from past events, the settlement of which is expected to result in an outflow from the entity of resources embodying economic benefits. |
| Equity | Decrease in economic benefits during the accounting period in the form of outflows or depletions of assets or incurrences of liabilities. |

**42    C**

Relevant information contains information which has both predictive and confirmatory value.

**43    D**

Faithful representation means presenting transactions according to their economic substance rather than their legal form. Items A to C all represent incorrect accounting treatments, and item D reflects that a sale and repurchase agreement with a bank is likely to represent a secured loan rather than a sale.

**44    B**

All other definitions include some part of the correct answer, but are incomplete.

**45    A**

There only has to be probable flow of economic benefits, rather than a certain flow. Also, the cost or value must be capable of reliable measurement, or no amount can be put into the financial statements.

**46    D**

Information is relevant if it influences the economic decisions of the users. The other definitions describe good treatment but are not explaining the concept of relevance.

**47**

|  | **True** | **False** |
|---|---|---|
| It is a principles-based framework | ✓ |  |
| It is a legal obligation |  | ✓ |

IFRS Standards are based on a principles-based framework, as they are based on the IASB's Conceptual Framework for Financial Reporting. It does not represent a legal obligation.

**48    D**

Harmonisation would not provide greater compatibility with legal systems, as legal systems differ worldwide. Greater compatibility would arise when a country develops its own accounting standards within the context of their specific legal framework.

**49    A, B, C**

A principles-based framework recognises that is not possible to draw up a set of rules to cover every eventuality and therefore does not attempt to do so. It is also harder to prove compliance as there are fewer prescriptive rules in place.

**50    D**

Where there is conflict between the conceptual framework and an IFRS Standard, the IFRS Standard will prevail. An example of this is IAS 20 *Government* grants, where deferred grant income is held as a liability, despite not satisfying the definition of a liability.

**51    C**

Receivables sold with recourse do not represent a transfer of control to the purchaser, as the purchaser does not carry the risk of irrecoverable debts. Thus the substance of the transaction is that the receivables have not been transferred and should not be derecognised.

**52    D**

The substance is that there is no free finance. Its cost is built into the selling price and this will represent a significant financing component.

**53    B**

By definition irredeemable preference shares do not have a contractual obligation to be repaid and thus do not meet the definition of a liability. They are therefore classed as equity.

**54    B**

Historical cost annual depreciation = $90,000 ((500,000 × 90%)/5 years).

After two years carrying amount would be $320,000 (500,000 – (2 × 90,000)).

Current cost annual depreciation = $108,000 ((600,000 × 90%)/5 years).

After two years carrying amount would be $384,000 (600,000 – (2 × 108,000)).

**55    A, C**

A is an onerous contract and C the provision is still required if there is no intention to sell.

**56    D**

As the receivable is 'sold' with recourse it must remain as an asset on the statement of financial position and is not derecognised.

**57    D**

As it is a new type of transaction, comparability with existing treatments is not relevant.

**58    B**

Historical cost is the easiest to verify as the cost can be proved back to the original transaction.  Fair value is often more difficult to verify as it may involve elements of estimation.

**59    C**

The prior period error is corrected by restating the comparative amounts for the previous period at their correct value. A note to the accounts should disclose the nature of the error, together with other details.

**60    B**

Level 3 inputs do include the best information available, but this is not regarded as the most reliable evidence of fair value, as level 1 inputs are likely to provide the most reliable evidence.

**61    B**

A change in the method of inventory valuation would be classed as a change in accounting policy under IAS 8.  The allowance for receivables, useful life and depreciation method are all accounting estimates.

**62    A, D**

A change in accounting policy may be made firstly if this is required by an IFRS Standard.  If there is no requirement, an entity can choose to change their accounting policy if they believe a new accounting policy would result in a more reliable and relevant presentation of events and transactions.

Entities cannot change their accounting policies simply to make financial reporting easier, or to try and show a more favourable picture of results.

**63**

|  | **Can be used** | **Cannot be used** |
|---|:---:|:---:|
| Historical cost | ✓ |  |
| Present value | ✓ |  |
| Realisable value | ✓ |  |

**64     A**

In times of rising prices, asset values will be understated, as historical cost will not be a true representation of the asset values. Additionally, the real purchase cost of replacement items will not be incorporated, meaning that profits are overstated.

B and D relate to asset values being overstated, which is incorrect. Unrecognised gains is irrelevant.

**65     D**

The capital maintenance concept aims to ensure that excess dividends are not paid in times of rising prices, by considering the effects of both inflation and specific price rises.

A, B and C are all key concepts regarding financial statements, but do not cover rising prices.

**66**

|  | **Change in accounting policy** | **Change in accounting estimate** |
|---|:---:|:---:|
| Classifying commission earned as revenue in the statement of profit or loss, having previously classified it as other operating income | ✓ |  |
| Revising the remaining useful life of a depreciable asset |  | ✓ |

A change of classification in presentation in financial statements is a change of accounting policy under IAS 8.

**67     B**

Item A is an adjustment when preparing consolidated financial statements. Item C is an accounting estimate, and item D is applying the same policy as previously, with a correction to the figure used.

**68     A**

IAS 10 defines adjusting events as those providing '**evidence of conditions existing at the end of the reporting period**' (IAS 10, para 3(a)). In the case of inventories, it may be sales of inventory in this period indicate that the net realisable value of some items of inventory have fallen below their cost and require writing down to their net realisable value as at 30 September 20X4.

**69**  **B**

The logs will be classed as inventory. The land will be classed as property, plant and equipment. The development costs will be treated as an intangible asset.

**70**  **B, D, E**

IAS 2 *Inventories* states that:

(a)  selling costs cannot be included in inventory cost, therefore item A cannot be included

(b)  general overheads cannot be included (item C)

(c)  overhead costs should be added to inventory cost on the basis of '**normal capacity of the production facilities**' (IAS 2, para 13), therefore item F cannot be included in cost

(d)  the cost of **factory** management and administration can be included, so that item D can be included in inventory values.

**71**  **$55,800**

|  | Cost | Net Realisable Value (NRV) | Lower of cost and NRV |
|---|---|---|---|
| Item 1 | $24,000 | (note 1) | $24,000 |
| Item 2 | $33,600 | $31,800 (note 2) | $31,800 |
|  |  |  | $55,800 |

**Notes:**

(1)  The recoverable amount is not known, but it must be above cost because the contract is 'expected to produce a high profit margin'. The subsequent fall in the cost price to $20,000 is irrelevant for the inventory valuation.

(2)  The recoverable amount is $36,000 minus 50% of $8,400.

**72**  **B**

The costs of inventory should include all costs of bringing inventory to its present location and condition, so Mario should include the raw material cost, import duties, direct labour, subcontracted labour and production overheads in its inventory.

Sales tax would not be included as it is recoverable.

Storage costs are specifically excluded from the value of inventory, as they are incurred once the inventory is ready to be sold.

Abnormal wastage costs are excluded from the valuation of inventory per IAS 2 *Inventories*.

**73    $970,000**

The normal selling price of the damaged inventory is $300,000 ($210,000/70%). This will now sell for $240,000 ($300,000 × 80%), less commission of $60,000 ($240,000 × 25%) to give a NRV of $180,000. The expected loss on the damaged inventory is $30,000 ($210,000 cost – $180,000 NRV) and therefore the total inventory should be valued at $970,000 ($1,000,000 – $30,000).

**74**

|  | **Accounted for under IAS 41** *Agriculture* | **Outside the scope of IAS 41** *Agriculture* |
|---|---|---|
| Dairy cattle | ✓ | |
| Milk | ✓ | |
| Cheese | | ✓ |

The cheese will be a product which is the result of processing after harvest, so will be outside the scope of IAS 41 *Agriculture*.

**75    D**

Biological assets should be revalued to fair value less point of sale costs at the year end, with the gain or loss being taken to the statement of profit or loss.

If you chose A, you have used the cost model. If you chose B or C, you have not deducted the point of sale costs.

**76    C**

Depreciation of leased plant $68,000 ($340,000/5 years)

Finance cost $25,000 (($340,000 – $90,000) × 10%)

Rental of equipment $13,500 ($18,000 × $^{9}/_{12}$)

Total $106,500.

**77    B**

|  | *B/f* | *Interest 7%* | *Payment* | *c/f* |
|---|---|---|---|---|
| Year end | $ | $ | $ | $ |
| 31 October 20X3 | 45,000 | 3,150 | (10,975) | 37,175 |
| 31 October 20X4 | 37,175 | 2,602 | (10,975) | 28,802 |

The figure to the right of the payment in the next year is the non-current liability. Once 20X4's payment has been made, $28,802 will still be owed, making this the non-current liability. The current liability will be the difference between the total liability of $37,175 and the non-current liability of $28,802, which is $8,373.

If you selected C, you chose the total year-end liability rather than the non-current liability. If you selected A, you deducted the payment of $10,975 from the total. If you selected D you recorded the payment in advance and chose the year end liability rather than the non-current liability.

**78    D**

Assets permitted to be exempted from recognition are low-value assets and those with a lease term of 12 months or less. The use of the asset is irrelevant, and, although IFRS 16 *Leases* does not define low-value, it is the cost when new that is considered rather than current fair value.

**79    A**

Initial value of lease liability is the present value of lease payments, $86,240.

|        | Balance b/f | Payment    | Subtotal | Interest @ 8% | Balance c/f |
|--------|-------------|------------|----------|---------------|-------------|
| 20X3   | 86,240      | (20,000)   | 66,240   | 5,299         | 71,539      |
| 20X4   | 71,539      | (20,000)   | 51,539   | 4,123*        | 55,662      |
| 20X5   | 55,662      | (20,000)*  | 35,662*  |               |             |

The non-current liability at 20X4 is the figure to the right of the payment in 20X5, $35,662. The current liability is the total liability of $55,662 less the non-current liability of $35,662, which is $20,000.

The finance cost is the figure in the interest column for 20X4, $4,123.

If you chose B you have done the entries for year one. If you chose C or D, you have recorded the payments in arrears, not in advance.

**80    C**

The transfer of ownership at the end of the lease indicates that Pigeon will have use of the asset for its entire life, and therefore 7 years is the appropriate depreciation period. Potential transactions at market rate would be ignored as they do not confer any benefit on Pigeon, and Pigeon's depreciation policy for purchased assets is irrelevant.

**81    A**

Reverse incorrect treatment of rental:

Dr Liability $210,000, Cr Retained Earnings $210,000

Charge asset depreciation ($635,000/5):

Dr Retained earnings $127,000, Cr Property, plant and equipment $127,000

Charge finance cost ($635,000 × 12.2%):

Dr Retained Earnings $77,470, Cr Liability $77,470

This gives a net adjustment of $5,530 to be credited to opening retained earnings.

If you selected B, you have missed the depreciation. If you selected C you have simply reversed the rental payment. If you selected D you assumed that the entries were correct.

**82    $58,000**

The asset would initially be capitalised at $87,000.  This is then depreciated over six years, being the shorter of the useful life and the lease term (including any secondary period).

This would give a depreciation expense of $14,500 a year.  After two years, accumulated depreciation would be $29,000 and therefore the carrying amount would be $58,000.

**83    A**

Sideshow is only leasing the asset for 5 years out of its remaining life of 20 years, so control of the asset has been passed to the purchaser.

The initial liability recognised will be the present value of lease rentals, $599,000, giving a finance cost for the year of $47,920 ($599,000 × 8%).

The proportion of the right-of-use asset retained by Sideshow will be equal to the initial liability as a proportion of the proceeds. So the initial value of the right-of-use asset will be

$(599,000/2,000,000) \times 1,600,000 = \$479,200$

Depreciation over 5 years would give an expense of $95,840.

The profit to be recognised on disposal can be calculated in one of two ways.

Create the initial recognition journal and calculate a balancing figure:

|  | Dr | Cr |
|---|---|---|
|  | $ | $ |
| Bank | 2,000,000 |  |
| Property, plant & equipment | 479,200 |  |
| Property plant & equipment |  | 1,600,000 |
| Lease liability |  | 599,000 |
| Profit on disposal (SPL) – balancing figure |  | 280,200 |

Alternatively the profit to be recognised could be calculated by taking the proportion of the asset not retained by Sideshow (i.e. difference between sale proceeds and lease liability):

$$\frac{(\$2,000,000 - \$599,000)}{\$2,000,000} \times (\$2,000,000 - \$1,600,000) = \$280,200$$

If you chose B you have not capitalised the leased asset.  If you chose C you recognised the full profit.  If you chose D you capitalised the asset at the present value of the lease payments.

**84    B**

| Year end | b/f $000 | Interest @ 10% $000 | Payment $000 | c/f $000 |
|---|---|---|---|---|
| 30 September 20X4 | 23,000 | 2,300 | (6,000) | 19,300 |
| 30 September 20X5 | 19,300 | 1,930 | (6,000) | 15,230 |

Current liability at 30 September 20X4 = 19,300,000 – 15,230,000 = $4,070,000

**85 D**

The value recognised in respect of the lease payments will be the present value of future lease payments rather than the total value.

**86 $1,090**

As Stark has retained control of the asset, the asset cannot be treated as sold, and will be retained at its carrying amount, depreciated over the remaining life of 10 years. The sale proceeds will effectively be treated as a loan of $7 million, on which interest will be charged at 7%. Therefore the following items will be included in the statement of profit or loss, all figures in $000:

Depreciation: $6,000/10 years = $600

Finance cost: $7,000 × 7% = $490

Total expense = $600 + $490 = $1,090

**87 B**

The loan notes should initially be recorded at their net proceeds, being the $100,000 raised less the $3,000 issue costs, giving $97,000. This should then be held at amortised cost, taking the effective rate of interest to the statement of profit or loss. The annual payment will be the coupon rate, which will be 5% × $100,000 = $5,000 a year.

Applying this to an amortised cost table gives $7,981, as shown below.

|  | B/f | Interest 8% | Payment | c/f |
|---|---|---|---|---|
|  | $ | $ | $ | $ |
| 20X4 | 97,000 | 7,760 | (5,000) | 99,760 |
| 20X5 | 99,760 | **7,981** |  |  |

If you chose C, you have done the calculation for 20X4. If you chose D, you have used 8% of the full $100,000 and done the calculation for 20X4. If you chose A, you have used 8% of the full $100,000.

**88 B**

The amount payable each year is based on the coupon rate of 7%, giving an amount of $210,000 payable each year ($3 million × 7%). This should be discounted at the market rate of interest of 9%, together with the capital repayment to find the value of the liability.

| | |
|---|---|
| Year 1 ($210,000 × 0.914) | 191,940 |
| Year 2 ($210,000 × 0.837) | 175,770 |
| Year 3 ($3,210,000 × 0.766) | 2,458,860 |
| Total present value of debt | **2,826,570** |
| Equity element (balance) | **173,430** |
| Total bond value | 3,000,000 |

If you chose A, you used the incorrect discount rate. If you chose C you forgot to calculate the repayment of $3 million. If you chose D you have not used split accounting.

**89    A**

The business model test must also be passed, which means that the objective is to hold the instrument to collect the cash flows rather than to sell the asset. The others are irrelevant.

**90    A**

The default position for equity investments is fair value through profit or loss, meaning the investment is revalued each year end, with the gain or loss being taken to the statement of profit or loss.

Fair value through other comprehensive income is the alternative position.

Amortised cost is an alternative treatment for debt instruments.

Net proceeds relates to financial liabilities.

**91    $9,500**

The investment should be classified as fair value through other comprehensive income.

As such, they will initially be valued inclusive of transaction costs.

Therefore, the initial value is 10,000 × $3.50 = $35,000 + $500 = $35,500.

At year-end, these will be revalued to fair value of $4.50 each, therefore 10,000 × $4.50 = $45,000.

The gain is therefore $45,000 – $35,500 = $9,500.

**92**

| Gain | | Where recorded |
|---|---|---|
| 18,750 | | Statement of profit or loss |

Financial assets held for trading will be valued at fair value through profit or loss. These are therefore valued excluding any transaction costs, which will be expensed to profit or loss.

The initial value of the investment is therefore 15,000 × $6.50 = $97,500

The shares will be revalued to fair value as at year-end, and the gain will be taken to profit or loss.  The year-end value of the shares is 15,000 × $7.75 = $116,250, giving a gain of $18,750. This is recognised within profit or loss.

**93    B**

Transaction costs are included when measuring all financial assets and liabilities at amortised cost, and when valuing financial assets valued at fair value through other comprehensive income.

Transaction costs for financial assets valued at fair value through profit or loss are expensed through the statement of profit or loss and not included in the initial value of the asset.

**94**   **$810,000**

| Year ended 30 September | Cash flow | Discount rate | Discounted cash flows |
|---|---|---|---|
| | $000 | at 8% | $000 |
| 20X4 | 500 | 0.93 | 465 |
| 20X5 | 500 | 0.86 | 430 |
| 20X6 | 10,500 | 0.79 | 8,295 |
| | | | ───── |
| Value of debt component | | | 9,190 |
| Equity (balance) | | | **810** |
| | | | ───── |
| Proceeds | | | 10,000 |
| | | | ───── |

**95**   **$768,000**

The initial liability should be recorded at the net proceeds of $9.6 million. The finance cost should then be accounted for using the effective rate of interest of 8%. Therefore the finance cost for the year is **$768,000** ($9.6 million × 8%).

**96**

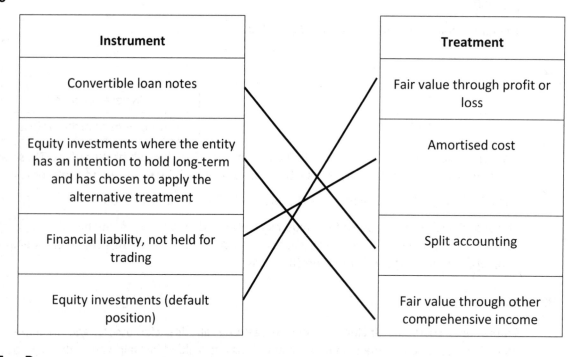

| Instrument | Treatment |
|---|---|
| Convertible loan notes | Fair value through profit or loss |
| Equity investments where the entity has an intention to hold long-term and has chosen to apply the alternative treatment | Amortised cost |
| Financial liability, not held for trading | Split accounting |
| Equity investments (default position) | Fair value through other comprehensive income |

**97**   **D**

Functional currency is defined as the currency of the primary economic environment in which an entity operates.

Answer A is the definition of presentation currency. Answer C is one of the primary methods of determining an entity's functional currency.

**98    A**

Overseas transactions are recorded in the functional currency using the spot rate of exchange. Therefore, the land is initially recorded at $10 million (30m dinars/3). Land is a non-monetary asset and so is not retranslated, meaning that its carrying amount remains at $10 million.

If you selected answer B then you retranslated the land at the closing rate of exchange. If you selected answer C then you translated the land at the average rate of exchange. If you selected answer D then you measured the land at its fair value, despite the fact that it is held using the cost model.

**99    B**

Statement (i) is false. Exchange gains and losses arising on the retranslation of monetary items are recognised in profit or loss in the period.

**100   $207,000**

The loan should initially be translated into dollars using the spot rate of 6.0.

The repayment of the loan should be translated using the spot rate of 5.0.

The outstanding loan at the reporting date is a monetary item so is retranslated using the closing rate of 5.6.

The exchange loss is calculated as follows:

|  | Dinar (000) | Rate | $000 |
|---|---|---|---|
| 1 January 20X1 | 12,000 | 6.0 | 2,000 |
| 30 November 20X1 | (3,000) | 5.0 | (600) |
| Foreign exchange loss | – |  | 207 |
| 31 December 20X1 | 9,000 | 5.6 | 1,607 |

**101   C**

The machine is recorded in the functional currency using the spot rate, giving an initial value of $10 million (20m dinars/2).

The machine is then depreciated over its useful life. By the reporting date, the carrying amount will be $9.5 million ($10m × 19/20). The machine is a non-monetary item held under a cost model so is not retranslated at the reporting date.

If you selected answer A then you have translated the depreciation at the closing rate of exchange. If you selected answer B then you have translated depreciation at the average rate of exchange. If you selected answer D then you have retranslated the machine at the closing rate of exchange.

**102  D**

The sale should be treated as a loan secured against the inventory. The inventory would remain with Mango, and a $500,000 loan would be recorded. This loan would incur interest at 10% a year. In year one $50,000 would therefore be recorded as a finance cost.

Answers A and B treat this as a sale, which is incorrect. Deferred income is not taken to the statement of profit or loss, so item C is incorrect.

**103  C**

Although the invoiced amount is $180,000, $30,000 of this has not yet been earned and must be deferred until the servicing work has been completed.

**104**

| | | $m |
|---|---|---:|
| Step 1 – Overall | | |
| Price | | 5.0 |
| Total cost | – incurred to date | (1.6) |
| | – estimated future | (2.4) |
| | | |
| Overall profit | | 1.0 |

Step 2 – Progress

Progress = work certified 1.8/total price 5 = 36%

Step 3 – Profit
Profit to recognise = $1m × 36% = $0.36m

| | $m |
|---|---:|
| Step 4 – Statement of financial position | |
| Costs to date | 1.60 |
| Profit to date | 0.36 |
| Less: Amount billed | (1.80) |
| | |
| Contract asset | 0.16 |

**105**

| Revenue | Cost of sales |
|:---:|:---:|
| $63 million | $83 million |

| | | $m |
|---|---|---:|
| Step 1 – Overall | | |
| Price | | 90 |
| Total cost | – incurred to date | (77) |
| | – estimated future | (33) |
| | | |
| Overall **loss** | | (20) |

Step 2 – Progress

Progress = work certified 63/total price 90 = 70%

|  | $m |
|---|---|
| Step 3 – SPL | |
| Revenue (70% of 90) | 63 |
| Cost of sales (balancing figure to recognise full loss) | (83) |
| **FULL** loss to be recognised immediately | (20) |

## 106 $90

The discount should be allocated to each part of the bundled sale. Applying the discount across each part gives revenue as follows:

| Goods | $50 | ($75 × $100/$150) |
|---|---|---|
| Installation | $20 | ($30 × $100/$150) |
| Service | $30 | ($45 × $100/$150) |

The revenue in relation to the goods and installation should be recognised on 1 May 20X1. As 8 months of the service has been performed (from 1 May to 31 December 20X1), then $20 should be recognised ($30 × $^8/_{12}$).

This gives a total revenue for the year of 50 + 20 + 20 = $90.

## 107

| Step | Correct order |
|---|---|
| Identify the separate performance obligations within a contract | Identify the contract |
| Identify the contract | Identify the separate performance obligations within a contract |
| Determine the transaction price | Determine the transaction price |
| Recognise revenue when (or as) a performance obligation is satisfied | Allocate the transaction price to the performance obligations in the contract |
| Allocate the transaction price to the performance obligations in the contract | Recognise revenue when (or as) a performance obligation is satisfied |

**108  D**

| | | $m |
|---|---|---|
| Price | | 40 |
| Total cost | – incurred to date | (16) |
| | – estimated future | (18) |
| | | ___ |
| Overall profit | | 6 |
| | | ___ |

Progress = 45%

| | $m |
|---|---|
| Revenue (45% of 40) | 18.0 |
| Cost of sales (45% of total costs of 34) | (15.3) |
| | ___ |
| Gross profit | 2.7 |
| | ___ |

Items A and B incorrectly include the full revenue. Item C includes the actual costs to date incorrectly.

**109  $30,000**

| | $ |
|---|---|
| Contract price | 200,000 |
| Total contract cost (130,000 + 20,000) | (150,000) |
| | _____ |
| Estimated total profit | 50,000 |
| | _____ |

Progress 180,000/200,000 = 90%

| | |
|---|---|
| Profit earned = 50,000 × 90% = | 45,000 |
| Recognised in previous year | (15,000) |
| | _____ |
| Current year profit | 30,000 |
| | _____ |

**110  B**

For item B the sale of the goods has fulfilled a contractual obligation so the revenue in relation to this can be recognised.  The service will be recognised over time, so the revenue should be deferred and recognised as the obligation is fulfilled.

For item A Hatton acts as an agent, so only the commission should be included in revenue.

For item C any profit or loss on disposal should be taken to the statement of profit or loss. The proceeds should not be included within revenue.

For item D the $1 million should be initially discounted to present value as there is a significant financing component within the transaction. The revenue would initially be recognised at $826,000, with an equivalent receivable. This receivable would then be held at amortised cost with finance income of 10% being earned each year.

**111** **$500,000**

|  | $000 |
|---|---|
| Costs to date | 4,500 |
| Loss | (2,000) |
| Less:  Amount billed | (3,000) |
| | |
| Contract liability | (500) |

As the contract is loss-making, Sugar should record the full loss immediately.

**112** **A**

Using the work certified basis, the progress of this contract is 1,050/1,500= 70%.

Therefore 70% of the total contract costs should be recognised, giving 800 × 70% = $560,000.

As $240,000 of costs were recognised in the prior year, costs of $320,000 ($560,000 – $240,000) should be recognised in the current year statement of profit or loss.

**113** **A**

| | |
|---|---|
| Contract price | 1,000,000 |
| Total contract cost (530,000 + 170,000) | (700,000) |
| | |
| Estimated total profit | 300,000 |
| | |
| Progress 600,000/1,000,000 = 60% | |
| Revenue (60% × 1,000,000) | 600,000 |
| Cost of sales (60% × 700,000) | (420,000) |
| | |
| Profit | 180,000 |
| | |
| Costs to date | 530,000 |
| Profit to date | 180,000 |
| Less: amount billed | (600,000) |
| | |
| Contract asset | 110,000 |

**114** **D**

At 31 March 20X5, the deferred consideration of $12,650 would need to be discounted by 10% for one year to $11,500 (effectively deferring a finance cost of $1,150). The total amount credited to profit or loss would be $24,150 (12,650 + 11,500).

**115  D**

The tax expense in the statement of profit or loss is made up of the current year estimate, the prior year overprovision and the movement in deferred tax. The prior year overprovision must be deducted from the current year expense, and the movement in deferred tax must be added to the current year expense, as the deferred tax liability has increased.

Tax expense = $60,000 – $4,500 + $600 = $56,100

If you chose A, you have deducted the movement in deferred tax, even though the liability has increased. If you chose C you have added the overprovision. If you chose B you have added the overprovision and the closing deferred tax liability.

**116**

| Statement of profit or loss | Statement of financial position |
|:---:|:---:|
| $88,000 | $83,000 |

The tax expense in the statement of profit or loss is made up of the current year estimate and the prior year underprovision. The year-end liability in the statement of financial position is made up of the current year estimate only.

Tax expense = $83,000 + $5,000 underprovision from previous year = $88,000

Tax liability = $83,000 year end estimate only.

**117  C**

| | |
|---|---|
| Deferred tax provision required | 9,000 (30,000 × 30%) |
| Opening balance per trial balance | 12,000 |
| | ———— |
| Reduction in provision | (3,000) |
| | ———— |

**Tax expense:**

| | |
|---|---|
| Current year estimate | 15,000 |
| Prior year overprovision | (4,000) |
| Deferred tax, as above | (3,000) |
| | ———— |
| Charge for year | 8,000 |
| | ———— |

If you chose A, you have added in the full deferred tax liability. If you chose B you have added the full liability and the overprovision. If you chose D, you have not dealt with the overprovision.

**118  A**

| | |
|---|---|
| Deferred taxation increase | 7,000  (23,000 – 16,000) |
| Less  tax on revaluation gain | (3,000) recognised as OCI (10,000 × 30%) |
| | ———— |
| Charge to SPL | 4,000 |
| | ———— |

**Tax expense:**

| | |
|---|---|
| Current year estimate | 12,000 |
| Prior year overprovision | (7,000) |
| Deferred tax, as above | 4,000 |
| | ———— |
| Charge for year | 9,000 |
| | ———— |

If you chose B, you have used the full deferred tax increase. If you chose C you have added the overprovision. If you chose D you have deducted the deferred tax movement.

**119  89.1¢**

EPS = $3,000,000/3,366,667 (W1) = 89.1¢

**(W1)  Weighted average number of shares**

Step 1 – Theoretical ex-rights price (TERP)

| | |
|---|---|
| 2 shares @ $2 = | $4.00 |
| 1 share @ $1.40 = | $1.40 |
| | ——— |
| 3 shares | $5.40 |

**TERP = $5.40/3 = $1.80**

Step 2 – Rights fraction = 2/1.8

Step 3 – Weighted average number of shares (WANS)

| Date | Number | Fraction of year | Rights fraction | Weighted average |
|---|---|---|---|---|
| 1 January | 2,400,000 | 3/12 | 2/1.8 | 666,667 |
| 1 April | 3,600,000 | 9/12 | | 2,700,000 |
| | | | | ————— |
| | | | | 3,366,667 |
| | | | | ————— |

**120  A**

EPS = $2,000,000/4,250,000 (W1) = 47.1¢

**(W1)  Weighted average number of shares**

| Date | Number | Fraction of year | Bonus fraction | Weighted average |
|---|---|---|---|---|
| 1 January | 3,000,000 | 5/12 | 4/3 | 1,666,667 |
| 1 June | 4,000,000 | 4/12 | | 1,333,333 |
| 30 September | 5,000,000 | 3/12 | | 1,250,000 |
| | | | | _____ |
| | | | | 4,250,000 |
| | | | | _____ |

If you chose C or D, you have failed to apply the bonus fraction correctly. If you chose B you have ignored the bonus fraction.

**121  75¢**

The prior year earnings per share figure must be restated by the inverse of the rights fraction that relates to the current year earnings per share calculation.

The current year rights fraction is calculated below.

Step 1 – Theoretical ex-rights price (TERP)

| | |
|---|---|
| 3 shares @ $2.20 = | $6.60 |
| 1 share @ $1.40 = | $1.60 |
| | _____ |
| 4 shares | $8.20 |

**TERP = $8.20/4 = $2.05**

Step 2 – Rights fraction

$$\frac{2.20}{2.05}$$

Therefore the restated earnings per share figure is 81c × 2.05/2.20 = 75¢.

**122  D**

Diluted EPS is calculated as 10,644,000/7,250,000 = 146.8¢

| The earnings adjustment is: | $ | |
|---|---|---|
| Earnings for basic EPS | 10,500,000 | |
| Plus interest saved (2.5m × 8%) | 200,000 | |
| Less tax (200,000 × 28%) | (56,000) | |
| Earnings for Diluted EPS | 10,644,000 | |
| | | |
| Shares for basic EPS | 6,000,000 | |
| Shares issued on conversion | 1,250,000 | (2,500,000/100) × 50 |
| Shares for diluted EPS | 7,250,000 | |

**123 C**

To calculate diluted earnings per share with an option, you need to work out the number of 'free' shares that will be issued if the options are exercised, and add that to the weighted average number of shares.

If the options are exercised, $3 million will be received ($3 × 1 million options).

At the market value of $5, $3 million would buy 600,000 shares ($3m/$5).

Therefore the cash received is the equivalent of 600,000 shares. As there are 1 million options, this means that 400,000 shares are being issued for free.

Diluted EPS = $2m/(4 million + 400,000) = **45.5¢**

**124 $2,250,000**

The Earnings figure for the EPS calculation is the profit attributable to the parent shareholders.

**125 A, E**

Redeemable preference dividends will already have been removed from net profit when arriving at this figure in a statement of profit or loss. Therefore this adjustment is not necessary. Dividends are simply the cash paid out of the earnings, and are often compared to the earnings per share. All the other items will need to be removed from the overall net profit figure in the statement of profit or loss.

**126**

| Considered within DEPS | Considered within Basic EPS |
|---|---|
| The issue during the year of a convertible (to equity shares) loan note | A 1 for 5 rights issue of equity shares during the year at $1.20 when the market price of the equity shares was $2.00 |
| The granting during the year of directors' share options exercisable in three years' time | Equity shares issued during the year as the purchase consideration for the acquisition of a new subsidiary |

**127 B**

A and D will give the same impression as overall profit for the year. C is incorrect as diluted EPS is not an indication of future profit.

**128 A**

(1,550/((2,500 × 2) + 1,200 see below))

2 million shares at $1.20 = $2.4 million which would buy 800,000 shares at full price of $3. Therefore, dilution element (free shares) is 1,200,000 (2,000 – 800).

**129**

| Legal action against AP | Legal action by AP |
|:---:|:---:|
| Provision | Contingent asset |

The legal action against AP has a probable outflow, so AP should make a provision. The legal action taken by AP is a contingent asset. As it is probable, it should be disclosed in a note. Assets should only be recognised when there is a virtually certain inflow.

**130 C**

A provision is only required when there is a present obligation arising as a result of a past event, it is probable that an outflow of resources embodying economic benefits will be required to settle the obligation, and a reliable estimate can be made of the amount. Only answer C meets all these criteria. Answer A is incorrect because the obligation does not exist at the reporting date and also cannot be reliably measured at present. Answer B is an example of an adjusting event after the reporting date as it provides evidence of conditions existing at the reporting. Answer D is a contingent liability. However, as its likelihood is remote no provision is necessary.

**131 C**

The warehouse fire is an adjusting event as it occurred before the reporting date. Settlement of the insurance claim should therefore be included in the financial statements.

The other events are non-adjusting as they occurred after the reporting date and do not provide evidence of conditions existing at the reporting date. Issue B is a brand new event, and therefore should not be adjusted. As it is clearly material the event should be disclosed in the notes to the accounts.

**132 $3,500,000**

Per IAS 37 *Provisions, Contingent Liabilities and Contingent Assets*, the amount payable relates to a past event (the sale of faulty products) and the likelihood of payout is probable (i.e. more likely than not). Hence, the full amount of the payout should be provided for.

**133 B**

The costs associated with ongoing activities (relocation and retraining of employees) should not be provided for.

**134 B**

Extraction provision at 30 September 20X4 is $2.5 million (250 × 10).

Dismantling provision at 1 October 20X3 is $20.4 million (30,000 × 0.68).

This will increase by an 8% finance cost by 30 September 20X4 = $22,032,000.

Total provision is $24,532,000.

**135 B, C**

The change in tax rate and the fire will be non-adjusting events as the conditions did not exist at the reporting date.

**136**

|  | Adjusting | Non-adjusting |
|---|:---:|:---:|
| A public announcement in April 20X5 of a formal plan to discontinue an operation which had been approved by the board in February 20X5. |  | ✓ |
| The settlement of an insurance claim for a loss sustained in December 20X4. | ✓ |  |

A board decision to discontinue an operation does not create a liability. A provision can only be made on the announcement of a formal plan (as it then raises a valid expectation that the action will be carried out). As this announcement occurs during the year ended 31 March 20X6, this a non-adjusting event for the year ended 31 March 20X5.

The insurance claim was in existence at the year end, so this will be an adjusting event as it provides further evidence of conditions in existence.

**137  D**

Deferred tax relating to the revaluation of an asset must be provided for even if there is no intention to sell the asset in accordance with IAS 12 *Income Taxes*.

**138**

|  | True | False |
|---|:---:|:---:|
| IAS 10 *Events After the Reporting Period* covers the period from the reporting date to the annual general meeting |  | ✓ |
| According to IAS 10 *Events After the Reporting Period*, any non-adjusting event should be disclosed as a note in the financial statements |  | ✓ |

Both are false. IAS 10 *Events After the Reporting Period* covers the period from the reporting date up to the date the financial statements are authorised for issue. Only material non-adjusting events need to be disclosed as notes in the financial statements.

**139**

| There is a present obligation from a past event | No |
|---|:---:|
| A reliable estimate can be made | Yes |
| There is a probable outflow of economic benefits | Yes |

Whilst there is an estimate of $500,000 and it is probable that Faubourg will make the changes, there is no present obligation at 31 December 20X4.

If Faubourg changes its mind and sells the building prior to June 20X5, no obligation would arise. Future obligations are not accounted for as provisions.

**140  A, D**

Changes in provisions are regarded as changes in accounting estimates so should be accounted for prospectively rather than retrospectively.

Provisions should be recorded at the best estimate, reflecting the amount most likely to be paid out, rather than the highest possible liability.

# CONSOLIDATED FINANCIAL STATEMENTS

**141**

|  | Consolidated | Not to be consolidated |
|---|---|---|
| Beta is a bank and its activity is so different from the engineering activities of the rest of the group that it would be meaningless to consolidate it. | ✓ | |
| Delta is located in a country where local accounting standards are compulsory and these are not compatible with IFRS Standards used by the rest of the group. | ✓ | |
| Gamma is located in a country where a military coup has taken place and Petre has lost control of the investment for the foreseeable future. | | ✓ |

The investment in Gamma no longer meets the definition of a subsidiary (ability to control) and therefore would not be consolidated.

**142  A**

Is the correct treatment for a bargain purchase (negative goodwill).

**143  C**

While having the majority of shares may be a situation which leads to control, it does not feature in the definition of control per IFRS 10 *Consolidated Financial Statements*.

**144  D**

At 31 December 20X2 the deferred consideration needs to be discounted to present value by one year.

$200,000/1.1 = $181,818

If you chose C, you have not discounted the consideration. If you chose A, you have not unwound the discount. If you chose B, you have only done the first year calculation.

**145  $371,000**

To work out the net assets at acquisition, the retained earnings at acquisition must be calculated.

The retained earnings at the end of the year are given as $180,000, and there has been a profit of $36,000 for the year.

As Philip has owned Stanley for 3 months, then 3 months of this profit is regarded as post-acquisition. Therefore $9,000 has been made since acquisition.

Once this has been worked out, the retained earnings at acquisition can be calculated by deducting the post-acquisition retained earnings of $9,000 from the closing retained earnings of $180,000 to give $171,000.

Net assets at acquisition = $200,000 share capital + $171,000 retained earnings = $371,000.

**146  $2,780,000**

The cost of investment is worked out as follows:

Shares: 800,000 × ¾ × $3.80 = $2,280,000

Deferred cash = $550,000 × $^1/_{1.1}$ = $500,000

The professional fees cannot be capitalised as part of the cost of investment. Therefore the total cost of investment is $2,280,000 + $500,000 = **$2,780,000**

**147  B**

The profit on the $800,000 sale is $160,000 ($800,000 × $^{25}/_{125}$).

As 75% of the goods have been sold on to third parties, 25% remain in inventory at the year end. Unrealised profits only arise on goods remaining in inventory at the year end, so the unrealised profit is $40,000 ($160,000 × 25%).

**148  $352,000**

The unrealised profit on the non-current asset transfer needs to be removed.

The carrying amount at the year-end after the transfer is $32,000 ($40,000 less 1 year's depreciation).

The carrying amount of the asset if it had not been transferred would have been $24,000 ($30,000 less 1 year's depreciation).

Therefore the unrealised profit on the non-current asset is $8,000 ($32,000 – $24,000)

The total property, plant and equipment is $300,000 + $60,000 – $8,000 = **$352,000**.

**149  B, E**

The fact that unanimous consent is required would suggest that there is no control over the investee. Preference shares carry no voting rights and therefore are excluded when considering the control held over an investee.

**150**

|  | Include in cost of investment | Do not include in the cost of investment |
|---|---|---|
| An agreement to pay a further $30,000 if the subsidiary achieves an operating profit of over $100,000 in the first 3 years after acquisition | ✓ |  |
| Professional fees of $10,000 in connection with the investment |  | ✓ |

Any incidental costs associated with the acquisition should be expensed as incurred. Contingent consideration can all be included as part of the cost of an investment in a subsidiary.

**151 D**

All of Paul's revenue and expenses will be time-apportioned from the date of acquisition to the date of consolidation to reflect the period for which these were controlled by Peter.

**152 A**

The asset has not been sold outside of the group and therefore there is an unrealised profit to adjust for on consolidation.

**153**

|  | True | False |
|---|---|---|
| It will always be deducted in full from the parent retained earnings |  | ✓ |
| It will be apportioned between the parent and the non-controlling interest (NCI) when the NCI is valued at fair value | ✓ |  |

Where the NCI is valued at fair value, the goodwill impairment will be split between the parent and the NCI in accordance with their shareholdings.

**154 A**

The activities of the subsidiary are irrelevant when making the decision as to whether to produce consolidated financial statements or not.

**155 $160m**

|  | $000 |  |
|---|---|---|
| Consideration – shares | 100,000 | (see below) |
| Consideration – cash | 60,000 |  |

Branch purchased 75% of Leaf's 80 million shares, giving them 60 million shares. Branch issued 2 shares for every 3 purchased, meaning 40 million shares have been issued (60m × 2/3). At a market value of $2.50 each, 40 million shares have a value of $100 million.

**156 $108,000**

NCI % × S's PAT = 20% × $600k = $120k

NCI% × PUP (S selling to P) = 20% × 60k = ($12k)

Total NCI = $120k – $12k = **$108k**

**157  D**

Cost of sales = $14.7m + $8.7m ($^9/_{12}$ × $11.6m) – $4.3m (intra-group sale) + $0.2m (PUP) = **$19.3m**

The PUP is $2.2m × $^{10}/_{110}$ = $0.2m.

If you chose B, you have not time-apportioned the results. If you chose A you have deducted the PUP rather than adding it. If you chose C, you have missed the PUP.

**158  $970,000**

Operating expenses = $600,000 + $350,000 + $20,000 (FV depreciation) = $970,000

The only adjustments to the statement of profit or loss should be the current year income or expenses. Therefore the prior year fair value depreciation and goodwill impairment are ignored.

**159  B**

The finance costs for the subsidiary must be time apportioned for six months, as A has only owned them for that period of time. Also, the intra-group interest must be split out. The intra-group interest would not have existed in the first half of the year, as the loan was only given to B in July.

The intra-group interest for the second 6 months would have been $20,000 ($500,000 × 8% × $^6/_{12}$). Without this, B's finance costs would have been $50,000 for the year. Splitting this evenly across the year would mean that $25,000 was incurred in each six month period.

Therefore the total finance costs would be $200,000 + $25,000 = **$225,000**.

**160  A**

|  | Impacts the NCI share of profit | Does not impact the NCI share |
|---|---|---|
| Goodwill impairment | ✓ | |
| The parent transferring an item of inventory to the subsidiary for $10,000 greater than its carrying amount, all of which remains in the group at the year end | | ✓ |
| The subsidiary having an item of plant with a fair value of $500,000 above its carrying amount, and a remaining life of 10 years | ✓ | |

The parent transferring inventory at a profit would mean that the parent's profits are overstated. This would have no impact on the non-controlling interest.

**161  $6,600,000**

Consolidated revenue: AB $5.5m + CD $2.1m – $1m intra-group= $6.6 million

All intra-group sales and cost of sales are removed from the group accounts.

**162 B**

The dividend would not have been in Allen's statement of profit or loss, so no adjustment to this would be made. The adjustment to remove the dividend would be made in investment income, where Burridge will have recorded the income in its individual financial statements.

The profit needs to be time-apportioned for the six months of ownership, with the $10,000 impairment then deducted.

Share of profit of associate = 30% × $200,000 ($400,000 × 6/12) – $10,000 = **$50,000**

If you chose D, you have not time-apportioned the associate. If you chose C, you have not deducted the impairment. If you chose A, you have only recognised 30% of the impairment.

**163 B**

Beasant own 30% of Arnie's shares, which is 30,000 shares (30% of Arnie's 100,000 shares).

As Beasant issued 1 share for every 3 purchased, Beasant issued 10,000 shares. These had a market value of $4.50 and were therefore worth $45,000.

In valuing an associate Beasant must include 30% of Arnie's post-acquisition movement in net assets. Arnie has made a post-acquisition loss of $40,000 (net assets at acquisition were $500,000 and net assets at 31 December were $460,000). Therefore Beasant's share of this is a $12,000 loss (30%).

| | |
|---|---|
| Cost of investment | $45,000 |
| Share of post-acquisition loss | ($12,000) |
| | ――――― |
| Investment in associate | $33,000 |
| | ――――― |

If you chose D, you based the consideration on 30,000 shares rather than 10,000. If you chose C, you have ignored share capital from the net assets movement. If you chose A, you have used the wrong share price for consideration.

**164**

| | Single entity concept | Going concern concept |
|---|:---:|:---:|
| Removing unrealised profits on group sales | ✓ | |
| Removing intra-group balances | ✓ | |

**165**

| | |
|---|---|
| 30% of the share capital of Hansen Co. The other 70% is owned by Lawro, another listed entity, whose directors make up Hansen's board. | Subsidiary |
| 80% of the share capital of Kennedy Co, whose activities are significantly different from the rest of the Nicol group. | Associate |
| 30% of the share capital of Bruce Co. The Nicol group have appointed 2 of the 5 board members of Bruce Co, with the other board members coming from three other entities. | Investment |

Normally 30% would suggest that Nicol have significant influence, making Hansen an associate. However, Lawro having 70% and controlling the entire board would mean that it is unlikely that Nicol have influence and therefore treat it as a trade investment.

**166  A**

| | $ |
|---|---|
| Cost of Investment | 5,500,000 |
| Badger % of post-acquisition profits | 46,875 |
| $30\% \times (625,000 \times {}^{3}/_{12})$ | |
| **Total** | **5,546,875** |

**167  $325,000**

| | $ |
|---|---|
| Share of Net Profit: $30\% \times 1,500,000$ | 450,000 |
| Share of PUP: $30\% \times ((2m \times 50\%) \times 30\%)$ | (90,000) |
| Current year impairment | (35,000) |
| **Total** | **325,000** |

**168  A**

IFRS 10 *Consolidated Financial Statements* states that where the reporting date for a parent is different from that of a subsidiary, the subsidiary should prepare additional financial information as of the same date as the financial statements of the parent unless it is impracticable to do so.

If it is impracticable to do so, IFRS 10 allows use of subsidiary financial statements made up to a date of not more than three months earlier or later than the parent's reporting date, with due adjustment for significant transactions or other events between the dates.

The companies do not have to have the same policies in their individual financial statements, but adjustments will be made to prepare the consolidated financial statements using the group policies.

Only the profit relating to goods remaining in the group at year end needs to be adjusted.

**169  A, B**

Items C and D would signify control.

**170 C, D**

While the same accounting policies must be used in the consolidated financial statements, the subsidiaries do not have to operate the same policies as the parent. Having different activities is not an acceptable reason for non-consolidation.

**171 B**

| | $000 |
|---|---|
| Cost (240,000 × $6) | 1,440 |
| Share of associate's profit (400 × $^6/_{12}$ × 240/800) | 60 |
| | ––––– |
| | 1,500 |
| | ––––– |

**172 $63,800,000**

| | $000 |
|---|---|
| Viagem | 51,200 |
| Greca (26,000 × $^9/_{12}$) | 19,500 |
| Intra-group purchases (800 × 9 months) | (7,200) |
| URP in inventory (1,500 × $^{25}/_{125}$) | 300 |
| | ––––– |
| | 63,800 |
| | ––––– |

**173 C**

Market price of Sact's shares at acquisition was $2.50 ($3 × $^{100}/_{120}$), therefore non-controlling interest (NCI) at acquisition was $50,000 (100,000 × 20% × $2.50). NCI share of the post-acquisition profit is $6,000 (40,000 × $^9/_{12}$ × 20%). Therefore non-controlling interest as at 31 March 20X5 is $56,000.

**174 C**

Germaine only owns 40% of Foll's voting shares so is unlikely to exercise control.

**175 $546,000**

| | $ |
|---|---|
| Wilmslow | 450,000 |
| Post-acquisition Zeta ((340 – 200) × 80%) | 112,000 |
| Inventory PUP (320,000 × ¼ × $^{25}/_{125}$) | (16,000) |
| | ––––– |
| | 546,000 |
| | ––––– |

**176  C, D**

The fair value of deferred consideration is its present value. Fair values are applied to the subsidiary's assets, liabilities and contingent liabilities.

While the use of fair value seems to not comply with the historical cost principle, this will effectively form part of the cost of the subsidiary to the parent, so the principle is still applied. Depreciation will not increase if the fair value of assets is lower than the current carrying amount. Patents can be recorded as intangible assets as they are separable.

**177**

|  | True | False |
|---|---|---|
| The profit made by a parent on the sale of goods to a subsidiary is only realised when the subsidiary sells the goods to a third party | ✓ | |
| Eliminating intra-group unrealised profits never affects non-controlling interests | | ✓ |
| The profit element of goods supplied by the parent to an associate and held in year-end inventory must be eliminated in full | | ✓ |

**178  $1,335,000**

|  | $000 | |
|---|---|---|
| Investment at cost | 1,200 | |
| Share of post-acq profit | 150 | $(750 \times {}^{8}/_{12} \times 30\%)$ |
| Inventory PUP | (15) | $(300 \times {}^{20}/_{120} \times 30\%)$ |
| | 1,335 | |

**179  $98,600,000**

The $1 million cash in transit should be treated as if received (Dr Cash $1 million, Cr Receivables $1 million). After this, an intra-group balance of $3 million will remain. This is then removed (Dr Payables $3 million, Cr Receivables $3 million).

Therefore consolidated receivables = 64.6 + 38.6 – 1.0 – 3.0 = **$98.6m**

**180**

|  | True | False |
|---|---|---|
| If a subsidiary is disposed of on the last day of the reporting period then its assets and liabilities must still be included in the consolidated statement of financial position | | ✓ |
| The gain or loss arising on the disposal of a subsidiary in the financial statements is recorded in other comprehensive income | | ✓ |

**181**

| Cash consideration of $4.8 million |

| Deferred cash consideration of $8.3 million |

The professional fees cannot be capitalised. The deferred cash should be discounted to present value at the date of acquisition, $10 million/$1.1^2$ = $8.3 million.

**182  B**

The profit or loss on the disposal is calculated as follows:

| Proceeds | 10m |
| Goodwill at disposal | (2m) |
| Net assets at disposal | (9m) |
| Non-controlling interest at disposal | 3m |
| Profit on disposal | 2m |

If you selected answer A you have incorrectly identified it as a loss. If you selected answer C you have added the goodwill instead of deducting it. If you selected answer D you have added the non-controlling interest onto the carrying amount of the subsidiary (rather than deducting it) when calculating the profit or loss on disposal.

**183  $6,000,000**

The profit arising in the individual financial statements of Wind will be the difference between the proceeds received of $10 million and the purchase price of $4 million.

**184  $2,500,000**

| | $m |
| Proceeds | 9.0 |
| Goodwill at disposal | (4.6) |
| Net assets at disposal | (5.0) |
| Non-controlling interest at disposal | 3.1 |
| Profit on disposal | 2.5 |

**185   A**

|                                      | $m | $m |
| ------------------------------------ | --- | --- |
| Proceeds                             |     | 15  |
| Goodwill at disposal                 |     | Nil |
| Net assets at disposal               |     | (8) |
| Non-controlling interest:            |     |     |
| At acquisition                       | 2.2 |     |
| NCI % of post-acquisition net assets | 1.2 |     |
| 40% × ($8m – $5m)                    |     |     |
| NCI % of goodwill impairment (40% × $1m) | (0.4) |  |
|                                      |     |     |
| Non-controlling interest at disposal |     | 3   |
|                                      |     |     |
| Profit on disposal                   |     | 10  |

If you selected answer B you have used the non-controlling interest at acquisition when calculating the profit or loss on disposal, instead of the non-controlling interest at disposal. If you selected answer C you have not reduced the non-controlling interest by its share of the goodwill impairment. If you selected answer D you have valued the non-controlling interest at its share of the disposal date net assets.

## INTERPRETATION OF FINANCIAL STATEMENTS

**186   A**

A not-for-profit entity is not likely to have shareholders or 'earnings'.

**187   B**

A, C and D are all ratios associated with profit. A charity is more likely to be concerned with liquidity rather than the profits made by the entity.

**188**

|                                                                         | Limitation | Not a limitation |
| ----------------------------------------------------------------------- | ---------- | ---------------- |
| Different ways of calculating certain ratios exist                      | ✓          |                  |
| Accounting policy choices can limit comparability between different companies | ✓     |                  |

**189   35**

Inventory turnover is six times, so inventory days must be 365/6 = 61 days.

The cash collection period is inventory days plus receivables days less payables days.

Therefore the trade payables period is 61 + 42 – 68 = 35 days.

**190 C, E**

A new website selling direct to the public is unlikely to be on credit terms, as payment will be taken on the order.

This should therefore reduce the receivables collection period, as will the new retail units to the public, which will be cash based.

**191 C**

Return on capital employed is calculated as profit from operations/capital employed. Capital employed consists of debt and equity.

The deferred tax and payables are not included. Therefore the return on capital employed = $240,000/$900,000 = **26.7%**.

**192 0.87:1**

The quick ratio is made up of the current assets excluding inventory divided by the current liabilities = ($80,000 + $10,000)/($70,000 + $34,000) = **0.87:1**.

**193 A**

While the website is new in the year, the additional delivery costs are likely to be incurred every year in the future, meaning it is not a 'one-off' item.

**194 C**

Delivery costs to customers are not part of cost of sales, so increased prices will have no impact on the gross profit margin.

**195**

| | Available to KRL to use | Not available to KRL to use |
| --- | --- | --- |
| Details of the overseas country in which the target entity operates | ✓ | |
| Recent financial statements of the entity | ✓ | |
| Internal business plans of the takeover target | | ✓ |

Internal business plans would be internal information for an entity so KRL would not be able to use this information.

**196 A**

P/E ratio is seen as a marker of risk, and a high P/E ratio is indicative of a lower perceived risk than an entity with a lower P/E ratio. Therefore Marcel is seen as less risky than the sector average.

P/E ratio is also indicative of market confidence, and a high P/E ratio means that high future growth is expected. Therefore, there is more confidence about the future prospects of Marcel than the sector average.

**197**

|  | True | False |
|---|---|---|
| It acts as a prediction of the future Earnings Per Share figure |  | ✓ |
| It discloses that Earnings Per Share could have been higher |  | ✓ |

Diluted EPS is not a prediction of the future EPS figure as firstly there is no forecast made of the earnings figure.

Secondly, if there were a range of conversion terms for a convertible, the terms giving the maximum number of issued shares would always be used in the diluted EPS calculation, rather than the most likely conversion terms.

Diluted EPS is a warning to shareholders that the EPS calculation could have been lower if the commitments to issue ordinary shares had been issued as shares in the current period.

**198  B**

The finance cost in the profit or loss account will be based on the effective interest rate, so the charge will be $2.5m × 8% = $200,000.

If the interest cover to be maintained is 9, then the minimum operating profit to be maintained must be $200 × 9 = $1.8m.

Option A used the coupon rate of 6% to calculate the finance cost, giving $150k.

Option C used the difference between the effective and coupon rate which is $50k.

Option D includes the transaction costs in the initial value of the loan, when calculating effective interest, giving $220k.

**199  5.6**

Price Earnings (P/E) Ratio is Current Market Price per share/Earnings Per Share.

The Earnings Per Share (EPS) for Rogers is net profit/number of ordinary shares in issue. The share capital is $1 million, and as the share capital is divided into 50¢ shares there must be 2 million shares in issue.

Therefore, EPS is 1,250/2,000 = $0.625, or 62.5c

P/E ratio is therefore 3.50/0.625 = 5.6

**200  21.4%**

The dividend yield is calculated as the Dividend per share/Current share price × 100%

Dividend per share is Total dividends/Total number of shares

Dividend per share is therefore $1.5m/2m = $0.75, or 75¢

The current share price is $3.50

Therefore the dividend yield is 0.75/3.5 × 100% = 21.4%

**201 B**

ROCE can be sub-divided into net profit × asset turnover.

Alco has a higher net profit, and therefore must be a high end retailer. Its asset turnover is 0.4 times, so it does not use assets intensively to generate a profit.

This would be expected of a high end retailer, as they are not volume driven.

Saleco has a low net profit, and therefore must be a lower end retailer. Its asset turnover is 5 times, so it uses assets intensively to generate a profit.

This would be expected of a lower end retailer, as they are volume driven.

**202**

|  | Limitation | Not a limitation |
|---|:---:|:---:|
| Financial statements often use historic cost, meaning that inflation is not taken into account | ✓ | |
| Complex items may not fit into any accounting standards and therefore may be omitted from the financial statements | | ✓ |

While complex items may exist which don't fit easily into an accounting standard, these cannot simply be omitted from the financial statements. The IFRS Conceptual Framework for Financial Reporting is a principles-based framework, so these would be accounted for using the principles contained within it.

**203 A**

Lepchem have not yet made any sales, so any ratio involving profit or revenue is irrelevant. The current ratio will be relevant, as Lepchem may have cash flow problems as they spend cash to develop new pharmaceuticals without any cash receipt until they are successful. This could threaten Lepchem's ability to continue as a going concern.

**204 C**

|  | Could be used to assess | Will not be used |
|---|:---:|:---:|
| The return given to investors | | ✓ |
| The success in achieving the organisation's stated aims | ✓ | |
| How well costs are being managed | ✓ | |

Not-for-profit entities do not exist to make profits, therefore the return given to investors is irrelevant.

## 205  D

With a property management business, the value of that business is linked to the properties and the income which they can generate. Therefore the revenue and profits generated will be relevant.

However, there is unlikely to be any inventory so inventory turnover will not be a key measure that is used.

## 206  B, C

Rising costs are likely to affect the whole industry and would still mean that Quartile could be compared to the sector.  As the error has been corrected, there will be no issues over comparability this year.

## 207  51

Year-end inventory of six times is 61 days (365/6).

Trade payables period is 42 days (230,000 × 365/2,000,000).

Therefore receivables collection period is 51 days (70 – 61 + 42).

## 208  B, D

Factoring with recourse means Trent still has the risk of an irrecoverable receivable and therefore could not derecognise the receivable. The cash sales are irrelevant as Trent does not include them within the calculation.

## 209  D

Acquisition of an asset under a lease agreement will increase debt and so increase gearing. The other options either increase equity or have no impact.

## 210  C

Use of average cost gives a higher cost of sales (and in turn lower operating profit) than FIFO during rising prices.

# STATEMENT OF CASH FLOWS

## 211  A

| PPE | | | |
|---|---|---|---|
| b/f | 14,400 | Disposal (CA) | 3,000 |
| Revaluation | 2,000 | Depreciation | 2,500 |
| Provision | 4,000 | | |
| **Additions (balance)** | **8,500** | b/f | 23,400 |
| | 28,900 | | 28,900 |

**212 B**

|  | $ |
|---|---|
| Accrued interest b/f | 12,000 |
| Interest per statement of profit or loss | 41,000 |
| Less unwinding (this is not cash, $150,000 × 6%) | (9,000) |
| Accrued interest c/f | (15,000) |
| | |
| Paid | 29,000 |

If you chose A, you have ignored the unwinding of the discount. If you chose C you have made an error between the opening and closing liability. If you chose D you have simply taken the expense for the year.

**213 $98,000**

**Tax liabilities**

|  |  |  |  |
|---|---|---|---|
| | | b/f (27 + 106) | 133 |
| **Paid (balance)** | **98** | Statement of profit or loss | 122 |
| c/f (38 + 119) | 157 | | |
| | 255 | | 255 |

**214 D**

Finance costs are added back in the indirect method but are not included in the direct method.

**215 A, C**

Purchase of investments and purchase of equipment would both be shown within cash flows from investing activities.

**216 D**

|  | $ |
|---|---|
| Profit | 37,500 |
| Depreciation | 2,500 |
| Increase in receivables | (2,000) |
| Decrease in inventory | 3,600 |
| Increase in payables | 700 |
| | |
| Cash generated from operations | 42,300 |
| Purchase of non-current assets | (16,000) |
| | |
| Net increase in cash and cash equivalents | 26,300 |

If you chose A, you have deducted depreciation. If you chose C you have deducted the payables movement. If you chose B, you have added the movement in receivables.

## 217  D

| | Add to profit before tax | Deduct from profit before tax |
|---|---|---|
| Decrease in trade receivables | ✓ | |
| Increase in inventories | | ✓ |
| Profit on sale of non-current assets | | ✓ |
| Depreciation | ✓ | |

Profit on disposal of non-current assets will be deducted from profit, as it relates to non-cash income. Increases in inventories would be deducted as they have a negative impact on cash flow. Decreases in receivables would have a positive impact on cash flow. Depreciation should be added to profit as it relates to a non-cash expense.

## 218  $10,000

There will be an inflow of $30,000 relating to a share issue (being the total movement in share capital and share premium), and a $20,000 outflow on repayment of the debentures. Therefore the overall movement will be a net $10,000 inflow.

## 219  A

**PPE**

| | | | | |
|---|---|---|---|---|
| b/f | 180 | Disposal | 60 |
| Revaluation | 25 | Depreciation | 20 |
| **Paid (balance)** | **125** | c/f | 250 |
| | —— | | —— |
| | 330 | | 330 |
| | —— | | —— |

The amounts to be shown in investing activities will be:

Purchase of PPE:     ($125,000) (See working above)

Sale of PPE:     $50,000 (Given in question)

This gives a **net outflow of $75,000**

If you chose B or D, you have only accounted for one of the cash flows. If you chose C, you have missed the disposal from your PPE working.

**220**

| Amortisation of government grant | Receipt of grant |
|---|---|
| | Cash received from grant $300,000 in investing activities |
| Decrease of 100,000 to cash generated from operations | |

The release of government grant should be deducted within the reconciliation of cash generated from operations, as this represents non-cash income. The grant received of $300,000 can be calculated using a working, as shown below.

### Grant liability

| | | | |
|---|---|---|---|
| | | b/f | 900,000 |
| Release to SPL | 100,000 | **Receipt of grant (balance)** | **300,000** |
| c/f | 1,100,000 | | |
| | ––––––– | | ––––––– |
| | 1,200,000 | | 1,200,000 |
| | ––––––– | | ––––––– |

# Section 5

# ANSWERS TO OBJECTIVE CASE QUESTIONS – SECTION B

## CONCEPTUAL FRAMEWORK/INTERNATIONAL FINANCIAL REPORTING STANDARDS

**221  $300,000**

The engine will be depreciated over the life of 36,000 flight hours. As the aircraft has flown for 1,200 hours in the first 6 months, the depreciation for the engine will be $9 million × 1,200/36,000 = $300,000.

**222  D**

Replacement components of complex assets can be capitalised. As the new engine has a life of 36,000 hours, the engine will be depreciated over this life rather than the based on the remaining life of the damaged engine.

**223**

|  | Capitalise | Expense |
|---|---|---|
| $3 million repair of the wing |  | ✓ |
| $2 million repainting of the exterior |  | ✓ |

Both costs will be regarded as repairs and must be expensed.

**224  B**

Cabin fittings – at 1 October 20X8 the carrying amount of the cabin fittings is $7.5 million $(25{,}000 - (25{,}000 \times {}^{3.5}/_5))$. The cost of improving the cabin facilities of $4.5 million should be capitalised as it led to enhanced future economic benefits in the form of substantially higher fares.

The cabin fittings would then have a carrying amount of $12 million (7,500 + 4,500) and an unchanged remaining life of 18 months. Thus depreciation for the six months to 31 March 20X9 is $4 million $(12{,}000 \times {}^6/_{18})$, giving a carrying amount of $8 million.

If you selected A, you have depreciated the upgrade over 5 years rather than the remaining life. If you selected C, you have not capitalised the upgrade. If you selected D, you have done a full year's depreciation on the upgrade.

## 225 Carrying amount

Recoverable amount is calculated by comparing value in use and fair value less costs to sell, so neither of those would be correct, and replacement cost is not relevant to an impairment calculation.

## 226 A

As Speculate uses the fair value model for investment properties, the asset should be revalued to fair value before being classed as an investment property. The gain on revaluation should be taken to other comprehensive income, as the asset is being revalued while held as property, plant and equipment.

At 1 October, the carrying amount of the asset is $1,950, being $2 million less 6 months' depreciation. As the fair value at 1 October is $2.3 million, this leads to a $350,000 gain which will be recorded in other comprehensive income.

## 227 B

Investment properties can be accounted for under the cost or fair value model but not the revaluation model, which applies to property, plant and equipment.

## 228 $190,000

|  | | $000 |
|---|---|---|
| Gain on investment properties: | A (2,340 – 2,300) | 40 |
| | B (1,650 – 1,500) | 150 |

## 229

| Individual | ✓ | Consolidated | ✓ |
|---|---|---|---|
| Investment property | ✓ | Investment property | |
| Property, plant & equipment | | Property, plant & equipment | ✓ |
| Within goodwill | | Cancelled as an intra-group item | |

In the individual financial statements Speculate would treat property B as an investment, but in Speculate's consolidated financial statements property B would be accounted for under IAS 16 *Property, Plant and Equipment* and be classified as owner-occupied. The group is regarded as a single entity, and the group use the building.

## 230 B

If Speculate uses the cost model, the asset would be transferred to investment properties at its carrying amount and then depreciated over its remaining life. This would mean that the asset would have a year's depreciation applied to it, 6 months while held as property, plant and equipment, 6 months while held as an investment property. Fair values would be irrelevant.

The depreciation would therefore be $2 million/20 years = $100,000, giving a carrying amount of $1.9 million.

If you selected A, you have only accounted for depreciation for 6 months. If you selected C or D, you have applied depreciation to the fair value of the asset.

**231 D**

Loans are regarded as financial liabilities and should be held at amortised cost.

**232 A, B**

Borrowing costs must be capitalised if they are directly attributable to qualifying assets, which are assets that take a substantial time to complete. Capitalisation should cease once substantially all the activities to prepare the asset are complete. Capitalisation commences when expenditure is incurred on the asset, borrowing costs are being incurred **and** preparation activities have commenced.

**233 $125,000**

The finance cost of the loan must be calculated using the effective rate of 7.5%, so the total finance cost for the year ended 31 March 20X8 is $750,000 ($10 million × 7.5%). As the loan relates to a qualifying asset, the finance cost (or part of it in this case) can be capitalised in accordance with IAS 23 *Borrowing Costs*.

Capitalisation commences from when expenditure is being incurred (1 May 20X7) and must cease when the asset is ready for its intended use (28 February 20X8), in this case a 10 month period.

The finance cost to be capitalised = $625,000 ($750,000 × $^{10}/_{12}$). The remaining two months finance costs of $125,000 must be expensed.

**234 $625,000**

The finance cost to be capitalised = $625,000 ($750,000 × $^{10}/_{12}$).

**235 B**

Temporary investment income earned during the construction period should be netted off the amount capitalised. However, the interest was earned **prior to the period of construction**. Therefore the investment income earned should be taken to the statement of profit or loss as investment income.

**236 B**

The dismantling costs should be capitalised at the present value of $4 million, with an equivalent liability created. In addition to this, the discount on the $4 million should be unwound by 8% each year, with the increase being taken to finance costs in the statement of profit or loss.

Therefore the finance cost is $320,000 unwinding of interest ($4 million × 8%).

If you selected A, you spread the cost over the life of the asset. If you selected C, you have expensed the full amount. If you selected D, you have discounted the $4 million, despite being told that this was already at its present value.

**237 A**

The $1.2 million government grant should be released over the 5 year life of the asset, meaning that $240,000 will be released to the statement of profit or loss each year. As Shawler only received the grant on 1 October 20X3, only $120,000 ($^{6}/_{12}$) should be released to the statement of profit or loss in the year.

Therefore there is a remaining balance of $1,080,000 at the year-end. Of this, $240,000 will be released in the next year, so $840,000 will be shown as a non-current liability.

If you selected B, you have not split the year-end liability into current and non-current. If you selected C, you have released a full year of the grant and then not split the year-end liability. If you selected D, you have split the year-end liability but have released a full year of the grant rather than 6 months.

**238 $3,000,000**

The land is initially translated using the spot rate of exchange and so is recognised at $3 million (12m dinar/4).

Land is a non-monetary asset and so is **not** retranslated at the reporting date.

**239 B**

Training costs cannot be capitalised as it is not possible to restrict the access of others to the economic benefit as staff could leave and take their skills elsewhere.

**240 A, B**

The deferred income should be removed, with an expense recorded in the statement of profit or loss. No prior year adjustment should be made. The plant cost would only be increased if the grant was accounted for using the netting off method.

**241 B, D**

Whilst items A and D are necessary for an item to be capitalised as an asset, they are not linked to the characteristic of them being identifiable.

**242**

|  | Capitalise | Expense |
|---|---|---|
| Training courses for staff |  | ✓ |
| Expenditure on processor chip |  | ✓ |

Training courses for staff cannot be capitalised as Darby will not be able to restrict the access of others to the economic benefit. The expenditure on the chip would be classed as research expenditure.

## 243  **$320,000**

The amounts incurred from 1 February to 30 April should be expensed, meaning that $300,000 (3 × $100,000) should be expensed. Following this, the costs from 1 May to 30 October should be capitalised, meaning that $600,000 should be capitalised.

The development asset should then be amortised over the 5-year remaining life, giving $120,000 amortisation each year. This should be amortised from 1 November, meaning that 2 months' amortisation should be expensed in the year, so $120,000 × $^2/_{12}$ = $20,000.

Therefore the total expense = $300,000 + $20,000 = **$320,000**.

## 244  **C**

The development costs will not be subject to an annual impairment review, but will be amortised over the 5 year useful life. The development costs will be held at the carrying value, and will not be revalued each year.

Plant used solely on the development project will result in the depreciation being a directly attributable cost of the project. Therefore any depreciation on the asset will be included in the costs to be capitalised and will be taken to the statement of profit or loss as the project is amortised over the 5 year life.

## 245  **D**

At the date of the impairment review, the asset had a carrying amount of $450,000 ($^9/_{10}$ × $500,000).

The recoverable amount of the asset is the **higher** of the fair value less costs to sell of $380,000 ($400,000 – $20,000) and the value in use of $480,000. The recoverable amount is therefore $480,000.

The carrying amount of the asset is **lower** than the recoverable amount, so no impairment is charged.

## 246  **D**

Depreciation 1 January to 30 June 20X4 (80,000/10 × $^6/_{12}$) = 4,000

Depreciation 1 July to 31 December 20X4 (81,000/9 × $^6/_{12}$) = 4,500

Total depreciation = 8,500

## 247  **D**

The entity's market capitalisation would not be reflected within the values on the statement of financial position.

## 248  **B**

Value in use of $38,685 is lower than fair value less costs to sell of $43,000, so recoverable amount is $43,000 and impairment is $60,750 – $43,000 = $17,750.

## 249  **D, E**

There is no requirement to test cash generating units (CGUs) more often than other assets. A CGU could be a subsidiary, but not necessarily, and the CGU needs to be consistently identified.

## 250 $262,500

The impairment loss of $220,000 ($1,170 − $950) is allocated: $35,000 to damaged plant and $85,000 to goodwill, the remaining $100,000 allocated proportionally to the building and the undamaged plant. The impairment to be allocated to the plant will be $37,500 ($100,000 × ($300/(300+500))), leaving an amended carrying amount of the plant of $262,500 ($300,000 − $37,500).

## 251 B

Profit or loss from discontinued operations will consist of the post-tax profit or loss, inclusive of any gains or losses on disposal of assets and any costs associated with the closure of the operation.

This figure should be shown underneath profit from continuing operations, but before other comprehensive income.

## 252 A

The disposal of outlets in country A represents a separate geographical location and should be treated as a discontinued operation. The change in focus in Country B is not regarded as a separate major line of business, as it is just targeting different customers.

## 253 D

Depreciation should cease on the date that the asset is classified as held for sale. In this case, this will be 1 January 20X3. Therefore depreciation would be $150,000 ($4 million/ 20 years × $9/12$), giving a carrying amount of $3,850,000.

As the asset is expected to sell for $4 million, the asset should be held at $3,850,000 as the asset should be held at the lower of carrying amount and fair value less costs to sell.

## 254 A

Costs relating to the ongoing activities of the entity cannot be provided for according to IAS 37 *Provisions, Contingent Liabilities and Contingent Assets*. Therefore only the redundancy costs of $300,000 can be provided.

## 255

|  | Adjusting event | Non-adjusting event |
|---|:---:|:---:|
| Disposal of plant | ✓ |  |
| Redundancy settlement | ✓ |  |

Both events relate to conditions in existence at the reporting date, so both events should be regarded as adjusting events.

## 256 B, C

Accounting policies should only be changed if required by a new IFRS Standards or if doing so results in the production of more reliable and relevant information.

**257**

The change in useful life of the plant will be a change in accounting **estimate** and should be applied **prospectively**.

**258 A**

A change in accounting policy must be accounted for as if the new policy had always been in place, retrospectively. In this case, for the year ended 30 September 20X9, both the opening and closing inventories would need to be measured at AVCO which would reduce reported profit by the movement in the values of the opening and closing inventories of $400,000 (($20 million – $18 million) – ($15 million – $13.4 million).

The other effect of the change will be on the retained earnings brought forward at 1 October 20X8. These will be restated (reduced) by the effect of the reduced inventory value at 30 September 20X8 i.e. $1.6 million ($15 million – $13.4 million). This adjustment would be shown in the statement of changes in equity.

**259 $88,000**

The inventories should be valued at the lower of cost and net realisable value (NRV). The items have a cost of $100,000 (20,000 at $5). The NRV is $88,000, being the 20,000 units at their net selling price of $44 ($55 less 20% commission).

**260 B**

The inventories should be held at the cost of $80,000 as the net realisable value of $150,000 less $20,000 to complete will be higher than the cost. The replacement cost of $50,000 is irrelevant.

**261 C**

The cattle will be classed as a biological asset and the milk will be classed as agricultural produce. The cheese is produced after processing so will be classed as inventory.

**262 $19,000**

The sheep will be held at fair value less point of sale costs. Initially the sheep would have been recognised at $95,000, being the $100,000 less 5% selling costs. At 31 March 20X6, they will be valued at $114,000, being $120,000 less 5% selling costs. Therefore a gain of $19,000 will be recorded in the statement of profit or loss.

**263 B**

Current cost accounting will apply the current cost of the asset less depreciation to date to reflect the age of the asset. As a new asset would cost $300,000, a 4 year old asset under current cost accounting will be valued at $180,000 ($300,000 – ($4/_{10} \times $300,000)).

**264 B**

This will be a level 2 input, as it is using the price of similar assets without adjustment.

**265  A, C**

The revaluation will increase equity, therefore affecting the gearing and return on capital employed. The depreciation will also increase. As Schrute charges depreciation to operating expenses, this will affect the net profit margin.

**266  C**

The lease grants the lessee the beneficial rights of asset use, meaning that a right-of-use asset and lease liability are recorded.

A is incorrect as it treats the rental as an expense, which is not permitted under IFRS 16 *Leases*.

B outlines incorrect treatment for interest, which should decrease over the life of the lease as the lease liability decreases.

D is incorrect as the payments reduce the lease liability rather than being treated as prepayments.

**267  A**

Leased assets are exempt from capitalisation where the lease period is for 12 months or less, or the assets are low-value assets.  IFRS 16 *Leases* does not give a value for what is meant by low-value assets, but gives examples, including telephones.  In this case the lease rentals would be charged as an expense within the statement of profit or loss.

**268  $306,250**

The plant would be capitalised at $350,000, equal to the lease liability plus the initial payment.  This would then be depreciated over the four year lease term, giving depreciation of $87,500 a year.

As Fino only entered into the lease halfway through the year, this would give depreciation of $43,750.  Therefore the carrying amount would be $350,000 less $43,750, which is $306,250.

**269  A**

|  | $ |
|---|---|
| Present value of total lease payments | 350,000 |
| Less initial lease rental | (100,000) |
| | ———— |
| Initial lease liability | 250,000 |
| | ———— |
| Interest to 30 September 20X7 (6 months at 10%) | 12,500 |

**270**

|  | **Increase** | **Decrease** |
|---|---|---|
| Return on Capital Employed |  | ✓ |
| Gearing | ✓ |  |
| Interest cover |  | ✓ |

Recognition of the lease liability would cause debt liabilities and finance costs to increase. This means that the capital employed would be higher, therefore decreasing return on capital employed. Gearing would increase due to the increased debt. Interest cover would decrease due to the higher level of finance costs.

**271  C**

The initial lease liability will be $1,263,000, on which 12 months interest at 6% would be $75,780.

**272  B**

|  | b/f | Interest @ 6% | Payment | c/f |
|---|---|---|---|---|
|  | $000 | $000 | $000 | $000 |
| 20X6 | 1,263 | 76 | (300) | 1,039 |
| 20X7 | 1,039 | 62 | (300) | 801 |

At 31 December 20X6 the total lease liability is $1,039,000. This must be split into current and non-current liabilities. The non-current liability is $801,000, being the amount remaining after the payment in 20X7. Therefore the current liability is $238,000, being the difference between $1,039,000 and $801,000.

If you selected A, you have calculated the liability as if payments were made in advance rather than in arrears.

If you selected C, you have chosen the total liability.

If you selected D, you have chosen the non-current liability.

**273  C**

A leased asset would normally be depreciated over the shorter of the lease term and useful life of the asset. However, as ownership transfers to Lotso at the end of the lease term, Lotso will be using the asset for the entire 6 year period. Therefore the asset is depreciated over 6 years, recognising $210,500 ($1,263,000/6) depreciation a year, and leaving a carrying amount as at 31 December 20X6 of $1,052,500.

**274  B**

This represents a sale and leaseback where the seller-lessee retains the full benefit of the asset over its remaining life.  The asset is not derecognised and remains on the statement of financial position at its carrying amount of $10 million, to be depreciated over the remaining 20 years at a rate of $500,000 ($10m/20) per annum.  The value after one year is therefore $9.5 million.

The sale proceeds of $11.5 million would be treated as a loan.

**275**

|  | True | False |
|---|---|---|
| Statement 1 |  | ✓ |
| Statement 2 |  | ✓ |

In a sale and leaseback where the seller-lessee does not retain use of the asset over its remaining life then the seller-lessee is deemed to have disposed of part of the asset, and any profit or loss would be recognised on this element of the asset no longer retained.

Sale proceeds in a sale and leaseback transaction would only be treated as a loan where the seller-lessee retains use of the asset over its remaining life.

**276  D**

Laidlaw should not 'derecognise' the receivables, but instead treat the $1.8 million cash received from Finease as a current liability (a loan or financing arrangement secured on the receivables).

This is a 'with recourse' factoring arrangement, as Finease can return the receivables to Laidlaw, meaning that Laidlaw carries the risk of these.

**277  $810,000**

The payments should be discounted at the market rate to find the split of the liability and equity, shown in the working below.

| Year ended 30 September | Cash flow | Discount rate at | Discounted cash flows |
|---|---|---|---|
|  | $000 | 8% | $000 |
| 20X3 | 500 | 0.93 | 465 |
| 20X4 | 500 | 0.86 | 430 |
| 20X5 | 10,500 | 0.79 | 8,295 |
|  |  |  | ———— |
| Liability component |  |  | 9,190 |
| **Equity ( balance)** |  |  | **810** |
|  |  |  | ———— |
| Total proceeds |  |  | 10,000 |
|  |  |  | ———— |

## 278 A, D

The substance of this transaction is that the bank has granted a loan of $5 million to Laidlaw. Control of the inventory has not been transferred, so the 'sale' should not be recognised as revenue. Therefore the loan should be recognised, in addition to the interest expense.

## 279 D

5% will not be charged to the statement of profit or loss, as the liability element will be held at amortised cost with 8% on the outstanding balance being charged to the statement of profit or loss each year.

## 280 A

Applying split accounting is essential for faithful representation, otherwise the correct accounting treatment is not being applied. While the disclosures may assist relevance, applying the correct accounting treatment is ensuring the fundamental characteristic of faithful representation is met.

## 281 D

All three items fall under the description of financial instruments. A financial instrument is a contract that gives rise to a financial asset of one entity and a financial liability or equity instrument of another entity. The convertible loan notes will be split between a financial liability and equity. The loan notes will be a financial liability and the investments will be a financial asset.

## 282 C

The liability should be held at amortised cost using the effective rate of interest at 10%.

|  | B/f | Interest 10% | Payment | c/f |
|---|---|---|---|---|
|  | $000 | $000 | $000 | $000 |
| 20X5 | 28,508 | 2,851 | (2,400) | 28,959 |

## 283 $768,000

|  | $ |
|---|---|
| Nominal value issued | 10,000,000 |
| Less: issue costs | (400,000) |
| Initial value | 9,600,000 |
| Interest at effective rate of 8% | $768,000 |

**284 B**

Howard should record the dividend income of $100,000 (10 cents × 1 million shares) as well as the gain in value of $1 million.

**285**

| | Capitalised | Not capitalised |
|---|---|---|
| Fair value through other comprehensive income investments | ✓ | |
| Fair value through profit or loss investments | | ✓ |
| Amortised cost investments | ✓ | |

Transaction costs relating to fair value through profit or loss investments should be expensed in the statement of profit or loss.

**286 C**

The payable should initially be translated at the spot rate of Kr10:$1, giving a payable of $1,000. As payables are a monetary liability, they should be retranslated at the closing rate of Kr8:$1. This gives a closing payable of $1,250. Therefore the foreign exchange loss is $250, as it will now cost $250 more to settle the liability. This will be charged to the statement of profit or loss.

**287 B**

The receivable should initially be translated at the spot rate of Kr10:$1, giving a receivable of $6,000. When the cash of Kr 30,000 is received, the foreign currency gain or loss should be recorded.

At the rate of Kr10.5:$1, this will give a value of $2,857. As the Kr 30,000 would have originally been included at $3,000, this gives a loss of $143.

Finally, the year-end balance must be retranslated at the closing rate of Kr8:$1. This gives a closing receivable of $3,750. As this would originally have been included at $3,000, this gives a gain of $750. Therefore the net gain is $750 – $143 = $607.

**288**

| | True | False |
|---|---|---|
| Statement 1 | | ✓ |
| Statement 2 | | ✓ |

Inventory should not be retranslated as it is not a monetary item. Foreign exchange gains will not be included in revenue.

## 289 $3,000

The tax expense in the statement of profit or loss consists of the current tax estimate and the movement on deferred tax in the year. The closing deferred tax liability is $90,000, being the temporary differences of $360,000 at the tax rate of 25%. This means that the deferred tax liability has decreased by $40,000 in the year. This decrease should be deducted from the current tax estimate of $43,000 to give a total expense of $3,000.

## 290 C

A debit balance represents an under-provision of tax from the prior year. This should be added to the current year's tax expense in the statement of profit or loss.

An under- or over-provision only arises when the prior year tax estimate is paid so there is no adjustment required to the current year liability.

## 291 A

Revenue should be recorded by multiplying the contract price by the progress to date. Therefore the revenue to be recorded is $10 million × 80% = $8 million.

If you selected B, you have ignored the progress figure given and calculated progress on the basis of costs to date compared to total contract costs.

If you selected C you have selected the amount billed.

If you selected D you have calculated the profit to be recognised rather than the revenue.

## 292 D

This is a loss making contract. In this situation, the loss should be recorded in full immediately. Revenue should be based on the progress to date.

| Step 1 – Overall | $000 |
|---|---|
| Price | 8,000 |
| Total cost  – incurred to date | (4,000) |
|             – estimated future | (6,000) |
| Overall loss | (2,000) |

Step 2 – Progress

60%

| Step 3 – SPL | $000 |
|---|---|
| Revenue (60% of 8,000) | 4,800 |
| **Cost of sales (Balancing figure)** | **(6,800)** |
| **FULL** loss to be recognised immediately | (2,000) |

**293 C**

See the workings below

| Step 1 – Overall | $000 |
|---|---:|
| Contract price | 4,000 |
| Total contract cost (500 + 2,000) | (2,500) |
| | |
| Estimated total profit | 1,500 |

Step 2 – Progress = 25%

| Step 3 – SPL | |
|---|---:|
| Revenue (25% × 4,000) | 1,000 |
| Cost of sales (25% × 2,500) | (625) |
| | |
| Profit | 375 |

| Step 4 – SFP | |
|---|---:|
| Costs to date | 500 |
| Profit to date | 375 |
| Less: Amount billed | (1,000) |
| | |
| Contract liability | (125) |

**294 B**

Where the progress and overall profit of a contract are uncertain, revenue must be recognised to the level of recoverable costs.

There may be a contract asset based on the amount spent to date compared to the amount billed to the customer.

**295** As a change in accounting **estimate**, applied **prospectively**.

IFRS 15 *Revenue from Contracts with Customers* explains that a change in the method of measuring progress is a change in accounting estimate. Changes in accounting estimate are always applied prospectively.

**296 D**

The revenue in relation to the installation and the machine itself can be recognised, with the revenue on the service recognised over time as the service is performed. The service will be recognised over the 2 year period. By 31 December 20X7, 2 months of the service has been performed. Therefore $20,000 can be recognised ($240,000 × $^2/_{24}$).

Total revenue is therefore $580,000, being the $800,000 less the $220,000 relating to the service which has not yet been recognised.

**297**

| Sales element | Discount applied | Discount not applied |
|---|---|---|
| Machine | ✓ | |
| Installation | ✓ | |
| Service | ✓ | |

Discounts should be applied evenly across the components of a sale unless any one element is regularly sold separately at a discount. As Creg does not sell the service and installation separately, the discount must be applied evenly to each of the three elements.

**298 B**

Revenue as an agent is made by earning commission. Therefore the revenue on these sales should only be $600,000 (10% of $6 million). As Creg currently has $6 million in revenue, $5.4 million needs to be removed, with $5.4 million also removed from cost of sales.

**299 $9,490,000**

The fact that Creg has given the customer a year to pay on such a large amount suggests there is a significant financing component within the sale.

The $990,000 received can be recognised in revenue immediately. The remaining $9.01 million must be discounted to its present value of $8.5 million. This is then unwound over the year, with the interest recognised as finance income.

Therefore total initial revenue = $990,000 + $8,500,000 = $9,490,000.

**300 D**

This does not represent a real sale as control has not passed to the bank. Creg still maintains responsibility for the upkeep of the goods.

The bank cannot benefit from the price rise as Creg holds the option to repurchase the goods for a price below the expected fair value.

Therefore this will be treated as a $3 million loan. The additional $630,000 represents interest of 10% a year over two years on the $3 million.

**301 D**

| | |
|---|---|
| EPS for the year ended 30 September 20X7 ($15 million/43.25 million × 100) | 35¢ |
| | |
| Step 1 – Theoretical ex rights price (TERP) | |
| 4 shares at $3.80 | 15.2 |
| 1 share at $2.80 | 2.8 |
| ——— | ——— |
| 5    shares at **$3.60** (TERP) | 18 |
| ——— | ——— |

Step 2 – Rights fraction

Market value before issue/TERP = \$3.80/\$3.60

Step 3 – Weighted average number of shares

| | | |
|---|---|---|
| 36 million × $^3/_{12}$ × $^{\$3.80}/_{\$3.60}$ | 9.50 | million |
| 45 million × $^9/_{12}$ | 33.75 | million |
| | 43.25 | million |

If you selected A, you have simply divided the profit for the year by the number of shares at the start of the year. If you selected B, you have used the inverse of the rights fraction. If you selected C, you have applied the rights fraction for the whole year rather than for the period up to the rights issue.

## 302 A

| | | |
|---|---|---|
| Diluted EPS for the year ended 30 September 2009 ($15.6 million/45.75 million × 100) | 34¢ | |
| Adjusted earnings | | |
| 15 million + (10 million × 8% × 75%) | \$15.6 | million |
| Adjusted number of shares | | |
| 43.25 million + (10 million × $^{25}/_{100}$) | 45.75 | million |

If you selected B, you have ignored the additional tax that would be payable on the interest saved. If you selected C, you have ignored the additional shares that would be issued. If you selected D, you have ignored the impact to the profit and simply increased the number of shares.

## 303 C

| | | | |
|---|---|---|---|
| EPS for the year ended 30 September 20X7 ($12 million/43.2 million × 100) | | 28¢ | |
| Weighted average number of shares | | | |
| 1 Oct | 34 million × $^4/_{12}$ × $^6/_5$ | 13.6 | million |
| 1 Feb | 37 million × $^5/_{12}$ × $^6/_5$ | 18.5 | million |
| 1 July | 44.4 million × $^3/_{12}$ | 11.1 | million |
| | | 43.2 | million |

The bonus fraction should be applied from the start of the year up to the date of the bonus issue. If you selected A, you have added the bonus issue in July to the number of shares in addition to the bonus fraction, effectively double counting the bonus issue. If you selected B, you have missed out the bonus fraction completely. If you selected D you have just added the 3 million market issue without considering the bonus issue.

**304**

| Company | Comparative restated | No restatement |
|---|:---:|:---:|
| Barstead | ✓ | |
| Cabott | | ✓ |
| Dunstan | ✓ | |

Prior year earnings per share figures must be restated when there is a bonus element to a share issue. Rights issues contain a bonus element so Barstead must restate the prior year figure. Dunstan performed a bonus issue so must restate the prior year figure.

**305**

| | Correct | Incorrect |
|---|:---:|:---:|
| Statement 1 | | ✓ |
| Statement 2 | ✓ | |

Diluted EPS uses the current year's profit, adjusted for items currently in existence such as options or convertibles. It is not a predictor of future earnings.

**306 C**

To recognise a provision, it must be **probable** that an outflow of resources will be required.

**307 C**

A provision is recognised at the best estimate of the expenditure required. For a single obligation, this should be the most likely outcome.

If you selected answer B you have calculated an expected value. This is used when the provision being measured involves a large population of items.

**308 $840,000**

The provision being measured involves a large population of items, so an expected value must be calculated:

(100,000 × 6% × $100) + (100,000 × 8% × $30) = $840,000

**309 A**

The employees affected have been told about the restructuring and therefore a constructive obligation exists. The provision must not include any costs related to the ongoing activities of the entity. This means that only the redundancy payments should be provided for.

**310**

|  | Provision | No provision |
|---|---|---|
| Situation 1 |  | ✓ |
| Situation 2 |  | ✓ |

A provision should not be recognised for situation 1 because it does not give rise to an obligation. Hermione could change its operations in order to avoid the legal requirement to fit smoke filters.

A provision should not be recognised for situation 2. Future operating losses can be avoided, meaning that no obligation exists.

**311  B**

Provisions must be made if a legal or constructive obligation exists. The provision will be made at present value and added to the cost of the asset.  Over the 10 year period, the asset will be depreciated and the discount on the provision will be unwound.

**312  $7,452,000**

The provision should be recorded at the present value of $6.9 million initially ($15 million × 0.46).  After this, the discount on the provision must be unwound, meaning the provision will increase by 8% a year. Therefore the year-end provision is $6.9 million × 1.08 = $7,452,000.

**313**

|  | Adjusting | Non-adjusting |
|---|---|---|
| Fire in the warehouse |  | ✓ |
| Sale of inventory | ✓ |  |

The fire will be a non-adjusting event as the condition did not exist at the year end.  The sale of inventory will be an adjusting event, as this shows that the net realisable value of the inventory is lower than its cost, meaning that inventory was incorrectly valued at the year end.

**314  C**

The date of the government announcement of the tax change is beyond the period of consideration in IAS 10 *Events After the Reporting Period*. Thus this would be neither an adjusting nor a non-adjusting event. The increase in the deferred tax liability will be provided for in the year to 30 September 20X9. Had the announcement been before 6 November 20X8, it would have been treated as a non-adjusting event requiring disclosure of the nature of the event and an estimate of its financial effect in the notes to the financial statements.

## 315  A

From Promoil's perspective, as a separate entity, the guarantee for Hamlet's loan is a contingent liability of $10 million. As Hamlet is a separate entity, Promoil has no liability for the secured amount of $15 million, not even for the potential shortfall for the security of $3 million. The $10 million contingent liability would be disclosed in the notes to Promoil's financial statements.

In Promoil's consolidated financial statements, the full liability of $25 million would be included in the statement of financial position as part of the group's non-current liabilities – there would be no contingent liability disclosed.

# CONSOLIDATED FINANCIAL STATEMENTS

## 316  B

Share for share exchange: 15m × 80% = 12m shares acquired × $^2/_5$ = 4.8m Penfold shares issued @ $5.30 = $25,440,000 consideration given for Superted.

Penfold have issued 4.8m shares so 4.8m will be added to share capital with the remaining $20.64m added to other components of equity. As Penfold currently has $6m other components of equity, the total will be $26,640,000.

If you selected C, you have added Superted's other components of equity, and the subsidiary's equity is not included in the consolidated equity.

If you selected A, you have added the entire share consideration, and if you selected D, you have added the entire share consideration and Superted's other components of equity.

## 317  $66,400,000

The cash-in-transit must be treated as if received. To do this, $2 million will be added to cash and deducted from receivables. This will leave a $6 million intra-group receivable balance, which will then be removed along with the $6 million intra-group payable balance.

Total receivables = 32,400 + 38,000 – 2,000 – 6,000 = $66,400,000.

## 318  A

The non-controlling interest **at acquisition** will be $7.2 million.

Penfold has owned Superted for 6 months so 6 months' profit should be included in the consolidated financial statements for the year. Therefore the NCI's share of this will be $2.4 million ($24 million × $^6/_{12}$ × 20%).

The sale of plant from Penfold to Superted requires an adjustment to the depreciation charge recorded within the accounts of Superted.  The increase in value of $5 million will result in an additional depreciation charge of $0.5 million ($5m × $^1/_5$ × $^6/_{12}$) to be reversed as part of the PUP adjustment.  The NCI's share of this is $0.5m × 20% = $0.1 million.

Therefore NCI = $7.2 million + $2.4 million + $0.1 million = $9.7 million.

If you selected B, you deducted the PUP adjustment.

If you selected C, you have taken the NCI at acquisition.

If you selected D, you have ignored the PUP adjustment.

**319** **$481,500,000**

The unrealised profit on the non-current asset transfer needs to be removed.

The carrying amount at the year-end after the transfer is $22.5 million ($25 million less 6 months depreciation).

The carrying amount of the asset if it had never been transferred would have been $18 million ($20 million less 6 months depreciation).

Therefore the unrealised profit on the non-current asset is $4.5 million.

The total PPE is therefore $345 million + $141 million − $4.5 million = $481.5 million.

**320** **C**

There is no control or significant influence as Arnold is controlled by the other investor. Therefore the investment in Arnold will be held as an equity investment, which is a financial instrument.

**321** **B**

The deferred consideration should be discounted to the present value at acquisition. $6 million$/1.08^2$ = $5.144 million.

At 31 March 20X5, 6 months have elapsed, so the discount needs to be unwound for 6 months. $5.144 million × 8% × $6/12$ = $206,000. Therefore the liability at 31 March 20X5 = $5,144 + 206 = $5,350,000.

If you selected A you have not unwound any interest.

If you selected C you have unwound a full year's interest.

If you selected D you have not discounted the consideration.

**322** **B**

(Workings in $000)

Cost of sales = 319,200 + (176,400 × $6/12$) − 6,000 (intra-group) + 360 (PUP) = 401,760

PUP = $6,000 × 20% margin × 30% remaining = $360

If you selected A, you have adjusted for all the profit, rather than the 30% remaining in the group at the year-end. If you selected C you have taken out a full year's sales rather than 6 months. If you selected D you have taken out a full year's sales and adjusted for all the profit rather than the amount remaining in the group.

**323** **D**

Operating expenses = 50,610 + (33,120 × $6/12$) + 100 FV depreciation* + 600 impairment = 67,870.

*Fair value depreciation = $4 million/20 years = $200,000 a year × $6/12$ = $100,000.

If you selected A, you have added a full year's fair value depreciation. If you selected B, you have deducted the fair value depreciation. If you selected C, you have either time apportioned the impairment or deducted a full year's fair value depreciation.

**324  C**

Unrealised profits from note (i) would only affect the non-controlling interest if the subsidiary sold goods to the parent, which is not the case. Fair value depreciation (note (ii)) always affects the NCI. Goodwill impairment (note (iii)) will affect the NCI if the NCI is measured at fair value, which it is here.

**325**

| | Correct | Incorrect |
|---|:---:|:---:|
| Statement 1 | ✓ | |
| Statement 2 | | ✓ |

A subsidiary's assets, liabilities and contingent liabilities must be included at fair value in the consolidated financial statements. Professional fees associated with the acquisition of a subsidiary cannot be capitalised, regardless of which method is used to measure the non-controlling interest.

**326  D**

Consolidated retained earnings will consist of 100% of Prunier's retained earnings plus 80% of Sheringham's post acquisition loss ($3.5m – $4m), including the fair value depreciation on Sheringham's assets ($800 × $\frac{1}{20}$).

| | $000 |
|---|---:|
| Prunier | 11,000 |
| Sheringham (500 + 40) × 80% | (432) |
| | ——— |
| | 10,568 |
| | ——— |

**327  $2,400,000**

The other comprehensive income attributable to the parent will be 100% of Prunier's revaluation gain in the year and 80% of Sheringham's post acquisition revaluation gain. Prunier has made a gain of $2 million in the year and Sheringham has made $500,000. Therefore the other comprehensive income attributable to the parent is $2 million plus 80% × $500,000 = $2,400,000.

**328**

| | Recognise | Not to be recognised |
|---|---|---|
| Sheringham's brand name, which was internally generated so not shown in Sheringham's financial statements but has a fair value of $3 million | ✓ | |
| A research project in progress, which was one of the main reasons Prunier purchased Sheringham and has a fair value of $2 million | ✓ | |
| An intangible asset related to an encryption process which has now been deemed illegal. This is included within intangibles at $1.5 million | | ✓ |

Internally generated assets and research projects can be recognised within consolidated financial statements if a fair value can be attached to them. The encryption process is now illegal so cannot be recognised as an asset.

**329  B**

Profit on all sales = 3,000 × 20/120 = $500,000. Anderson has a quarter left, so this is $125,000. As Anderson is an associate, only 30% of this needs to be removed, which is $37,500. If you selected A, you have used margin and not mark-up, and not adjusted for the associate. If you selected C, you have taken all of the unrealised profit, rather than 30%. If you selected D, you have used margin and not mark-up.

**330  A**

The profit or loss on the disposal is calculated as follows:

| | $000 |
|---|---|
| Proceeds | 9,000 |
| Goodwill at disposal | (1,000) |
| Net assets at disposal | (10,600) |
| Non-controlling interest at disposal | 2,500 |
| | ——— |
| Loss on disposal | (100) |
| | ——— |

If you selected B, you have added the goodwill instead of deducting it. If you selected C, you have deducted the non-controlling interest at disposal. If you selected D, you have deducted 80% of the net assets, rather than all of them.

# INTERPRETATION OF FINANCIAL STATEMENTS

**331 B**

B is correct, as follows:

| | A | | B |
|---|---|---|---|
| | $m | | $m |
| Gross profit = 26% × $160m | 41.6 | Gross profit = 17% × $300m | 51 |
| Operating profit = 9% × $160m | 14.4 | Operating profit = 11% × $300m | 33 |
| | ——— | | ——— |
| Operating expenses | 27.2 | | 18 |
| | ——— | | ——— |

A is incorrect. A's revenue is significantly lower than B's and therefore B is more likely to be benefiting from economies of scale.

C is incorrect. A has higher gearing than B and would therefore be considered a higher risk by lenders. (The low interest rate may however explain why A are using debt finance in the first place.)

D is incorrect. LOP's gross profit margin is higher than both A's and B's and therefore acquisition of either entity is likely to reduce the overall margin of the combined business (unless cost savings can be achieved as a result of the acquisition).

**332 A, D**

B is incorrect. A has higher gearing than B and therefore reduced capacity for additional borrowings.

C is incorrect. LOP's P/E ratio is higher than B's suggesting that the market is more confident about the future performance of LOP.

E is incorrect. The share price may react positively or negatively, depending on the investor's view of the impact the acquisition will have on LOP.

**333 B**

A and B may target different customers, but that would not mean that their financial statements are incomparable. It may lead to different margins earned, but comparison could still be made, and would help LOP to assess which type of customer and market they made wish to target.

**334 24.5%**

| | LOP | | B |
|---|---|---|---|
| | $m | | $m |
| Gross profit = 28% × $500m | 140 | Gross profit = 17% × $300m | 51 |

Without the cost savings, LOP and B are making a gross profit of $191 million on revenue of $800 million. If the cost savings of $5 million are taken into account, the gross profit will increase to $196 million. This will give a gross profit margin of **24.5%** (196/800).

**335**

| | Correct | Incorrect |
|---|---|---|
| Statement 1 | | ✓ |
| Statement 2 | ✓ | |

If B has treated the leases incorrectly, then B's liabilities will be understated, meaning that gearing would be understated. B would also not have included any finance costs in the statement of profit or loss, meaning the average interest rate expensed will not have included the interest on the lease.

**336  7.5%**

1,500/(15,000 + 3,000 + 2,000) = 1,500/20,000 = 7.5%

**337  D**

Combined profit from operations = $1,5m – $0.6m = $900,000.

Combined revenue = $9.4m + $1.2m = $10,600,000.

Operating margin = 900/10,600 = 8.5%.

If you selected C, you have just used Franck's profit. If you selected B, you have added the loss of 600 rather than deducting it. If you selected A, you have just used Franck's revenue rather than the combined revenue.

**338**

| | Correct | Incorrect |
|---|---|---|
| Statement 1 | ✓ | |
| Statement 2 | ✓ | |

Return on capital employed will clearly decrease, as Franck has made a loss. The capital employed will increase, but overall profit will decrease. Duik has a higher level of gearing (4,000/22,800 = 17.5%) compared to Franck (2,000/18,000 = 11%), which means gearing will increase when the two companies are combined.

**339  C**

Individual entity financial statements should not contain errors, and if they do, this is not a problem specific to being a subsidiary of another entity.

**340  C**

The upcoming projects are unlikely to be publicly available information, whereas A, B and D can all be assessed from looking at Duik's financial statements for the current or previous periods.

# STATEMENT OF CASH FLOWS

**341  C**

Cooper has used the indirect method. The direct method is an alternative method of calculating cash generated from operations.

Classification by function and nature relate to the way that items are presented in the statement of profit or loss.

**342**

|  | $000 |
|---|---|
| Profit from operations | 3,500 |
| Depreciation | 4,600 |
| Release of government grant | 1,400 |
| Profit on disposal of property | (3,700) |
| Increase in inventories | (400) |
| Decrease in trade and other receivables | (300) |
| Increase in trade and other payables | 900 |

The release of government grant is non-cash income, so should be deducted from profit from operations.

The decrease in trade receivables is good for cash so would be added to profit rather than being deducted.

**343  A**

| **Property** | | | |
|---|---|---|---|
| b/f | 39,500 | Depreciation | 4,600 |
| | | **Disposal (balance)** | **5,900** |
| | | c/f | 29,000 |
| | ——— | | ——— |
| | 39,500 | | 39,500 |
| | ——— | | ——— |

The carrying amount of the property disposed was $5.9 million. As Cooper made a profit of $3.7 million on disposal, the sale proceeds must have been **$9.6 million**.

If you selected B, you have deducted the profit on disposal rather than adding it.

If you selected C, you have used the profit on disposal.

If you selected D, you have selected the carrying amount disposed rather than the sale proceeds.

**344** **$3,400,000**

### Grant deferred income

|  |  |  |  |
|---|---|---|---|
|  |  | b/f | 6,000 |
| Released in year | 1,400 | **Received (balance)** | **3,400** |
| c/f | 8,000 |  |  |
|  | 9,400 |  | 9,400 |

**345** **B**

A rights issue will mean that cash has been raised, increasing the cash from financing activities. Intangible assets can affect the statement of cash flow if they are purchased as this will lead to an outflow of cash.

**346** **A**

### Retained earnings

|  |  |  |  |
|---|---|---|---|
|  |  | b/f | 940 |
| **Dividend paid (balance)** | **145** | Revaluation surplus | 20 |
| c/f | 900 | Profit for the year | 85 |
|  | 1,045 |  | 1,045 |

When the land is disposed, the remaining revaluation surplus will be taken to retained earnings. If you selected B, you have deducted the revaluation surplus. If you selected C, you have taken the movement in retained earnings. If you selected D, you have missed out the revaluation surplus transfer into retained earnings.

**347** **C**

The loan notes should be held at amortised cost, with the effective rate of interest being taken to the statement of profit or loss. As these have an effective rate of 8%, $40,000 has been taken to the statement of profit or loss. However, it is only the coupon rate of 5% which has been paid in the year, so $500,000 × 5% = $25,000.

In addition Depay has paid interest on the lease. The total interest charge for the year is $60,000, comprising loan note and lease interest. The loan note interest charged is $40,000, which means that the lease interest, paid as part of the lease payment on 30 September 20X2, must be the balance, $20,000.

So the total interest paid in the year is $45,000.

**348  $42,000**

**Tax liabilities ($000)**

| | | | |
|---|---|---|---|
| | | b/f (40 + 125) | 165 |
| Tax paid (balance) | 42 | Tax expense | 57 |
| c/f (30 + 150) | 180 | | |
| | ––––– | | ––––– |
| | 222 | | 222 |
| | ––––– | | ––––– |

**349  B**

Dividends received are shown within cash flows from investing activities.

**350  $80,000**

**Lease liabilities ($000)**

| | | | |
|---|---|---|---|
| | | b/f | 310 |
| Paid (balance) | **80** | New asset additions | 70 |
| c/f | 300 | | |
| | ––––– | | ––––– |
| | 380 | | 380 |
| | ––––– | | ––––– |

As the interest has been both charged and paid during the year we may ignore it in our T-account calculation.  The resulting calculation above uses the capital balances to identify the capital repaid.

# Section 6

# ANSWERS TO CONSTRUCTED RESPONSE QUESTIONS – SECTION C

## PREPARATION OF SINGLE ENTITY FINANCIAL STATEMENTS

**351   CANDEL**  *Walk in the footsteps of a top tutor*

(a)   **Candel – Revised profit for the year**

|  | $000 |
|---|---|
| Draft profit before tax | 59,100 |
| Depreciation (W3)   – leasehold property | (2,500) |
|    – plant and equipment | (9,600) |
| Removal of disposal proceeds | (2,500) |
| Loss on disposal of plant (4,000 – 2,500) | (1,500) |
| Amortisation of development costs (W3) | (4,000) |
| Research and development expenses (1,400 + 2,400 (W3)) | (3,800) |
| Removal of legal provision (W1) | 400 |
| Inclusion of provision for legal costs (W1) | (100) |
| Finance costs (W2) | (1,200) |
| Income tax expense (11,400 + (6,000 – 5,800 deferred tax)) | (11,600) |
| | ——— |
| Profit for the year | 22,700 |
| | ——— |

(b)    **Candel – Statement of financial position as at 30 September 20X8**

| Assets | $000 | $000 |
|---|---:|---:|
| Non-current assets (W3) | | |
| Property, plant and equipment (43,000 + 38,400) | | 81,400 |
| Development costs (W3) | | 14,800 |
| | | 96,200 |
| Current assets | | |
| Inventory | 20,000 | |
| Trade receivables | 43,100 | 63,100 |
| Total assets | | 159,300 |
| | | |
| Equity and liabilities: | | |
| Equity shares of 25 cents each | | 50,000 |
| Revaluation surplus (10,000 – 4,500) | 5,500 | |
| Retained earnings (18,500 + 22,700) | 41,200 | 46,700 |
| | | 96,700 |
| Non-current liabilities | | |
| Deferred tax | 6,000 | |
| 8% redeemable preference shares (20,000 + 400 (W2)) | 20,400 | 26,400 |
| Current liabilities | | |
| Trade payables (23,800 – 400 + 100 – re legal action (W2)) | 23,500 | |
| Bank overdraft | 1,300 | |
| Current tax payable | 11,400 | 36,200 |
| Total equity and liabilities | | 159,300 |

**Workings** (figures in brackets in $000)

**(W1)    Legal case**

As it is considered that the outcome of the legal action against Candel is unlikely to succeed (only a 20% chance) it is inappropriate to provide for any damages. The potential damages are an example of a contingent liability which should be disclosed (at $2 million) as a note to the financial statements. Therefore the legal provision of $400,000 should be removed. The unrecoverable legal costs are a liability (the start of the legal action is a past event) and should be provided for in full at $100,000.

**(W2)  Preference shares**

**Tutorial note**

This requires knowledge of accounting for financial instruments under IAS 32 Financial Instruments: Presentation and IFRS 9 Financial Instruments.

The finance cost of $1.2 million for the preference shares is based on the effective rate of 12% applied to $20 million issue proceeds of the shares for the six months they have been in issue (20m × 12% × 6/12). The dividend paid of $800,000 is based on the nominal rate of 8%. The additional $400,000 (accrual) is added to the carrying amount of the preference shares in the statement of financial position. As these shares are redeemable they are treated as debt and their dividend is treated as a finance cost.

**(W3)  Non-current assets:**

Leasehold property

| | |
|---|---:|
| Valuation at 1 October 20X7 | 50,000 |
| Depreciation for year (20 year life) | (2,500) |
| | ———— |
| Carrying amount at date of revaluation | 47,500 |
| Valuation at 30 September 20X8 | (43,000) |
| | ———— |
| Revaluation deficit | 4,500 |
| | ———— |

**Tutorial note**

Remember to write off the disposed asset, both cost and b/fwd accumulated depreciation before calculating the current year depreciation charge.

| | $000 |
|---|---:|
| Plant and equipment per trial balance (76,600 – 24,600) | 52,000 |
| Disposal (8,000 – 4,000) | (4,000) |
| | ———— |
| | 48,000 |
| Depreciation for year (20%) | (9,600) |
| | ———— |
| Carrying amount at 30 September 20X8 | 38,400 |
| | ———— |

**Tutorial note**

Remember research costs are to be expensed and development costs are to be capitalised only when the recognition criteria in IAS38 Intangible Assets are met. In this question- the directors do not become confident that the project will be successful until 1 April – therefore development costs on the new project in January – March must be expensed.

Capitalised/deferred development costs

| | |
|---|---|
| Carrying amount at 1 October 20X7 (20,000 – 6,000) | 14,000 |
| Amortised for year (20,000 × 20%) | (4,000) |
| Capitalised during year (800 × 6 months) | 4,800 |
| | ——— |
| Carrying amount at 30 September 20X8 | 14,800 |
| | ——— |

**Note:** Development costs can only be treated as an asset from the point where they meet the recognition criteria in IAS 38 *Intangible Assets*. Thus development costs from 1 April to 30 September 20X8 of $4.8 million (800 × 6 months) can be capitalised. These will not be amortised as the project is still in development. The research costs of $1.4 million plus three months' development costs of $2.4 million (800 × 3 months) (i.e. those incurred before the criteria were met) must be expensed.

## 352 PRICEWELL

(a) **Pricewell – Statement of profit or loss for the year ended 31 March 20X9**

| | $000 |
|---|---|
| Revenue (310,000 + 22,000 (W1) – 6,400 (W2)) | 325,600 |
| Cost of sales (W3) | (255,100) |
| | ——— |
| Gross profit | 70,500 |
| Distribution costs | (19,500) |
| Administrative expenses | (27,500) |
| Finance costs (W5) | (1,248) |
| | ——— |
| Profit before tax | 22,252 |
| Income tax expense (700 + 4,500 – 2,800 (W7)) | (2,400) |
| | ——— |
| Profit for the year | 19,852 |
| | ——— |

**(b)** **Pricewell – Statement of financial position as at 31 March 20X9**

| Assets | $000 | $000 |
|---|---:|---:|
| Non-current assets | | |
| Property, plant and equipment (W4) | | 66,400 |
| | | |
| Current assets | | |
| Inventory | 28,200 | |
| Trade receivables | 33,100 | |
| Contract asset (W1) | 17,100 | |
| Bank | 5,500 | 83,900 |
| | | ——— |
| Total assets | | 150,300 |
| | | ——— |
| Equity and liabilities | | |
| Equity shares of 50 cents each | | 40,000 |
| Retained earnings (W6) | | 55,952 |
| | | ——— |
| | | 95,952 |
| | | |
| Non-current liabilities | | |
| Deferred tax (W7) | 5,600 | |
| Lease liability (W5) | 5,716 | |
| | ——— | 11,316 |
| | | |
| Current liabilities | | |
| Trade payables | 33,400 | |
| Lease liability (W5) | 5,132 | |
| Current tax payable | 4,500 | 43,032 |
| | ——— | ——— |
| Total equity and liabilities | | 150,300 |
| | | ——— |

**Workings**

**(W1) Contract with customer:**

**(i)     Overall**

| | $000 |
|---|---:|
| Selling price | 50,000 |
| Estimated cost | |
| To date | (12,000) |
| To complete | (10,000) |
| Plant | (8,000) |
| | ——— |
| Estimated profit | 20,000 |
| | ——— |

**(ii)   Progress**

Work completed to date has been agreed at $22 million so the contract is 44% complete ($22m/$50m).

**(iii)   Statement of profit or loss**

| | |
|---|---:|
| Revenue | 22,000 |
| Cost of sales (44% × $30m total costs) | (13,200) |
| | ——— |
| Profit to date | 8,800 |
| | ——— |

**(iv)   Statement of financial position**

| | |
|---|---:|
| Costs to date (12,000 + 2,000 depreciation (W4)) | 14,000 |
| Profit to date | 8,800 |
| Payment from customer | (5,700) |
| | ——— |
| Contract asset | 17,100 |
| | ——— |

**(W2)** Pricewell is acting as an agent (not the principal) for the sales on behalf of Trilby. Therefore the statement of comprehensive income should only include $1.6 million (20% of the sales of $8 million). Therefore $6.4 million ($8m – $1.6m) should be deducted from revenue and cost of sales. It would also be acceptable to show agency sales (of $1.6 million) separately as other income.

**(W3) Cost of sales**

| | $000 |
|---|---:|
| Per question | 234,500 |
| Contract (W1) | 13,200 |
| Agency cost of sales (W2) | (6,400) |
| Depreciation (W4)   – leasehold property | 1,800 |
| – owned plant | 8,500 |
| – right-of-use asset (20,000 × 25%) | 5,000 |
| Surplus on revaluation of leasehold property (W4) | (1,500) |
| | ——— |
| | 255,100 |
| | ——— |

**(W4) Non-current assets**

Property, plant and equipment

| | Leasehold property | Owned plant & equipment | Right-of-use plant | Specialist plant for contract | Total |
|---|---|---|---|---|---|
| | $000 | $000 | | $000 | $000 |
| Valuation/cost 1 April 20X8 | 25,200 | 46,800 | 20,000 | | |
| Depreciation 1 April 20X8 | | (12,800) | (5,000) | | |
| Acquisition | | | | 8,000 | |
| | | ——— | | | |
| | | 34,000 | | | |
| Depreciation charge | | | | | |
| $25,200 \times {}^1/_{14}$ | (1,800) | | | | |
| $34,000 \times 25\%$ | | (8,500) | | | |
| $8,000 \times \frac{1}{2} \times {}^6/_{12}$ | | | | (2,000) | |
| $20,000 \times 25\%$ | | | (5,000) | | |
| | ——— | | | | |
| | 23,400 | | | | |
| Revaluation surplus | 1,500 | | | | |
| | ——— | ——— | ——— | ——— | ——— |
| Revaluation/carrying amount 31 March 20X9 | 24,900 | 25,500 | 10,000 | 6,000 | 66,400 |
| | ——— | ——— | ——— | ——— | ——— |

The leasehold property has 14 years useful life remaining at the beginning of the year. The specialist plan was acquired on 1 October 20X8 and is therefore only depreciated for 6 months.

The $1.5 million revaluation surplus is credited to cost of sales (W3) in the statement of profit or loss because this represents the partial reversal of the $2.8 million impairment loss recognised in the statement of profit or loss in the previous year ended 31 March 20X8.

**(W5) Lease liability ($000)**

| | Balance b/f | Interest 8% | Payment | Balance c/f |
|---|---|---|---|---|
| Year to 31 March 20X9 | 15,600 | 1,248 | (6,000) | 10,848 |
| Year to 31 March 20Y0 | 10,848 | 868 | (6,000) | 5,716 |

| | |
|---|---|
| Finance cost to profit or loss | 1,248 |
| Non-current liability | 5,716 |
| Current liability (10,848 – 5,716) | 5,132 |

### (W6) Retained earnings

|  | $000 |
|---|---|
| Balance at 1 April 20X8 | 44,100 |
| Profit for year per part (a) | 19,852 |
| Equity dividend paid per trial balance | (8,000) |
| Balance at 31 March 20X9 | 55,952 |

### (W7) Deferred taxation

|  | $000 |
|---|---|
| Provision required at 31 March 20X9 | 5,600 |
| Balance b/f per trial balance | (8,400) |
| Credit to tax expense | (2,800) |

| Marking scheme | | |
|---|---|---|
|  |  | *Marks* |
| (a) | Statement of profit or loss |  |
|  | Revenue | 2 |
|  | Cost of sales | 4½ |
|  | Distribution costs | ½ |
|  | Administrative expenses | ½ |
|  | Finance costs | 1 |
|  | Income tax expense | 1½ |
|  | Maximum | 10 |
| (b) | Statement of financial position |  |
|  | Property, plant and equipment | 1½ |
|  | Right-of-use asset | ½ |
|  | Inventory | ½ |
|  | Due on construction contract | 2 |
|  | Trade receivables and bank | ½ |
|  | Equity shares | ½ |
|  | Retained earnings | 1 |
|  | Deferred tax | 1 |
|  | Lease – non-current liability | ½ |
|  | Trade payables | ½ |
|  | Lease – current liability | 1 |
|  | Current tax payable | ½ |
|  | Maximum | 10 |
| **Total** |  | **20** |

## 353 HIGHWOOD

(a) **Highwood – Statement of profit or loss and other comprehensive income for the year ended 31 March 20X1**

|  | $000 |
|---|---|
| Revenue | 339,650 |
| Cost of sales (W1) | (206,950) |
| Gross profit | 132,700 |
| Distribution costs | (27,500) |
| Administrative expenses (30,700 – 1,300 + 600 allowance (W4)) | (30,000) |
| Finance costs (W5) | (2,848) |
| Profit before tax | 72,352 |
| Income tax expense (19,400 – 800 + 400 (W4)) | (19,000) |
| Profit for the year | 53,352 |
| Other comprehensive income: | |
| Gain on revaluation of property (W3) | 15,000 |
| Deferred tax on revaluation (W3) | (3,750) |
| Total comprehensive income | 64,602 |

(b) **Highwood – Statement of changes in equity for the year ended 31 March 20X1**

|  | Share capital $000 | Equity option $000 | Revaluation reserve $000 | Retained earnings $000 | Total equity $000 |
|---|---|---|---|---|---|
| Balance at 1 April 20X0 (see below) | 6,000 | nil | nil | 1,400 | 7,400 |
| 8% loan note issue (W5) |  | 1,524 |  |  | 1,524 |
| Comprehensive income |  |  | 11,250 | 53,352 | 64,602 |
| Balance at 31 March 20X1 | 6,000 | 1,524 | 11,250 | 54,752 | 73,526 |

**(c)    Highwood – Statement of financial position as at 31 March 20X1**

| | $000 | $000 |
|---|---|---|
| Assets | | |
| Non-current assets | | |
| Property, plant and equipment (W2) | | 77,500 |
| Current assets | | |
| Inventory (36,000 – 2,700 + 6,000) (W3)) | 39,300 | |
| Trade receivables (47,100 + 10,000 – 600 allowance (W4)) | 56,500 | 95,800 |
| | | _____ |
| Total assets | | 173,300 |
| | | _____ |
| | | |
| Equity and liabilities | | |
| Equity (see answer (b)) | | |
| Equity shares of 50 cents each | | 6,000 |
| Other component of equity – equity option | | 1,524 |
| Revaluation surplus | | 11,250 |
| Retained earnings | | 54,752 |
| | | _____ |
| | | 73,526 |
| Non-current liabilities | | |
| Deferred tax (W6) | 6,750 | |
| 8% convertible loan note (28,476 + 448 (W3)) | 28,924 | 35,674 |
| | _____ | |
| Current liabilities | | |
| Trade payables | 24,500 | |
| Liability to Easyfinance (W4) | 8,700 | |
| Bank overdraft | 11,500 | |
| Current tax payable | 19,400 | 64,100 |
| | _____ | _____ |
| Total equity and liabilities | | 173,300 |
| | | _____ |

**Workings** (figures in brackets in $000)

**(W1)  Cost of sales**

| | $000 |
|---|---|
| Per question | 207,750 |
| Depreciation – building (W2) | 2,500 |
| Adjustment/increase to closing inventory (W3) | (3,300) |
| | _____ |
| | 206,950 |
| | _____ |

**(W2) Freehold property**

The revaluation of the property will create an initial revaluation reserve of $15 million (80,000 – (75,000 – 10,000)). $3.75 million of this (25%) will be transferred to deferred tax leaving a net revaluation reserve of $11.25 million. The building valued at $50 million will require a depreciation charge of $2.5 million (50,000/20 years remaining) for the current year. This will leave a carrying amount in the statement of financial position of $77.5 million (80,000 – 2,500).

**(W3) Inventory adjustment**

| | |
|---|---:|
| Goods delivered (deduct from closing inventory) | (2,700) |
| Cost of goods sold (7,800 × 100/130) (add to closing inventory) | 6,000 |
| | —— |
| Net increase in closing inventory | 3,300 |
| | —— |

**(W4) Factored receivables**

As Highwood still bears the risk of the non-payment of the receivables, the substance of this transaction is a loan. Thus the receivables must remain on Highwood's statement of financial position and the proceeds of the 'sale' treated as a current liability. The difference between the factored receivables (10,000) and the loan received (8,700) of $1.3 million, which has been charged to administrative expenses, should be reversed except for $600,000 which should be treated as an allowance for uncollectible receivables.

**(W5) 8% convertible loan note**

This is a compound financial instrument having a debt (liability) and an equity component. These must be quantified and accounted for separately:

| Year ended 31 March | Outflow | 10% factor | Present value |
|---|---:|---:|---:|
| | $000 | | $000 |
| 20X1 | 2,400 | 0.91 | 2,184 |
| 20X2 | 2,400 | 0.83 | 1,992 |
| 20X3 | 32,400 | 0.75 | 24,300 |
| | | | —— |
| Liability component | | | 28,476 |
| Equity component (balance) | | | 1,524 |
| | | | —— |
| Proceeds of issue | | | 30,000 |
| | | | —— |

The finance cost for the year will be $2,848,000 (28,476 × 10% rounded). Thus $448,000 ($2,848k – $2,400k interest paid) will be added to the carrying amount of the loan note in the statement of financial position.

### (W6) Deferred tax

| | |
|---|---:|
| Credit balance required at 31 March 20X1 (27,000 × 25%) | 6,750 |
| Revaluation of property (W1) | (3,750) |
| Balance at 1 April 20X0 | (2,600) |
| | ———— |
| Charge to statement of profit or loss | 400 |
| | ———— |

<table>
<tr><th colspan="4" align="center">Marking scheme</th></tr>
<tr><td></td><td></td><td></td><td>Marks</td></tr>
<tr><td>(a)</td><td colspan="2">Statement of profit or loss</td><td></td></tr>
<tr><td></td><td colspan="2">Revenue</td><td>½</td></tr>
<tr><td></td><td colspan="2">Cost of sales</td><td>3</td></tr>
<tr><td></td><td colspan="2">Distribution costs</td><td>½</td></tr>
<tr><td></td><td colspan="2">Administrative expenses</td><td>1</td></tr>
<tr><td></td><td colspan="2">Finance costs</td><td>1½</td></tr>
<tr><td></td><td colspan="2">Income tax expense</td><td>1½</td></tr>
<tr><td></td><td colspan="2">Other comprehensive income</td><td>1</td></tr>
<tr><td></td><td></td><td></td><td>———</td></tr>
<tr><td></td><td></td><td>Maximum</td><td>9</td></tr>
<tr><td></td><td></td><td></td><td>———</td></tr>
<tr><td>(b)</td><td colspan="2">Statement of changes in equity</td><td></td></tr>
<tr><td></td><td colspan="2">Opening balances</td><td>1</td></tr>
<tr><td></td><td colspan="2">Other component of equity (equity option)</td><td>1</td></tr>
<tr><td></td><td colspan="2">Total comprehensive income (½ each)</td><td>1</td></tr>
<tr><td></td><td></td><td></td><td>———</td></tr>
<tr><td></td><td></td><td>Maximum</td><td>3</td></tr>
<tr><td></td><td></td><td></td><td>———</td></tr>
<tr><td>(c)</td><td colspan="2">Statement of financial position</td><td></td></tr>
<tr><td></td><td colspan="2">Property, plant and equipment</td><td>1</td></tr>
<tr><td></td><td colspan="2">Inventory</td><td>1</td></tr>
<tr><td></td><td colspan="2">Trade receivables</td><td>1</td></tr>
<tr><td></td><td colspan="2">Deferred tax</td><td>1</td></tr>
<tr><td></td><td colspan="2">Issue of 8% loan note</td><td>1½</td></tr>
<tr><td></td><td colspan="2">Liability to Easyfinance</td><td>1</td></tr>
<tr><td></td><td colspan="2">Bank overdraft</td><td>½</td></tr>
<tr><td></td><td colspan="2">Trade payables</td><td>½</td></tr>
<tr><td></td><td colspan="2">Current tax payable</td><td>½</td></tr>
<tr><td></td><td></td><td></td><td>———</td></tr>
<tr><td></td><td></td><td>Maximum</td><td>8</td></tr>
<tr><td></td><td></td><td></td><td>———</td></tr>
<tr><td>Total</td><td></td><td></td><td>20</td></tr>
<tr><td></td><td></td><td></td><td>———</td></tr>
</table>

## 354 KEYSTONE

(a) **Keystone – Statement of profit or loss and other comprehensive income for the year ended 30 September 20X1**

|  | $000 | $000 |
|---|---|---|
| Revenue |  | 377,600 |
| Cost of sales (W1) |  | (258,100) |
|  |  | ———— |
| Gross profit |  | 119,500 |
| Distribution costs |  | (14,200) |
| Administrative expenses |  |  |
| (46,400 – 24,000 dividend (50,000 × 5 × $2.40 × 4%)) |  | (22,400) |
|  |  | ———— |
| Profit from operations |  | 82,900 |
| Investment income |  | 800 |
| Finance costs |  | (350) |
|  |  | ———— |
| Profit before tax |  | 83,350 |
| Income tax expense (24,300 + 1,800 (W3)) |  | (26,100) |
|  |  | ———— |
| Profit for the year |  | 57,250 |
| Other comprehensive income |  |  |
| Revaluation of leased property | 8,000 |  |
| Transfer to deferred tax (W3) | (2,400) | 5,600 |
|  | ———— | ———— |
| Total comprehensive income for the year |  | 62,850 |
|  |  | ———— |

(b) **Keystone – Statement of financial position as at 30 September 20X1**

|  | $000 | $000 |
|---|---|---|
| Assets |  |  |
| Non-current assets |  |  |
| Property, plant and equipment (W2) |  | 78,000 |
| Current assets |  |  |
| Inventory | 56,600 |  |
| Trade receivables | 31,150 | 87,750 |
|  | ——— | ——— |
| Total assets |  | 165,750 |
|  |  | ——— |

Equity and liabilities

| | | |
|---|---:|---:|
| Equity shares of 20 cents each | | 50,000 |
| Revaluation surplus (W2) | 5,600 | |
| Retained earnings (15,600 + 57,250 – 24,000 dividend paid) | 48,850 | 54,450 |
| | | 104,450 |
| Non-current liabilities | | |
| Deferred tax (W3) | | 6,900 |
| Current liabilities | | |
| Trade payables | 27,800 | |
| Bank overdraft | 2,300 | |
| Current tax payable | 24,300 | 54,400 |
| Total equity and liabilities | | 165,750 |

**Workings** (figures in brackets in $000)

**(W1) Cost of sales**

| | $000 |
|---|---:|
| Opening inventory | 46,700 |
| Materials (64,000 – 3,000) | 61,000 |
| Production labour (124,000 – 4,000) | 120,000 |
| Factory overheads (80,000 – (4,000 × 75%)) | 77,000 |
| Amortisation of leased property (W2) | 3,000 |
| Depreciation of plant (1,000 + 6,000 (W2)) | 7,000 |
| Closing inventory | (56,600) |
| | 258,100 |

The cost of the self-constructed plant is $10 million (3,000 + 4,000 + 3,000 for materials, labour and overheads respectively that have also been deducted from the above items in cost of sales). It is not permissible to add a profit margin to self-constructed assets.

**(W2) Non-current assets**

The leased property has been amortised at $2.5 million per annum (50,000/ 20 years). The accumulated amortisation of $10 million therefore represents four years, so the remaining life at the date of revaluation is 16 years.

| | $000 |
|---|---:|
| Carrying amount at date of revaluation (50,000 – 10,000) | 40,000 |
| Revalued amount | 48,000 |
| Gross gain on revaluation | 8,000 |
| Transfer to deferred tax at 30% | (2,400) |
| Net gain to revaluation surplus | 5,600 |

The revalued amount of $48 million will be amortised over its remaining life of 16 years at $3 million per annum.

The self-constructed plant will be depreciated for six months by $1 million ($10m × 20% × 6/12) and have a carrying amount at 30 September 20X1 of $9 million. The plant in the trial balance will be depreciated by $6 million ((44.5m – 14.5m) × 20%) for the year and have a carrying amount at 30 September 20X1 of $24 million.

In summary:

|  | $000 |
|---|---|
| Leased property (48,000 – 3,000) | 45,000 |
| Plant (9,000 + 24,000) | 33,000 |
| | |
| Property, plant and equipment | 78,000 |

**(W3)  Deferred tax**

|  |  |
|---|---|
| Provision required at 30 September 20X1 ((15,000 + 8,000) × 30%) | 6,900 |
| Provision at 1 October 20X0 | (2,700) |
| | |
| Increase required | 4,200 |
| Transferred from revaluation surplus (W2) | (2,400) |
| | |
| Charge to statement of profit or loss | 1,800 |

| Marking scheme | | |
|---|---|---|
| | | *Marks* |
| (a) | Statement of profit or loss | |
| | Revenue | ½ |
| | Cost of sales | 5½ |
| | Distribution costs | ½ |
| | Administrative expenses | 1½ |
| | Investment income | 1 |
| | Finance costs | ½ |
| | Income tax expense | 1½ |
| | Other comprehensive income | 1 |
| | | |
| | Maximum | 12 |
| (b) | Statement of financial position | |
| | Property, plant and equipment | 1 |
| | Inventory | ½ |
| | Trade receivables | ½ |
| | Equity shares | ½ |
| | Revaluation surplus | 1½ |
| | Retained earnings | 1½ |
| | Deferred tax | 1 |
| | Trade payables & overdraft | 1 |
| | Current tax payable | ½ |
| | | |
| | Maximum | 8 |
| **Total** | | **20** |

## 355  FRESCO

(a)  **Fresco – Statement of profit or loss and other comprehensive income for the year ended 31 March 20X2**

| | $000 |
|---|---|
| Revenue | 350,000 |
| Cost of sales (W1) | (311,000) |
| Gross profit | 39,000 |
| Distribution costs | (16,100) |
| Administrative expenses (26,900 + 3,000 re fraud) | (29,900) |
| Finance costs (300 + 2,300 (W3)) | (2,600) |
| Loss before tax | (9,600) |
| Income tax relief (2,400 + 200 (W4) – 800) | 1,800 |
| Loss for the year | (7,800) |
| Other comprehensive income | |
| Revaluation of leased property (W2) | 4,000 |
| Total comprehensive losses | (3,800) |

(b)  **Fresco – Statement of changes in equity for the year ended 31 March 20X2**

| | Share capital $000 | Share premium $000 | Revaluation surplus $000 | Retained earnings $000 | Total equity $000 |
|---|---|---|---|---|---|
| Balances at 1 April 20X1 | 45,000 | 5,000 | nil | 5,100 | 55,100 |
| Prior period adjustment (re fraud) | | | | (1,000) | (1,000) |
| Restated balance | | | | 4,100 | |
| Rights share issue (see below) | 9,000 | 4,500 | | | 13,500 |
| Total comprehensive losses (see (i) above) | | | 4,000 | (7,800) | (3,800) |
| Transfer to retained earnings | | | (500) | 500 | |
| Balances at 31 March 20X2 | 54,000 | 9,500 | 3,500 | (3,200) | 63,800 |

The rights issue was 18 million shares (45,000/50 cents each × $^1/_5$) at 75 cents = $13.5 million. This equates to the balance on the suspense account. This should be recorded as $9 million equity shares (18,000 × 50 cents) and $4.5 million share premium (18,000 × (75 cents – 50 cents)).

The discovery of the fraud represents an error part of which is a prior period adjustment ($1 million) in accordance with IAS 8 *Accounting Policies, Changes in Accounting Estimates and Errors*.

**(c)**     **Fresco – Statement of financial position as at 31 March 20X2**

| Assets | $000 | $000 |
|---|---|---|
| Non-current assets | | |
| Property, plant and equipment (W2) | | 62,700 |
| | | |
| Current assets | | |
| Inventory | 25,200 | |
| Trade receivables (28,500 – 4,000 re fraud) | 24,500 | |
| Current tax refund | 2,400 | |
| | ——— | 52,100 |
| | | |
| Total assets | | 114,800 |
| | | |
| **Equity and liabilities** | | |
| Equity (see (ii) above) | | |
| Equity shares of 50 cents each | | 54,000 |
| Share premium | | 9,500 |
| Revaluation | | 3,500 |
| Retained earnings | | (3,200) |
| | | ——— |
| | | 63,800 |
| | | |
| Non-current liabilities | | |
| Lease liability (W3) | 15,230 | |
| Deferred tax (W4) | 3,000 | |
| | ——— | 18,230 |
| Current liabilities | | |
| Trade payables | 27,300 | |
| Lease liability (W3) | 4,070 | |
| Bank overdraft | 1,400 | |
| | ——— | 32,770 |
| | | |
| Total equity and liabilities | | 114,800 |

**Workings** (figures in brackets are in $000)

**(W1)  Cost of sales**

| | $000 |
|---|---|
| Per question | 298,700 |
| Amortisation of leased property (W2) | 4,500 |
| Depreciation of right-of-use asset (W2) | 5,000 |
| Depreciation of other plant and equipment ((47,500 – 33,500) × 20%) | 2,800 |
| | ——— |
| | 311,000 |

**(W2)  Property, plant and equipment**

|  | Leasehold property | Plant & Equipment | Right-of-use plant | Total |
|---|---|---|---|---|
|  | $000 | $000 | $000 | $000 |
| 1 April 20X1 Cost b/f | 48,000 | 47,500 |  |  |
| Depreciation b/f | (16,000) | (33,500) |  |  |
| Addition |  |  | 25,000 |  |
|  | ——— | ——— |  |  |
|  | 32,000 | 14,000 |  |  |
| Revaluation gain | 4,000 |  |  |  |
|  | ——— |  |  |  |
| Revaluation | 36,000 |  |  |  |
| Amortisation/depreciation |  |  |  |  |
| $36,000 \times \frac{1}{8}$ | (4,500) |  |  |  |
| $14,000 \times 20\%$ |  | (2,800) |  |  |
| $25,000 \times \frac{1}{5}$ |  |  | (5,000) |  |
|  | ——— | ——— | ——— | ——— |
|  | 31,500 | 11,200 | 20,000 | 62,700 |
|  | ——— | ——— | ——— | ——— |

$500,000 (4,000/8 years) of the revaluation surplus will be transferred to retained earnings (reported in the statement of changes in equity).

**(W3)  Lease liability**

|  | Balance b/f | Interest @ 10% | Payment | Balance c/f |
|---|---|---|---|---|
| Year to 31 March 20X2 | 23,000 | 2,300 | (6,000) | 19,300 |
| Year to 31 March 20X3 | 19,300 | 1,930 | (6,000) | 15,230 |

| | |
|---|---|
| Finance cost: | $2,300 |
| Non-current liability: | $15,230 |
| Current liability: (19,300 – 15,230) | $4,070 |

**(W4)  Deferred tax**

| | |
|---|---|
| Provision required at 31 March 20X2 (12,000 × 25%) | 3,000 |
| Provision at 1 April 20X1 | (3,200) |
|  | ——— |
| Credit (reduction in provision) to statement of profit or loss | (200) |
|  | ——— |

## 356 QUINCY

(a)    **Quincy – Statement of profit or loss and other comprehensive income for the year ended 30 September 20X2**

|  | $000 |
|---|---|
| Revenue (213,500 – 1,600 (W1)) | 211,900 |
| Cost of sales (W2) | (144,300) |
| | |
| Gross profit | 67,600 |
| Distribution costs | (12,500) |
| Administrative expenses (19,000 – 1,000 loan issue costs (W4)) | (18,000) |
| Loss on fair value of equity investments (17,000 – 15,700) | (1,300) |
| Investment income | 400 |
| Finance costs (W4) | (1,920) |
| | |
| Profit before tax | 34,280 |
| Income tax expense (7,400 + 1,100 – 200 (W5)) | (8,300) |
| | |
| Profit for the year | 25,980 |

(b)    **Quincy – Statement of changes in equity for the year ended 30 September 20X2**

| | Share capital $000 | Retained earnings $000 | Total equity $000 |
|---|---|---|---|
| Balance at 1 October 20X1 | 60,000 | 6,500 | 66,500 |
| Total comprehensive income | | 25,980 | 25,980 |
| Dividend paid (60,000 × 4 × 8 cents) | | (19,200) | (19,200) |
| | | | |
| Balance at 30 September 20X2 | 60,000 | 13,280 | 73,280 |

(c)    **Quincy – Statement of financial position as at 30 September 20X2**

| **Assets** | $000 | $000 |
|---|---|---|
| Non-current assets | | |
| Property, plant and equipment (W3) | | 42,500 |
| Equity financial asset investments | | 15,700 |
| | | |
| | | 58,200 |
| Current assets | | |
| Inventory | 24,800 | |
| Trade receivables | 28,500 | |
| Bank | 2,900 | 56,200 |
| | | |
| Total assets | | 114,400 |

**Equity and liabilities**

| | | |
|---|---:|---:|
| Equity shares of 25 cents each | | 60,000 |
| Retained earnings | | 13,280 |
| | | ——— |
| | | 73,280 |
| | | |
| Non-current liabilities | | |
| Deferred tax (W5) | 1,000 | |
| Deferred revenue (W1) | 800 | |
| 6% loan note (20X4) (W4) | 24,420 | 26,220 |
| | ——— | |
| | | |
| Current liabilities | | |
| Trade payables | 6,700 | |
| Deferred revenue (W1) | 800 | |
| Current tax payable | 7,400 | 14,900 |
| | ——— | ——— |
| | | |
| Total equity and liabilities | | 114,400 |
| | | ——— |

**Workings** (figures in brackets in $000)

**(W1)** The revenue for the service must be deferred. The deferred revenue must include the normal profit margin (25%) for the deferred work. At 30 September 20X2, there are two more years of servicing work, thus $1.6 million ((600 × 2) × $^{100}/_{75}$) must be deferred, split between current and non-current liabilities.

**(W2) Cost of sales**

| | $000 |
|---|---:|
| Per trial balance | 136,800 |
| Depreciation of plant (W3) | 7,500 |
| | ——— |
| | 144,300 |
| | ——— |

**(W3) Plant and equipment:**

| | $000 |
|---|---:|
| Carrying amount as at 1 October 20X1 (83,700 – 33,700) | 50,000 |
| Depreciation at 15% per annum | (7,500) |
| | ——— |
| Carrying amount as at 30 September 20X2 | 42,500 |
| | ——— |

**(W4) Loan note**

The finance cost of the loan note is charged at the effective rate of 8% applied to the carrying amount of the loan. The issue costs of the loan ($1 million) should be deducted from the proceeds of the loan ($25 million) and not treated as an administrative expense. This gives an initial carrying amount of $24 million and a finance cost of $1,920,000 (24,000 × 8%). The interest actually paid is $1.5 million (25,000 × 6%) and the difference between these amounts, of $420,000 (1,920 – 1,500), is accrued and added to the carrying amount of the loan note. This gives $24.42 million (24,000 + 420) for inclusion as a non-current liability in the statement of financial position.

**Note:** The loan interest paid of $1.5 million plus the dividend paid of $19.2 million (see (b)) equals the $20.7 million shown in the trial balance for these items.

**(W5) Deferred tax**

| | $000 |
|---|---|
| Provision required as at 30 September 20X2 (5,000 × 20%) | 1,000 |
| Less provision b/f | (1,200) |
| Credit to statement of profit or loss | (200) |

| **Marking scheme** | | |
|---|---|---|
| | | *Marks* |
| (a) | Statement of profit or loss | |
| | Revenue | 1½ |
| | Cost of sales | 1½ |
| | Distribution costs | ½ |
| | Administrative expenses | 1½ |
| | Loss on investments | 1 |
| | Investment income | ½ |
| | Finance costs | 1½ |
| | Income tax expense | 2 |
| | Maximum | 10 |
| (b) | Statement of changes in equity | |
| | Balances b/f | 1 |
| | Total comprehensive income | ½ |
| | Dividend paid | ½ |
| | | 2 |
| (c) | Statement of financial position | |
| | Property, plant and equipment | 1 |
| | Equity investments | 1 |
| | Inventory | ½ |
| | Trade receivables | ½ |
| | Bank | ½ |
| | Deferred tax | 1 |
| | Deferred revenue | 1 |
| | 6% loan note | 1½ |
| | Trade payables | ½ |
| | Current tax payable | ½ |
| | Maximum | 8 |
| | | **20** |

**357 ATLAS**

(i)   **Atlas – Statement of profit or loss and other comprehensive income for the year ended 31 March 20X3**

**Monetary figures in brackets are in $000**

|  | $000 |
|---|---|
| Revenue (550,000 – 10,000 in substance loan (W3)) | 540,000 |
| Cost of sales (W1) | (420,600) |
| | |
| Gross profit | 119,400 |
| Distribution costs | (21,500) |
| Administrative expenses (30,900 + 5,400 re directors' bonus of 1% of sales made) | (36,300) |
| Finance costs (700 + 500 (10,000 × 10% × $^6/_{12}$ re in substance loan)) | (1,200) |
| | |
| Profit before tax | 60,400 |
| Income tax expense (27,200 – 1,200 + (9,400 – 6,200) deferred tax) | (29,200) |
| | |
| Profit for the year | 31,200 |
| Other comprehensive income | |
| Revaluation gain on land and buildings (W2) | 7,000 |
| | |
| Total comprehensive income for the year | 38,200 |

(ii)  **Atlas – Statement of financial position as at 31 March 20X3**

| Assets | $000 | $000 |
|---|---|---|
| Non-current assets | | |
| Property, plant and equipment (44,500 + 52,800 (W2)) | | 97,300 |
| Current assets | | |
| Inventory (43,700 + 7,000 re in substance loan (W3)) | 50,700 | |
| Trade receivables | 42,200 | 92,900 |
| | | |
| Plant held for sale (W2) | | 3,600 |
| | | |
| Total assets | | 193,800 |

**Equity and liabilities**

Equity

| | |
|---|---:|
| Equity shares of 50 cents each | 50,000 |
| Revaluation surplus | 7,000 |
| Retained earnings (11,200 + 31,200) | 42,400 |
| | 99,400 |

Non-current liabilities

In-substance loan from Xpede

| | | |
|---|---:|---:|
| (10,000 + 500 accrued interest (W3)) | 10,500 | |
| Deferred tax | 9,400 | |
| | | 19,900 |

Current liabilities

| | | |
|---|---:|---:|
| Trade payables | 35,100 | |
| Income tax | 27,200 | |
| Accrued directors' bonus | 5,400 | |
| Bank overdraft | 6,800 | |
| | | 74,500 |
| Total equity and liabilities | | 193,800 |

**Workings** (figures in brackets are in $000)

**(W1)  Cost of sales**

| | $000 |
|---|---:|
| Per question | 411,500 |
| Closing inventory re in substance loan (W3) | (7,000) |
| Depreciation of buildings (W2) | 2,500 |
| Depreciation of plant and equipment (W2) | 13,600 |
| | 420,600 |

**(W2)  Non-current assets**

**Land and buildings**

The gain on revaluation and carrying amount of the land and buildings will be:

| | $000 |
|---|---:|
| Carrying amount at 1 April 20X2 (60,000 – 20,000) | 40,000 |
| Revaluation at that date (12,000 + 35,000) | 47,000 |
| Gain on revaluation | 7,000 |
| Buildings depreciation (35,000/14 years) | (2,500) |
| Carrying amount of land and buildings at 31 March 20X3 (47,000 – 2,500) | 44,500 |

**Plant**

The plant held for sale should be shown separately and not be depreciated after 1 October 20X2.

Other plant

| | |
|---|---:|
| Carrying amount at 1 April 20X2 (94,500 – 24,500) | 70,000 |
| Plant held for sale (9,000 – 5,000) | (4,000) |
| | —— |
| | 66,000 |
| Depreciation for year ended 31 March 20X3 (20% reducing balance) | (13,200) |
| | —— |
| Carrying amount at 31 March 20X3 | 52,800 |
| | —— |

| | |
|---|---:|
| Plant held for sale: | |
| At 1 April 20X2 (from above) | 4,000 |
| Depreciation to date of reclassification (4,000 × 20% × $^6/_{12}$) | (400) |
| | —— |
| Carrying amount at 1 October 20X2 | 3,600 |
| | —— |
| Total depreciation of plant for year ended 31 March 20X3 (13,200 + 400) | 13,600 |

As the fair value of the plant held for sale at 1 October 20X2 is $4.2 million, it should continue to be carried at its (lower) carrying amount, and no longer depreciated.

**(W3)** The transaction with Xpede will not be recognised as a sale. The presence of the option suggests that control of the goods has not passed to Xpede. Therefore this transaction will be recognised as a financial liability, with interest of 10% accruing each year.

As the transaction occurred partway through the year, 6 months interest ($500k) should be included within finance costs and added to the liability.

As this is not a sale, the goods should be transferred back into inventory at the cost of $7 million. This amount should also be deducted from cost of sales.

| Marking scheme | | | Marks |
|---|---|---|---|
| (i) | Statement of profit or loss and other comprehensive income | | |
| | Revenue | | 1 |
| | Cost of sales | | 3 |
| | Distribution costs | | ½ |
| | Administrative expenses | | 1 |
| | Finance costs | | 1 |
| | Income tax | | 1½ |
| | Other comprehensive income | | 1 |
| | | Maximum | 9 |
| (ii) | Statement of financial position | | |
| | Property, plant and equipment | | 2½ |
| | Inventory | | 1 |
| | Trade receivables | | ½ |
| | Plant held for sale (at 3,600) | | 1 |
| | Retained earnings | | 1 |
| | Revaluation surplus | | 1 |
| | In substance loan | | 1 |
| | Deferred tax | | 1 |
| | Trade payables | | ½ |
| | Current tax | | ½ |
| | Directors' bonus | | ½ |
| | Bank overdraft | | ½ |
| | | Maximum | 11 |
| **Total** | | | **20** |

## 358 MOBY

**(a)** **Moby – Statement of profit or loss and other comprehensive income for the year ended 30 September 20X3**

| | $000 |
|---|---|
| Revenue (227,800 + 10,000 (W1)) | 237,800 |
| Cost of sales (W2) | (181,900) |
| Gross profit | 55,900 |
| Administrative expenses (29,850 – 150 (W6)) | (29,700) |
| Profit from operations | 26,200 |
| Finance costs (4,000 loan + 2,930 (W4)) | (6,930) |
| Profit before tax | 19,270 |
| Income tax expense (3,400 – 2,000 (W5)) | (1,400) |
| Profit for the year | 17,870 |

Other comprehensive income

Items which will not be reclassified to profit or loss

| | |
|---|---:|
| Gain on revaluation of land and buildings (W3) | 4,400 |
| Deferred tax on gain (4,400 × 25%) | (1,100) |
| | ———— |
| Total comprehensive income for the year | 21,170 |
| | ———— |

**(b) Moby – Statement of financial position as at 30 September 20X3**

| Assets | $000 | $000 |
|---|---:|---:|
| Non-current assets | | |
| Property, plant and equipment (W3) | | 73,000 |
| Current assets | | |
| Inventory | 56,600 | |
| Trade receivables | 38,500 | |
| Contract asset (W1) | 6,000 | 101,100 |
| | ———— | ———— |
| Total assets | | 174,100 |
| | | ———— |
| **Equity and liabilities** | | |
| Equity shares of 20 cents each | | 27,000 |
| Revaluation surplus | 3,300 | |
| Retained earnings (19,800 + 17,870) | 37,670 | 40,970 |
| | ———— | ———— |
| | | 67,970 |
| Non-current liabilities | | |
| Lease liability (W4) | 16,133 | |
| Deferred tax (W5) | 7,100 | |
| Loan note (40,000 × 1.1) | 44,000 | 67,233 |
| | ———— | |
| Current liabilities | | |
| Lease liability (W4) | 6,897 | |
| Trade payables | 21,300 | |
| Bank overdraft | 7,300 | |
| Current tax payable | 3,400 | 38,897 |
| | ———— | ———— |
| Total equity and liabilities | | 174,100 |
| | | ———— |

**Workings** (monetary figures in brackets in $000)

**(W1) Contract with customer**

### Step 1 – Overall

|  | $000 | $000 |
|---|---|---|
| Total contract revenue |  | 25,000 |
| Costs incurred to date | 14,000 |  |
| Estimated costs to complete | 6,000 |  |
|  | ——— | (20,000) |
| Total contract profit |  | 5,000 |

### Step 2 – Progress

Percentage of completion is 40% (10,000/25,000)

### Step 3 – Statement of profit or loss

| | |
|---|---|
| Revenue | 10,000 |
| Cost of sales (40% × 20,000 total costs) | (8,000) |
| Profit for year | 2,000 |

### Step 4 – Statement of financial position

| | |
|---|---|
| Costs to date | 14,000 |
| Profit to date | 2,000 |
| Billed to date | (10,000) |
| Contract asset | 6,000 |

**(W2) Cost of sales**

| | $000 |
|---|---|
| Per question | 164,500 |
| Contract with customer (W1) | 8,000 |
| Depreciation of building (W3) | 2,400 |
| Depreciation of right-of-use plant (W3) | 7,000 |
| | 181,900 |

### (W3) Property, plant & equipment

| | Land | Building | Right-of-use plant | Total |
|---|---|---|---|---|
| | $000 | $000 | $000 | $000 |
| 1 October 20X2 Cost | 12,000 | 48,000 | 35,000 | |
| Accumulated depreciation | | (10,000) | (7,000) | |
| | 12,000 | 38,000 | 28,000 | |
| Revaluation gain | 4,000 | 400 | | |
| Revalued amount | 16,000 | 38,400 | | |
| Depreciation charge | | | | |
| $38,400 \times \frac{1}{16}$ | | (2,400) | | |
| $35,000 \times \frac{1}{5}$ | | | (7,000) | |
| | 16,000 | 36,000 | 21,000 | 73,000 |

### (W4) Lease liability

| | Balance b/f | Interest @ 10% | Payment | Balance c/f |
|---|---|---|---|---|
| Year to 30 September 20X3 | 29,300 | 2,930 | (9,200) | 23,030 |
| Year to 30 September 20X4 | 23,030 | 2,303 | (9,200) | 16,133 |

| | |
|---|---|
| Finance cost: | $2,930 |
| Non-current liability: | $16,133 |
| Current liability: (23,030 – 16,133) | $6,897 |

### (W5) Deferred tax

| | $000 | $000 |
|---|---|---|
| Provision b/f at 1 October 20X2 | | (8,000) |
| Provision c/f required at 30 September 20X3 | | |
| Temporary differences per question | 24,000 | |
| Revaluation of land and buildings | 4,400 | |
| | 28,400 | |
| × 25% | | 7,100 |
| Net reduction in provision | | (900) |
| Charged to other comprehensive income on revaluation gain (4,400 × 25%) | | (1,100) |
| Credit to profit or loss | | 2,000 |

**(W6) Insurance provision**

The remaining provision balance of $150,000 does not meet the criteria to be recognised as a provision as there is no present obligation. The balance is therefore reversed through administration expenses, removing the provision and reducing the expense.

| Marking scheme | | Marks |
|---|---|---|
| (a) Statement of profit or loss and other comprehensive income | | |
| Revenue | | 1½ |
| Cost of sales | | 2½ |
| Operating expenses | | 1 |
| Finance costs | | 1½ |
| Income tax expense | | 1½ |
| Gain on revaluation of land and buildings | | 1 |
| Deferred tax on gain | | 1 |
| | Maximum | 10 |
| (b) Statement of financial position | | |
| Property, plant and equipment | | 1½ |
| Inventory | | ½ |
| Amount due on contract | | 1 |
| Trade receivables | | ½ |
| Equity shares | | ½ |
| Revaluation surplus | | ½ |
| Retained earnings | | ½ |
| Non-current lease obligation | | 1 |
| Deferred tax | | 1 |
| Loan note | | 1 |
| Current lease obligation | | ½ |
| Bank overdraft | | ½ |
| Trade payables | | ½ |
| Current tax payable | | ½ |
| | Maximum | 10 |
| **Total** | | **20** |

## 359 XTOL

### (a) Xtol – Statement of profit or loss for the year ended 31 March 20X4

| | $000 |
|---|---|
| Revenue (490,000 –- 20,000 agency sales (W1)) | 470,000 |
| Cost of sales (W1) | (289,600) |
| Gross profit | 180,400 |
| Distribution costs | (33,500) |
| Administrative expenses | (36,800) |
| Other operating income – agency sales | 2,000 |
| Finance costs (900 overdraft + 3,676 (W2)) | (4,576) |
| Profit before tax | 107,524 |
| Income tax expense (28,000 + 3,200 + 3,700 (W3)) | (34,900) |
| Profit for the year | 72,624 |

### (b) Xtol – Statement of financial position as at 31 March 20X4

| | $000 | $000 |
|---|---|---|
| Non-current assets | | |
| Property, plant and equipment (75,000 + 155,500 – 57,500) | | 173,000 |
| Current assets | | |
| Inventory | 61,000 | |
| Trade receivables | 63,000 | 124,000 |
| Total assets | | 297,000 |
| **Equity and liabilities** | | |
| Equity shares of $1 each | | 66,000 |
| Share premium | | 15,000 |
| Other component of equity – equity option | | 4,050 |
| Retained earnings (15,200 + 72,624 profit for year) | | 87,824 |
| | | 172,874 |
| Non-current liabilities | | |
| Deferred tax | 8,300 | |
| 5% convertible loan note (W2) | 47,126 | 55,426 |
| Current liabilities | | |
| Trade payables (32,200 + 3,000 re Francais (W1)) | 35,200 | |
| Bank overdraft | 5,500 | |
| Current tax payable | 28,000 | 68,700 |
| Total equity and liabilities | | 297,000 |

**(c)**   **Basic earnings per share for the year ended 31 March 20X4**

| | |
|---|---:|
| Profit per statement of profit or loss | $72.624 million |
| Weighted average number of shares (W4) | 62.255 million |
| Earnings per share | 117¢ |

**Workings (figures in brackets in $000)**

**(W1) Cost of sales (including the effect of agency sales on cost of sales and trade payables)**

| | $000 |
|---|---:|
| Cost of sales per question | 290,600 |
| Remove agency costs | (15,000) |
| Depreciation of plant and equipment ((155,500 – 43,500) × 12½%) | 14,000 |
| | ——— |
| | 289,600 |
| | ——— |

The agency sales should be removed from revenue (debit $20 million) and their 'cost' from cost of sales (credit $15 million). Instead, Xtol should report the commission earned of $2 million (credit) as other operating income (or as revenue would be acceptable). This leaves a net amount of $3 million ((20,000 – 15,000) – 2,000) owing to Francais as a trade payable.

**(W2) 5% convertible loan note**

The convertible loan note is a compound financial instrument having a debt and an equity component which must be accounted for separately:

| Year ended 31 March | Outflow | 8% | Present value |
|---|---:|---:|---:|
| | $000 | | $000 |
| 20X4 | 2,500 | 0.93 | 2,325 |
| 20X5 | 2,500 | 0.86 | 2,150 |
| 20X6 | 52,500 | 0.79 | 41,475 |
| | | | ——— |
| Debt component | | | 45,950 |
| Equity component (= balance) | | | 4,050 |
| | | | ——— |
| Proceeds of issue | | | 50,000 |
| | | | ——— |

The finance cost for the year will be $3,676,000 (45,950 × 8%) and the carrying amount of the loan as at 31 March 20X4 will be $47,126,000 (45,950 + (3,676 – 2,500)).

**(W3) Deferred tax**

| | $000 |
|---|---:|
| Provision at 31 March 20X4 | 8,300 |
| Balance at 1 April 20X3 | (4,600) |
| | ——— |
| Charge to statement of profit or loss | 3,700 |
| | ——— |

**(W4) Earnings per share**

Step 1 – Theoretical ex-rights price (TERP)

| | |
|---|---|
| 5 shares @ $2.50 = | $12.50 |
| 1 share @ $1.60 = | $1.60 |
| | ——— |
| 6 shares | $14.10 |

**TERP = $14.10/6 = $2.35**

Step 2 – Rights fraction = $^{2.50}/_{2.35}$

Step 3 – Weighted average number of shares

| Date | Number | Fraction of year | Rights fraction | Weighted average |
|---|---|---|---|---|
| 1 April | 55,000,000 | $^{6}/_{12}$ | $^{2.50}/_{2.35}$ | 29,255,319 |
| 1 October | 66,000,000 | $^{6}/_{12}$ | | 33,000,000 |
| | | | | ——— |
| | | | | 62,255,319 |

There are 66 million shares at 31 March 20X4. This is after the 1 for 5 rights issue. Therefore anyone who held 5 shares at the start of the year now has 6 shares. Therefore the opening number of shares would be 55 million (66 million × $^{5}/_{6}$).

| Marking scheme | | Marks |
|---|---|---|
| (a) | Statement of profit or loss | |
| | Revenue | 1 |
| | Cost of sales | 1½ |
| | Distribution costs | ½ |
| | Administrative expenses | ½ |
| | Operating income agency sales | ½ |
| | Finance costs | 1½ |
| | Income tax expense | 1½ |
| (b) | Statement of financial position | |
| | Property, plant and equipment | ½ |
| | Inventory | ½ |
| | Trade receivables | ½ |
| | Deferred tax | ½ |
| | Share capita/share premium | ½ |
| | Retained earnings | ½ |
| | Convertible option – Equity component | 1 |
| | 5% loan note | 1½ |
| | Trade payables | 1½ |
| | Bank overdraft | ½ |
| | Current tax | ½ |
| (c) | Calculation of opening shares | 1 |
| | Calculation of TERP | 1 |
| | Application of fraction to first 6 months only | 1 |
| | Time apportionment | 1 |
| | Use of own profit from SPL | 1 |
| **Total** | | **20** |

## 360 DUNE

**Key answer tips**

This question contained many of the usual adjustments that you would expect with a published accounts question such as depreciation and tax adjustments. You were also expected to demonstrate your knowledge of accounting for held for sale assets and financial assets and liabilities in this time-consuming question.

**(a)** **Dune – Statement of profit or loss for the year ended 31 March 20X4**

|  | $000 |
|---|---|
| Revenue (400,000 | 400,000 |
| Cost of sales (W1) | (306,100) |
|  | ———— |
| Gross profit | 93,900 |
| Distribution costs | (26,400) |
| Administrative expenses (34,200 – 500 loan note issue costs) | (33,700) |
| Investment income | 1,200 |
| Gain on investments at fair value through profit or loss (28,000 – 26,500) | 1,500 |
| Finance costs (200 + 1,950 (W3) | (2,150) |
|  | ———— |
| Profit before tax | 34,350 |
| Income tax expense (12,000 – 1,400 – 1,800 (W4)) | (8,800) |
|  | ———— |
| Profit for the year | 25,550 |
|  | ———— |

**Dune – Statement of financial position as at 31 March 20X4**

|  | $000 | $000 |
|---|---|---|
| **Assets** |  |  |
| Non-current assets |  |  |
| Property, plant and equipment (W5) |  | 37,400 |
| Investments at fair value through profit or loss |  | 28,000 |
|  |  | ———— |
|  |  | 65,400 |
| Current assets |  |  |
| Inventory | 48,000 |  |
| Trade receivables | 40,700 |  |
| Bank | 15,500 | 104,200 |
|  | ———— |  |
| Non-current assets held for sale (W2) |  | 33,500 |
|  |  | ———— |
| Total assets |  | 203,100 |
|  |  | ———— |

**Equity and liabilities**

Equity

| | |
|---|---:|
| Equity shares of $1 each | 40,000 |
| Other components of equity | 20,000 |
| Retained earnings (38,400 + 25,550 – 10,000 dividend) | 53,950 |
| | 113,950 |

Non-current liabilities

| | | |
|---|---:|---:|
| Deferred tax (W4) | 4,200 | |
| 5% loan notes (W3) | 20,450 | 24,650 |

Current liabilities

| | | |
|---|---:|---:|
| Trade payables | 52,000 | |
| Accrued loan note interest (W3) | 500 | |
| Current tax payable | 12,000 | 64,500 |

| | |
|---|---:|
| Total equity and liabilities | 203,100 |

**(b)** **Earnings per share:**

EPS = $25,550,000/36,594,595 (W6)) = $0.70

Re-stated 20X3 EPS = 68c × $(^{0.74}/_{0.82})$ = $0.61

**Workings** (figures in brackets in $000)

**(W1) Cost of sales**

| | $000 |
|---|---:|
| Per question | 294,000 |
| Depreciation of leasehold property (see below) | 1,500 |
| Impairment of leasehold property (see below) | 4,000 |
| Depreciation of plant and equipment ((67,500 – 23,500) × 15%) | 6,600 |
| | 306,100 |

**(W2)** The leasehold property must be classed as a non-current asset held for sale from 1 October 20X3 at its fair value less costs to sell. It must be depreciated for six months up to this date (after which depreciation ceases). This is calculated at $1.5 million (45,000/15 years × $^{6}/_{12}$). Its carrying amount at 1 October 20X3 is therefore $37.5 million (45,000 – (6,000 + 1,500)).

Its fair value less cost to sell at this date is $33.5 million ((40,000 × 85%) – 500). It is therefore impaired by $4 million (37,500 – 33,500).

**(W3)** The finance cost of the loan note, at the effective rate of 10% applied to the correct carrying amount of the loan note of $19.5 million, is $1.95 million. The issue costs must be deducted from the proceeds of the loan note as they are not an administrative expense. The interest actually paid is $500,000 (20,000 × 5% × $^6/_{12}$) but a further $500,000 needs to be accrued as a current liability (as it will be paid soon). The difference between the total finance cost of $1.95 million and the $1 million interest payable is added to the carrying amount of the loan note to give $20.45 million (19,500 + 950) for inclusion as a non-current liability in the statement of financial position.

**(W4) Deferred tax**

| | |
|---|---:|
| Provision required at 31 March 20X4 (14,000 × 30%) | 4,200 |
| Less provision at 1 April 20X3 | (6,000) |
| | ——— |
| Credit (reduction in provision) to statement of profit or loss | (1,800) |
| | ——— |

**(W5) Property, plant and equipment**

| | |
|---|---:|
| Property, plant and equipment (67,500 – 23,500 – 6,600) | 37,400 |

**(W6) Weighted average number of shares**

Step 1 – Theoretical ex-rights price (TERP)

| | |
|---|---:|
| 4 shares @ $0.82 = | $3.28 |
| 1 share @ $0.42 = | $0.42 |
| | ——— |
| 5 shares | $3.70 |

**TERP = $3.70/5 = $0.74**

Step 2 – Rights fraction = $^{0.82}/_{0.74}$

Step 3 – Weighted average number of shares

| Date | Number | Fraction of year | Rights fraction | Weighted average |
|---|---|---|---|---|
| 1 April | 32,000,000 | $^9/_{12}$ | $^{0.82}/_{0.74}$ | 26,594,595 |
| 1 January | 40,000,000 | $^3/_{12}$ | | 10,000,000 |
| | | | | ————— |
| | | | | 36,594,595 |
| | | | | ————— |

Based on 40 million shares in issue at 31 March 20X4, a rights issue of 1 for 4 on 1 January 20X4 would have resulted in the issue of 8 million new shares (40 million × $^1/_5$). Therefore there would have been 32 million shares at the start of the year.

| | Marking scheme | | Marks |
|---|---|---|---|
| (a) | **Statement of profit or loss** | | |
| | Revenue | | ½ |
| | Cost of sales | | 2 |
| | Distribution costs | | ½ |
| | Administrative expenses | | 1 |
| | Investment income | | ½ |
| | Gain on investments | | ½ |
| | Finance costs | | 1½ |
| | Income tax expense | | 2 |
| | | | ___ |
| | | Maximum | 7½ |
| | **Statement of financial position** | | |
| | Property, plant and equipment | | ½ |
| | Investments | | ½ |
| | Inventory | | ½ |
| | Trade receivables | | ½ |
| | Bank | | ½ |
| | Non-current asset held for sale | | 1 |
| | Equity shares | | ½ |
| | Retained earnings (1 for dividend) | | 1 |
| | Deferred tax | | 1 |
| | 5% loan note | | 1 |
| | Trade payables | | ½ |
| | Accrued loan note interest | | ½ |
| | Current tax payable | | ½ |
| | | | ___ |
| | | Maximum | 7½ |
| (b) | Number of shares at start of year | | 1 |
| | TERP | | 1 |
| | Application of rights fraction and time apportionment | | 1 |
| | Use of own profit | | 1 |
| | Restatement of prior year | | 1 |
| | | | ___ |
| **Total** | | | **20** |

**Examiner's comments**

This was a question of preparing financial statements from a trial balance with various adjustments required. These involved the dealing with the use of the effective interest rate for a loan, a fair value investment, an impairment of a leasehold property (including presenting it as 'held for sale'), and accounting for taxation. The most common errors were:

- loan: the issue costs were often ignored and calculating the finance charge at the nominal rate of 5% instead of the effective rate of 10%. Omission of accrued interest from current liabilities or including it at the incorrect amount

- leasehold property: a failure to depreciate it up to the date it became 'held for sale', not calculating the subsequent impairment loss, and most candidates continuing to show it as a non-current, rather than a current, asset

- there were many errors in the treatment of the taxation, including debiting the over provision of the previous year's tax instead of crediting, treating the closing provision of deferred tax as the charge in the statement of profit or loss and confusion over SFP entries.

## 361 KANDY

### (a) Kandy – Schedule of retained earnings of Kandy as at 30 September 20X4

| | | $000 |
|---|---|---:|
| Retained earnings per trial balance | | 19,500 |
| Adjustments re: | | |
| Note (i) | Add back issue costs of loan note (W1) | 1,000 |
| | Loan finance costs (W1) | (2,610) |
| Note (ii) | Depreciation of buildings (W2) | (2,600) |
| | Depreciation of plant and equipment (W2) | (3,000) |
| Note (iii) | Income tax expense (W3) | (800) |
| Note (iv) | Gain on investments at fair value through profit or loss ($2.6m – $2m) | 600 |
| | Adjusted retained earnings | 12,090 |

### (b) Kandy – Statement of financial position as at 30 September 20X4

| Assets | $000 | $000 |
|---|---:|---:|
| Non-current assets | | |
| Property, plant and equipment (W2) | | 65,400 |
| Investments at fair value through profit or loss (per note (iv)) | | 2,600 |
| Current assets (per trial balance) | | 68,700 |
| | | ––––––– |
| Total assets | | 136,700 |
| | | ––––––– |
| **Equity and liabilities** | | |
| Equity | | |
| Equity shares of $1 each | | 40,000 |
| Revaluation surplus (12,000 – 2,400 (W2 and W3)) | 9,600 | |
| Retained earnings (from (a)) | 12,090 | |
| | ––––––– | 21,690 |
| | | ––––––– |
| | | 61,690 |
| Non-current liabilities | | |
| Deferred tax (W3) | 4,400 | |
| 6% loan note (W1) | 29,810 | |
| | ––––––– | 34,210 |
| Current liabilities (per trial balance) | 38,400 | |
| Current tax payable | 2,400 | 40,800 |
| | ––––––– | ––––––– |
| Total equity and liabilities | | 136,700 |
| | | ––––––– |

**Workings**

**(W1) Loan note**

| | $000 |
|---|---|
| Proceeds | 30,000 |
| Less issue costs incorrectly charged as expense | (1,000) |
| | |
| Initial liability | 29,000 |
| Interest at 9% effective rate | 2,610 |
| Less interest paid per trial balance | (1,800) |
| | |
| | 29,810 |

The loan note is carried at amortised cost, calculated as above. The initial value is calculated by deducting the issue costs from the proceeds of the loan note. Interest is always calculated using the effective rate.

**(W2) Non-current assets**

| | Land | Buildings | Plant & equipment | Total |
|---|---|---|---|---|
| | $000 | $000 | $000 | $000 |
| Cost b/f | 5,000 | 50,000 | 58,500 | |
| Depreciation b/f | – | (20,000) | (34,500) | |
| | | | | |
| | 5,000 | 30,000 | 24,000 | |
| Gain on revaluation | 3,000 | 9,000 | | |
| | | | | |
| Revaluation | 8,000 | 39,000 | | |
| Depreciation charge | | | | |
| $39,000 \times {}^{1}/_{15}$ | | (2,600) | | |
| $24,000 \times 12{}^{1}/_{2}\%$ | | | (3,000) | |
| | | | | |
| | 8,000 | 36,400 | 21,000 | 65,400 |

Total revaluation gain is $12 million ($3m + $9m).

**(W3) Taxation**

| **Income tax expense** | $000 |
|---|---|
| Provision for year ended 30 September 20X4 | 2,400 |
| Less over-provision in previous year | (1,100) |
| Deferred tax (see below) | (500) |
| | |
| | 800 |

| **Deferred tax** | $000 |
|---|---|
| Provision required at 30 September 20X4 ((\$10m temporary differences + \$12m revaluation) × 20%) | 4,400 |
| Provision b/f at 1 October 20X3 | (2,500) |
| | ——— |
| Movement in provision | 1,900 |
| Charge to revaluation of land and buildings (\$12m × 20%) | (2,400) |
| | ——— |
| Balance – credit to profit or loss above | (500) |
| | ——— |

| **Marking scheme** | | |
|---|---|---|
| | | *Marks* |
| (a) | Schedule of retained earnings as at 30 September 20X4 | |
| | Retained earnings per trial balance | 1 |
| | Issue costs | 1 |
| | Loan finance costs | 2 |
| | Depreciation charges | 2 |
| | Income tax expense | 2 |
| | Investments | 1 |
| | | ——— |
| | Maximum | 9 |
| | | ——— |
| (b) | Statement of financial position | |
| | Property, plant and equipment | 2 |
| | Investments | 1 |
| | Current assets | 1½ |
| | Equity shares | ½ |
| | Revaluation surplus | 2 |
| | Deferred tax | 1 |
| | 6% loan note | 1½ |
| | Current liabilities (per trial balance) | ½ |
| | Current tax payable | 1 |
| | | ——— |
| | Maximum | 11 |
| | | ——— |
| **Total** | | **20** |
| | | ——— |

## 362 CLARION

### (a)  Clarion – Statement of profit or loss for the year ended 31 March 20X5

|  | $000 |
|---|---|
| Revenue | 132,000 |
| Cost of sales (W1) | (105,300) |
| Gross profit | 26,700 |
| Distribution costs | (7,400) |
| Administrative expenses | (8,000) |
| Finance costs (W2) | (2,790) |
| Investment income (W3) | 1,000 |
| Profit before tax | 9,510 |
| Income tax expense (3,500 – 400 + 300 (W4)) | (3,400) |
| Profit for the year | 6,110 |

### (b)  Clarion – Statement of financial position as at 31 March 20X5

| Assets | $000 | $000 |
|---|---|---|
| Property, plant and equipment (85,000 – 19,000 – 17,000 (W1)) | | 49,000 |
| Investments through profit or loss | | 6,500 |
| | | 55,500 |
| Current assets | | |
| Inventory | 11,700 | |
| Trade receivables | 20,500 | |
| | | 32,200 |
| Total assets | | 87,700 |
| Equity | | |
| Equity shares of $1 each | | 35,000 |
| Retained earnings (4,700 + 6,110) | | 10,810 |
| | | 45,810 |
| Non-current liabilities | | |
| 8% loan notes | 15,000 | |
| Deferred tax (W4) | 3,000 | |
| Environmental provision (4,000 + 320 (W2)) | 4,320 | |
| Lease liability (W5) | 3,747 | |
| | | 26,067 |
| Current liabilities | | |
| Trade payables | 9,400 | |
| Lease liability (W5) | 1,023 | |
| Bank overdraft | 1,900 | |
| Current tax payable | 3,500 | |
| | | 15,823 |
| Total equity and liabilities | | 87,700 |

(c)   **Clarion – Extracts from the statement of cash flows for the year ended 31 March 20X5**

|  | $000 |
|---|---|
| **Cash flows from investing activities** |  |
| Purchase of plant and equipment | (14,000) |
| Sale of investments | 1,600 |
| **Cash flows from financing activities** |  |
| Redemption of loan notes (W6) | (5,000) |
| Repayment of lease liability (2,300 + (1,500 – 570)) (W5) | (3,230) |

**Workings (figures in brackets in $000)**

**(W1)**

|  | $000 |
|---|---|
| Cost of sales (per question) | 88,300 |
| Depreciation of plant and equipment (85,000 × 20%) | 17,000 |
|  | 105,300 |

**(W2)   Finance costs**

|  |  |
|---|---|
| 8% loan notes (800 trial balance + 800 suspense account (W6) | 1,600 |
| Lease interest (W5) | 570 |
| Bank interest | 300 |
| Environmental provision (4,000 × 8%) | 320 |
|  | 2,790 |

**(W3)   Investment income**

|  |  |
|---|---|
| Dividends received and profit on sale | 500 |
| Gains on fair value (6,500 – 6,000) | 500 |
|  | 1,000 |

**(W4)   Deferred tax**

|  |  |
|---|---|
| Provision required as at 31 March 20X5 (12,000 × 25%) | 3,000 |
| Balance at 1 April 20X4 | (2,700) |
| Charge to profit or loss | 300 |

**(W5) Lease liability**

| | Balance b/f | Interest at 10% | Paid | Balance c/f |
|---|---|---|---|---|
| | $000 | $000 | $000 | $000 |
| Year to 31 March 20X5 | 5,700 | 570 | (1,500) | 4,770 |
| Year to 31 March 20X6 | 4,770 | 477 | (1,500) | 3,747 |

| | | |
|---|---|---|
| Interest charge | | $570 |
| Non-current liability | | $3,747 |
| Current liability | (4,770 – 3747) | $1,023 |

**(W6) Elimination of suspense account**

| | $000 |
|---|---|
| Cash cost of loan note redemption (20,000 × 25%) | 5,000 |
| Six months' interest on loan note (20,000 × 8% × $^6/_{12}$) | 800 |
| | ———— |
| | 5,800 |
| | ———— |

| **Marking scheme** | |
|---|---|
| | *Marks* |
| **(a)** Statement of profit or loss | |
| Revenue | ½ |
| Cost of sales | 2 |
| Distribution costs | ½ |
| Administrative expenses | ½ |
| Investment income | 1½ |
| Finance costs | 1½ |
| Income tax expense | 1½ |
| | —— |
| | 8 |
| | —— |
| **(b)** Statement of financial position | |
| Property, plant and equipment | 1 |
| Investments through profit or loss | ½ |
| Unamortised lease premium | 1 |
| Inventory and receivables | ½ |
| Share capital | ½ |
| Retained earnings | ½ |
| 8% loan notes | 1 |
| Deferred tax | 1 |
| Environmental provision | ½ |
| Non-current lease obligation | ½ |
| Trade payables and overdraft | ½ |
| Current lease obligation | 1 |
| Current tax payable | ½ |
| | —— |
| | 9 |
| | —— |
| **(c)** Purchase of property, plant and equipment | ½ |
| Sale of investments | ½ |
| Redemption of loan notes | ½ |
| Payment of lease liability | 1½ |
| | —— |
| **Total** | **20** |
| | —— |

**363 MOSTON**  *Walk in the footsteps of a top tutor*

(a) **Moston – Statement of profit or loss and other comprehensive income for the year ended 30 June 20X5**

|  | $000 |
|---|---|
| Revenue (113,500 – 3,000 see below) | 110,500 |
| Cost of sales (W1) | (95,700) |
| Gross profit | 14,800 |
| Distribution costs | (3,600) |
| Administrative expenses (6,800 – 500 loan note issue costs) | (6,300) |
| Investment income | 300 |
| Gain on financial asset equity investments (9,600 – 8,800) | 800 |
| Finance costs (W2) | (1,710) |
| Profit before tax | 4,290 |
| Income tax expense (1,200 + 800) | (2,000) |
| Profit for the year | 2,290 |
| Other comprehensive income | |
| Items that will not be reclassified to profit or loss | |
| Gain on revaluation of property (29,000 – (28,500 – 1,900) (W1)) | 2,400 |
| Total comprehensive income for the year | 4,690 |

**Tutorial note**

The 'sale' of the maturing goods is a $3 million loan in substance, carrying 10% interest per annum. This is a loan as the option is almost certain to be exercised. This means control of the goods has not passed over from Moston. Therefore the $3 million should be removed from revenue and included as a loan.

(b) **Moston – Statement of changes in equity for the year ended 30 June 20X5**

|  | Share capital | Other components of equity | Revaluation surplus | Retained earnings | Total equity |
|---|---|---|---|---|---|
|  | $000 | $000 | $000 | $000 | $000 |
| Balance at 1 July 20X4 | 20,000 | 2,300 | 3,000 | 6,200 | 31,500 |
| Share issue | 10,000 | 7,000 | | | 17,000 |
| Total comprehensive income for the year | | | 2,400 | 2,290 | 4,690 |
| Dividends paid (20,000 × 20 cents) | | | | (4,000) | (4,000) |
| Balance at 30 June 20X5 | 30,000 | 9,300 | 5,400 | 4,490 | 49,190 |

(c)    **Moston – Statement of cash flows for the year ended 30 June 20X5**

| | $000 |
|---|---|
| **Cash flows from investing activities** | |
| Capitalised development costs | (3,200) |
| **Cash flows from financing activities** | |
| Shares issued | 17,000 |
| Dividends paid | (4,000) |
| Loan notes issued | 19,500 |

**Tutorial note**

It is crucial that you know what each section of the statement of cash flows contains so that you are able to produce extracts if required. This is likely to contain a number of figures given to you in the question, such as the loan notes and shares issued so there is scope to pick up some simpler marks here.

**Workings (monetary figures in brackets in $000)**

**(W1)  Cost of sales**

| | $000 |
|---|---|
| Per trial balance | 88,500 |
| Goods re in-substance loan | (2,000) |
| Depreciation of property (28,500/15 years) | 1,900 |
| Depreciation of plant and equipment ((27,100 – 9,100) × 15%) | 2,700 |
| Research and development expenses (see below) | 4,600 |
| | ——— |
| | 95,700 |
| | ——— |

**Tutorial note**

Development costs can only be capitalised from the date the directors became confident that the new product would be commercially successful, which is 1 May. Research of $3 million (3 months at $1 million per month) from January to March and April's costs of $1.6 million should be expensed. This leaves $3.2 million (2 months at $1.6 million per month) to be capitalised at the year end.

**(W2)  Loan interest**

| | |
|---|---|
| 5% loan note ((20,000 – 500) × 8% see below) | 1,560 |
| In-substance loan (3,000 × 10% × $^6/_{12}$) | 150 |
| | ——— |
| | 1,710 |
| | ——— |

The 5% loan note issue costs should not be charged to administrative expenses, but deducted from the proceeds of the loan.

## 364  TRIAGE

(a)  **Triage – schedule of adjustments to profit for the year ended 31 March 20X6**

|  | $000 |
|---|---:|
| Draft profit before interest and tax per trial balance | 30,000 |
| Adjustments re: | |
| Note (i) | |
| Convertible loan note finance costs (W1) | (3,023) |
| Note (ii) | |
| Amortisation of leased property (1,500 + 1,700 (W2) | (3,200) |
| Depreciation of plant and equipment (W2) | (6,600) |
| Note (iii) | |
| Current year loss on fraud (700 – 450 see below) | (250) |
| Note (iv) | |
| Income tax expense (2,700 + 700 – 800 (W3)) | (2,600) |
| | ——— |
| Profit for the year | 14,327 |
| | ——— |

(b)  **Triage– Statement of financial position as at 31 March 20X6**

|  | $000 | $000 |
|---|---:|---:|
| Assets | | |
| Non-current assets | | |
| Property, plant and equipment (64,600 + 37,400 (W2)) | | 102,000 |
| Current assets | | |
| Trade receivables (28,000 – 700 fraud) | 27,300 | |
| Other current assets per trial balance | 9,300 | 36,600 |
| | ——— | ——— |
| Total assets | | 138,600 |
| | | ——— |
| Equity and liabilities | | |
| Equity | | |
| Equity shares of $1 each | | 50,000 |
| Other component of equity (W1) | 2,208 | |
| Revaluation surplus (7,800 – 1,560 (W2)) | 6,240 | |
| Retained earnings (W4) | 17,377 | 25,825 |
| | ——— | ——— |
| | | 75,825 |
| Non-current liabilities | | |
| Deferred tax (W3) | 3,960 | |
| 6% convertible loan notes (W1) | 38,415 | 42,375 |
| | ——— | |
| Current liabilities | | |
| Per trial balance | 17,700 | |
| Current tax payable | 2,700 | 20,400 |
| | ——— | ——— |
| Total equity and liabilities | | 138,600 |
| | | ——— |

**(c)** Diluted earnings per share (W5)                                    28.9 cents

**Workings (monetary figures in brackets in $000)**

**Note:**

The $450,000 fraud loss in the previous year is a prior period adjustment (reported in the statement of changes in equity). The possible insurance claim is a contingent asset and should be ignored.

**(W1) 6% convertible loan notes**

The convertible loan notes are a compound financial instrument having a debt and an equity component which must both be quantified and accounted for separately:

| Year ended 31 March | Outflow | 8% factor | Present value |
|---|---|---|---|
| | $000 | | $000 |
| 20X6  Interest – $4m × 6% | 2,400 | 0.93 | 2,232 |
| 20X7  Interest | 2,400 | 0.86 | 2,064 |
| 20X8  Capital + interest | 42,400 | 0.79 | 33,496 |
| | | | |
| Debt component | | | 37,792 |
| Equity component (= balance) | | | 2,208 |
| | | | |
| Proceeds of issue | | | 40,000 |

The finance cost will be $3,023,000 (37,792 × 8%) and the carrying amount of the loan notes at 31 March 20X6 will be $38,415,000 (37,792 + 3,023 – 2,400).

**(W2) Non-current assets**

| | $000 |
|---|---|
| Carrying amount at 1 April 20X5 (75,000 – 15,000) | 60,000 |
| Amortisation to date of revaluation (1 October 20X5) $(75,000 \times {}^6/_{12})$ | (1,500) |
| | |
| Carrying amount at revaluation | 58,500 |
| Gain on revaluation = balance | 7,800 |
| | |
| Revaluation at 1 October 20X5 | 66,300 |
| Amortisation to year ended 31 March 20X6 (66,300/19.5 years $\times {}^6/_{12}$) | (1,700) |
| | |
| Carrying amount at 31 March 20X6 | 64,600 |

Prior to the revaluation annual amortisation is $3m (75,000/25 years). Therefore the accumulated amortisation at 1 April 20X5 of $15m represents five years' amortisation. At the date of revaluation (1 October 20X5), there will be a remaining life of 19.5 years.

Of the revaluation gain, $6.24m (80%) is credited to the revaluation surplus and $1.56m (20%) is credited to deferred tax.

**Plant and equipment**

|  | $000 |
|---|---:|
| Carrying amount at 1 April 20X5 (72,100 – 28,100) | 44,000 |
| Depreciation for year ended 31 March 20X6 (15% reducing balance) | (6,600) |
| Carrying amount at 31 March 20X6 | 37,400 |

**(W3) Deferred tax**

|  | $000 |
|---|---:|
| Provision required at 31 March 20X6: | |
| Revalued property and other assets (7,800 + 12,000) × 20%) | 3,960 |
| Provision at 1 April 20X5 | (3,200) |
| Increase in provision | 760 |
| Revaluation of land and buildings (7,800 × 20%) | (1,560) |
| Balance credited to profit or loss | 800 |

**(W4) Retained earnings**

|  | |
|---|---:|
| Balance at 1 April 20X5 | 3,500 |
| Prior period adjustment (fraud) | (450) |
| Adjusted profit for year (from (a)) | 14,327 |
| Balance at 31 March 20X6 | 17,377 |

**(W5)** The maximum additional shares on conversion is 8 million (40,000 × $^{20}/_{100}$), giving total shares of 58 million. The notional saving in loan interest is $2.418m (3,023 (from (W1) above × 80% (i.e. after tax)), giving adjusted earnings of $16.745m (14,327 + 2,418).

Therefore diluted EPS is $\dfrac{\$16,745,000 \times 100}{58 \text{ million shares}} = 28.9 \text{ cents}$

| Marking scheme | | |
|---|---|---|
| | | *Marks* |
| **(a)** | Schedule of adjustments to profit for year ended 31 March 20X6 | |
| | Profit before interest and tax b/f | ½ |
| | Loan finance costs | 1 |
| | Depreciation charges | 1½ |
| | Fraud loss | ½ |
| | Income tax expense | 1½ |
| | | ─── |
| | | 5 |
| | | ─── |
| **(b)** | Statement of financial position | |
| | Property, plant and equipment | 2½ |
| | Trade receivables | 1 |
| | Other current assets (per trial balance) | ½ |
| | Equity shares | ½ |
| | Equity option | 1 |
| | Revaluation surplus | 1 |
| | Retained earnings | 1½ |
| | Deferred tax | 1 |
| | 6% loan note | 1½ |
| | Current liabilities (per trial balance) | ½ |
| | Current tax payable | 1 |
| | | ─── |
| | | 12 |
| | | ─── |
| **(c)** | Diluted earnings per share | 3 |
| | | ─── |
| **Total** | | **20** |
| | | ─── |

**Examiner's comments**

The question was reasonably well answered with many candidates scoring at least half marks.

In part (a) a significant number of candidates prepared a series of workings but did not attempt to either summarise these or state their effect on the statement of profit or loss, which restricted the number of marks that could be awarded. The requirement for a schedule is an alternative approach to the preparation of a full statement of profit or loss, whilst still testing key principles of profit measurement. Future candidates should ensure that they avoid the common errors noted in this session:

- Some candidates did not attempt to calculate the debt component of the convertible loan note and a few calculated interest paid at the underlying rate rather than the "coupon" rate.

- A number of candidates did not correctly split the amortisation of the leased property between the two halves of the year and often used an incorrect remaining useful life to determine the amortisation charge for the second half of the year.

- Many candidates did not correctly split the fraud between the amount related to the current year and the remainder which related to the previous year and therefore was not relevant to profit or loss.

- Some candidates included the estimated amount the directors hoped could be recovered from insurers. This was a contingent asset and, as many candidates correctly noted, should be ignored.

- Candidates' understanding of current and deferred tax issues seems to have been a particular problem.

Part (b) required the preparation of the statement of financial position incorporating figures in the given trial balance and the adjustments from part (a). Common errors noted were:

- Some candidates did not include the equity component of the convertible loan note as an "other component of equity" and sometimes included it as a liability rather than equity.

- A number of candidates did not reduce the revaluation surplus by the deferred tax element or did not report the revaluation surplus at all.

- Candidates also incorrectly showed an incomplete (or omitted to show) deferred tax provision.

- Some candidates omitted the current tax liability or incorrectly adjusted it by the underprovision for the previous year.

Part (c) required a calculation of Triage's potential diluted earnings per share for the year. Many candidates either did not attempt this part of the question or made no adjustment for dilution. As the question did not ask for the basic earnings per share no marks were awarded for calculating it – the marks were specifically for the diluting adjustments.

# STATEMENT OF CASH FLOWS

365    TABBA   *Walk in the footsteps of a top tutor*

**Key answer tips**

The statement of cash flows has the usual standard calculations but take care with the government grant and leases which have balances in both current and non-current liabilities.

(a)    **Statement of cash flows of Tabba for the year ended 30 September 20X5**

| | $000 | $000 |
|---|---|---|
| Cash flows from operating activities | | |
| Profit before tax | | 50 |
| Adjustments for: | | |
| Depreciation (W1) | | 2,200 |
| Amortization of government grant (W3) | | (250) |
| Profit on sale of factory (12,000 – 7,400) | | (4,600) |
| Increase in insurance claim provision (1,500 – 1,200) | | (300) |
| Interest receivable | | (40) |
| Finance cost | | 260 |
| | | ‾‾‾‾‾‾ |
| | | (2,680) |
| Working capital adjustments: | | |
| Increase in inventories (2,550 – 1,850) | | (700) |
| Increase in trade receivables (3,100 – 2,600) | | (500) |
| Increase in trade payables (4,050 – 2,950) | | 1,100 |
| | | ‾‾‾‾‾‾ |
| Cash outflow from operations | | (2,780) |
| Interest paid | | (260) |
| Income taxes paid (W4) | | (1,350) |
| | | ‾‾‾‾‾‾ |
| Net cash outflow used in operating activities | | (4,390) |
| Cash flows from investing activities | | |
| Sale of factory | 12,000 | |
| Purchase of non-current assets (W1) | (2,900) | |
| Receipt of government grant (from question) | 950 | |
| Interest received | 40 | |
| | ‾‾‾‾‾‾ | |
| Net cash from investing activities | | 10,090 |

| Cash flows from financing activities | | |
|---|---|---|
| Issue of 6% loan notes | 800 | |
| Redemption of 10% loan notes | (4,000) | |
| Lease payments (W2) | (1,100) | |
| | ——— | |
| Net cash used in financing activities | | (4,300) |
| | | ——— |
| Net increase in cash and cash equivalents | | 1,400 |
| Cash and cash equivalents at beginning of period | | (550) |
| | | ——— |
| Cash and cash equivalents at end of period | | 850 |
| | | ——— |

**Note:** Interest paid may also be presented as a financing activity and interest received as an operating cash flow.

**Workings (T-account format)**

### (W1)  Non-current assets – Cost

| | | | |
|---|---|---|---|
| b/f | 20,200 | | |
| Right-of-use asset additions (W2) | 1,500 | Disposals | 8,600 |
| **Cash paid (balance)** | **2,900** | | |
| | | c/f | 16,000 |
| | ——— | | ——— |
| | 24,600 | | 24,600 |
| | ——— | | ——— |

### Non-current assets – Accumulated depreciation

| | | | |
|---|---|---|---|
| | | b/f | 4,400 |
| Disposal | 1,200 | **Charge for year (balance)** | **2,200** |
| c/f | 5,400 | | |
| | ——— | | ——— |
| | 6,600 | | 6,600 |
| | ——— | | ——— |

### (W2) Lease liability

| | | | | |
|---|---|---|---|---|
| Paid (balance) | **1,100** | b/f (800 + 1,700) | | 2,500 |
| | | New right-of-use assets | | 1,500 |
| c/f (900 + 2,000) | 2,900 | (W1) | | |
| | ───── | | | ───── |
| | 4,000 | | | 4,000 |
| | ───── | | | ───── |

### (W3) Government grants

| | | | | |
|---|---|---|---|---|
| | | b/f (400 + 900) | | 1,300 |
| Amortisation in SPL (balance) | **250** | New grants | | 950 |
| c/f (600 + 1,400) | 2,000 | | | |
| | ───── | | | ───── |
| | 2,250 | | | 2,250 |
| | ───── | | | ───── |

### (W4) Tax liabilities

| | | | | |
|---|---|---|---|---|
| | | b/f (1,200 + 500) | | 1,700 |
| SPL credit | 50 | | | |
| Cash paid (balance) | **1,350** | | | |
| c/f (100 + 200) | 300 | | | |
| | ───── | | | ───── |
| | 1,700 | | | 1,700 |
| | ───── | | | ───── |

### (W5) Retained earnings

| | | | | |
|---|---|---|---|---|
| | | b/f | | 850 |
| | | Profit per SPL | | 100 |
| | | Transfer from revaluation reserve | | 1,600 |
| c/f | 2,550 | | | |
| | ───── | | | ───── |
| | 2,550 | | | 2,550 |
| | ───── | | | ───── |

This working turns out to be unnecessary, but proves that no dividend was paid during the year.

**Workings (columnar format)**

**(W1) Non-current assets**

| | |
|---|---:|
| Cost/valuation b/f | 20,200 |
| New right-of-use assets (from question) | 1,500 |
| Disposals | (8,600) |
| **Acquisitions – balancing figure** | **2,900** |
| | |
| Cost/valuation c/f | 16,000 |
| | |
| Depreciation b/f | 4,400 |
| Disposal | (1,200) |
| **Charge for year – balancing figure** | **2,200** |
| | |
| Depreciation c/f | 5,400 |
| | |
| Sale of factory: | |
| Proceeds (from question) | 12,000 |
| Carrying amount (from question) | (7,400) |
| | |
| Profit on sale | 4,600 |

**(W2) Lease liability**

| | | |
|---|---|---:|
| Balance b/f | – current | 800 |
| | – non-current | 1,700 |
| New leases (from question) | | 1,500 |
| Balance c/f | – current | (900) |
| | – non-current | (2,000) |
| | | |
| Cash repayments – balancing figure | | 1,100 |

**(W3) Government grant**

| | | |
|---|---|---:|
| Balance b/f | – current | 400 |
| | – non-current | 900 |
| Grants received in year (from question) | | 950 |
| Balance c/f | – current | (600) |
| | – non-current | (1,400) |
| | | |
| Difference – amortisation credited to statement of comprehensive income | | 250 |

**(W4) Taxation**

| | |
|---|---:|
| Current provision b/f | 1,200 |
| Deferred tax b/f | 500 |
| Tax credit in statement of comprehensive income | (50) |
| Current provision c/f | (100) |
| Deferred tax c/f | (200) |
| | ───── |
| Tax paid – balancing figure | 1,350 |
| | ───── |

**(W5) Reconciliation of retained earnings**

| | |
|---|---:|
| Balance b/f | 850 |
| Transfer from revaluation reserve | 1,600 |
| Profit for period | 100 |
| | ───── |
| Balance c/f | 2,550 |
| | ───── |

**(b)** There is a huge net cash outflow from operating activities of $4,390,000 despite Tabba reporting a modest operating profit of $270,000. More detailed analysis of this difference reveals some worrying concerns for the future. Many businesses experience higher operating cash flows than the underlying operating profit mainly due to depreciation charges being added back to profits to arrive at the cash flows. This is certainly true in Tabba's case, where operating profits have been 'improved' by $2.2 million during the year in terms of the underlying cash flows.

However, the major reconciling difference is the profit on the sale of Tabba's factory of $4.6 million. This amount has been credited in the statement of profit or loss and has dramatically distorted the profit from operations. If the sale of the factory had not taken place, Tabba would show losses of $4.33 million (4,600 – 270 ignoring any possible tax effects). When Tabba publishes its financial statements this profit will almost certainly require separate disclosure which should make the effects of the transaction more transparent to the users of the financial statements. A further indication of poor operating profits is that they have been boosted by $300,000 due to an increase in the insurance claim provision (again this is not a cash flow) and $250,000 release of government grants.

Another relevant point is that there has been a very small increase in working capital of $100,000 (700 + 500 – 1,100). However, underlying this is the fact that both inventories and trade receivables are showing substantial increases (despite the profit deterioration), which may indicate the presence of bad debts or obsolete inventories, and trade payables have also increased substantially (by $1.1 million) which may be a symptom of liquidity problems prior to the sale of the factory.

**366 COALTOWN**  *Walk in the footsteps of a top tutor*

**Key answer tips**

This proved to be a relatively straightforward statement of cash flow. Watch out for the disposal, Coaltown has an unexpected COST associated with disposal that will represent a cash outflow rather than an inflow.

**Coaltown – Statement of cash flows for the year ended 31 March 20X9:**

**Note:** Figures in brackets in $000

| | $000 | $000 |
|---|---|---|
| Cash flows from operating activities | | |
| Profit before tax | | 10,200 |
| Adjustments for: | | |
| depreciation of non-current assets (W1) | 6,000 | |
| loss on disposal of displays (W1) | 1,500 | |
| | ——— | |
| Interest expense | | 600 |
| Increase in warranty provision (1,000 – 180) | | 820 |
| increase in inventory (5,200 – 4,400) | | (800) |
| increase in receivables (7,800 – 2,800) | | (5,000) |
| Decrease in payables (4,500 – 4,200) | | (300) |
| Negligence claim previously provided | | (120) |
| | | ——— |
| Cash generated from operations | | 12,900 |
| Interest paid | | (600) |
| Income tax paid (W2) | | (5,500) |
| | | ——— |
| Net cash from operating activities | | 6,800 |
| Cash flows from investing activities (W1) | | |
| Purchase of non-current assets | (20,500) | |
| Disposal cost of non-current assets | (500) | |
| | ——— | |
| Net cash used in investing activities | | (21,000) |
| | | ——— |
| | | (14,200) |
| Cash flows from financing activities | | |
| Issue of equity shares (10,500 capital (W5) + 4,000 premium (W6)) | 14,500 | |
| Issue of 10% loan notes | 1,000 | |
| Convertible loan repaid | (1,600) | |
| Equity dividends paid (W4) | (4,000) | |
| | ——— | |
| Net cash from financing activities | | 9,900 |
| | | ——— |
| Net decrease in cash and cash equivalents | | (4,300) |
| Cash and cash equivalents at beginning of period | | 700 |
| | | ——— |
| Cash and cash equivalents at end of period | | (3,600) |
| | | ——— |

**Workings (Columnar format)**

**(W1)  Non-current assets**

| Cost | $000 |
|---|---:|
| Balance b/f | 80,000 |
| Revaluation (5,000 – 2,000 depreciation) | 3,000 |
| Disposal | (10,000) |
| Balance c/f | (93,500) |
| **Cash flow for acquisitions** | **20,500** |

| Depreciation | $000 |
|---|---:|
| Balance b/f | 48,000 |
| Revaluation | (2,000) |
| Disposal | (9,000) |
| Balance c/f | (43,000) |
| **Difference – charge for year** | **6,000** |

| Disposal of displays | $000 |
|---|---:|
| Cost | 10,000 |
| Depreciation | (9,000) |
| Cost of disposal | 500 |
| **Loss on disposal** | **1,500** |

**(W2)  Income tax paid**

| | $000 |
|---|---:|
| Provision b/f | (5,300) |
| Statement of profit or loss tax charge | (3,200) |
| Provision c/f | 3,000 |
| **Difference – cash paid** | **(5,500)** |

**(W3)  Revaluation surplus**

| | $000 |
|---|---:|
| Balance b/f | 2,500 |
| Gain on revaluation | 5,000 |
| Balance c/f | (6,500) |
| **Difference – reserves transfer to retained earnings** | **(1,000)** |

**(W4) Retained earnings**

| | $000 |
|---|---|
| Balance b/f | 15,800 |
| Profit for year | 7,000 |
| Reserves transfer from revaluation surplus (W3) | 1,000 |
| Balance c/f | (19,800) |
| | |
| **Difference – dividend paid** | **(4,000)** |

**(W5) Share capital**

| | $000 |
|---|---|
| Balance b/f | 6,000 |
| Loan note converted to shares (see below) | 100 |
| Balance c/f | (16,600) |
| | |
| **Difference – shares issued** | **10,500** |

**(W6) Other components of equity**

| | $000 |
|---|---|
| Balance b/f | 500 |
| Loan note converted to shares (see below) | 300 |
| Balance c/f | 4,800 |
| | |
| **Difference – shares issued** | **4,000** |

**Therefore the total cash from share issue = 10,500 + 4,000 = $14,500.**

**Note:**

The $2 million convertible has 20% of it converted into shares. As each holder choosing conversion gets 25 shares for every $100 held, the entries for this will be:

Dr Convertible loan $400,000

    Cr Share Capital               $100,000 ($400,000 × 25/100)

    Cr Other components of equity    $300,000

The remaining 80% has been repaid, and the double entries for this would be:

Dr Convertible loan $1,600,000

    Cr Cash $1,600,000

### Workings (T-account format)

#### (W1) Non-current assets – Cost

| | | | |
|---|---|---|---|
| b/f | 80,000 | | |
| Revaluation | 3,000 | Disposals | 10,000 |
| **Cash additions (balance)** | **20,500** | | |
| | | c/f | 93,500 |
| | _____ | | _____ |
| | 103,500 | | 103,500 |
| | _____ | | _____ |

#### Non-current assets – Accumulated depreciation

| | | | |
|---|---|---|---|
| Revaluation | 2,000 | b/f | 48,000 |
| Disposal | 9,000 | **Charge for year (balance)** | **6,000** |
| c/f | 43,000 | | |
| | _____ | | _____ |
| | 54,000 | | 54,000 |
| | _____ | | _____ |

**Note:** The disposal had a carrying amount of $1m at disposal (cost $10m, accumulated depreciation $9m), and cost $500k to dispose, making a loss on disposal of $1,500k.

#### (W2) Tax Liabilities

| | | | |
|---|---|---|---|
| | | b/f | 5,300 |
| **Tax paid (balance)** | **5,500** | Charge from P/L | 3,200 |
| c/f | 3,000 | | |
| | _____ | | _____ |
| | 8,500 | | 8,500 |
| | _____ | | _____ |

#### (W3) Revaluation surplus

| | | | |
|---|---|---|---|
| | | b/f | 2,500 |
| **Retained earnings (balance)** | **1,000** | PP&E | 5,000 |
| c/f | 6,500 | | |
| | _____ | | _____ |
| | 7,500 | | 7,500 |
| | _____ | | _____ |

#### (W4) Retained earnings

| | | | |
|---|---|---|---|
| | | b/f | 15,800 |
| **Dividend paid (balance)** | **4,000** | Profit for the year | 7,000 |
| c/f | 19,800 | Revaluation surplus (W3) | 1,000 |
| | _____ | | _____ |
| | 23,800 | | 23,800 |
| | _____ | | _____ |

### (W5) Share capital

|  |  | b/f | 6,000 |
|---|---|---|---|
|  |  | Convertible loan (see note under (W6) in columnar format | 100 |
| c/f | 16,600 | **Shares issued (balance)** | **10,500** |
|  | ——— |  | ——— |
|  | 16,600 |  | 16,600 |
|  | ——— |  | ——— |

### (W6) Other components of equity

|  |  | b/f | 500 |
|---|---|---|---|
|  |  | Convertible (see note under (W6) in columnar format | 300 |
| c/f | 4,800 | **Shares issued (balance)** | **4,000** |
|  | ——— |  | ——— |
|  | 4,800 |  | 4,800 |
|  | ——— |  | ——— |

| Marking scheme | |
|---|---|
|  | *Marks* |
| Profit from operations (PBT + finance costs) | 1 |
| Depreciation charge | 2 |
| Loss on disposal | 1 |
| Warranty adjustment | 1 |
| Negligence claim | 1 |
| Working capital items | 1½ |
| Finance costs | 1 |
| Income tax paid | 1 |
| Purchase of non-current assets | 2 |
| Disposal cost of non-current assets | 1 |
| Issue of equity shares | 2 |
| Convertible repaid | 1 |
| Issue of 10% loan note | 1 |
| Dividend paid | 2 |
| Cash and cash equivalents b/f and c/f, movement | 1½ |
|  | — |
| **Total** | **20** |
|  | — |

## 367 MONTY

**Monty – Statement of cash flows for the year ended 31 March 20X3:**

**(Note: Figures in brackets are in $000)**

| | $000 | $000 |
|---|---:|---:|
| Cash flows from operating activities: | | |
| Profit before tax | | 3,000 |
| Adjustments for: | | |
| depreciation of non-current assets | | 900 |
| amortisation of non-current assets | | 200 |
| release of government grant | | (25) |
| finance costs (400 + 150) | | 550 |
| decrease in inventories (3,800 – 3,300) | | 500 |
| increase in receivables (2,950 – 2,200) | | (750) |
| increase in payables (2,650 – 2,100) | | 550 |
| | | ——— |
| Cash generated from operations | | 4,925 |
| Finance costs paid (320 (W6) + 150 lease) | | (470) |
| Income tax paid (W1) | | (425) |
| | | ——— |
| Net cash from operating activities | | 4,030 |
| Cash flows from investing activities: | | |
| Purchase of property, plant and equipment (W2) | (700) | |
| Deferred development expenditure (1,000 + 200) | (1,200) | |
| Receipt of government grant (W5) | 150 | |
| | ——— | |
| Net cash used in investing activities | | (1,750) |
| Cash flows from financing activities: | | |
| Repayment of lease liabilities (W3) | (1,050) | |
| Equity dividend paid (W4) | (550) | |
| | ——— | |
| Net cash used in financing activities | | (1,600) |
| | | ——— |
| Net increase in cash and cash equivalents | | 680 |
| Cash and cash equivalents at beginning of period | | 1,300 |
| | | ——— |
| Cash and cash equivalents at end of period | | 1,980 |
| | | ——— |

**Workings (columnar format)**

**(W1) Income tax paid**

| | $000 |
|---|---|
| Provision b/f – current | (725) |
| – deferred | (800) |
| Tax charge | (1,000) |
| Transfer from revaluation reserve | (650) |
| Provision c/f – current | 1,250 |
| – deferred | 1,500 |
| **Balance – cash paid** | **(425)** |

**(W2) Property, plant and equipment**

| | $000 |
|---|---|
| Balance b/f | 10,700 |
| Revaluation | 2,000 |
| New right-of-use asset | 1,500 |
| Depreciation | (900) |
| Balance c/f | (14,000) |
| **Balance – cash purchases** | **(700)** |

**(W3) Lease liabilities**

| | $000 |
|---|---|
| Balances b/f – current | (600) |
| – non-current | (900) |
| New lease | (1,500) |
| Balances c/f – current | 750 |
| – non-current | 1,200 |
| **Balance cash repayment** | **(1,050)** |

**(W4) Equity dividend**

| | $000 |
|---|---|
| Retained earnings b/f | 1,750 |
| Profit for the year | 2,000 |
| Retained earnings c/f | (3,200) |
| **Balance – dividend paid** | **(550)** |

**(W5) Government grant**

| | $000 |
|---|---|
| Liabilities b/f (100 + 25) | 125 |
| Released to statement of profit or loss in the year | (25) |
| Liabilities c/f | (250) |
| **Balance – receipt of government grant** | **150** |

**(W6) Finance costs**

As the loan notes are repayable at a premium, the effective rate of interest of 10% will be expensed to the statement of profit or loss each year. However, it is only the amount paid (the coupon rate of 8%) which will be taken to the statement of cash flows.

| Loan notes | $000 |
|---|---|
| Balance b/f | 4,000 |
| Statement of profit or loss expense | 400 |
| Liabilities c/f | (4,080) |
| | ——— |
| **Balance – interest paid** | **(320)** |
| | ——— |

**Workings (T-account format)**

### (W1) Tax Liabilities

| | | | |
|---|---|---|---|
| | | b/f (725 + 800) | 1,525 |
| **Tax paid (balance)** | **425** | Charge from SPL | 1,000 |
| c/f (1,250 + 1,500) | 2,750 | Transfer from revaluation surplus | 650 |
| | ——— | | ——— |
| | 3,175 | | 3,175 |
| | ——— | | ——— |

### (W2) Property, plant and equipment

| | | | |
|---|---|---|---|
| b/f | 10,700 | | |
| Revaluation | 2,000 | Depreciation | 900 |
| Right-of-use additions (W3) | 1,500 | | |
| **Cash additions (balance)** | **700** | | |
| | | c/f | 14,000 |
| | ——— | | ——— |
| | 14,900 | | 14,900 |
| | ——— | | ——— |

### (W3) Lease liabilities

| | | | |
|---|---|---|---|
| | | b/f (600 + 900) | 1,500 |
| **Liabilities repaid (balance)** | **1,050** | New PP&E (W2) | 1,500 |
| c/f (750 + 1,200) | 1,950 | | |
| | ——— | | ——— |
| | 3,000 | | 3,000 |
| | ——— | | ——— |

### (W4) Retained earnings

| | | | |
|---|---|---|---|
| | | b/f | 1,750 |
| **Dividend paid (balance)** | 550 | Profit for year | 2,000 |
| c/f | 3,200 | | |
| | 3,750 | | 3,750 |

### (W5) Government grants

| | | | |
|---|---|---|---|
| | | b/f (100 + 25) | 125 |
| Release of grant | 25 | **Receipt of grant (balance)** | **150** |
| c/f (200 + 50) | 250 | | |
| | 275 | | 275 |

### (W6) Loan note

| | | | |
|---|---|---|---|
| | | b/f | 4,000 |
| **Interest paid (balance)** | 320 | Interest expensed | 400 |
| c/f | 4,080 | | |
| | 4,400 | | 4,400 |

| Marking scheme | |
|---|---|
| | *Marks* |
| Profit from operations (PBT + finance costs) | 1 |
| Depreciation | 1 |
| Amortisation | 1 |
| Release of grant | 1 |
| Working capital items | 1½ |
| Interest paid | 2 |
| Tax paid | 2 |
| Purchase of PPE | 3 |
| Development costs | 1 |
| Grant received | 2 |
| Lease payment | 2 |
| Dividends paid | 1 |
| Movement in cash | 1½ |
| **Total** | **20** |

## 368 KINGDOM

(a)    **Kingdom – Statement of cash flows for the year ended 30 September 20X3:**

|  | $000 | $000 |
|---|---|---|
| Cash flows from operating activities: | | |
| Profit before tax | | 2,400 |
| Adjustments for: | | |
| depreciation of property, plant and equipment | | 1,500 |
| loss on sale of property, plant and equipment (2,300 – 1,800) | | 500 |
| finance costs | | 600 |
| investment properties – rentals received | | (350) |
| – fair value changes | | 700 |
| | | _____ |
| | | 5,350 |
| decrease in inventory (3,100 – 2,300) | | 800 |
| decrease in receivables (3,400 – 3,000) | | 400 |
| increase in payables (4,200 – 3,900) | | 300 |
| | | _____ |
| Cash generated from operations | | 6,850 |
| Interest paid (600 – 100 + 50) | | (550) |
| Income tax paid (W1) | | (1,950) |
| | | _____ |
| Net cash from operating activities | | 4,350 |
| Cash flows from investing activities: | | |
| Purchase of property, plant and equipment (W2) | (5,000) | |
| Sale of property, plant and equipment | 1,800 | |
| Purchase of investment property | (1,400) | |
| Investment property rentals received | 350 | |
| | _____ | |
| Net cash used in investing activities | | (4,250) |
| Cash flows from financing activities: | | |
| Issue of equity shares (17,200 – 15,000) | 2,200 | |
| Equity dividends paid (W3) | (2,800) | |
| | _____ | |
| Net cash used in financing activities | | (600) |
| | | _____ |
| Net decrease in cash and cash equivalents | | (500) |
| Cash and cash equivalents at beginning of period | | 300 |
| | | _____ |
| Cash and cash equivalents at end of period | | (200) |
| | | _____ |

**Workings – columnar format**

**(W1) Income tax**

|  |  |
|---|---:|
|  | $000 |
| Provision b/f | (1,850) |
| Profit or loss charge | (600) |
| Provision c/f | 500 |
|  | ————— |
| **Balance – tax paid** | **(1,950)** |
|  | ————— |

**(W2) Property, plant and equipment**

|  |  |
|---|---:|
|  | $000 |
| Balance b/f | (25,200) |
| Depreciation | 1,500 |
| Revaluation (downwards) | 1,300 |
| Disposal (at carrying amount) | 2,300 |
| Transfer from investment properties | (1,600) |
| Balance c/f | 26,700 |
|  | ————— |
| **Balance – acquired during year** | **(5,000)** |
|  | ————— |

**(W3) Equity dividends**

|  |  |
|---|---:|
|  | $000 |
| Retained earnings b/f | 8,700 |
| Profit for the year | 1,800 |
| Retained earnings c/f | (7,700) |
|  | ————— |
| **Balance – dividends paid** | **2,800** |
|  | ————— |

**Note:** For tutorial purposes the reconciliation of the investment properties is:

|  |  |
|---|---:|
|  | $000 |
| Balance b/f | 5,000 |
| Acquired during year (from question) | 1,400 |
| Loss in fair value | (700) |
| Transfer to property, plant and equipment | (1,600) |
|  | ————— |
| Balance c/f | 4,100 |
|  | ————— |

**Workings – T account format**

**(W1) Tax liabilities**

| | | | |
|---|---:|---|---:|
| | | b/f | 1,850 |
| **Tax paid (balance)** | **1,950** | Charge from SPL | 600 |
| c/f | 500 | | |
| | ————— | | ————— |
| | 2,450 | | 2,450 |
| | ————— | | ————— |

### (W2) Property, plant and equipment

| | | | |
|---|---|---|---|
| b/f | 25,200 | Revaluation | 1,300 |
| Transfer from investment properties | 1,600 | Depreciation | 1,500 |
| | | Disposal | 2,300 |
| **Cash additions (balance)** | **5,000** | | |
| | | c/f | 26,700 |
| | 31,800 | | 31,800 |

### (W3) Retained earnings

| | | | |
|---|---|---|---|
| | | b/f | 8,700 |
| **Dividend paid (balance)** | **2,800** | Profit for year | 1,800 |
| c/f | 7,700 | | |
| | 10,500 | | 10,500 |

### (W4) Investment properties

| | | | |
|---|---|---|---|
| b/f | 5,000 | Transfer to PP&E | 1,600 |
| Additions | 1,400 | Loss in fair value | 700 |
| | | c/f | 4,100 |
| | 6,400 | | 6,400 |

**(b)** The fall in the Kingdom's profit before tax can be analysed in three elements: changes at the gross profit level, the effect of overheads and the relative performance of the investment properties. The absolute effect on profit before tax of these elements are reductions of $1.4 million (15,000 – 13,600), $2.25 million (10,250 – 8,000) and $1.25 million (900 + 350) respectively, amounting to $4.9 million in total. Many businesses would consider returns on investment properties as not being part of operating activities, however these returns do impact on profit before tax.

**Gross profit**

Despite slightly higher revenue, gross profit fell by $1.4 million. This is attributable to a fall in the gross profit margin (down from 34.1% to 30.3%). Applying the stated 8% rise in the cost of sales, last year's cost of sales of $29 million would translate to an equivalent figure of $31.32 million in the current year which is almost the same as the actual figure ($31.3 million). This implies that the production activity/volume of sales has remained the same as last year. As the increase in revenue in the current year is only 2%, the decline in gross profitability has been caused by failing to pass on to customers the percentage increase in the cost of sales. This may be due to management's slow response to rising prices and/or to competitive pressures in the market.

Although there has been a purchase of new plant of $5 million (from the statement of cash flows), it would seem that this is a replacement of the $2.3 million of plant sold during the year. This is supported by the stagnation in the (apparent) volume of sales. The replacement of plant has probably led to slightly higher depreciation charges.

### Operating costs/overheads

The administrative expenses and distribution costs are the main culprit of the fall in profit before tax as these are $2.25 million (or 28%) higher than last year. Even if they too have increased 8%, due to rising prices, they are still much higher than would have been expected, which implies a lack of cost control of these overheads.

### Performance of investment properties

The final element of the fall in profit before tax is due to declining returns on the investment properties. This has two elements. First, a reduction in rentals received which may be due to the change in properties under rental (one transferred to owner-occupation and one newly let property) and/or a measure of falling rentals generally. The second element is clearer: there has been a decrease in the fair values of the properties in the current year compared to a rise in their fair values in the previous year. The fall in investment properties mirrors a fall in the value of Kingdom's other properties within property, plant and equipment (down $1.3 million), which suggests problems in the commercial property market.

| | Marking scheme | |
|---|---|---|
| | | *Marks* |
| (a) | Profit from operations (PBT + finance costs – investment income) | 2 |
| | Depreciation/loss on sale | 1 |
| | Working capital items | 1½ |
| | Interest paid | 1 |
| | Tax paid | 1½ |
| | Purchase of PPE | 3 |
| | Sale of PPE | ½ |
| | Purchase of investment property | 1 |
| | Investment property rentals | 1 |
| | Share issue | ½ |
| | Dividends paid | 1 |
| | Movement in cash | 1 |
| (b) | One per point made | 5 max |
| **Total** | | **20** |

# BUSINESS COMBINATIONS

**369 PREMIER**  *Walk in the footsteps of a top tutor*

**Key answer tip**

Remember the statement of profit or loss is for a period, so the results of the subsidiary must be time apportioned to reflect the post-acquisition period but in the statement of financial position, the subsidiary's results must not be time apportioned.

**(a)** **Consolidated statement of profit or loss and other comprehensive income for the year ended 30 September 20X0**

|  | $000 |
|---|---:|
| Revenue (92,500 + (45,000 × 4/12) – 4,000 intra-group sales) | 103,500 |
| Cost of sales (W6) | (78,850) |
|  | ——— |
| Gross profit | 24,650 |
| Other expenses (12,000 + (5,100 × 4/12)) | (13,700) |
|  | ——— |
| Profit for the year | 10,950 |
|  | ——— |
| Other comprehensive income: |  |
| Gain on FVTOCI investments | 300 |
|  | ——— |
| Total other comprehensive income for the year | 300 |
|  | ——— |
| Total comprehensive income | 11,250 |
|  | ——— |
| Profit for year attributable to: |  |
| Equity holders of the parent | 10,760 |
| Non-controlling interest (W7) | 190 |
|  | ——— |
|  | 10,950 |
|  | ——— |
| Total comprehensive income attributable to: |  |
| Equity holders of the parent (10,760 + 300 + 500) | 11,060 |
| Non-controlling interest (from above) | 190 |
|  | ——— |
|  | 11,250 |
|  | ——— |

**(b)** **Consolidated statement of financial position as at 30 September 20X0**

| | $000 |
|---|---|
| Non-current assets | |
| Property, plant and equipment | 38,250 |
| (25,500 + 13,900 – 1,200 (FV adj) + 50 (FV adj)) | |
| Goodwill (W3) | 9,300 |
| Investments (1,800 – 800 (consideration) + 300 (gain on FVOCI)) | 1,300 |
| | ——— |
| | 48,850 |
| Current assets (12,500 + 2,400 +130 – 130 (cash in transit) – 350 (intra-group) – 400 (W2)) | 14,150 |
| | ——— |
| | 63,000 |
| | ——— |
| Equity | |
| Equity shares of $1 each ((12,000 + 2,400 (W3)) | 14,400 |
| Share premium (W3) | 9,600 |
| Other equity reserve (500 + 300 (gain on FVOCI)) | 800 |
| Retained earnings (W5) | 13,060 |
| | ——— |
| | 39,860 |
| Non-controlling interest (W4) | 3,690 |
| | ——— |
| | 43,550 |
| Current liabilities (15,000 + 6,800 – 350 intra group balance) | 21,450 |
| | ——— |
| | 63,000 |
| | ——— |

**Tutorial note**

FVOCI investment gains are shown in other comprehensive income at the foot of the SPLOCI.

**Workings** in $000

**(W1) Group structure**

Premier

1 June 20X0 ($^{4}/_{12}$)   80%

Sanford

**(W2)  Net assets**

|  | At acquisition | At reporting date | Post-acquisition |
|---|---|---|---|
| Share capital | 5,000 | 5,000 | – |
| Retained earnings $(4,500 - (3900 \times {}^4/_{12}))$ | 3,200 | 4,500 | 1,300 |
| Property fair value | (1,200) | (1,200) | – |
| Depreciation reduction (below) |  | 50 | 50 |
| PUP (below) |  | (400) | (400) |
|  | ——— | ——— | ——— |
|  | 7,000 | 7,950 | 950 |
|  | ——— | ——— | ——— |
|  | W3 |  | W4/W5 |

The depreciation reduction is calculated as $1,200/8 years × ${}^4/_{12}$ = $50,000.

The unrealised profit in inventory is calculated as $2m × ${}^{25}/_{125}$ = $400,000.

**Tutorial note**

The fair value adjustment for property is a downwards fair value adjustment and therefore should be deducted from W2 and non-current assets.  The reduction in depreciation should be added back in W2 and added back to non-current assets.

**(W3)  Goodwill**

| Parent holding (investment) at fair value: |  |
|---|---|
| Shares $((5,000 \times 80\%) \times {}^3/_5 \times \$5)$ | 12,000 |
| Cash | 800 |
| NCI value at acquisition | 3,500 |
|  | ——— |
|  | 16,300 |
| Less: Fair value of net assets at acquisition (W2) | (7,000) |
|  | ——— |
| Goodwill on acquisition | 9,300 |
|  | ——— |

**Tutorial note**

The 2.4 million shares $(5,000 \times 80\% \times {}^3/_5)$ issued by Premier at $5 each would be recorded as share capital of $2.4 million and share premium of $9.6 million.

**(W4)  Non-controlling interest (SFP)**

| NCI value at acquisition | 3,500 |
|---|---|
| NCI share of post-acquisition reserves (W2) $(950 \times 20\%)$ | 190 |
|  | ——— |
|  | 3,690 |
|  | ——— |

**(W5)  Consolidated retained earnings**

| | |
|---|---|
| Premier | 12,300 |
| Share of Sanford post-acquisition reserves (W2) (950 × 80%) | 760 |
| | 13,060 |

**(W6)  Cost of sales**

| | |
|---|---|
| Premier | 70,500 |
| Sanford (36,000 × $^4/_{12}$) | 12,000 |
| Intra-group purchases | (4,000) |
| PUP in inventory (W2) | 400 |
| Reduction of depreciation charge (W2) | (50) |
| | 78,850 |

**(W7)  NCI (in SPL):**

| | |
|---|---|
| Subsidiary profit (3,900 × $^4/_{12}$) | 1,300 |
| Less PUP (W2) | (400) |
| Add reduction in depreciation (W2) | 50 |
| | 950 |
| | |
| NCI share at 20% | 190 |

| Marking scheme | | Marks |
|---|---|---|
| **(a)** Statement of profit or loss: | | |
| Revenue | | 1 |
| Cost of sales | | 2 |
| Other expenses | | ½ |
| Other comprehensive income – gain on investments | | ½ |
| NCI split of profit for the year | | 1½ |
| NCI split of total comprehensive income | | ½ |
| | Maximum | 6 |
| **(b)** Statement of financial position: | | |
| Property, plant and equipment | | 2 |
| Goodwill | | 3 |
| Investments | | 1 |
| Current assets | | 2 |
| Equity shares | | 1 |
| Share premium | | 1 |
| Other equity reserve | | ½ |
| Retained earnings | | 1½ |
| Non-controlling interest | | 1 |
| Current liabilities | | 1 |
| | Maximum | 14 |
| **Total** | | **20** |

**370 PATRONIC**  *Walk in the footsteps of a top tutor*

**Key answer tip**

Part (a) requires the calculation of the purchase consideration, testing the commonly examined areas of share exchanges and deferred cash payments. Part (b) requires the preparation of a consolidated statement of profit or loss – be careful to ensure that you pro-rate the subsidiary's results to take into account that they have only been a subsidiary for eight months.

**(a)** **Cost of control in Sardonic:**

| | $000 |
|---|---|
| Parent holding (investment) at fair value: | |
| Share exchange (18,000 × $^2/_3$ × $5.75) | 69,000 |
| Deferred payment ((18,000 × 2.42) × $1/1.1^2$) | 36,000 |
| | 105,000 |

**Tutorial note**

The acquisition of 18 million out of a total of 24 million equity shares is a 75% interest.

**(b)** **Patronic Group**

**Consolidated statement of profit or loss for the year ended 31 March 20X8**

| | $000 |
|---|---|
| Revenue (150,000 + (78,000 × $^8/_{12}$) – (1,250 × 8 months intra group)) | 192,000 |
| Cost of sales (W1) | (119,100) |
| Gross profit | 72,900 |
| Distribution costs (7,400 + (3,000 × $^8/_{12}$)) | (9,400) |
| Administrative expenses (12,500 + (6,000 × $^8/_{12}$)) | (16,500) |
| Finance costs (W2) | (5,000) |
| Impairment of goodwill | (2,000) |
| Share of profit from associate (6,000 × 30%) | 1,800 |
| Profit before tax | 41,800 |
| Income tax expense (10,400 + (3,600 × $^8/_{12}$)) | (12,800) |
| Profit for the year | 29,000 |

Attributable to:

| | |
|---|---|
| Equity holders of the parent (balance) | 27,400 |
| Non-controlling interest (W3) | 1,600 |
| | |
| | 29,000 |

**Workings**

**(W1) Cost of sales**

| | $000 | $000 |
|---|---|---|
| Patronic | | 94,000 |
| Sardonic (51,000 × $^8/_{12}$) | | 34,000 |
| Intra group purchases (1,250 × 8 months) | | (10,000) |
| Additional depreciation: plant (2,400/4 years × $^8/_{12}$) | 400 | |
| property (per question) | 200 | 600 |
| | | |
| Unrealised profit in inventories (3,000 × $^{20}/_{120}$) | | 500 |
| | | |
| | | 119,100 |

**Tutorial note**

For both sales revenues and cost of sales, only the post-acquisition intra-group trading should be eliminated.

**(W2) Finance costs**

| | $000 |
|---|---|
| Patronic per question | 2,000 |
| Unwinding interest – deferred consideration (36,000 × 10% × $^8/_{12}$) | 2,400 |
| Sardonic (900 × $^8/_{12}$) | 600 |
| | |
| | 5,000 |

**(W3) Non-controlling interest**

| | |
|---|---|
| Sardonic post-acquisition profit (13,500 × $^8/_{12}$) | 9,000 |
| Fair value depreciation (W1) | (600) |
| Impairment | (2,000) |
| | |
| Sardonic adjusted profit | 6,400 |
| | |
| Non-controlling interest at 25% | 1,600 |

**Examiner's comments**

The main areas where candidates went wrong were:

In **part (a)** – cost of investment

- most candidates correctly calculated the share exchange consideration, but failed to discount (for two years) the deferred cash consideration correctly.

**Part (b)** – consolidated statement of profit or loss

- a surprisingly common error was not time-apportioning (for 8 months) the subsidiary's results, instead a full year's results were often included. This is a fundamental error showing a lack of understanding of the principle that a subsidiary's results are only included the consolidated accounts from date it becomes a member of the group. A small minority of candidates proportionally consolidated, rather than equity accounted, the associate (some even proportionately consolidated the subsidiary), however this error is now becoming much less common.

- many candidates did not correctly eliminate the intra-group trading, with either no adjustment at all or eliminating pre-acquisition trading as well.

- the unrealised profit in inventory was often calculated as a gross profit percentage, whereas the question stated it was a mark-up was on cost. It was also common for this adjustment to be deducted from cost of sales rather than added.

- impairment/amortisation of goodwill was often omitted.

- the finance cost relating to the unwinding of the deferred consideration was omitted by most candidates.

- the calculation of the non-controlling interest (now called non-controlling interest) was sometimes ignored or did not take account the post-acquisition additional depreciation adjustment or time apportionment.

| **Marking scheme** | | |
|---|---|---|
| | | *Marks* |
| (a) | Goodwill of Sardonic: | |
| | Consideration | 3 |
| (b) | Statement of profit or loss: | |
| | Revenue | 2 |
| | Cost of sales | 5 |
| | Distribution costs and administrative expenses | 1 |
| | Finance costs | 2 |
| | Impairment of goodwill | 1 |
| | Share of associate's profit | 2 |
| | Income tax | 1 |
| | Parent's share | 1 |
| | Non-controlling interest | 2 |
| | Maximum | 17 |
| **Total** | | **20** |

**371 PEDANTIC**

**(a)** **Consolidated statement of profit or loss for the year ended 30 September 20X8**

|  | $000 |
|---|---|
| Revenue (85,000 + (42,000 × $^6/_{12}$) – 8,000 intra-group sales) | 98,000 |
| Cost of sales (W8) | (72,000) |
|  |  |
| Gross profit | 26,000 |
| Operating expenses (8,300 + (5,600 × $^6/_{12}$) + 1,000 impairment)) | (12,100) |
|  |  |
| Profit before tax | 13,900 |
| Income tax expense (4,700 + (1,400 × $^6/_{12}$)) | (5,400) |
|  |  |
| Profit for the year | 8,500 |
|  |  |
| Attributable to: |  |
| Equity holders of the parent (balance) | 8,700 |
| Non-controlling interest (W9) | (200) |
|  |  |
|  | 8,500 |

**(b)** **Consolidated statement of financial position as at 30 September 20X8**

|  |  |
|---|---|
| Non-current assets |  |
| Property, plant and equipment |  |
| (40,600 + 12,600 + 2,000 – 200 depreciation adjustment (W2)) | 55,000 |
| Goodwill (W3) | 3,500 |
|  |  |
|  | 58,500 |
| Current assets (W7) | 21,400 |
|  |  |
| Total assets | 79,900 |
|  |  |
| Equity and liabilities |  |
| Equity shares of $1 each (10, 000 + 1,600 (W3)) | 11,600 |
| Share premium (W3) | 8,000 |
| Retained earnings (W5) | 35,100 |
|  |  |
|  | 54,700 |
| Non-controlling interest (W4) | 5,700 |
|  |  |
| Total equity | 60,400 |
| Non-current liabilities |  |
| 10% loan notes (4,000 + 3,000) | 7,000 |
| Current liabilities (8,200 + 4,700 – 400 intra-group balance) | 12,500 |
|  |  |
| Total equity and liabilities | 79,900 |

**Workings**

**(W1) Group structure**

Pedantic

60%

Sophistic

Investment acquired on 1 April 20X8 so has been held for 6 months.

**(W2) Net assets of Sophistic**

|  | At acquisition | At reporting date | Post acq |
|---|---|---|---|
|  | $000 | $000 | $000 |
| Share capital | 4,000 | 4,000 | – |
| Retained earnings | 5,000 | 6,500 | 1,500 |
| Fair value adjustment: |  |  |  |
| Plant | 2,000 | 2,000 | – |
| Depreciation (2,000/5 years) × $^6/_{12}$ |  | (200) | (200) |
| PUP on inventory (W6) |  | (800) | (800) |
|  | ——— | ——— | ——— |
|  | 11,000 | 11,500 | 500 |
|  | ——— | ——— | ——— |

**(W3) Goodwill**

|  | $000 |
|---|---|
| Parent holding (investment) at fair value: |  |
| Share exchange ((4,000 × 60%) × $^2/_3$ × $6) | 9,600 |
| NCI value at acquisition (given) | 5,900 |
| Less: Fair value of net assets at acquisition (W2) | (11,000) |
|  | ——— |
|  | 4,500 |
| Less impairment | (1,000) |
|  | ——— |
| Goodwill as at 30 September 20X8 | 3,500 |
|  | ——— |

**(W4) Non-controlling interest (SFP)**

|  | $000 |
|---|---|
| NCI value at acquisition | 5,900 |
| NCI share of post-acquisition reserves (W2) (500 × 40%) | 200 |
| NCI share of impairment (1,000 × 40%) | (400) |
|  | ——— |
|  | 5,700 |
|  | ——— |

**(W5) Consolidated reserves**

|  | $000 |
|---|---|
| Pedantic | 35,400 |
| Sophistic (W2) (500 × 60%) | 300 |
| Pedantic share of impairment (1,000 × 60%) | (600) |
|  | 35,100 |

**(W6) Provision for unrealised profit on inventory**

The unrealised profit (PUP) in inventory is calculated as ($8 million – $5.2 million) × $^{40}/_{140}$ = $800,000.

**(W7) Current assets**

|  | $000 |
|---|---|
| Pedantic | 16,000 |
| Sophistic | 6,600 |
| PUP in inventory (W6) | (800) |
| Cash in transit | 200 |
| Intra-group balance | (600) |
|  | 21,400 |

**(W8) Cost of sales**

|  | $000 |
|---|---|
| Pedantic | 63,000 |
| Sophistic (32,000 × $^{6}/_{12}$) | 16,000 |
| Intra-group sales | (8,000) |
| PUP in inventory (W6) | 800 |
| Additional depreciation (W2) | 200 |
|  | 72,000 |

**(W9) Non-controlling interest (SPL)**

|  |  |
|---|---|
| Sophistic's post acquisition profit (3,000 × $^{6}/_{12}$) | 1,500 |
| Fair value depreciation (W8) | (200) |
| PUP (W6) | (800) |
| Impairment | (1,000) |
| Sophistic adjusted loss | (500) |
| Non-controlling interest at 40% | (200) |

**372 PANDAR**  *Walk in the footsteps of a top tutor*

**(a)    Carrying amount of investment in Ambra at 30 September 20X9**

|  | $000 |
|---|---:|
| Cost (40 million × 40% × $2) | 32,000 |
| Share of post-acquisition losses (5,000 × 40% × $^6/_{12}$) | (1,000) |
| Impairment charge | (3,000) |
| Unrealised profit (6,000 × 20% × ½ × 40%  ) | (240) |
|  | 27,760 |

**(b)    Pandar Group**

**Consolidated statement of profit or loss for the year ended 30 September 20X9**

|  | $000 | $000 |
|---|---:|---:|
| Revenue (210,000 + (150,000 × $^6/_{12}$) − 15,000 intra-group sales) |  | 270,000 |
| Cost of sales (W1) |  | (162,500) |
| Gross profit |  | 107,500 |
| Distribution costs (11,200 + (7,000 × $^6/_{12}$)) |  | (14,700) |
| Administrative expenses (18,300 + (9,000 × $^6/_{12}$) + 2,000 impairment) |  | (24,800) |
| Investment income (W2) |  | 1,100 |
| Finance costs (W3) |  | (2,300) |
| Share of loss from associate (5,000 × 40% × $^6/_{12}$) | (1,000) |  |
| Impairment of investment in associate | (3,000) |  |
| Unrealised profit in associate (see (a)) | (240) | (4,240) |
| Profit before tax |  | 62,560 |
| Income tax expense (15,000 + (10,000 × $^6/_{12}$)) |  | (20,000) |
| Profit for the year |  | 42,560 |
| Attributable to: |  |  |
| Owners of the parent |  | 41,160 |
| Non-controlling interest (W4) |  | 1,400 |
|  |  | 42,800 |

**Workings** (figures in brackets in $000)

**(W1) Cost of sales**

|  | $000 |
|---|---|
| Pandar | 126,000 |
| Salva ($100{,}000 \times {}^6/_{12}$) | 50,000 |
| Intra-group purchases | (15,000) |
| Additional depreciation: plant ($5{,}000/5$ years $\times {}^6/_{12}$) | 500 |
| Unrealised profit in inventories ($15{,}000/3 \times 20\%$) | 1,000 |
|  | 162,500 |

**Tutorial note**

As the registration of the domain name is renewable indefinitely (at only a nominal cost) it will not be amortised.

**(W2) Investment income**

|  | $000 |
|---|---|
| Per statement of comprehensive income | 9,500 |
| Intra-group interest ($50{,}000 \times 8\% \times {}^6/_{12}$) | (2,000) |
| Intra-group dividend ($8{,}000 \times 80\%$) | (6,400) |
|  | 1,100 |

**(W3) Finance costs**

|  | $000 |
|---|---|
| Pandar | 1,800 |
| Salva post-acquisition ($((3{,}000 - 2{,}000) \times {}^6/_{12}) + 2{,}000$) | 2,500 |
| Intra-group interest (W2) | (2,000) |
|  | 2,300 |

**Tutorial note**

The interest on the loan note is $2 million ($50 million $\times 8\% \times {}^6/_{12}$). This is in Salva's profit in the post-acquisition period. Thus Salva's profit of $21 million has a split of $11.5 million pre-acquisition (($21$ million + $2$ million interest) $\times {}^6/_{12}$) and $9.5 million post-acquisition.

**(W4) Non-controlling interest**

| | |
|---|---:|
| Salva's post-acquisition profit (see tutorial note above) | 9,500 |
| Fair value depreciation (W1) | (500) |
| Impairment (W1) | (2,000) |
| | ───── |
| | 7,000 |
| | ───── |
| Non-controlling interest share at 20% | 1,400 |
| | ───── |

<table>
<tr><th colspan="4" align="center">Marking scheme</th></tr>
<tr><td colspan="3"></td><td align="center">Marks</td></tr>
<tr><td>(a)</td><td colspan="2">Carrying amount of Ambra</td><td></td></tr>
<tr><td></td><td colspan="2">Cost</td><td align="center">1</td></tr>
<tr><td></td><td colspan="2">Share of post-acquisition losses</td><td align="center">1</td></tr>
<tr><td></td><td colspan="2">Unrealised profit</td><td align="center">1</td></tr>
<tr><td></td><td colspan="2">Impairment charge</td><td align="center">1</td></tr>
<tr><td></td><td></td><td align="right">Maximum</td><td align="center">4</td></tr>
<tr><td>(b)</td><td colspan="2">Statement of comprehensive income:</td><td></td></tr>
<tr><td></td><td colspan="2">Revenue</td><td align="center">1½</td></tr>
<tr><td></td><td colspan="2">Cost of sales</td><td align="center">3</td></tr>
<tr><td></td><td colspan="2">Distribution costs and administrative expenses</td><td align="center">½</td></tr>
<tr><td></td><td colspan="2">Administrative expenses</td><td align="center">1½</td></tr>
<tr><td></td><td colspan="2">Investment income</td><td align="center">2½</td></tr>
<tr><td></td><td colspan="2">Finance costs</td><td align="center">1½</td></tr>
<tr><td></td><td colspan="2">Share of associate's losses and impairment charge</td><td align="center">1½</td></tr>
<tr><td></td><td colspan="2">Income tax</td><td align="center">1</td></tr>
<tr><td></td><td colspan="2">Non-controlling interests</td><td align="center">3</td></tr>
<tr><td></td><td></td><td align="right">Maximum</td><td align="center">16</td></tr>
<tr><td>Total</td><td colspan="2"></td><td align="center">20</td></tr>
</table>

**Examiner's comments**

The main areas where candidates made errors were:

In **part (a)** calculation of associate:

- the calculation of the carrying amount of the associate was also very good, often gaining full marks. The main problems were not apportioning (by $^6/_{12}$) the losses in the year of acquisition and not applying the 40% group holding percentage. Some treated the losses as profits.

**The consolidated statement of profit or loss (b)**. Again well-prepared candidates gained good marks with most understanding the general principles. The main errors were with the more complex adjustments:

- a full year's additional depreciation of the plant was charged, but it should have been only for the post-acquisition period of six months

- many candidates incorrectly amortised the domain name. Its registration was renewable indefinitely at negligible cost so it should not have been amortised
- surprisingly a number of candidates incorrectly calculated the PUP on inventory by treating the gross profit of 20% as if it were a mark-up on cost of 20%
- the elimination of intra-group dividend was often ignored or the full $8 million was eliminated instead
- often the trading and impairment losses of the associate were ignored in preparing the statement of comprehensive income
- the non-controlling interest was frequently ignored and where it was calculated, many forgot to adjust for the additional depreciation on the fair value of the plant.

Despite the above, this was the best answered question and many candidates gained good marks.

## 373  PICANT

**Key answer tips**

Part (a) required the preparation of a statement of financial position that is relatively straightforward. Ensure that you do not include the associate on a line-by-line basis and equity account instead. One of the complications in this question is the contingent consideration. The contingent consideration should be accounted for at the acquisition date regardless of its probability providing it can be reliably measured. The fair value of the consideration has then changed at the year end. Under IFRS 3 Business Combinations the change in the consideration is taken via group retained earnings and the goodwill calculation is not adjusted for.

**(a)  Consolidated statement of financial position of Picant as at 31 March 20X4**

|  | $000 | $000 |
|---|---|---|
| Non-current assets: |  |  |
| Property, plant and equipment (37,500 + 24,500 + 2,000 FV adj – 100 FV depn) |  | 63,900 |
| Goodwill (16,000 – 3,800 (W3)) |  | 12,200 |
| Investment in associate (W6)) |  | 13,200 |
|  |  | ——— |
|  |  | 89,300 |
| Current assets |  |  |
| Inventory (10,000 + 9,000 + 1,800 GIT – 600 PUP (W7))) | 20,200 |  |
| Trade receivables (6,500 + 1,500 – 3,400 intra-group (W7)) | 4,600 | 24,800 |
|  | ——— | ——— |
| Total assets |  | 114,100 |
|  |  | ——— |

| | | |
|---|---|---|
| Equity and liabilities | | |
| Equity attributable to owners of the parent | | |
| Equity shares of $1 each | | 25,000 |
| Share premium | 19,800 | |
| Retained earnings (W5)) | 27,500 | 47,300 |
| | | 72,300 |
| Non-controlling interest (W4)) | | 8,400 |
| Total equity | | 80,700 |
| Non-current liabilities | | |
| 7% loan notes (14,500 + 2,000) | | 16,500 |
| Current liabilities | | |
| Contingent consideration | 2,700 | |
| Other current liabilities (8,300 + 7,500 – 1,600 intra-group (W7)) | 14,200 | 16,900 |
| Total equity and liabilities | | 114,100 |

**Workings** (all figures in $ million)

**(W1)  Group structure**

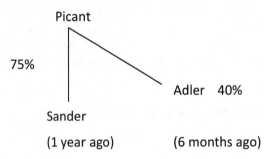

Picant

75%

Sander

(1 year ago)

Adler   40%

(6 months ago)

**(W2)  Net assets**

| | Acquisition | Reporting date | Post-acq |
|---|---|---|---|
| | $000 | $000 | $000 |
| Share capital | 8,000 | 8,000 | – |
| Retained earnings | 16,500 | 17,500 | 1,000 |
| Fair value adjustments: | | | |
| Factory | 2,000 | 2,000 | – |
| Fair value depreciation | | (100) | (100) |
| Software written off | (500) | | 500 |
| | 26,000 | 27,400 | 1,400 |
| | W3 | | W4/W5 |

**(W3) Goodwill**

Parent holding (investment) at fair value

|  | $000 |
|---|---|
| – Share exchange (8,000 × 75% × $^3/_2$ × $3.20) | 28,800 |
| – Contingent consideration | 4,200 |
|  | 33,000 |
| NCI value at acquisition (8,000 × 25% × $4.50) | 9,000 |
|  | 42,000 |
| Less: |  |
| Fair value of net assets at acquisition (W2) | (26,000) |
|  |  |
| Goodwill on acquisition | 16,000 |
| Impairment | (3,800) |
|  |  |
|  | 12,200 |

**(W4) Non-controlling interest**

|  | $000 |
|---|---|
| NCI value at acquisition (W3) | 9,000 |
| NCI share of post-acquisition reserves (1,400 × 25% (W2)) | 350 |
| NCI share of impairment (3,800 × 25%) | (950) |
|  |  |
|  | 8,400 |

**(W5) Group retained earnings**

|  | $000 |
|---|---|
| Picant's retained earnings | 27,200 |
| Sanders post-acquisition profits (1,400 × 75% (W2)) | 1,050 |
| Group share of impairment (3,800 × 75%) | (2,850) |
| Adler's post-acquisition profits (6,000 × $^6/_{12}$ × 40%) | 1,200 |
| PUP in inventories (1,800 × $^{50}/_{150}$) | (600) |
| Gain from reduction of contingent consideration (4,200 – 2,700) | 1,500 |
|  |  |
|  | 27,500 |

### (W6) Investment in associate

| | $000 |
|---|---|
| Investment at cost: | |
| Cash consideration (5,000 × 40% × $4) | 8,000 |
| 7% loan notes (5,000 × 40% × $100/50) | 4,000 |
| | 12,000 |
| Adler's post-acquisition profits (6,000 × 6/12 × 40%) | 1,200 |
| | 13,200 |

### (W7) Goods in transit and unrealised profit (PUP)

The intra-group current accounts differ by the goods-in-transit sales of $1.8 million on which Picant made a profit of $600,000 (1,800 × 50/150). Thus inventory must be increased by $1.2 million (its cost), $600,000 is eliminated from Picant's profit, $3.4 million is deducted from trade receivables and $1.6 million (3,400 – 1,800) is deducted from trade payables (other current liabilities).

**(b)** An associate is defined by IAS 28 *Investments in Associates and Joint Ventures* as an investment over which an investor has significant influence. There are several indicators of significant influence, but the most important are usually considered to be a holding of 20% or more of the voting shares and board representation. Therefore it was reasonable to assume that the investment in Adler (at 31 March 20X4) represented an associate and was correctly accounted for under the equity accounting method.

The current position (from May 20X4) is that although Picant still owns 30% of Adler's shares, Adler has become a subsidiary of Spekulate as it has acquired 60% of Adler's shares. Adler is now under the control of Spekulate (part of the definition of being a subsidiary), therefore it is difficult to see how Picant can now exert significant influence over Adler. The fact that Picant has lost its seat on Adler's board seems to reinforce this point. In these circumstances the investment in Adler falls to be treated under IFRS 9 *Financial Instruments*. It will cease to be equity-accounted from the date of loss of significant influence. Its carrying amount at that date will be its initial recognition value under IFRS 9 (fair value) and thereafter it will be accounted for in accordance with IFRS 9.

**374 PRODIGAL**

(a) **Prodigal – Consolidated statement of profit or loss and other comprehensive income for the year ended 31 March 20X1**

|  | $000 |
|---|---|
| Revenue (450,000 + (240,000 × $^6/_{12}$) – 40,000 intra-group sales) | 530,000 |
| Cost of sales (W1) | (278,800) |
|  | ––––––– |
| Gross profit | 251,200 |
| Distribution costs (23,600 + (12,000 × $^6/_{12}$)) | (29,600) |
| Administrative expenses (27,000 + (23,000 × $^6/_{12}$)) | (38,500) |
| Finance costs (1,500 + (1,200 × $^6/_{12}$)) | (2,100) |
|  | ––––––– |
| Profit before tax | 181,000 |
| Income tax expense (48,000 + (27,800 × $^6/_{12}$)) | (61,900) |
|  | ––––––– |
| Profit for the year | 119,100 |
|  | ––––––– |
| Other comprehensive income |  |
| Gain on revaluation of land (2,500 + 1,000) | 3,500 |
|  | ––––––– |
| Total comprehensive income | 122,600 |
|  | ––––––– |
| Profit attributable to: |  |
| Owners of the parent (balance) | 111,550 |
| Non-controlling interest (W2) | 7,550 |
|  | ––––––– |
|  | 119,100 |
|  | ––––––– |
| Total comprehensive income attributable to: |  |
| Owners of the parent (balance) | 114,800 |
| Non-controlling interest (W2) | 7,800 |
|  | ––––––– |
|  | 122,600 |
|  | ––––––– |

**(b)** **Prodigal – Equity section of the consolidated statement of financial position as at 31 March 20X1**

| | $000 |
|---|---|
| Equity attributable to owners of the parent | |
| Revaluation surplus (land) (W6) | 11,650 |
| Retained earnings (W5) | 201,550 |
| | 213,200 |
| Non-controlling interest (W4) | 107,800 |
| | 321,000 |
| Total equity | |

**Workings**

**(W1) Cost of sales**

| | $000 |
|---|---|
| Prodigal | 260,000 |
| Sentinel (110,000 × $^6/_{12}$) | 55,000 |
| Intra-group purchases | (40,000) |
| Unrealised profit on sale of plant | 1,000 |
| Depreciation adjustment on sale of plant (1,000/2½ years × $^6/_{12}$) | (200) |
| Unrealised profit in inventory (12,000 × 10,000/40,000) | 3,000 |
| | 278,800 |

**(W2) NCI (SPL)**

| | $000 |
|---|---|
| Sentinel's post-acquisition profit (66,000 × $^6/_{12}$) | 33,000 |
| PUP – inventory (W1) | (3,000) |
| PUP – plant depreciation (W1) | 200 |
| Sentinel's adjusted profit | 30,200 |
| Non-controlling interest at 25% | 7,550 |
| NCI (Total comprehensive income) | |
| As above | 7,550 |
| Other comprehensive income (1,000 × 25%) | 250 |
| | 7,800 |

**(W3) Net assets**

| | Acquisition | Reporting date | Post-acquisition | |
|---|---|---|---|---|
| | $000 | $000 | $000 | |
| Retained earnings | 158,000 | 191,000 | 33,000 | |
| Revaluation surplus | – | 1,000 | 1,000 | (W6) |
| PUP – inventory | – | (3,000) | (3,000) | |
| PUP – plant depreciation | – | 200 | 200 | |
| | 158,000 | 189,200 | 31,200 | |

**Note:** Only the post-acquisition impact on retained earnings should go to the group retained earnings. This will be the 33,000 post acquisition profits less the 3,000 PUP on inventory plus the PUP on plant depreciation. Therefore Prodigal's share of Sentinel's post-acquisition retained earnings = 75% × 30,200 = 22,650.

**(W4) Non-controlling interest**

| | $000 |
|---|---|
| NCI value at acquisition (note (iv)) | 100,000 |
| NCI share of post-acquisition reserves (31,200 × 25% (W3)) | 7,800 |
| | 107,800 |

**(W5) Group retained earnings**

| | $000 |
|---|---|
| Prodigal's retained earnings (90,000 b/f + 89,900 profit for year) | 179,900 |
| Sentinel's post-acquisition profits (30,200 (W3) × 75%) | 22,650 |
| NCA PUP | (1,000) |
| | 201,550 |

**(W6) Revaluation surplus**

| | $000 |
|---|---|
| Prodigal's revaluation surplus (8,400 + 2,500 gain in year) | 10,900 |
| Sentinel's post-acquisition surplus (1,000 (W3) × 75%) | 750 |
| | 11,650 |

Alternative workings for the equity section:

**Prodigal – Equity section**

| | $000 |
|---|---|
| Equity attributable to owners of the parent | |
| Revaluation surplus (land) (8,400 + 2,500 + (1,000 × 75%)) | 11,650 |
| Retained earnings (see below) | 201,550 |
| | 213,200 |
| Non-controlling interest (see below) | 107,800 |
| Total equity | 321,000 |

**Retained earnings**

| | $000 |
|---|---|
| Prodigal at 1 April 20X0 | 90,000 |
| Per statement of profit or loss | 111,550 |
| | 201,550 |

**NCI**

| | $000 |
|---|---|
| At acquisition | 100,000 |
| Per statement of profit or loss | 7,800 |
| | 107,800 |

| Marking scheme | | |
|---|---|---|
| | | *Marks* |
| **(a)** | **Statement of profit or loss and other comprehensive income** | |
| | Revenue | 2 |
| | Cost of sales | 5 |
| | Distribution costs and administrative expenses | 1 |
| | Finance costs | 1 |
| | Income tax expense | 1 |
| | Non-controlling interest in profit for year | 2 |
| | Other comprehensive income | 1 |
| | Non-controlling interest in other comprehensive income | 2 |
| | Maximum | 15 |
| **(b)** | **Consolidated equity** | |
| | Revaluation surplus | 1½ |
| | Retained earnings | 2 |
| | Non-controlling interest | 1½ |
| | Maximum | 5 |
| **Total** | | **20** |

## 375 PALADIN

**Consolidated statement of financial position of Paladin as at 30 September 20X1**

|  | $000 |
|---|---|
| Assets | |
| Non-current assets: | |
| Property, plant and equipment (40,000 + 31,000 + 4,000 FV – 1,000 FV depreciation) | 74,000 |
| Intangible assets | |
| – goodwill (W3) | 15,000 |
| – other intangibles (7,500 + 3,000 FV – 500 FV amortisation) | 10,000 |
| Investment in associate (W6) | 7,700 |
|  | 106,700 |
| Current assets (22,000 + 13,700 – 600 PUP (W7)) | 35,100 |
| Total assets | 141,800 |
| Equity and liabilities | |
| Equity attributable to owners of the parent | |
| Equity shares of $1 each | 50,000 |
| Retained earnings (W5) | 35,200 |
|  | 85,200 |
| Non-controlling interest (W4) | 7,900 |
| Total equity | 93,100 |
| Non-current liabilities | |
| Deferred tax (15,000 + 8,000) | 23,000 |
| Current liabilities (11,600 + 8,700 + 5,400 deferred consideration) | 25,700 |
| Total equity and liabilities | 141,800 |

**Workings**

**(W1) Group structure**

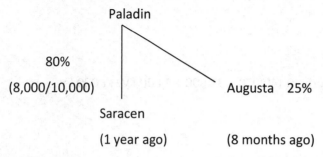

Paladin

80%
(8,000/10,000)

Saracen

(1 year ago)

Augusta   25%

(8 months ago)

**(W2) Net assets**

| | Acquisition | Reporting date | Post-acquisition |
|---|---|---|---|
| | $000 | $000 | $000 |
| Share capital | 10,000 | 10,000 | – |
| Retained earnings | 12,000 | 18,000 | 6,000 |
| Fair value adjustment to plant | 4,000 | 4,000 | – |
| Fair value depreciation (4,000/4 years) | | (1,000) | (1,000) |
| Fair value adjustment to intangible | 3,000 | 3,000 | – |
| Fair value amortisation (3,000/6 years) | | (500) | (500) |
| | 29,000 | 33,500 | 4,500 |
| | W3 | | W4/W5 |

**(W3) Goodwill**

| | $000 |
|---|---|
| Cash on acquisition | 32,000 |
| Deferred consideration ($5,400 \times {}^{100}/_{108}$) | 5,000 |
| NCI at acquisition (2,000 shares owned × $3.50 ) | 7,000 |
| Less: Fair value of net assets at acquisition (W2) | (29,000) |
| Goodwill on acquisition | 15,000 |

**(W4) Non-controlling interest**

| | $000 |
|---|---|
| Fair value on acquisition (W3) | 7,000 |
| Post-acquisition profits (4,500 (W2) × 20%) | 900 |
| | 7,900 |

**(W5) Group retained earnings**

|  | $000 |
|---|---|
| Paladin's retained earnings (25,700 + 9,200) | 34,900 |
| Saracen's post-acquisition profits (4,500 (W2) × 80%) | 3,600 |
| Augusta's post-acquisition profits (W6) | 200 |
| Augusta's impairment loss | (2,500) |
| PUP (W7) | (600) |
| Finance cost of deferred consideration (5,000 × 8%) | (400) |
|  | 35,200 |

**(W6) Investment in associate**

|  | $000 |
|---|---|
| Cash consideration | 10,000 |
| Share of post-acquisition profits (1,200 × $^{8}/_{12}$ × 25%) | 200 |
| Impairment loss | (2,500) |
|  | 7,700 |

**(W7) PUP**

The PUP in Saracen's inventory is $600,000 (2,600 × $^{30}/_{130}$).

| Marking scheme | |
|---|---|
|  | *Marks* |
| Property, plant and equipment | 2 |
| Goodwill | 5 |
| Other intangibles | 1½ |
| Investment in associate | 1½ |
| Current assets | 1½ |
| Equity shares | ½ |
| Retained earnings | 5 |
| Non-controlling interest | 1 |
| Deferred tax | ½ |
| Current liabilities | 1½ |
| **Total** | **20** |

## 376 PYRAMID

**Pyramid – Consolidated statement of financial position as at 31 March 20X2**

|  | $000 | $000 |
|---|---|---|
| **Assets** | | |
| Non-current assets: | | |
| Property, plant and equipment (38,100 + 28,500 + 3,000 fair value – 600 depreciation) | | 69,000 |
| Goodwill (W3) | | 7,400 |
| – fair value equity investments | | 2,800 |
| | | 79,200 |
| Current assets | | |
| Inventory (13,900 + 10,400 + 1,500 GIT (W7) – 500 PUP (W6)) | 25,300 | |
| Trade receivables (11,400 + 5,500 – 1,200 CIT – 3,200 intra group (W7)) | 12,500 | |
| Bank (9,400 + 600 + 1,200 CIT (W7)) | 11,200 | |
| | | 49,000 |
| Total assets | | 128,200 |
| **Equity and liabilities** | | |
| Equity attributable to owners of the parent | | |
| Equity shares of $1 each | | 25,000 |
| Reserves: | | |
| Share premium | 17,600 | |
| Retained earnings (W5) | 35,780 | |
| | | 53,380 |
| | | 78,380 |
| Non-controlling interest (W4) | | 8,480 |
| Total equity | | 86,860 |
| Non-current liabilities (16,500 + 4,000 + 1,000 deferred tax) | | 21,500 |
| Current liabilities | | |
| Deferred consideration (6,400 + 640 unwinding of discount (W5)) | 7,040 | |
| Other current liabilities (9,500 + 5,000 + 1,500 GIT – 3,200 intra group (W7) | 12,800 | |
| | | 19,840 |
| Total equity and liabilities | | 128,200 |

**Workings**

**(W1)  Group structure**

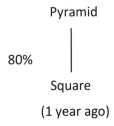

Pyramid

80%

Square

(1 year ago)

**(W2)  Net assets**

|  | Acquisition | Reporting date | Post-acquisition |
|---|---|---|---|
|  | $000 | $000 | $000 |
| Share capital | 10,000 | 10,000 | – |
| Retained earnings | 18,000 | 26,000 | 8,000 |
| Fair value: plant | 3,000 | 3,000 | – |
| Fair value plant depreciation |  | (600) | (600) |
| Fair value: deferred tax | (1,000) | (1,000) | – |
|  | 30,000 | 37,400 | 7,400 |
|  | W3 |  | W4/W5 |

**(W3)  Goodwill**

|  | $000 |
|---|---|
| Shares | 24,000 |
| Deferred consideration (8,000 × 88c × $^1/_{1.1}$) | 6,400 |
|  | 30,400 |
| NCI at acquisition (2,000 shares owned × $3.50 ) | 7,000 |
|  | 37,400 |
| Less: |  |
| Fair value of net assets at acquisition (W2) | (30,000) |
| Goodwill on acquisition | 7,400 |

**(W4)  Non-controlling interest**

|  | $000 |
|---|---|
| Fair value on acquisition (W3) | 7,000 |
| Post-acquisition profits (7,400 (W2) × 20%) | 1,480 |
|  | 8,480 |

**(W5)  Group retained earnings**

|  | $000 |
|---|---|
| Pyramid's retained earnings  (16,200 + 14,000) | 30,200 |
| Square's post-acquisition profits (7,400 (W2) × 80%) | 5,920 |
| Gain on equity investments (2,800 – 2,000) | 800 |
| PUP (W7) | (500) |
| Finance cost of deferred consideration (6,400 × 10%) | (640) |
|  | 35,780 |

**(W6)  PUP**

The PUP in inventory is $500,000 ($1.5m × $^{50}/_{150}$).

**(W7)  Intra-group current accounts**

The goods-in-transit and cash-in-transit need to be dealt with first.

Goods in transit:          Dr Inventory 1,500, Cr Payables 1,500

Cash in transit:           Dr Cash 1,200, Cr Receivables 1,200

This leaves $3,200 in receivables/payables, which can now be cancelled down.

| Marking scheme | |
|---|---|
|  | *Marks* |
| Statement of financial position: | |
| Property, plant and equipment | 2 |
| Goodwill | 4½ |
| Other equity investments | 1 |
| Inventory | 1½ |
| Receivables | 1½ |
| Bank | 1 |
| Share capital and share premium | ½ |
| Retained earnings | 3½ |
| Non-controlling interest | 1 |
| Non-current liabilities | 1 |
| Deferred consideration | 1 |
| Other current liabilities | 1½ |
| **Total** | **20** |

## 377 VIAGEM

**(a)** **Viagem consolidated goodwill on acquisition of Greca as at 1 January 20X2**

|  | $000 | $000 |
|---|---|---|
| Investment at cost |  |  |
| Shares (10,000 × 90% × $^2/_3$ × $6.50) |  | 39,000 |
| Deferred consideration (9,000 × $1.76/1.1) |  | 14,400 |
| Non-controlling interest (10,000 × 10% × $2.50) |  | 2,500 |
|  |  | ––––––– |
|  |  | 55,900 |
| Net assets (based on equity) of Greca as at 1 January 20X2 |  |  |
| Equity shares | 10,000 |  |
| Retained earnings b/f at 1 October 20X1 | 35,000 |  |
| Earnings 1 October 20X1 to acquisition (6,200 × $^3/_{12}$) | 1,550 |  |
| Fair value adjustments:   plant | 1,800 |  |
| contingent liability recognised | (450) |  |
|  | ––––––– |  |
| Net assets at date of acquisition |  | (47,900) |
|  |  | ––––––– |
| Consolidated goodwill |  | 8,000 |
|  |  | ––––––– |

**(b)** **Viagem Consolidated statement of profit or loss for year ended 30 September 20X2**

|  | $000 |
|---|---|
| Revenue (64,600 + (38,000 × $^9/_{12}$) – 7,200 intra-group sales) | 85,900 |
| Cost of sales (W1) | (64,250) |
|  | ––––––– |
| Gross profit | 21,650 |
| Distribution costs (1,600 + (1,800 × $^9/_{12}$)) | (2,950) |
| Administrative expenses (3,800 + (2,400 × $^9/_{12}$) + 2,000 goodwill impairment) | (7,600) |
| Income from associate (2,000 × 40% based on underlying earnings) | 800 |
| Finance costs (420 + (14,400 × 10% × $^9/_{12}$ re deferred consideration)) | (1,500) |
|  | ––––––– |
| Profit before tax | 10,400 |
| Income tax expense (2,800 + (1,600 × $^9/_{12}$)) | (4,000) |
|  | ––––––– |
| Profit for the year | 6,400 |
|  | ––––––– |
| Profit for year attributable to: |  |
| Equity holders of the parent (balance) | 6,180 |
| Non-controlling interest (W2) | 220 |
|  | ––––––– |
|  | 6,400 |
|  | ––––––– |

**Workings**

**(W1)  Cost of sales**

|  |  | $000 |
|---|---|---:|
| Viagem |  | 51,200 |
| Greca (26,000 × $^9/_{12}$) |  | 19,500 |
| Intra-group purchases (800 × 9 months) |  | (7,200) |
| PUP in inventory (1,500 × $^{25}/_{125}$) |  | 300 |
| Additional depreciation (1,800/3 years × $^9/_{12}$) |  | 450 |
|  |  | ———— |
|  |  | 64,250 |
|  |  | ———— |

**(W2)  NCI**

|  | $000 |
|---|---:|
| Greca post-acquisition profit (6,200 × $^9/_{12}$) | 4,650 |
| Fair value depreciation | (450) |
| Impairment | (2,000) |
|  | ———— |
| Greca adjusted profit | 2,200 |
|  | ———— |
| Non-controlling interest at 10% | 220 |
|  | ———— |

| **Marking scheme** | | | |
|---|---|---|---:|
| | | | *Marks* |
| (a) | Consolidated goodwill: | | |
| | Consideration – share exchange | | 1½ |
| | – deferred | | 1½ |
| | – NCI | | 1 |
| | Net assets – equity | | ½ |
| | – retained at acquisition | | 1 |
| | – fair value adjustments | | 1½ |
| | | | —— |
| | | Maximum | 7 |
| (b) | Consolidated statement of profit or loss | | |
| | Revenue | | 1½ |
| | Cost of sales | | 3½ |
| | Distribution costs | | ½ |
| | Administrative expenses | | 1½ |
| | Income from associate | | 1½ |
| | Finance costs | | 2 |
| | Income tax | | ½ |
| | NCI | | 2 |
| | | | —— |
| | | Maximum | 13 |
| **Total** | | | —— |
| | | | **20** |
| | | | —— |

## 378 PARADIGM

(a)    **Paradigm – Consolidated statement of financial position as at 31 March 20X3**

|  | $000 | $000 |
|---|---|---|
| **Assets** | | |
| Non-current assets: | | |
| Property, plant and equipment (47,400 + 25,500 – 3,000 fair value + 500 depreciation) | | 70,400 |
| Goodwill (W3) | | 8,500 |
| Financial asset: equity investments (7,100 + 3,900) | | 11,000 |
| | | 89,900 |
| **Current assets** | | |
| Inventory (20,400 + 8,400 – 600 PUP (W6)) | 28,200 | |
| Trade receivables (14,800 + 9,000) | 23,800 | |
| Bank | 2,100 | |
| | | 54,100 |
| **Total assets** | | 144,000 |
| | | |
| **Equity and liabilities** | | |
| Equity attributable to owners of the parent | | |
| Equity shares of $1 each (40,000 + 6,000 (W3) | | 46,000 |
| Share premium (W3) | | 6,000 |
| Retained earnings (W5) | | 33,925 |
| Non-controlling interest (W4) | | 8,800 |
| | | |
| **Total equity** | | 94,725 |
| 10% loan notes (8,000 + 1,500 (W3) | | 9,500 |
| Current liabilities | | |
| Trade payables (17,600 + 13,000 + 75 interest (W7)) | 30,675 | |
| Bank overdraft | 9,100 | |
| | | 39,775 |
| | | |
| **Total equity and liabilities** | | 144,000 |

**Workings**

**(W1)  Group structure**

Paradigm

75%

Strata
(6 months)

### (W2) Net assets

|  | At acquisition | At reporting date | Post-acquisition |
|---|---|---|---|
|  | $000 | $000 | $000 |
| Share capital | 20,000 | 20,000 | – |
| Retained earnings | (6,000) | 4,000 | 10,000 |
| Fair value adjustment | (3,000) | (3,000) | – |
| Fair value depreciation $(3,000 \times {}^6/_{36})$ |  | 500 | 500 |
| Gain on equity investment |  | 700 | 700 |
|  | 11,000 | 22,200 | 11,200 |

### (W3) Goodwill

|  | $000 |
|---|---|
| Share exchange $((20,000 \times 75\%) \times {}^2/_5 \times \$2)$ | 12,000 |
| 10% loan notes $(15,000 \times {}^{\$100}/_{1,000})$ | 1,500 |
| Non-controlling interest $(20,000 \times 25\% \times \$1.20)$ | 6,000 |
| Less: Fair value of net assets at acquisition (W2) | (11,000) |
| Goodwill on acquisition | 8,500 |

The market value of the shares issued of $12 million would be recorded as $6 million share capital and $6 million share premium as the shares have a nominal value of $1 each and an issue value of $2 each.

### (W4) Non-controlling interest

|  | $000 |
|---|---|
| Fair value on acquisition (W3) | 6,000 |
| Post-acquisition profits (11,200 (W2) × 25%) | 2,800 |
|  | 8,800 |

### (W5) Group retained earnings

|  | $000 |
|---|---|
| Paradigm's retained earnings  (19,200 + 7,400) | 26,600 |
| Strata's post-acquisition profit (11,200 (W2) × 75%) | 8,400 |
| PUP in inventory (W6) | (600) |
| Loss on equity investments (7,500 – 7,100) | (400) |
| Interest on unrecorded loan notes (W7) | (75) |
|  | 33,925 |

**(W6) PUP**

Strata's inventory (from Paradigm) at 31 March 20X3 is $4.6 million (one month's supply). At a mark-up on cost of 15%, there would be $600,000 of profit $(4,600 \times {}^{15}/_{115})$ in the inventory.

**(W7) Interest**

Paradigm must accrue for the interest on the loan notes issued to Strata's previous owners. This is $1,500 \times 10\% \times {}^{6}/_{12} = 75$.

**(b)** IFRS 3 *Business Combinations* requires the purchase consideration for an acquired entity to be allocated to the fair value of the assets, liabilities and contingent liabilities acquired (henceforth referred to as net assets) with any residue being allocated to goodwill. This also means that those net assets will be recorded at fair value in the consolidated statement of financial position. This is entirely consistent with the way other net assets are recorded when first transacted (i.e. the initial cost of an asset is normally its fair value). This ensures that individual assets and liabilities are correctly valued in the consolidated statement of financial position. Whilst this may sound obvious, consider what would happen if say a property had a carrying amount of $5 million, but a fair value of $7 million at the date it was acquired. If the carrying amount rather than the fair value was used in the consolidation it would mean that tangible assets (property, plant and equipment) would be understated by $2 million and intangible assets (goodwill) would be overstated by the same amount.

There could also be a 'knock-on' effect with incorrect depreciation charges in the years following an acquisition and incorrect calculation of any goodwill impairment. Thus the use of carrying amounts rather than fair values would not give a 'faithful representation' as required by the Framework.

The assistant's comment regarding the inconsistency of value models in the consolidated statement of financial position is a fair point, but it is really a deficiency of the historical cost concept rather than a flawed consolidation technique. Indeed the fair value of the subsidiary's net assets represent the historical cost to the parent. To overcome much of the inconsistency, there would be nothing to prevent the parent from applying the revaluation model to its property, plant and equipment.

| Marking scheme | | Marks |
|---|---|---|
| **(a)** | Property, plant and equipment | 1½ |
| | Goodwill | 3½ |
| | Equity investments | 1 |
| | Inventory | ½ |
| | Receivables | ½ |
| | Bank | ½ |
| | Equity shares | 1 |
| | Share premium | ½ |
| | Retained earnings | 2½ |
| | Non-controlling interest | 1½ |
| | 10% loan notes | 1 |
| | Trade payables | ½ |
| | Bank overdraft | ½ |
| **(b)** | One mark per point made | 5 |
| **Total** | | **20** |

## 379 POLESTAR

(a) **Consolidated statement of profit or loss for the year ended 30 September 20X3**

|  | $000 |
|---|---|
| Revenue $(110,000 + (66,000 \times {}^6/_{12}) - (4,000 + 9,000 \text{ intra-group sales}))$ | 130,000 |
| Cost of sales (W6) | (109,300) |
|  |  |
| Gross profit | 20,700 |
| Operating expenses $(8,500 + (4,400 \times {}^6/_{12}) - 3,400 \text{ negative goodwill (W3)})$ | (7,300) |
| Decrease in contingent consideration $(1,800 - 1,500)$ | 300 |
|  |  |
| Profit before tax | 13,700 |
| Income tax expense $(3,500 - (1,000 \times {}^6/_{12}))$ | (3,000) |
|  |  |
| Profit for the year | 10,700 |
|  |  |
| Profit for year attributable to: |  |
| Equity holders of the parent | 11,450 |
| Non-controlling interest losses (W7) | (750) |
|  |  |
|  | 10,700 |

(b) **Consolidated statement of financial position as at 30 September 20X3**

|  | $000 |
|---|---|
| **Assets** |  |
| Non-current assets |  |
| Property, plant and equipment $(41,000 + 21,000 + 2,000 \text{ FV} - 100 \text{ dep'n})$ | 63,900 |
| Investments $(13,500 - (13,500 \text{ cash consideration}))$ | – |
|  |  |
|  | 63,900 |
| Current assets $(19,000 + 4,800 - 600 \text{ PUP})$ | 23,200 |
|  |  |
| Total assets | 87,100 |

Equity attributable to owners of the parent

| | |
|---|---:|
| Equity shares of 50 cents each | 30,000 |
| Retained earnings (W5) | 29,950 |
| | ——— |
| | 59,950 |
| Non-controlling interest (W4) | 2,850 |
| | ——— |
| Total equity | 62,800 |
| Current liabilities | |
| Contingent consideration | 1,500 |
| Other (15,000 + 7,800) | 22,800 |
| | ——— |
| Total equity and liabilities | 87,100 |
| | ——— |

## Workings

### (W1) Group structure

Polestar

75%

Southstar

(6 months)

### (W2) Net assets

| | At acquisition | At reporting date | Post-acquisition |
|---|---:|---:|---:|
| | $000 | $000 | $000 |
| Share capital | 6,000 | 6,000 | – |
| Retained earnings | 14,300 | 12,000 | (2,300) |
| Fair value adjustment | 2,000 | 2,000 | – |
| Fair value depreciation | | | |
| $(2,000/10 \text{ years} \times {}^{6}/_{12})$ | | (100) | (100) |
| PUP (W6) | | (600) | (600) |
| | ——— | ——— | ——— |
| | 22,300 | 19,300 | (3,000) |
| | ——— | ——— | ——— |
| | W3 | | W4/W5 |

**(W3) Goodwill**

| | $000 |
|---|---:|
| Cash consideration (6,000/0.5 × 75% × $1.50) | 13,500 |
| Contingent consideration | 1,800 |
| Non-controlling interest | 3,600 |
| | 18,900 |
| Fair value of net assets at acquisition (W2) | (22,300) |
| Gain on bargain purchase | (3,400) |

**(W4) Non-controlling interest**

| | $000 |
|---|---:|
| Fair value on acquisition (W3) | 3,600 |
| Post-acquisition losses ((3,000) (W2) × 25%) | (750) |
| | 2,850 |

**(W5) Group retained earnings**

| | $000 |
|---|---:|
| Polestar's retained earnings | 28,500 |
| Southstar's post-acquisition losses((3,000) (W2) × 75%) | (2,250) |
| Change in contingent consideration | 300 |
| Gain on bargain purchase (W3) | 3,400 |
| | 29,950 |

**(W6) Cost of sales**

| | $000 |
|---|---:|
| Polestar | 88,000 |
| Southstar (67,200 × 6/12) | 33,600 |
| Intra-group purchases (4,000 + 9,000) | (13,000) |
| PUP in inventory (see below) | 600 |
| Additional depreciation on leased property (W2) | 100 |
| | 109,300 |

The profit on the sale of the goods back to Polestar is $3.6 million (9,000 − (4,000 + 1,400)). Therefore the unrealised profit in the inventory of $1.5 million at 30 September 20X3 is $600,000 $(3,600 \times {}^{1,500}/_{9,000})$.

### (W7)  NCI (SPL)

|  | $000 |
|---|---:|
| Southstar post-acquisition loss ($(4,600) \times {}^{6}/_{12}$) | (2,300) |
| PUP (W6) | (600) |
| Fair value depreciation (W2) | (100) |
|  | ————— |
| Southstar adjusted profit | (3,000) |
|  | ————— |
| Non-controlling interest at 25% | (750) |
|  | ————— |

**Note:**  IFRS 3 *Business Combinations* says negative goodwill should be credited to the acquirer, thus none of it relates to the non-controlling interests.

| Marking scheme | | | |
|---|---|---|---:|
| | | | *Marks* |
| (a) | Consolidated statement of profit or loss | | |
| | Revenue | | 1½ |
| | Cost of sales | | 3 |
| | Operating expenses | – other than negative goodwill | ½ |
| | | – negative goodwill finance costs | 3½ |
| | Decrease in contingent consideration | | ½ |
| | Income tax expense | | ½ |
| | Non-controlling interest | | 1½ |
| | | | ——— |
| | | Maximum | 11 |
| | | | ——— |
| (b) | Consolidated statement of financial position | | |
| | Property, plant and equipment | | 1½ |
| | Current assets | | 1½ |
| | Equity shares | | ½ |
| | Retained earnings | | 3 |
| | Non-controlling interest | | 1 |
| | Contingent consideration | | 1 |
| | Other current liabilities | | ½ |
| | | | ——— |
| | | Maximum | 9 |
| | | | ——— |
| **Total** | | | **20** |
| | | | ——— |

## 380 PENKETH

### (a) Goodwill

|  | $000 |
|---|---|
| Deferred consideration $(1.54 \times 90{,}000 \times {}^1/_{1.1})$ | 126,000 |
| Non-controlling interest $(1.25 \times 60{,}000)$ | 75,000 |
| Less: Fair value of net assets at acquisition (W1) | (196,000) |
| Goodwill on acquisition | 5,000 |

### (b) Penketh – Consolidated statement of profit or loss and other comprehensive income for the year ended 31 March 20X4

|  | $000 |
|---|---|
| Revenue $(620{,}000 + (310{,}000 \times {}^6/_{12}) - 20{,}000$ intra-group sales) | 755,000 |
| Cost of sales (W2) | (457,300) |
| Gross profit | 297,700 |
| Distribution costs $(40{,}000 + (20{,}000 \times {}^6/_{12}))$ | (50,000) |
| Administrative expenses $(36{,}000 + (25{,}000 \times {}^6/_{12}) + (5{,}000/5 \times {}^6/_{12}$ re customer list)) | (49,000) |
| Investment income $(5{,}000 + (1{,}600 \times {}^6/_{12}))$ | 5,800 |
| Finance costs $(2{,}000 + (5{,}600 \times 6/12) + (126{,}000 \times 10\% \times {}^6/_{12}$ re deferred consideration)) | (11,100) |
| Profit before tax | 193,400 |
| Income tax expense $(45{,}000 + (31{,}000 \times {}^6/_{12}))$ | (60,500) |
| Profit for the year | 132,900 |
| Other comprehensive income |  |
| Loss on revaluation of land (2,200 – 1,000 gain for Sphere) | (1,200) |
| Total comprehensive income for the year | 131,700 |

| Profit attributable to: |  |
|---|---|
| Owners of the parent (balance) | 117,700 |
| Non-controlling interest (W2) | 15,200 |
|  | 132,900 |

| Total comprehensive income attributable to: |  |
|---|---|
| Owners of the parent (balance) | 116,100 |
| Non-controlling interest (W3) | 15,600 |
|  | 131,700 |

**Workings**

**(W1) Net assets of Sphere at acquisition**

|  | $000 |
|---|---|
| Share capital | 75,000 |
| Retained earnings (70,000 b/f + 40,000 pre-acquisition) | 110,000 |
| Fair value adjustment – plant | 6,000 |
| Fair value adjustment – customer relationships | 5,000 |
|  | 196,000 |

**(W2) Cost of sales**

|  | $000 |
|---|---|
| Penketh | 400,000 |
| Sphere $(150,000 \times {}^6/_{12})$ | 75,000 |
| Intra-group purchases | (20,000) |
| Additional depreciation of plant $(6,000/2 \text{ years} \times {}^6/_{12})$ | 1,500 |
| Unrealised profit in inventory $(20,000 \times {}^1/_5 \times {}^{25}/_{125})$ | 800 |
|  | 457,300 |

**(W3) Non-controlling interest in profit for the year**

|  | $000 |
|---|---|
| Sphere's profit $(80,000 \times {}^6/_{12})$ | 40,000 |
| Fair value depreciation – plant | (1,500) |
| Fair value amortisation – customer list | (500) |
| Sphere adjusted profit | 38,000 |
| Non-controlling interest at 40% | 15,200 |

**Non-controlling interest in total comprehensive income**

|  | $000 |
|---|---|
| Non-controlling interest in statement of profit or loss (above) | 15,200 |
| Other comprehensive income $(1,000 \times 40\%)$ | 400 |
|  | 15,600 |

| Marking scheme | | Marks |
|---|---|---|
| **(a)** Goodwill | | |
| Consideration paid | | 1 |
| NCI at acquisition | | 1 |
| Net assets at acquisition (½ share capital, 1½ RE, 1 FV adjustments) | | 3 |
| **(b)** Consolidated statement of profit or loss and other comprehensive income | | |
| Revenue | | 2 |
| Cost of sales | | 3 |
| Distribution costs | | ½ |
| Administrative expenses | | 1½ |
| Investment income | | 1 |
| Finance costs | | 1½ |
| Income tax expense | | 1 |
| Other comprehensive income | | 1½ |
| Non-controlling interest in profit for year | | 2 |
| Non-controlling interest in other comprehensive income | | 1 |
| **Total** | | **20** |

## 381 PLASTIK

**(a)** **Plastik – Extracts from consolidated statement of profit or loss for the year ended 30 September 20X4**

|  | | $000 |
|---|---|---|
| (i) | Revenue $(62{,}600 + (30{,}000 \times {}^9/_{12}) - (300 \times 9$ months intra-group sales)) | 82,400 |
| (ii) | Cost of sales $(45{,}800 + (24{,}000 \times {}^9/_{12}) - 2{,}700$ intra-group sales $+ 120$ PUP (W7) $+ 100$ FV dep'n) | (61,320) |
| (iii) | Finance costs $(200 + 135$ (W5)) | (335) |

**(b)** **Plastik – Consolidated statement of financial position as at 30 September 20X4**

**Assets**

| Non-current assets | $000 |
|---|---|
| Property, plant and equipment $(18{,}700 + 13{,}900 + 4{,}000$ FV $- 100$ FV dep'n $+ 600$ revaluation) | 37,100 |
| Intangible asset: goodwill (W3) | 5,700 |
| | 42,800 |
| | |
| Current assets | |
| $(9{,}000 + 4{,}000 - 120$ (W5) $- 400$ cash in transit $- 800$ intra-group) | 11,680 |
| | |
| Total assets | 54,480 |

**Equity and liabilities**

| | |
|---|---:|
| Equity shares of $1 each (10, 000 + 4,800) | 14,800 |
| Other component of equity (share premium) | 9,600 |
| Revaluation surplus (2,000 + (600 × 80%)) | 2,480 |
| Retained earnings (W5) | 7,165 |
| Non-controlling interest (W4) | 4,900 |
| | ——— |
| Total equity | 38,945 |
| | ——— |
| Non-current liabilities | |
| 10% loan notes (2,500 + 1,000 – 1,000 intra-group) | 2,500 |
| | ——— |
| Current liabilities | |
| Trade payables (7,900 + 4,400 – 400 cash in transit – 800 intra-group) | 11,100 |
| Deferred consideration (1,800 + 135 (W5)) | 1,935 |
| | ——— |
| | 13,035 |
| | ——— |
| Total equity and liabilities | 54,480 |
| | ——— |

**Workings** (note figure in brackets are in $000)

**(W1) Group structure**

Plastik

80% – owned for 9 months

Subtrak

**(W2) Net assets**

| | Acquisition | Reporting date | Post-acquisition |
|---|---:|---:|---:|
| | $000 | $000 | $000 |
| Share capital | 9,000 | 9,000 | – |
| Retained earnings | 2,000 | 3,500 | 1,500 |
| Fair value – property | 4,000 | 4,000 | – |
| Fair value depreciation | | (100) | (100) |
| | ——— | ——— | ——— |
| | 15,000 | 16,400 | 1,400 |
| | ——— | ——— | ——— |
| | W3 | | W4/W5 |

**(W3) Goodwill**

| | $000 |
|---|---:|
| Shares (9,000 × 80% × $^2/_3$ × $3) | 14,400 |
| Deferred consideration (9,000 × 80% × $0.275 × $^1/_{1.1}$) | 1,800 |
| Non-controlling interest (9,000 × 20% × $2.50) | 4,500 |
| Less: Fair value of net assets at acquisition (W2) | (15,000) |
| | ——— |
| Goodwill on acquisition | 5,700 |
| | ——— |

The 4.8 million shares issued by Plastik represents share capital of $4.8 million (4,800 × $1) and share premium of $9.6 million (4,800 × $2).

**(W4) Non-controlling interest (SFP)**

| | $000 |
|---|---:|
| At date of acquisition (W3) | 4,500 |
| NCI % × S post acquisition (20% × 1,400 (W2)) | 280 |
| NCI % × S post acquisition revaluation (20% × 600) | 120 |
| | ——— |
| | 4,900 |
| | ——— |

**(W5) Group retained earnings**

| | $000 |
|---|---:|
| Plastik's retained earnings | 6,300 |
| Subtrak's post-acquisition (1,400 (W2) × 80%) | 1,120 |
| Unwinding discount on deferred consideration (1,800 × 10% × $^9/_{12}$) | (135) |
| PUP 600 x $^{25}/_{125}$ | (120) |
| | ——— |
| | 7,165 |
| | ——— |

| **Marking scheme** | | |
|---|---|---|
| | | *Marks* |
| (a) | Consolidated statement of profit or loss and other comprehensive income: | |
| | Revenue | 1½ |
| | Cost of sales | 2½ |
| | Finance costs | 1 |
| | Maximum | 5 |
| (b) | Consolidated statement of financial position: | |
| | Property, plant and equipment | 2 |
| | Goodwill | 2 |
| | Current assets | 2 |
| | Equity shares | 1 |
| | Other component of equity (share premium) | 1 |
| | Revaluation surplus | 1 |
| | Retained earnings | 1½ |
| | Non-controlling interest | 1 |
| | 10% loan notes | 1 |
| | Current liabilities | 1½ |
| | Deferred consideration | 1 |
| | Maximum | 15 |
| **Total** | | **20** |

## 382 BYCOMB

**(a)    Bycomb: Goodwill on acquisition of Cyclip as at 1 July 20X4**

| | $000 |
|---|---|
| Investment at cost: | |
| Shares (12,000 × 80% × $\frac{2}{3}$ × $3.00) | 19,200 |
| Deferred consideration (12,000 × 80% × $^{\$1.54}/_{1.1}$) | 13,440 |
| Non-controlling interest (12,000 × 20% × $2.50) | 6,000 |
| | 38,640 |
| Net assets at date of acquisition (W1) | (26,845) |
| Consolidated goodwill | 11,795 |

**(b)    Extracts from Bycomb consolidated statement of profit or loss for the year ended 31 March 20X5**

| | | $000 |
|---|---|---|
| (i) | Revenue (24,200 + (10,800 × $^9/_{12}$) – 3,000 intra-group sales) | 29,300 |
| (ii) | Cost of sales (W2) | (20,830) |
| (iii) | Finance costs (W3) | (1,558) |
| (iv) | Profit for year attributable to non-controlling interest (1,015 × 20% (W4)) or see (W5) | 203 |

**(c)** IFRS 3 *Business Combinations* allows as an option a non-controlling interest to be valued at its proportionate share of the acquired subsidiary's identifiable net assets. This carries forward the only allowed method in the previous version of this Standard. Its effect on the statement of financial position is that the resulting carrying amount of purchased goodwill only relates to the parent's element of such goodwill and as a consequence the non-controlling interest does not reflect its share of the subsidiary's goodwill. Some commentators feel this is an anomaly as the principle of a consolidated statement of financial position is that it should disclose the whole of the subsidiary's assets that are under the control of the parent rather than just the parent's share. This principle is applied to all of a subsidiary's other identifiable assets, so it seems logical to extend that treatment to goodwill.

Any impairment of goodwill under this method would only be charged against the parent's interest, as the non-controlling interest's share of goodwill is not included in the consolidated financial statements.

The second, more recent, method of valuing the non-controlling interest at its fair value would normally increase the value of the goodwill calculated on acquisition. This increase reflects the non-controlling interest's ownership of the subsidiary's goodwill and has the effect of 'grossing up' the goodwill and the non-controlling interests in the statement of financial position by the same amount. It is argued that this method reflects the whole of the subsidiary's goodwill/premium on acquisition and is thus consistent with the principles of consolidation.

Under this method any impairment of the subsidiary's goodwill is charged against both the parent and non-controlling interest in proportion to their shareholding in the subsidiary.

**Workings**

**(W1) Net assets of Cyclip at acquisition**

|  | $000 |
|---|---|
| Share capital | 12,000 |
| Retained earnings 1 April 20X4 | 13,500 |
| Earnings 1 April 20X4 to acquisition: | |
| $((2,400 + 100) \times {}^3/_{12})$ – see note below | 625 |
| Fair value adjustment – plant | 720 |
|  | ——— |
|  | 26,845 |
|  | ——— |

**Note:** The profit for the year for Cyclip would be increased by $100,000 due to interest capitalised, in accordance with IAS 23 *Borrowing Costs*.

Alternatively, the profit for the year could have been calculated as:

$(2,400 \times {}^3/_{12}) + 25$. As the interest to be capitalised has accrued evenly throughout the year, $25,000 would relate to pre-acquisition profits and $75,000 to post-acquisition profits.

**(W2) Cost of sales**

| | |
|---|---:|
| Bycomb | 17,800 |
| Cyclip (6,800 × $^9/_{12}$) | 5,100 |
| Intra-group purchases | (3,000) |
| URP in inventory (420 × 20/120) | 70 |
| Impairment of goodwill per question | 500 |
| Additional depreciation of plant (720 × $^9/_{18}$ months) | 360 |
| | ——— |
| | 20,830 |
| | ——— |

**(W3) Finance costs**

| | |
|---|---:|
| Bycomb per question | 400 |
| Unwinding of deferred consideration (13,440 × 10% × $^9/_{12}$) | 1,008 |
| Cyclip ((300 – 100 see below) × $^9/_{12}$) | 150 |
| | ——— |
| | 1,558 |
| | ——— |

The interest capitalised in accordance with IAS 23 *Borrowing Costs* of $100,000 would reduce the finance costs of Cyclip for consolidation purposes.

**(W4) Post-acquisition profit of Cyclip**

| | |
|---|---:|
| Profit plus interest capitalised and time apportioned ((2,400 + 100) × $^9/_{12}$) – see note in (W1) | 1,875 |
| Impairment of goodwill (per question) | (500) |
| Additional depreciation of plant (W2) | (360) |
| | ——— |
| | 1,015 |
| | ——— |

**(W5) Alternative working for non-controlling interest share of profit**

| | |
|---|---:|
| NCI share of profit ((2,400 + 100) × $^9/_{12}$ × 20%) | 375 |
| NCI share of impairment (500 × 20%) | (100) |
| NCI share of FV depreciation of plant (360 × 20%) | (72) |
| | ——— |
| | 203 |
| | ——— |

| Marking scheme | | | Marks |
|---|---|---|---|
| (a) | Goodwill at acquisition | | 6 |
| | | | ___ |
| (b) | (i) | Revenue | 1 |
| | (ii) | Cost of sales | 3 |
| | (iii) | Finance costs | 2½ |
| | (iv) | Profit or loss attributable to non-controlling interests. | 2½ |
| | | | ___ |
| | | | 9 |
| | | | ___ |
| (c) | One mark per point made | | 5 |
| | | | ___ |
| **Total** | | | **20** |
| | | | ___ |

## 383 PALISTAR

### Palistar – Consolidated statement of financial position as at 30 June 20X5

| Assets | $000 |
|---|---|
| Non-current assets: | |
| Property, plant and equipment (55,000 + 28,600) | 83,600 |
| Goodwill (W3) | 3,000 |
| Game rights (12,000 – 1,200 (W2)) | 10,800 |
| Financial asset equity investments (13,200 + 7,900) | 21,100 |
| | ———— |
| | 118,500 |
| | |
| Current assets | |
| Inventory (17,000 + 15,400 + 800 GIT – 600 (W6)) | 32,600 |
| Trade receivables (14,300 + 10,500 – 2,400 intra-group) | 22,400 |
| Bank (2,200 + 1,600) | 3,800 |
| | ———— |
| | 58,800 |
| | ———— |
| Total assets | 177,300 |
| | ———— |
| | |
| Equity and liabilities | |
| Equity attributable to owners of the parent | |
| Equity shares of $1 each (20,000 + 6,000 (W3)) | 26,000 |
| Other components of equity (share premium) (4,000 + 18,000 (W3)) | 22,000 |
| Retained earnings (W5) | 52,425 |
| | ———— |
| | 100,425 |
| Non-controlling interest (W4) | 15,675 |
| | ———— |
| Total equity | 116,100 |

Current liabilities

| | |
|---|---|
| Deferred consideration (18,000 + 900 finance cost (W5)) | 18,900 |
| Other current liabilities (25,800 + 18,100 – (2,400 intra-group – 800 GIT)) | 42,300 |
| | 61,200 |

Total equity and liabilities 177,300

**Workings**

**(W1) Group structure**

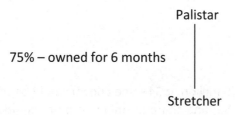

Palistar

75% – owned for 6 months

Stretcher

**(W2) Net assets**

| | Acquisition | Reporting date | Post-acquisition |
|---|---|---|---|
| | $000 | $000 | $000 |
| Share capital | 20,000 | 20,000 | – |
| Retained earnings (see below) | 18,000 | 24,000 | 6,000 |
| Fair value: game rights | 12,000 | 12,000 | – |
| Amortisation $\times \frac{1}{5} \times \frac{6}{12}$ | | (1,200) | (1,200) |
| Fair value investments | 1,000 | 1,900 | 900 |
| | 51,000 | 56,700 | 5,700 |
| | W3 | | W4/W5 |

Stretcher makes 60% of its profit in the period from 1 June. Therefore the post-acquisition retained earnings is $6 million (60% × $10 million), making the retained earnings at acquisition $18 million ($24 million less $6 million).

### (W3) Goodwill in Stretcher

|  | $000 |
|---|---|
| Share exchange (20,000 × 75% × $^2/_5$) = (6,000 × $4) | 24,000 |
| Deferred consideration (20,000 × 75% × $^{\$1.32}/_{1.1}$) | 18,000 |
| Non-controlling interest (20,000 × 25% × $3) | 15,000 |
|  | 57,000 |
| Net assets at acquisition | (51,000) |
|  | |
| Goodwill on acquisition | 6,000 |
| Impairment | (3,000) |
|  | |
| Goodwill at 30 June 20X5 | 3,000 |

The shares issued by Palistar (6 million at $4 – see above) would be recorded as share capital of $6 million (6,000 × $1) and share premium in other components of equity of $18 million (6,000 × $3).

### (W4) Non-controlling interest

|  | $000 |
|---|---|
| Fair value on acquisition (W3) | 15,000 |
| Post-acquisition profit (5,700 × 25% (W2)) | 1,425 |
| NCI share of impairment (3,000 × 25%) | (750) |
|  | |
|  | 15,675 |

### (W5) Consolidated retained earnings:

|  | $000 |
|---|---|
| Palistar's retained earnings (26,200 + 24,000) | 50,200 |
| Stretcher's adjusted post-acquisition profit (5,700 (W2) × 75%) | 4,275 |
| Palistar's share of impairment (3,000 × 75%) | (2,250) |
| Finance cost on deferred consideration (18,000 × 10% × $^6/_{12}$) | (900) |
| URP in inventory (W6) | (600) |
| Gain on equity investments (13,200 – 11,500) | 1,700 |
|  | |
|  | 52,425 |

### (W6) Provision for unrealised profit (PUP)

The inventory of Stretcher at 30 June 20X5 (adjusted for goods-in-transit (GIT) sale of $800,000) is $2.6 million (1,800 + 800). The unrealised profit on this will be $600,000 ($2.6m × $^{30}/_{130}$).

| **Marking scheme** | |
|---|---|
| | *Marks* |
| Consolidated statement of financial position: | |
| Property, plant and equipment | ½ |
| Goodwill | 5 |
| Game rights | 1 |
| Financial asset investments | 1 |
| Inventory | 2 |
| Receivables | 1 |
| Bank | ½ |
| Equity shares | 1 |
| Other component of equity | 1 |
| Retained earnings | 4 |
| Non-controlling interest | 1 |
| Deferred consideration | 1 |
| Other current liabilities | 1 |
| | —— |
| **Total** | **20** |
| | —— |

## 384   LAUREL

(a)   **Laurel: Consolidated goodwill on acquisition of Rakewood**

| | $000 | $000 |
|---|---|---|
| Investment at cost | | |
| Shares (15,000 × 60% × $^3/_5$ × $7.00) | | 37,800 |
| Deferred consideration (9,000 × $1.62/1.08) | | 13,500 |
| Non-controlling interest (15,000 × 40% × $2.00) | | 12,000 |
| | | ——— |
| | | 63,300 |
| Net assets (based on equity) of Rakewood as at 1 January 20X6 | | |
| Equity shares | 15,000 | |
| Retained earnings at 1 October 20X5 | 25,000 | |
| Earnings 1 October 20X5 to acquisition (10,400 × $^3/_{12}$) | 2,600 | |
| Fair value adjustments: | | |
|    plant | 4,000 | |
|    inventory | 200 | |
| | ——— | |
| Net assets at date of acquisition | | (46,800) |
| | | ——— |
| Consolidated goodwill | | 16,500 |
| | | ——— |

**(b)** **Laurel consolidated statement of profit or loss for the year ended 30 September 20X6**

|  | $000 |
|---|---|
| Revenue (84,500 + (52,000 × $^9/_{12}$) − (1,200 × 9 months) intra-group sales) | 112,700 |
| Cost of sales (see working below) | (74,900) |
| | |
| Gross profit | 37,800 |
| Distribution costs (2,000 + (1,600 × $^9/_{12}$)) | (3,200) |
| Administrative expenses (4,100 + (2,800 × $^9/_{12}$)) | (6,200) |
| Investment income (400 × $^9/_{12}$) | 300 |
| Income from associate (2,400 × 25% based on underlying earnings) | 600 |
| Finance costs (300 + (13,500 × 8% × $^9/_{12}$ re deferred consideration)) | (1,110) |
| | |
| Profit before tax | 28,190 |
| Income tax expense (4,800 + (3,600 × $^9/_{12}$)) | (7,500) |
| | |
| Profit for the year | 20,690 |
| | |
| Profit for year attributable to: | |
| Equity holders of the parent | 18,370 |
| Non-controlling interest | |
| ((10,400 × $^9/_{12}$) − 200 re inventory − 1,500 depreciation − 300 PUP) × 40%)) | |
| | 2,320 |
| | |
| | 20,690 |

**Working**

**Cost of sales**

|  | $000 |
|---|---|
| Laurel | 58,200 |
| Rakewood (34,000 × $^9/_{12}$) | 25,500 |
| Intra-group purchases (1,200 × 9 months) | (10,800) |
| Fair value inventory adjustment | 200 |
| PUP in inventory at 30 September 20X6 (1,800 × $^{20}/_{120}$) | 300 |
| Additional depreciation (4,000/2 years × $^9/_{12}$) | 1,500 |
| | |
| | 74,900 |

| **ACCA Marking scheme** | | |
|---|---|---|
| | | *Marks* |
| (a) | Consolidated goodwill: | |
| | Consideration – share exchange | 1 |
| |                – deferred consideration | 1 |
| |                – NCI | 1 |
| | Net assets    – equity shares | ½ |
| |                – retained earnings at acquisition | 1½ |
| |                – fair value adjustments | 2 |
| | | —— |
| | | 7 |
| | | —— |
| (b) | Consolidated statement of profit or loss: | |
| | Revenue | 1½ |
| | Cost of sales | 4½ |
| | Distribution costs | ½ |
| | Administrative expenses | ½ |
| | Investment income | 1½ |
| | Finance costs | 1½ |
| | Income tax expense | 1 |
| | NCI | 2 |
| | | —— |
| | | 13 |
| | | —— |
| **Total** | | **20** |
| | | —— |

## 385 DARGENT CO

### Consolidated statement of financial position as at 31 March 20X6

| Assets | $000 | $000 |
|---|---|---|
| Non-current assets: | | |
| Property, plant and equipment (75,200 + 31,500 + 4,000 mine – 200 dep) | | 110,500 |
| Goodwill (W3) | | 11,000 |
| Investment in associate (4,500 + 1,200 (W5)) | | 5,700 |
| | | ——— |
| | | 127,200 |
| Current assets | | |
| Inventory (19,400 + 18,800 + 700 GIT – 800 PUP (W6)) | 38,100 | |
| Trade receivables (14,700 + 12,500 – 3,000 intra group) | 24,200 | |
| Bank (1,200 + 600) | 1,800 | |
| | ——— | |
| | | 64,100 |
| | | ——— |
| Total assets | | 191,300 |
| | | ——— |

Equity and liabilities

| | |
|---|---:|
| Equity shares of $1 each (50,000 + 10,000 (W3)) | 60,000 |
| Other equity reserves (share premium) (W3) | 22,000 |
| Retained earnings (W5) | 37,390 |
| | 119,390 |
| Non-controlling interest (W4) | 9,430 |
| | |
| Total equity | 128,820 |

Non-current liabilities

| | | |
|---|---:|---:|
| 8% loan notes (5,000 + 15,000 consideration (W3)) | 20,000 | |
| Accrued loan interest (W5) | 300 | |
| Environmental provision (4,000 + 80 interest (W2)) | 4,080 | |
| | | 24,380 |
| Current liabilities (24,000 + 16,400 + 700 GIT – 3,000 intra group) | | 38,100 |
| | | |
| Total equity and liabilities | | 191,300 |

Workings (figures in brackets are in $000)

**(W1) Group structure**

Dargent

75%

Latree

(1 Jan 20X6)

**(W2) Net assets of Latree Co**

| | Acquisition | Reporting date | Post-acquisition |
|---|---:|---:|---:|
| | $000 | $000 | $000 |
| Equity shares | 20,000 | 20,000 | |
| Retained earnings at 1 April 20X5 | 19,000 | 19,000 | |
| Earnings 1 April to acquisition (8,000 × 9/12) | 6,000 | 8,000 | 2,000 |
| Fair value adjustment: Mine asset | 4,000 | 4,000 | |
| Mine depreciation (4,000 × 1/5 × 3/12) | | (200) | (200) |
| Mine provision | (4,000) | (4,000) | |
| Interest on provision (4,000 × 8% × 3/12) | | (80) | (80) |
| | 45,000 | 46,720 | 1,720 |

Applying the group policy to the environmental provision would mean adding $4 million to the carrying amount of the mine and the same amount recorded as a provision at the date of acquisition. This has no overall effect on the net assets at acquisition, but it does affect the consolidated statement of financial position and post-acquisition profit.

**(W3) Goodwill in Latree Co**

|  | $000 |
|---|---|
| Controlling interest | |
| Share exchange (20,000 × 75% × 2/3 × $3.20) | 32,000 |
| 8% loan notes (20,000 × 75% × $100/100) | 15,000 |
| Non-controlling interest (20,000 × 25% × $1.80) | 9,000 |
| | 56,000 |
| Net assets at acquisition (W2) | (45,000) |
| | 11,000 |

The share exchange of $32 million would be recorded as share capital of $10 million (10,000 × $1) and share premium of $22 million (10,000 × ($320 – $1)).

**(W4) Non-controlling interest**

|  | $000 |
|---|---|
| Value at acquisition (W3) | 9,000 |
| Post-acquisition profit (1,720 (W2) × 25%) | 430 |
| | 9,430 |

**(W5) Retained earnings**

|  | $000 |
|---|---|
| Dargent Co retained earnings | 36,000 |
| Latree Co post-acquisition profit (1,720 (W2) × 75%) | 1,290 |
| Amery unrecorded share of profit ((6,000 – 2,000) × 30%) | 1,200 |
| Unpaid loan interest (15,000 (W3) × 8% × 3/12) | (300) |
| PUP (W6) | (800) |
| | 37,390 |

**(W6) Provision for Unrealised Profit (PUP)**

|  | $000 |
|---|---|
| Inventory held by Latree | 2,100 |
| Goods in transit | 700 |
| Total intra-group inventory held | 2,800 |
| Profit included (2,800 × 40/140) | 800 |

| ACCA Marking scheme | |
| --- | --- |
| | *Marks* |
| Property, plant and equipment | 2 |
| Goodwill: consideration | 2½ |
| Goodwill: fair value net assets | 2 |
| Investments in associate | 1 |
| Inventory | 1½ |
| Receivables | 1 |
| Bank | ½ |
| Equity shares and share premium | 1 |
| Retained earnings: post-acquisition sub | 2 |
| Retained earnings: other | 2 |
| Non-controlling interests | 1½ |
| 8% loan notes | ½ |
| Environmental provision | 1½ |
| Current liabilities | 1 |
| | ─── |
| **Total** | **20** |
| | ─── |

# ANALYSING FINANCIAL STATEMENTS

**386 HARDY**  *Walk in the footsteps of a top tutor*

**Key answer tips**

This question requires an appraisal of a business that is experiencing problems as a result of a global recession, so do not be surprised when some profitability ratios produce negative results. A weak answer will simply refer to ratio movements as having increased or decreased, whereas a strong answer will refer to improvements or deteriorations in the ratios and will aim to relate it to the scenario provided by the examiner, explaining possible causes for the movements.

**Note:** references to 20X5 and 20X6 should be taken as being to the years ended 30 September 20X5 and 20X6 respectively.

**Profitability:**

**Statement of profit or loss performance:**

Hardy's statement of profit or loss results dramatically show the effects of the downturn in the global economy. Revenues are down by 18% (6,500/36,000 × 100), gross profit has fallen by 60% and a healthy after tax profit of $3.5 million has reversed to a loss of $2.1 million. These are reflected in the profit (loss) margin ratios shown in the appendix (the 'as reported' figures for 20X6). This in turn has led to a 15.2% return on equity being reversed to a negative return of 11.9%. However, a closer analysis shows that the results are not quite as bad as they seem. The downturn has directly caused several additional costs in 20X6: employee severance, property impairments and losses on investments (as quantified in the appendix). These are probably all non-recurring costs and could therefore justifiably be excluded from the 20X6 results to assess Hardy's 'underlying' performance. If this is done the results of Hardy for 20X6 appear to be much better than on first sight, although still not as good as those reported for 20X5. A gross margin of 27.8% in 20X5 has fallen to only 23.1% (rather than the reported margin of 13.6%) and the profit for period has fallen from $3.5 million (9.7%) to only $2.3 million (7.8%). It should also be noted that as well as the fall in the value of the investments, the related investment income has also shown a sharp decline which has contributed to lower profits in 20X6.

Given the economic climate in 20X6 these are probably reasonably good results and may justify the Chairman's comments. It should be noted that the cost saving measures which have helped to mitigate the impact of the downturn could have some unwelcome effects should trading conditions improve. It may not be easy to re-hire employees and a lack of advertising may cause a loss of market share.

**Statement of financial position:**

Perhaps the most obvious aspect of the statement of financial position is the fall in value ($8.5 million) of the non-current assets, most of which is accounted for by losses of $6 million and $1.6 million respectively on the properties and investments. Ironically, because these falls are reflected in equity, this has mitigated the fall in the return of the equity (from 15.2% to 13.1% underlying) and contributed to a perhaps unexpected improvement in asset turnover from 1.6 times to 1.7 times.

**Liquidity:**

Despite the downturn, Hardy's liquidity ratios now seem at acceptable levels (though they should be compared to manufacturing industry norms) compared to the low ratios in 20X5. The bank balance has improved by $1.1 million. This has been helped by a successful rights issue (this is in itself a sign of shareholder support and confidence in the future) raising $2 million and keeping customer's credit period under control. Some of the proceeds of the rights issue appear to have been used to reduce the bank loan which is sensible as its financing costs have increased considerably in 20X6. Looking at the movement on retained earnings (6,500 – 2,100 – 3,600) it can be seen that Hardy paid a dividend of $800,000 during 20X6. Although this is only half the dividend per share paid in 20X5, it may seem unwise given the losses and the need for the rights issue. A counter view is that the payment of the dividend may be seen as a sign of confidence of a future recovery. It should also be mentioned that the worst of the costs caused by the downturn (specifically the property and investments losses) are not cash costs and have therefore not affected liquidity.

The increase in the inventory and work-in-progress holding period and the trade receivables collection period being almost unchanged appear to contradict the declining sales activity and should be investigated. Although there is insufficient information to calculate the trade payables credit period as there is no analysis of the cost of sales figures, it appears that Hardy has received extended credit which, unless it had been agreed with the suppliers, has the potential to lead to problems obtaining future supplies of goods on credit.

**Gearing:**

On the reported figures debt to equity shows a modest increase due to statement of profit or loss losses and the reduction of the revaluation reserve, but this has been mitigated by the repayment of part of the loan and the rights issue.

**Conclusion:**

Although Hardy's results have been adversely affected by the global economic situation, its underlying performance is not as bad as first impressions might suggest and supports the Chairman's comments. Hardy still retains a relatively strong statement of financial position and liquidity position which will help significantly should market conditions improve. Indeed the impairment of property and investments may well reverse in future. It would be a useful exercise to compare Hardy's performance during this difficult time to that of its competitors – it may well be that its 20X6 results were relatively very good by comparison.

**Appendix:**

An important aspect of assessing the performance of Hardy for 20X6 (especially in comparison with 20X5) is to identify the impact that several 'one off' charges have had on the results of 20X6. These charges are $1.3 million redundancy costs and a $1.5 million (6,000 – 4,500 previous surplus) property impairment, both included in cost of sales and a $1.6 million loss on the market value of investments, included in administrative expenses. Thus in calculating the 'underlying' figures for 20X6 (below) the adjusted cost of sales is $22.7 million (25,500 – 1,300 – 1,500) and the administrative expenses are $3.3 million (4,900 – 1,600). These adjustments feed through to give an underlying gross profit of $6.8 million (4,000 + 1,300 + 1,500) and an underlying profit for the year of $2.3 million (−2,100 + 1,300 + 1,500 + 1,600).

Note:it is not appropriate to revise Hardy's equity (upwards) for the one-off losses when calculating equity based underlying figures, as the losses will be a continuing part of equity (unless they reverse) even if/when future earnings recover.

|  | 20X6 underlying | 20X6 as reported | 20X5 |
|---|---|---|---|
| Gross profit % (6,800/29,500 × 100) | 23.1% | 13.6% | 27.8% |
| Profit (loss) for period % (2,300/29,500 × 100) | 7.8% | (7.1)% | 9.7% |
| Return on equity (2,300/17,600 × 100) | 13.1% | (11.9)% | 15.2% |
| Net asset (taken as equity) turnover (29,500/17,600) | 1.7 times | same | 1.6 times |
| Debt to equity (4,000/17,600) | 22.7% | same | 21.7% |
| Current ratio (6,200:3,400) | 1.8:1 | same | 1.0:1 |
| Quick ratio (4,000:3,400) | 1.2:1 | same | 0.6:1 |
| Receivables collection (in days) (2,200/29,500 × 365) | 27 days | same | 28 days |
| Inventory and work-in-progress holding period (2,200/25,500 × 365) | 31 days | same | 27 days |

**Note:** the figures for the calculation of the 20X6 'underlying' ratios have been given, those of 20X6 'as reported' and 20X5 are based on equivalent figures from the summarised financial statements provided.

Alternative ratios/calculations are acceptable, for example net asset turnover could be calculated using total assets less current liabilities.

| Marking scheme | |
|---|---|
|  | *Marks* |
| Comments – 1 mark per valid point, up to | 13 |
| Ratio calculations – up to | 7 |
|  | ─── |
| **Total** | **20** |
|  | ─── |

## 387 PINTO

(a) **Comments on the cash management of Pinto**

**Operating cash flows:**

Pinto's operating cash inflows at $940,000 (prior to investment income, finance costs and taxation) are considerably higher than the equivalent profit before investment income, finance costs and tax of $430,000. This shows a satisfactory cash generating ability and is more than sufficient to cover finance costs, taxation (see later) and dividends. The major reasons for the cash flows being higher than the operating profit are due to the (non-cash) increases in the depreciation and warranty provisions. Working capital changes are relatively neutral, with a large increase in inventory appearing to be being financed by a substantial increase in trade payables and a modest reduction in trade receivables. The reduction in trade receivables is perhaps surprising as other indicators point to an increase in operating capacity which has not been matched with an increase in trade receivables. This could be indicative of good control over the cash management of the trade receivables (or a disappointing sales performance).

An unusual feature of the cash flow is that Pinto has received a tax refund of $60,000 during the current year. This would indicate that in the previous year Pinto was making losses (hence obtaining tax relief). Whilst the current year's profit performance is an obvious improvement, it should be noted that next year's cash flows are likely to suffer a tax payment as a consequence.

**Investing activities:**

There has been a dramatic investment/increase in property, plant and equipment. The carrying amount at 31 March 20X8 is substantially higher than a year earlier. It is difficult to be sure whether this represents an increase in operating capacity or is the replacement of the plant disposed of. (The voluntary disclosure encouraged by IAS 7 *Statement of Cash Flows* would help to assess this issue more accurately). However, judging by the level of the increase and the (apparent) overall improvement in profit position, it seems likely that there has been a successful increase in capacity. It is not unusual for there to be a time lag before increased investment reaches its full beneficial effect and in this context it could be speculated that the investment occurred early in the accounting year (because its effect is already making an impact) and that future periods may show even greater improvements.

The investment property is showing a good return, generating rental income of $40,000 in the year.

**Financing activities:**

It would appear that Pinto's financial structure has changed during the year. Debt of $400,000 has been redeemed (for $420,000) and there has been a share issue raising $1 million. The share issue has covered the cost of redemption and contributed to the investment in property, plant and equipment. The remainder of the finance for the property, plant and equipment has come from the very healthy operating cash flows. If ROCE is higher than the finance cost of the loan note at 6% (nominal) it may call into question the wisdom of the early redemption especially given the penalty cost (which has been classified within financing activities) of the redemption.

**Cash position:**

The overall effect of the year's cash flows is that they have improved the cash position dramatically. A sizeable overdraft of $120,000, which may have been a consequence of the (likely) losses in the previous year, has been reversed to a modest bank balance of $10,000 even after the payment of a $150,000 dividend.

**Summary**

The above analysis indicates that Pinto has invested substantially in renewing and/or increasing its property, plant and equipment. This has been financed largely by operating cash flows, and appears to have brought a dramatic turnaround in Pinto's fortunes. All the indications are that the future financial position and performance will continue to improve.

**(b)** The accruals/matching concept applied in preparing a statement of profit or loss has the effect of smoothing cash flows for reporting purposes. This practice arose because interpreting 'raw' cash flows can be very difficult and the accruals process has the advantage of helping users to understand the underlying performance of a business. For example if an item of plant with an estimated life of five years is purchased for $100,000, then in the statement of cash flows for the five year period there would be an outflow in year 1 of the full $100,000 and no further outflows for the next four years. Contrast this with the statement of profit or loss where by applying the accruals principle, depreciation of the plant would give a charge of $20,000 per annum (assuming straight-line depreciation). Many would see this example as an advantage of a statement of profit or loss, but it is important to realise that profit is affected by many items requiring judgements. This has led to accusations of profit manipulation or creative accounting, hence the disillusionment of the usefulness of the statement of profit or loss.

Another example of the difficulty in interpreting cash flows is that counter-intuitively a decrease in overall cash flows is not always a bad thing (it may represent an investment in increasing capacity which would bode well for the future), nor is an increase in cash flows necessarily a good thing (this may be from the sale of non-current assets because of the need to raise cash urgently).

The advantages of cash flows are:

- it is difficult to manipulate cash flows, they are real and possess the characteristic of objectivity (as opposed to profits affected by judgements).

- cash flows are an easy concept for users to understand, indeed many users misinterpret statement of profit or loss items as being cash flows.

- cash flows help to assess an entity's liquidity, solvency and financial adaptability. Healthy liquidity is vital to a going concern.

- many business investment decisions and valuations are based on projected cash flows.

- the 'quality' of profit is said to be confirmed by closely correlated cash flows. Some analysts take the view that if a business shows a healthy profit from operations, but has low or negative operating cash flows, there is a suspicion of profit manipulation or creative accounting.

**388 HARBIN**  *Walk in the footsteps of a top tutor*

**Key answer tip**

Be aware that the examiner specifically asks you to draw your attention to the chief executives report and the purchase of Fatima – if you do not discuss this at all you will be limited in the overall marks that you can achieve. You may choose to calculate further ratios to support your analysis (marks would be awarded where relevant). The highlighted words are key phrases that markers are looking for.

**Note:** Figures in the calculations of the ratios are in $million

**(a)**

|  | 20X7 | Workings |
|---|---|---|
| Return on year end capital employed | 11.2% | 24/(114 + 100) × 100 |
| Current ratio | 0.86 | 38/44 |
| Closing inventory holding period | 46 days | 25/200 × 365 |
| Trade receivables' collection period | 19 days | 13/250 × 365 |
| Gearing | 46.7% | 100/214 × 100 |

**(b)** **Analysis of the comparative financial performance and position of Harbin for the year ended 30 September 20X7**

> **Note:** References to 20X7 and 20X6 should be taken as the years ended 30 September 20X7 and 20X6.

**Introduction**

The figures relating to the comparative performance of Harbin 'highlighted' in the Chief Executive's report may be factually correct, but they take a rather biased and one dimensional view. They focus entirely on the performance as reflected in the statement of comprehensive income without reference to other measures of performance, notably the ROCE. There is no reference to the purchase of Fatima at the beginning of the year which has had a favourable effect on profit for 20X7. Due to this purchase, it is not consistent to compare Harbin's statement of comprehensive income results in 20X7 directly with those of 20X6 because it does not match like with like. Immediately before the $100 million purchase of Fatima, the carrying amount of the net assets of Harbin was $112 million. Thus the investment represented an increase of nearly 90% of Harbin's existing capital employed. The following analysis of performance will consider the position as shown in the reported financial statements (based on the ratios required by part (a) of the question) and then go on to consider the impact the purchase has had on this analysis.

**Profitability**

The ROCE is often considered to be the primary measure of operating performance, because it relates the profit made by an entity (return) to the capital (or net assets) invested in generating those profits. On this basis the ROCE in 20X7 of 11.2% represents a 58% improvement (i.e. 4.1% on 7.1%) on the ROCE of 7.1% in 20X6. Given there were no disposals of non-current assets, the ROCE on Fatima's net assets is 18.9% (22m/100m + 16.5m). **Note:** The net assets of Fatima at the year end would have increased by profit after tax of $16.5 million (i.e. 22m × 75% (at a tax rate of

25%)). Put another way, without the contribution of $22 million to profit before tax, Harbin's 'underlying' profit would have been a loss of $6 million which would give a negative ROCE. The principal reasons for the beneficial impact of Fatima's purchase is that its profit margins at 42.9% gross and 31.4% net (before tax) are far superior to the profit margins of the combined business at 20% and 6.4% respectively. It should be observed that the other contributing factor to the ROCE is the net asset turnover and in this respect Fatima's is actually inferior at 0.6 times (70m/116.5m) to that of the combined business of 1.2 times.

It could be argued that the finance costs should be allocated against Fatima's results as the proceeds of the loan note appear to be the funding for the purchase of Fatima. Even if this is accepted, Fatima's results still far exceed those of the existing business.

Thus the Chief Executive's report, already criticised for focussing on the statement of comprehensive income alone, is still highly misleading. Without the purchase of Fatima, underlying sales revenue would be flat at $180 million and the gross margin would be down to 11.1% (20m/180m) from 16.7% resulting in a loss before tax of $6 million. This sales performance is particularly poor given it is likely that there must have been an increase in spending on property plant and equipment beyond that related to the purchase of Fatima's net assets as the increase in property, plant and equipment is $120 million (after depreciation).

### Liquidity

Harbin's liquidity position as measured by the current ratio has deteriorated dramatically during the period. A relatively healthy 2.5:1 is now only 0.9:1 which is rather less than what one would expect from the quick ratio (which excludes inventory) and is a matter of serious concern. A consideration of the component elements of the current ratio suggests that increases in the inventory holding period and trade payables payment period have largely offset each other. There is a small increase in the collection period for trade receivables (up from 16 days to 19 days) which would actually improve the current ratio. This ratio appears unrealistically low, it is very difficult to collect credit sales so quickly and may be indicative of factoring some of the receivables, or a proportion of the sales being cash sales. Factoring is sometimes seen as a consequence of declining liquidity, although if this assumption is correct it does also appear to have been present in the previous year. The changes in the above three ratios do not explain the dramatic deterioration in the current ratio, the real culprit is the cash position, Harbin has gone from having a bank balance of $14 million in 20X6 to showing short-term bank borrowings of $17 million in 20X7.

A statement of cash flow would give a better appreciation of the movement in the bank/short term borrowing position.

It is not possible to assess, in isolation, the impact of the purchase of Fatima on the liquidity of the business.

**Dividends**

A dividend of 10 cents per share in 20X7 amounts to $10 million (100m × 10 cents), thus the dividend in 20X6 would have been $8 million (the dividend in 20X7 is 25% up on 20X6). It may be that the increase in the reported profits led the Board to pay a 25% increased dividend, but the dividend cover is only 1.2 times (12m/10m) in 20X7 which is very low. In 20X6 the cover was only 0.75 times (6m/8m) meaning previous years' reserves were used to facilitate the dividend. The low retained earnings indicate that Harbin has historically paid a high proportion of its profits as dividends, however in times of declining liquidity, it is difficult to justify such high dividends.

**Gearing**

Harbin has gone from a position of nil gearing (i.e. no long-term borrowings) in 20X6 to a relatively high gearing of 46.7% in 20X7. This has been caused by the issue of the $100 million 8% loan note which would appear to be the source of the funding for the $100 million purchase of Fatima's net assets. At the time the loan note was issued, Harbin's ROCE was 7.1%, slightly less than the finance cost of the loan note. In 20X7 the ROCE has increased to 11.2%, thus the manner of the funding has had a beneficial effect on the returns to the equity holders of Harbin. However, it should be noted that high gearing does not come without risk. Any future downturn in the results of Harbin would expose the equity holders to much lower proportionate returns and continued poor liquidity may mean payment of the loan interest could present a problem. Harbin's gearing and liquidity position would have looked far better had some of the acquisition been funded by an issue of equity shares.

**Conclusion**

There is no doubt that the purchase of Fatima has been a great success and appears to have been a wise move on the part of the management of Harbin. However, it has disguised a serious deterioration of the underlying performance and position of Harbin's existing activities which the Chief Executive's report may be trying to hide. It may be that the acquisition was part of an overall plan to diversify out of what has become existing loss making activities. If such a transition can continue, then the worrying aspects of poor liquidity and high gearing may be overcome.

| Marking scheme | | Marks |
|---|---|---|
| (a) | One mark per required ratio | 5 |
| (b) | For consideration of Chief Executive's report | 3 |
| | Remaining issues 1 mark per valid point | 12 |
| | | ── |
| **Total** | | **20** |
| | | ── |

N/A

### 389  VICTULAR  *Walk in the footsteps of a top tutor*

**Key answer tips**

This style of question is naturally time consuming – ensure you answer all parts of the question and do not spend too much time calculating ratios. Part (c) offers easy marks and is independent of the rest of the question – try doing part (c) first to ensure you do not miss out on such easy marks. When interpreting the results in part (b) be wary of making generalisations – you must ensure that you relate it to the information given in the question. Presentation is also crucial in part (b), so make it easy for the marker to read by being as neat as possible, with short paragraphs and spaces between paragraphs. The highlighted words are key phrases that markers are looking for.

(a)    **Equivalent ratios from the financial statements of Merlot (workings in $000)**

| | | |
|---|---|---|
| Return on year end capital employed (ROCE) | 20.9% | (1,400 + 590)/(2,800 + 3,200 + 500 + 3,000) × 100 |
| Pre-tax return on equity (ROE) | 50% | 1,400/2,800 × 100 |
| Net asset turnover | 2.3 times | 20,500/(14,800 – 5,700) |
| Gross profit margin | 12.2% | 2,500/20,500 × 100 |
| Operating profit margin | 9.8% | 2,000/20,500 × 100 |
| Current ratio | 1.3:1 | 7,300/5,700 |
| Closing inventory holding period | 73 days | 3,600/18,000 × 365 |
| Trade receivables' collection period | 66 days | 3,700/20,500 × 365 |
| Trade payables' payment period | 77 days | 3,800/18,000 × 365 |
| Gearing | 71% | (3,200 + 500 + 3,000)/9,500 × 100 |
| Interest cover | 3.3 times | 2,000/600 |
| Dividend cover | 1.4 times | 1,000/700 |

As required by the question, Merlot's lease liabilities (3,200 + 500) have been treated as debt when calculating the ROCE and gearing ratios.

(b)    **Assessment of the relative performance and financial position of Grappa and Merlot for the year ended 30 September 20X8**

**Introduction**

This report is based on the draft financial statements supplied and the ratios shown in (a) above. Although covering many aspects of performance and financial position, the report has been approached from the point of view of a prospective acquisition of the entire equity of one of the two entities.

**Profitability**

The ROCE of 20.9% of Merlot is far superior to the 14.8% return achieved by Grappa. ROCE is traditionally seen as a measure of management's overall efficiency in the use of the finance/assets at its disposal. More detailed analysis reveals that Merlot's superior performance is due to its efficiency in the use of its net assets. It achieved a net asset turnover of 2.3 times compared to only 1.2 times for Grappa. Put another way, Merlot makes sales of $2.30 per $1 invested in net assets compared to sales of only $1.20 per $1 invested for Grappa. The other element contributing to the ROCE is profit margins. In this area Merlot's overall performance is slightly inferior to that of Grappa, gross profit margins are almost identical, but Grappa's operating profit margin is 10.5% compared to Merlot's 9.8%. In this situation, where one entity's ROCE is superior to another's it is useful to look behind the figures and consider possible reasons for the superiority other than the obvious one of greater efficiency on Merlot's part.

A major component of the ROCE is normally the carrying amount of the non-current assets. Consideration of these in this case reveals some interesting issues. Merlot does not own its premises whereas Grappa does. Such a situation would not necessarily give a ROCE advantage to either entity as the increase in capital employed of an entity owning its factory would be compensated by a higher return due to not having a rental expense, and vice versa. If Merlot's rental cost, as a percentage of the value of the related factory, was less than its overall ROCE, then it would be contributing to its higher ROCE. There is insufficient information to determine this. Another relevant point may be that Merlot's owned plant is nearing the end of its useful life (carrying amount is only 22% of its cost) and they seem to be replacing owned plant with leased plant. Again this does not necessarily give Merlot an advantage, but the finance cost of the leased assets at only 7.5% is much lower than the overall ROCE (of either entity) and therefore this does help to improve Merlot's ROCE. The other important issue within the composition of the ROCE is the valuation basis of the entities' non-current assets. From the question, it appears that Grappa's factory is at current value (there is a property revaluation reserve) and note (ii) of the question indicates the use of historical cost for plant. The use of current value for the factory (as opposed to historical cost) will be adversely impacting on Grappa's ROCE. Merlot does not suffer this deterioration as it does not own its factory.

The ROCE measures the overall efficiency of management. However, as Victular is considering buying the equity of one of the two entities, it would be useful to consider the return on equity (ROE) – as this is what Victular is buying. The ratios calculated are based on pre-tax profits, which takes into account finance costs, but does not cause taxation issues to distort the comparison. Clearly Merlot's ROE at 50% is far superior to Grappa's 19.1%. Again the issue of the revaluation of Grappa's factory is making this ratio appear comparatively worse than it would be if there had not been a revaluation. In these circumstances it would be more meaningful if the ROE was calculated based on the asking price of each entity (which has not been disclosed) as this would effectively be the carrying amount of the relevant equity for Victular.

### Gearing

From the gearing ratio it can be seen that 71% of Merlot's assets are financed by borrowings (39% is attributable to Merlot's policy of leasing its plant). This is very high in absolute terms and double Grappa's level of gearing. The effect of gearing means that all of the profit after finance costs is attributable to the equity even though (in Merlot's case) the equity represents only 29% of the financing of the net assets. Whilst this may seem advantageous to the equity shareholders of Merlot, it does not come without risk. The interest cover of Merlot is only 3.3 times whereas that of Grappa is 6 times. Merlot's low interest cover is a direct consequence of its high gearing and it makes profits vulnerable to relatively small changes in operating activity. For example, small reductions in sales, profit margins or small increases in operating expenses could result in losses and mean that interest charges would not be covered.

Another observation is that Grappa has been able to take advantage of the receipt of government grants, Merlot has not. This may be due to Grappa purchasing its plant (which may then be eligible for grants) whereas Merlot leases its plant. It may be that the lessor has received any grants available on the purchase of the plant and passed some of this benefit on to Merlot via lower lease finance costs (at 7.5% per annum, this is considerably lower than Merlot has to pay on its 10% loan notes).

### Liquidity

Both entities have relatively low liquid ratios of 1.2 and 1.3 for Grappa and Merlot respectively, although at least Grappa has $600,000 in the bank whereas Merlot has a $1.2 million overdraft. In this respect Merlot's policy of high dividend payouts (leading to a low dividend cover and low retained earnings) is very questionable. Looking in more depth, both entities have similar inventory days. Merlot collects its receivables one week earlier than Grappa (perhaps its credit control procedures are more active due to its large overdraft), and of notable difference is that Grappa receives (or takes) a significantly longer credit period from its suppliers (108 days compared to 77 days). This may be a reflection of Grappa being able to negotiate better credit terms because it has a higher credit rating.

### Summary

Although both entities may operate in a similar industry and have similar profits after tax, they would represent very different purchases. Merlot's sales revenues are over 70% more than those of Grappa, it is financed by high levels of debt, it rents rather than owns property and it chooses to lease rather than buy its replacement plant. Also its remaining owned plant is nearing the end of its life. Its replacement will either require a cash injection if it is to be purchased (Merlot's overdraft of $1.2 million already requires serious attention) or create even higher levels of gearing if it continues its policy of leasing. In short although Merlot's overall return seems more attractive than that of Grappa, it would represent a much more risky investment. Ultimately the investment decision may be determined by Victular's attitude to risk, possible synergies with its existing business activities, and not least, by the asking price for each investment (which has not been disclosed to us).

**(c)**    The generally recognised potential problems of using ratios for comparison purposes are:

- inconsistent definitions of ratios

- financial statements may have been deliberately manipulated (creative accounting)

- different entities may adopt different accounting policies (e.g. use of historical costs compared to current values)

- different managerial policies (e.g. different entities offer customers different payment terms)

- statement of financial position figures may not be representative of average values throughout the year (this can be caused by seasonal trading or a large acquisition of non-current assets near the year-end)

- the impact of price changes over time/distortion caused by inflation.

When deciding whether to purchase a business, Victular should consider the following additional useful information:

- in this case the analysis has been made on the draft financial statements. These may be unreliable or change when being finalised. Audited financial statements would add credibility and reliance to the analysis (assuming they receive an unmodified Auditors' Report)

- forward-looking information such as profit and financial position forecasts, capital expenditure and cash budgets and the level of orders on the books

- the current (fair) values of assets being acquired

- the level of risk within a business. Highly profitable businesses may also be highly risky, whereas a less profitable business may have more stable 'quality' earnings

- not least would be the expected price to acquire the entity. It may be that a poorer performing business may be a more attractive purchase because it is relatively cheaper and may offer more opportunity for improving efficiencies and profit growth.

## 390 QUARTILE

(a) Below are the specified ratios for Quartile and (for comparison) those of the business sector average:

|  |  | Quartile | Sector average |
|---|---|---|---|
| Return on year-end capital employed | | | |
| $((3,400 + 800)/(26,600 + 8,000) \times 100)$ | | 12.1% | 16.8% |
| Net asset turnover | (56,000/34,600) | 1.6 times | 1.4 times |
| Gross profit margin | (14,000/56,000 × 100) | 25% | 35% |
| Operating profit margin | (4,200/56,000 × 100) | 7.5% | 12% |
| Current ratio | (11,200:7,200) | 1.6:1 | 1.25:1 |
| Average inventory (8,300 + 10,200/2) = 9,250) turnover | (42,000/9,250) | 4.5 times | 3 times |
| Trade payables' payment period | (5,400/43,900 × 365) | 45 days | 64 days |
| Debt to equity | (8,000/26,600 × 100) | 30% | 38% |

(b) **Assessment of comparative performance**

**Profitability**

The primary measure of profitability is the return on capital employed (ROCE) and this shows that Quartile's 12.1% is considerably underperforming the sector average of 16.8%. The main cause of this seems to be a much lower gross profit margin (25% compared to 35%). A possible explanation for this is that Quartile is deliberately charging a lower mark-up in order to increase its sales by undercutting the market. There is supporting evidence for this in that Quartile's average inventory turnover at 4.5 times is 50% better than the sector average of three times. An alternative explanation could be that Quartile has had to cut its margins due to poor sales which have had a knock-on effect of having to write down closing inventory.

Quartile's lower gross profit percentage has fed through to contribute to a lower operating profit margin at 7.5% compared to the sector average of 12%. However, from the above figures, it can be deduced that Quartile's operating costs at 17.5% (25% − 7.5%) of revenue appear to be better controlled than the sector average operating costs of 23% (35% − 12%) of revenue. This may indicate that Quartile has a different classification of costs between cost of sales and operating costs than the entities in the sector average or that other entities may be spending more on advertising/selling commissions in order to support their higher margins.

The other component of ROCE is asset utilisation (measured by net asset turnover). If Quartile's business strategy is indeed to generate more sales to compensate for lower profit margins, a higher net asset turnover would be expected. At 1.6 times, Quartile's net asset turnover is only marginally better than the sector average of 1.4 times. Whilst this may indicate that Quartile's strategy was a poor choice, the ratio could be partly distorted by the property revaluation and also by whether the deferred development expenditure should be included within net assets for this purpose, as the net revenues expected from the development have yet to come on stream. If these two aspects were adjusted for, Quartile's net asset turnover would be 2.1 times (56,000/(34,600 – 5,000 – 3,000)) which is 50% better than the sector average.

In summary, Quartile's overall profitability is below that of its rival businesses due to considerably lower profit margins, although this has been partly offset by generating proportionately more sales from its assets.

### Liquidity

As measured by the current ratio, Quartile has a higher level of cover for its current liabilities than the sector average (1.6:1 compared to 1.25:1). Quartile's figure is nearer the 'norm' of expected liquidity ratios, often quoted as between 1.5 and 2:1, with the sector average (at 1.25:1) appearing worryingly low. The problem of this 'norm' is that it is generally accepted that it relates to manufacturing rather than retail entities, as applies to Quartile (and presumably also to the sector average). In particular, retail entities have very little, if any, trade receivables as is the case with Quartile. This makes a big difference to the current ratio and makes the calculation of a quick ratio largely irrelevant. Consequently, retail entities operate comfortably with much lower current ratios as their inventory is turned directly into cash. Thus, if anything, Quartile has a higher current ratio than might be expected. As Quartile has relatively low inventory levels (deduced from high inventory turnover figures), this means it must also have relatively low levels of trade payables (which can be confirmed from the calculated ratios). The low payables period of 45 days may be an indication of suppliers being cautious with the credit period they extend to Quartile, but there is no real evidence of this (e.g. Quartile is not struggling with an overdraft). In short, Quartile does not appear to have any liquidity issues.

### Gearing

Quartile's debt to equity at 30% is lower than the sector average of 38%. Although the loan note interest rate of 10% might appear quite high, it is lower than the ROCE of 12.1% (which means shareholders are benefiting from the borrowings) and the interest cover of 5.25 times ((3,400 + 800)/800) is acceptable. Quartile also has sufficient tangible assets to give more than adequate security on the borrowings, therefore there appear to be no adverse issues in relation to gearing.

### Conclusion

Quartile may be right to be concerned about its declining profitability. From the above analysis, it seems that Quartile may be addressing the wrong market (low margins with high volumes). The information provided about its rival businesses would appear to suggest that the current market appears to favour a strategy of higher margins (probably associated with better quality and more expensive goods) as being more profitable. In other aspects of the appraisal, Quartile is doing well compared to other businesses in its sector.

## 391  BENGAL

**Note:**  references to 20X1 and 20X0 refer to the periods ending 31 March 20X1 and 20X0 respectively.

It is understandable that the shareholder's observations would cause concern. A large increase in sales revenue has not led to a proportionate increase in profit. To assess why this has happened requires consideration of several factors that could potentially explain the results.

Perhaps the most obvious would be that Bengal has increased its sales by discounting prices, and thereby cutting profit margins. Interpreting the ratios rules out this possible explanation as the gross profit margin has in fact increased in 20X1 (up from 40% to 42%).

Another potential cause of the disappointing profit could be overheads (distribution costs and administrative expenses) getting out of control, perhaps due to higher advertising costs or more generous incentives to sales staff. Again, when these expenses are expressed as a percentage of sales, this does not explain the disparity in profit as the ratio has remained at approximately 19%.

What is evident is that there has been a very large increase in finance costs which is illustrated by the interest cover deteriorating from 36 times to only 9 times.

The other 'culprit' is the taxation expense: expressed as a percentage of pre-tax accounting profit, the effective rate of tax has gone from 28.6% in 20X0 to 42.9% in 20X1. There are a number of factors that can affect a period's effective tax rate (including under- or over-provisions from the previous year), but judging from the figures involved, it would seem likely that either there was a material adjustment from an under-provision of tax in 20X0 or there has been a considerable increase in the rate levied by the taxation authority.

As an illustration of the effect, if the same effective tax rate in 20X0 had applied in 20X1, the after-tax profit would have been $3,749,000 (5,250 × (100% − 28.6%) rounded) and, using this figure, the percentage increase in profit would be 50% ((3,749 − 2,500)/2,500 × 100) which is slightly higher than the percentage increase in revenue.

Thus an increase in the tax rate and increases in finance costs due to much higher borrowings more than account for the disappointing profit commented upon by the concerned shareholder.

The other significant observation in comparing 20X1 with 20X0 is that Bengal has almost certainty acquired another business. The increased expenditure on property, plant and equipment of $6,740,000 and the newly acquired intangibles (probably goodwill) of $6.2 million are not likely to be attributable to organic or internal growth.

Indeed the decrease in the bank balance of $4.2 million and the issue of $7 million loan notes closely match the increase in non-current assets. This implies that the acquisition has been financed by cash resources (which Bengal looks to have been building up) and issuing debt (no equity was issued).

It may be that these assets were part of the acquisition of a new business and are 'surplus to requirements', hence they have been made available for sale.

They are likely to be valued at their 'fair value less cost to sell' and the prospect of their sale should be highly probable (normally within one year). That said, if the assets are not sold in the near future, it would call into question the acceptability of the current ratio which may cause short-term liquidity problems.

In summary, although reported performance has deteriorated, it may be that future results will benefit from the current year's investment and show considerable improvement. Perhaps some equity should have been issued to lower the finance costs and if the dividend of $750,000 had been postponed for a year there would be a better liquid position.

### Appendix

| Calculation of ratios (figures in $000): | 20X1 | 20X0 |
|---|---|---|
| Gross profit margin (10,700/25,500 × 100) | 42.0% | 40.0 % |
| Operating expenses % (4,800/25,500 × 100) | 18.8% | 19.1% |
| Interest cover ((5,250 + 650)/650) | 9 times | 36 times |
| Effective rate of tax (2,250/5,250) | 42.9% | 28.6% |
| Net profit (before tax) margin (5,250/25,500 × 100) | 20.6% | 20.3% |

The figures for the calculation of 20X1's ratios are given in brackets, the figures for 20X0 are derived from the equivalent figures.

## 392 WOODBANK

**Key answer tips**

This style of question is naturally time consuming – ensure you answer all parts of the question and do not spend too much time calculating ratios. When interpreting the results in part (b) be wary of making generalisations – you must ensure that you relate it to the information given in the question. Presentation is also crucial in part (b), so make it easy for the marker to read by being as neat as possible, with short paragraphs and spaces between paragraphs. The highlighted words are key phrases that markers are looking for.

**(a)** **Note: Figures in the calculations of the ratios are in $million**

| | 20X4 Excluding Shaw | 20X3 | 20X4 |
|---|---|---|---|
| Return on capital employed (ROCE) (profit before interest and tax/year-end total assets less current liabilities) | 13% (13/100) | 10.5% | 12.0% |
| Net asset (equal to capital employed) turnover | 1.2 times (120/100) | 1.16 times | 1.0 times |
| Gross profit margin | 20% (24/120) | 22.0% | 22.0% |
| Profit before interest and tax margin | 10.8% (13/120) | 9.1% | 12.0% |
| Current ratio | – | 1.7:1 | 1.08:1 |
| Gearing (debt/(debt + equity)) | – | 5.3% | 36.7% |

**(b)** **Analysis of the comparative financial performance and position of Woodbank for the year ended 31 March 20X4**

### Introduction

When comparing current performance and position with the previous year (or years), using trend analysis, it is necessary to take into account the effect of any circumstances which may create an inconsistency in the comparison. In the case of Woodbank, the purchase of Shaw is an example of such an inconsistency.

20X4's figures include, for a three-month period, the operating results of Shaw, and Woodbank's statement of financial position includes all of Shaw's net assets (including goodwill) together with the additional 10% loan notes used to finance the purchase of Shaw. None of these items were included in the 20X3 financial statements.

The net assets of Shaw when purchased were $50 million, which represents one third of Woodbank's net assets (capital employed) as at 31 March 20X4. It therefore represents a major investment for Woodbank and any analysis necessitates careful consideration of its impact.

### Profitability

ROCE is considered by many analysts to be the most important profitability ratio. A ROCE of 12.0% in 20X4, compared to 10.5% in 20X3, represents a creditable 14.3% (12.0 – 10.5)/10.5) improvement in profitability.

When ROCE is calculated excluding the contribution from Shaw, at 13.0%, it shows an even more favourable performance. Although this comparison (13.0% from 10.5%) is valid, it would seem to imply that the purchase of Shaw has had a detrimental effect on Woodbank's ROCE.

However, caution is needed when interpreting this information as ROCE compares the return (profit for a period) to the capital employed (equivalent to net assets at a single point in time).

In the case of Woodbank, the statement of profit or loss only includes three months' results from Shaw whereas the statement of financial position includes all of Shaw's net assets, which is inconsistent.

It would be fair to speculate that in future years, when a full year's results from Shaw are reported, the ROCE effect of Shaw will be favourable.

Indeed, assuming a continuation of Shaw's current level of performance, profit in a full year could be $20 million. On an investment of $50 million, this represents a ROCE of 40% (based on the initial capital employed) which is much higher than Woodbank's pre-existing business.

The cause of the improvement in ROCE is revealed by consideration of the secondary profitability ratios: asset turnover and profit margins. For Woodbank this reveals a complicated picture.

Woodbank's results, as reported, show that it is the increase in the profit before interest and tax margin (12.0% from 9.1%) which is responsible for the improvement in ROCE, as the asset turnover has actually decreased (1.0 times from 1.16 times) and gross profit is exactly the same in both years (at 22.0%).

When the effect of the purchase of Shaw is excluded the position changes. The overall improvement in ROCE (13.0% from 10.5%) is caused by both an increase in profit margin (at the before interest and tax level, at 10.8% from 9.1 %), despite a fall in gross profit (20.0% from 22.0%) and a very slight improvement in asset turnover (1.2 times from 1.16 times). This means that the purchase of Shaw has improved Woodbank's overall profit margins, but caused a fall in asset turnover.

Again, as with the ROCE, this is misleading because the calculation of asset turnover only includes three months' revenue from Shaw, but all of its net assets. When a full year of Shaw's results are reported, asset turnover will be much improved (assuming its three-months performance is continued).

### Liquidity

The liquidity position, as measured by the current ratio, has fallen considerably in 20X4 and is a cause for concern.

At 1.67:1 in 20X3, it was within the acceptable range (normally between 1.5:1 and 2.0:1) but the 20X4 ratio of 1.08:1 is very low, indeed it is more like that which would be expected for the quick ratio (acid test).

Without needing to calculate the component ratios of the current ratio (for inventory, receivables and payables), it can be seen from the statements of financial position that the main causes of the deterioration in the liquidity position are the reduction in the cash (bank) position and the dramatic increase in trade payables. The bank balance has fallen by $4.5 million (5,000 – 500) and the trade payables have increased by $8 million.

An analysis of the movement in the retained earnings shows that Woodbank paid a dividend of $5.5 million (10,000 + 10,500 – 15,000) or 6.88 cents per share. It could be argued that during a period of expansion, with demands on cash flow, dividends could be suspended or heavily curtailed.

Had no dividend been paid, the 20X4 bank balance would be $6.0 million and the current ratio would have been 1.3:1 ((27,000 + 5,500):25,000). This would be still on the low side, but much more reassuring to credit suppliers than the reported ratio of 1.08:1.

### Gearing

Woodbank has gone from a position of very modest gearing at 5.3% in 20X3 to 36.7% in 20X4. This has largely been caused by the issue of the additional 10% loan notes to finance the purchase of Shaw.

Arguably, it might have been better if some of the finance had been raised from a share issue, but the level of gearing is still acceptable and the financing cost of 10% should be more than covered by the prospect of future high returns from Shaw, thus benefiting shareholders overall.

**Conclusion**

The overall operating performance of Woodbank has improved during the period (although the gross profit margin on sales other than those made by Shaw has fallen) and this should be even more marked next year when a full year's results from Shaw will be reported (assuming that Shaw can maintain its current performance). The changes in the financial position, particularly liquidity, are less favourable and call into question the current dividend policy. Gearing has increased substantially, due to the financing of the purchase of Shaw but it is still acceptable and has benefited shareholders. It is interesting to note that of the $50 million purchase price, $30 million of this is represented by goodwill. Although this may seem high, Shaw is certainly delivering in terms of generating revenue with good profit margins.

(c)    Below are a number of issues/items of information in relation to the acquisition of Shaw which would be useful in producing a better analysis of Woodbank.

- Did the acquisition of Shaw include any consideration payable dependent on Shaw's results? If so, this should be recorded as a liability at its fair value.

- Shaw's statement of financial position would be useful. This would be useful in assessing the working capital cycle of Shaw compared to Woodbank, as the Woodbank group has a low cash balance as at 31 March 20X4.

- Shaw's statement of cash flows would be useful (as would the statement of cash flow for Woodbank). This would help assess the reasons for the significant fall in cash during the year.

- Any one-off costs associated with the acquisition of Shaw, such as professional fees. These will have been expensed and will have affected the profit margins in the year.

- Whether there are any potential savings to be made following the acquisition of Shaw, such as reduction in staff costs or shared properties. These may involve one-off costs such as redundancies or lease termination costs but could lead to improved margins in future periods.

- The nature of Shaw's business should be looked at in comparison to Woodbank. It will be useful to know if Shaw was a competitor of Woodbank, or maybe a supplier of goods to Woodbank. This would help with further analysis regarding market share or the potential future cost of goods if Shaw was either of these.

- A breakdown of Shaw's major customers would be useful, to see if any have left following the change of ownership in Shaw.

| Marking scheme | | | |
|---|---|---|---|
| | | | *Marks* |
| (a) | 1 mark per ratio | Maximum | 4 |
| (b) | 1 mark per relevant point to maximum | | 12 |
| (c) | 1 mark per relevant point to maximum | | 4 |
| **Total** | | | **20** |

## 393 HYDAN

(a) **For comparison**

|  | Hydan adjusted | Hydan as reported | Sector average |
|---|---|---|---|
| Return on equity (ROE) | 21.7% | 47.1% | 22.0% |
| Net asset turnover | 1.75 times | 2.36 times | 1.67 times |
| Gross profit margin | 28.6% | 35.7% | 30.0% |
| Net profit margin | 9.3% | 20.0% | 12.0% |

**Hydan's adjusted ratios**

On the assumption that after the purchase of Hydan, the favourable effects of the transactions with other businesses owned by the family would not occur, the following adjustments to the statement of profit or loss should be made:

|  | $000 |
|---|---|
|  |  |
| Cost of sales (45,000/0.9) | 50,000 |
| Directors' remuneration | 2,500 |
| Loan interest (10% × 10,000) | 1,000 |

These adjustments would give a revised statement of profit or loss:

|  | $000 |
|---|---|
| Revenue | 70,000 |
| Cost of sales | (50,000) |
|  | ——— |
| Gross profit | 20,000 |
| Operating costs | (7,000) |
| Directors' remuneration | (2,500) |
| Loan interest | (1,000) |
|  | ——— |
| Profit before tax | 9,500 |
| Income tax expense | (3,000) |
|  | ——— |
| Profit for the year | 6,500 |
|  | ——— |

In the statement of financial position:

|  |  |
|---|---|
| Equity would be the purchase price of Hydan (per question) | 30,000 |
| The commercial loan (replacing the directors' loan) would now be debt | 10,000 |

From these figures the adjusted ratios above are calculated as:

|  |  |  |
|---|---|---|
| Return on equity | ((6,500 /30,000) × 100) | 21.7% |
| Net asset turnover | (70,000/(30,000 + 10,000)) | 1.75 times |
| Gross profit margin | ((20,000)/70,000) × 100) | 28.6% |
| Net profit margin | ((6,500/70,000) × 100) | 9.30% |

**(b)** An analysis of Hydan's ratios based on the financial statements provided reveals a strong position, particularly in relation to profitability when compared to other businesses in this retail sector. Hydan has a very high ROE which is a product of higher-than-average profit margins (at both the gross and net profit level) and a significantly higher net asset turnover. Thus, on the face of it, Hydan is managing to achieve higher prices (or reduced cost of sales), has better control of overheads and is using its net assets more efficiently in terms of generating revenue.

However, when adjustments are made for the effects of its favourable transactions with other businesses owned by the family, the position changes somewhat. The effect of purchasing its inventory from another family-owned supplier at favourable market prices means that its reported gross profit percentage of 35.7% is flattering. Had these purchases been made at market prices, it would fall to 28.6% which is below the sector average of 30.0%. The effects of the favourable inventory purchases carry through to net profit. Based on Xpand's estimate of future directors' remuneration, it would seem the existing directors of Hydan are not charging commercial rates for their remuneration. When Xpand replaces the board of Hydan, it will have to increase directors' remuneration by $1.5 million. Additionally, when the interest free directors' loans are replaced with a commercial loan, with interest at 10% per annum, this would reduce net profit by a further $1 million. The accumulation of these adjustments means that the ROE which Xpand should expect would be 21.7% (rather than the reported 47.1%) which is almost exactly in line with the sector average of 22.0%.

In a similar vein, when the asset turnover is calculated based on the equity purchase price and the commercial loan (equating to net assets), it falls from 2.36 times to 1.75 times which is above, but much closer to, the sector average of 1.67 times. In summary, Hydan's adjusted results would still be slightly ahead of the sector averages in most areas and may well justify the anticipated purchase price of $30 million. However, Hydan will be nowhere near the excellently performing business suggested by the reported figures and Xpand needs to exercise a degree of caution in its negotiations.

**(c)** The consolidated financial statements of Lodan are of little value when trying to assess the performance and financial position of its subsidiary, Hydan. Therefore the main source of information on which to base any investment decision would be Hydan's own entity financial statements. However, where an entity is part of a group, there is the potential for the financial statements to have been subject to the influence of related-party transactions. In the case of Hydan, there has been a considerable amount of post-acquisition trading with Lodan and, because of the related-party relationship, it appears that this trading is not at arm's length (i.e. not at commercial rates).

There may be other aspects of the relationship where Lodan gives Hydan a benefit that may not have happened had Hydan not been part of the group, e.g. access to technology/research, cheap finance.

The operations of Hydan may now be centralised and run by Lodan. If Lodan doesn't allocate some of these costs to Hydan then Hydan's expenses will be understated. It could also be difficult for a purchaser to assess whether additional property would be required if Hydan share this with other group entities.

The main concern is that any information about the 'benefits' Lodan may have passed on to Hydan through related party transactions is difficult to obtain from published sources. It may be that Lodan would deliberately 'flatter' Hydan's financial statements specifically in order to obtain a high sale price and a prospective purchaser would not necessarily be able to determine that this had happened from either the consolidated or entity financial statements. There are suggestions of this in the fact that Hydan's directors are not charging market rates for their remuneration and are giving interest-free loans.

| Marking scheme | | Marks |
|---|---|---|
| (a) | 1½ marks per ratio | 6 |
| (b) | 1 mark per valid point. A good answer must emphasise the different interpretation when using adjusted figures | 9 |
| (c) | 1 mark per valid point, emphasising potential distortion of true trading performance | 5 |
| **Total** | | **20** |

## 394 YOGI

**Note:** References to 20X5 and 20X4 refer to the periods ended 31 March 20X5 and 20X4 respectively.

**(a)** **Calculation of equivalent ratios (figures in $000):**

| | (i) 20X4 excluding division | (ii) 20X5 as reported | 20X4 per question |
|---|---|---|---|
| Gross profit margin ((20,000 – 8,000)/(50,000 – 18,000) × 100) | 37.5% | 33.3% | 40.0% |
| Operating profit margin ((11,800 – 5,800)/32,000 × 100) | 18.8% | 10.3% | 23.6% |
| Return on capital employed (ROCE) ((11,800 – 5,800)/(29,200 – 7,200 – 7,000 see below) × 100) | 40.0% | 21.8% | 53.6% |
| Net asset turnover (32,000/15,000) | 2.13 times | 2.12 times | 2.27 times |

**Note:** The capital employed in the division sold at 31 March 20X4 was $7 million ($8 million sale proceeds less $1 million profit on sale).

The figures for the calculations of 20X4's adjusted ratios (i.e. excluding the effects of the sale of the division) are given in brackets, the figures for 20X5 are derived from the equivalent figures in the question. However, the operating profit margin and ROCE calculations exclude the profit from the sale of the division (as stated in the requirement) as it is a 'one-off' item.

**(b)** The most relevant comparison is the 20X5 results (excluding the profit on disposal of the division) with the results of 20X4 (excluding the results of the division), otherwise like is not being compared with like.

### Profitability

Although comparative sales have increased (excluding the effect of the sale of the division) by $4 million (36,000 – 32,000), equivalent to 12.5%, the gross profit margin has fallen considerably (from 37.5% in 20X4 down to 33.3% in 20X5) and this deterioration has been compounded by the sale of the division, which was the most profitable part of the business (which earned a gross profit margin of 44.4% (8/18)). The deterioration of the operating profit margin (from 18.8% in 20X4 down to 10.3% in 20X5) is largely due to poor gross profit margins, but operating expenses are proportionately higher (as a percentage of sales) in 20X5 (23.0% compared to 18.8%) which has further reduced profitability. This is due to higher administrative expenses (as distribution costs have fallen), perhaps relating to the sale of the division.

Yogi's performance as measured by ROCE has deteriorated dramatically from 40.0% in 20X4 (as adjusted) to only 21.8% in 20X5. As the net asset turnover has remained broadly the same at 2.1 times (rounded), it is the fall in the operating profit which is responsible for the overall deterioration in performance. Whilst it is true that Yogi has sold the most profitable part of its business, this does not explain why the 20X5 results have deteriorated so much (by definition the adjusted 20X4 figures exclude the favourable results of the division). Consequently, Yogi's management need to investigate why profit margins have fallen in 20X5. It may be that customers of the sold division also bought (more profitable) goods from Yogi's remaining business and they have taken their custom to the new owners of the division, or it may be related to external issues which are also being experienced by other businesses such as an economic recession. A study of industry sector average ratios could reveal this.

### Other issues

It is very questionable to have offered shareholders such a high dividend (half of the disposal proceeds) to persuade them to vote for the disposal. At $4 million (4,000 + 3,000 – 3,000, i.e. the movement on retained earnings or 10 million shares at 40 cents) the dividend represents double the profit for the year of $2 million (3,000 – 1,000) if the gain on the disposal is excluded. Another effect of the disposal is that Yogi appears to have used the other $4 million (after paying the dividend) from the disposal proceeds to pay down half of the 10% loan notes. This has reduced finance costs and interest cover, but, as the finance cost at 10% is much lower than the 20X5 ROCE of 21.8%, it will have had a detrimental effect on overall profit available to shareholders.

### Summary

In retrospect, it may have been unwise for Yogi to sell the most profitable part of its business at what appears to be a very low price. It has coincided with a remarkable deterioration in profitability (not solely due to the sale) and the proceeds of the disposal have not been used to replace capacity or improve long-term prospects. By returning a substantial proportion of the sale proceeds to shareholders, it represents a downsizing of the business.

**(c)** Although the sports club is a not-for-profit organisation, the request for a loan is a commercial activity that should be decided on according to similar criteria as would be used for other profit-orientated entities.

The main aspect of granting a loan is how secure the loan would be. To this extent a form of capital gearing ratio should be calculated, say existing long-term borrowings to net assets (i.e. total assets less current liabilities). Clearly if this ratio is high, further borrowing would be at an increased risk. The secondary aspect is to measure the sports club's ability to repay the interest (and ultimately the principal) on the loan. This may be determined from information in the statement of comprehensive income. A form of interest cover should be calculated, say the excess of income over expenditure (broadly the equivalent of profit) compared to (the forecast) interest payments. The higher this ratio the less risk of interest default. The calculations would be made for all four years to ascertain any trends that may indicate a deterioration or improvement in these ratios. As with other profit-oriented entities the nature and trend of the income should be investigated: for example, are the club's sources of income increasing or decreasing, does the reported income contain 'one-off' donations (which may not be recurring) etc? Also matters such as the market value of, and existing prior charges against, any assets intended to be used as security for the loan would be relevant to the lender's decision-making process. It may also be possible that the sports club's governing body (perhaps the trustees) may be willing to give a personal guarantee for the loan.

| Marking scheme | | | |
|---|---|---|---|
| | | | *Marks* |
| (a) | (i) and (ii) | Gross profit margin | 1 |
| | | Operating profit margin | 1½ |
| | | Return on capital employed | 1½ |
| | | Net asset turnover | 1 |
| | | | 5 |
| (b) | 1 mark per point (a good answer must consider the effect of the sale of the division) | | 10 |
| (c) | 1 mark per point | | 5 |
| **Total** | | | **20** |

## 395 XPAND

(a)     **Missing ratios for Kovert:**

| | |
|---|---:|
| Return on year-end capital employed (ROCE) | 31.0% |
| (4,900/(5,600 + 9,200 + 1,000 × 100) | |
| Profit margin (before interest and tax) (4,900/40,000 × 100) | 12.3% |
| Trade payables' payment period (2,100/32,800 × 365) | 23 days |
| Gearing (debt/(debt + equity)) (10,200/15,800 × 100) | 64.6% |

(b)     **Assessment of the comparative performance and financial position of Kandid and Kovert for the year ended 30 September 20X5**

### Introduction

This assessment of the two entities will look at the areas of profitability, liquidity and gearing with reference to some differences which may make the comparison of the reported figures potentially invalid.

### Profitability

ROCE is usually considered as the most important measure of profitability and is often described as a measure of management's overall efficiency in the use of the assets at its disposal. The ROCE of 62.5% of Kandid is far superior (more than double) to the 31.0% return achieved by Kovert. This superior return of Kandid can be analysed into its component parts of profit margin and asset turnover and in both of these areas Kandid's performance is better than that of Kovert. Kandid is generating $3.30 for every dollar invested, compared to only $2.50 per dollar invested in Kovert and earning a profit margin of 19.0% compared to just 12.3% by Kovert. Additionally, Kandid's gross profit margin at 24% is a third (6%/18%) higher than the 18% of Kovert. This may be, at least in part, due to marketing policy.  Kovert may be deliberately charging lower selling prices in order to generate greater revenue. This is evidenced by Kovert's turnover of $40 million compared to only $25 million for Kandid. The superior gross margin of Kandid continues into the operating profit level indicating that Kandid has better control of its overheads.

There are, however, a number of areas relating to the capital employed which may bring this superiority into question. Kandid has deducted the receipt of a government grant directly from the carrying amount of the related plant, which is allowed but is rather unusual. Normally, plant is shown gross less accumulated depreciation and related government grants are shown as a separate deferred credit. It also appears that Kandid rents its property whereas Kovert has purchased its property (and indeed revalued it which has increased its capital employed). Kandid also holds proportionately less inventory and receivables than Kovert. Whilst these factors may not necessarily result in a higher profit for Kandid (e.g. property rental may be higher than the equivalent depreciation of property), they would act to give Kandid lower net assets, and thus lower capital employed and in turn a higher ROCE than Kovert.

Bearing in mind these differences, it may be more helpful if Xpand were to calculate a return on its potential equity investment (ROE) of $12 million as this would be more relevant should it acquire either of the entities. Using profit after tax, Kandid's ROE would be 30% (3,600/12,000 × 100) whereas Kovert's ROE would be 25% (3,000/12,000). This still supports Kandid's superior return, but this introduces further differences. Both entities have $5 million in loan notes but the interest rate on Kandid's loan is only 5% compared to 10% for Kovert, presumably this reflects the difference in the creditworthiness of the two entities which is something that Xpand should take note of. There also appears to be a favourable tax discrepancy with Kandid paying a nominal rate of tax on its profit of 20% compared with 25% paid by Kovert. This may be due to be adjustments relating to previous years' profits or other tax issues. If Kandid had a comparable finance cost and tax rate to Kovert, its ROE would be nearer that of Kovert.

**Liquidity**

The given ratios show that both entities have healthy liquidity positions. Kandid's current ratio is slightly higher than Kovert's, perhaps too high. This seems to be down to holding more cash than Kovert as it has better inventory and receivables control, though arguably the current lease liability of Kovert should not be included in this ratio for comparative purposes. The individual components of the current ratio could suggest that Kovert holds a greater range of inventory, perhaps enabling it to achieve more sales, and the relatively high receivables collection period could be indicative of an uncollectable customer balance which should have been written off, or may just be due to poor credit control.

**Gearing**

At around 65%, both entities are highly geared. The relatively low equity, particularly retained earnings, may be due to the entities having a policy of paying most of their earnings as dividends. Kovert's high gearing is in part due to its policy of using leases to acquire its plant. Xpand should be aware that, for both entities, the $5 million loans are due for repayment in the near future which will represent a substantial further cash outlay on top of the purchase price it may pay.

**Summary**

Although both entities operate in a same industry sector and have a similar level of after-tax profits, and indeed have the same indicative valuation, they would represent very different investments. Kovert's revenue is over 60% (15,000/25,000 × 100) higher than that of Kandid, it is financed by high levels of debt (loans and leases), and it also owns, rather than rents, its property. Another point of note is that Kovert's plant is 80% depreciated and will need replacement in the near future, with consequent financing implications. Ultimately, the investment decision may be determined by Xpand's attitude to risk and how well each investment would fit in with existing activities and management structure.

(c) Basing an investment decision solely on one year's summarised financial statements is fraught with danger. Below are a number of issues and items of information to which Xpand may wish to seek clarification before making an offer.

**General:**

- in addition to using different strategies (e.g. buying property or renting it, targeting low mark-up/high volume sales), the two entities may use different accounting policies

- the availability of non-published forward-looking information such as profit forecasts, capital commitments and the size of orders on the books (providing this information should not be unreasonable if the shareholders are receptive to a takeover)

- is either entity established or a relatively young and growing entity, with more risk, but potentially more reward?

**Specific:**

- as noted above, the owned assets of Kovert are nearing the end of their useful life. Will these need replacing soon, or have they already been replaced by the leased assets?

- how much of the profit is due to the reputation or contacts of the current management and would they continue in their role after a takeover (and indeed would Xpand want this or would it prefer to use its own managers)?

- the fair value of the assets, compared to their carrying amounts, which will impact on the calculation of goodwill.

| Marking scheme | | Marks |
|---|---|---|
| (a) | 1 mark per ratio | 4 |
| (b) | 1 mark per value point up to | 12 |
| (c) | 1 mark per valid point up to | 4 |
| **Total** | | **20** |

## 396 SCHRUTE

**Ratios for Schrute for the year ended 30 September 20X3**

| | | | 20X2 |
|---|---|---|---|
| Gross profit margin | 51.1% | (48,000/94,000) × 100 | 59.1% |
| Operating profit margin | 1.3% | (1,200/94,000) × 100 | 8.5% |
| Return on Capital Employed | 1.0% | (1,200/(99,010 + 20,000)) × 100 | 7.4% |
| Current ratio | 2.6:1 | (24,110/9,100) | 4.6:1 |
| Inventory turnover period | 52 days | (6,500/46,000) × 365 | 60 days |
| Receivables collection period | 66 days | (17,000/94,000) × 365 | 83 days |

**Performance**

Revenue and expenses have all increased during the year, due to the acquisition of Howard, the new subsidiary. Howard would have contributed a full year's results to 20X3 that would not have been included within 20X2.

Whilst revenue has increased significantly, it can be seen that higher expenses have meant that the Schrute group has made less profit than in previous years.

It is also worth noting that the new hotel was only opened in March, so a full year's revenue has not yet been generated by the hotel.

The gross profit margin has fallen. It may well be that the hotel business generates much lower margins than the farming side of things. It may also be that the new hotel had to offer low room rates to attract new business as it was set up, or to bring customers back with special offers following the poor feedback. As the hotel establishes itself, the need to cut prices will hopefully not be a common issue.

The improvement in online feedback should lead to increased future bookings, so it may be that the new hotel generates a significantly improved return in the next year.

The operating profit margin has also deteriorated in the year. In addition to this fall, there is a significant one-off $4.5 million income relating to the disposal of investments, which shows a false position.

Without this gain on disposal, Schrute would have made a worrying loss from operations of $3.3 million. Analysing this further, it can be seen that the reason for the loss would be due to a significant increase in administrative expenses, which would be $30.1 million if the investment disposal is ignored.

Some of these expenses may be linked to the acquisition of Howard, such as professional fees, which will not be incurred in future years. There may also be some redundancy costs included if Schrute has merged administrative departments with Howard such as human resources.

A number of expenses are likely to be linked to the new hotel project in the year.

A large amount of these administrative expenses will hopefully relate to set up costs for the hotel and can be regarded as one-off expenses. Schrute has undertaken a significant marketing campaign to reverse their reputation.

Whilst these could be classed as one-off expenses, there will be many expenses included that will remain high in future periods. Staff numbers will have increased due to the hotel, and costs such as heating, lighting, and repairs will continue to be incurred each year.

There has not been a significant increase in distribution costs in the year. This could suggest that Schrute has done significantly less business from the farming side of the business, or that Howard has extremely low distribution costs.

While the distribution costs may have been saved, it is questionable whether it is wise to have diversified to avoid the impact of fuel prices. Howard appears to have smaller margins, and will incur significant heating and lighting costs, which are likely to rise in a similar manner to fuel costs.

The return on capital employed (ROCE) has also deteriorated in the year. This would actually be negative if the gain on investments had not been included, as Schrute would have been loss-making.

As well as making less profit, the capital employed by Schrute has also increased significantly. New shares have been issued by Schrute, and a new loan has been taken out. All of this seems to have been due to the acquisition of Howard and the new hotel, which has not been operational for a full year.

It actually appears that Howard is a loss-making entity, as the non-controlling interest share of the profit is negative. This could mean that the rest of the Schrute group has remained profitable, with Howard generating a loss.

It could also be that there has been a significant impairment in the goodwill of Howard since acquisition. If Schrute uses the fair value method for valuing the non-controlling interest, the non-controlling interest will have an allocation of the impairment.

It may well be that in 20X4 the performance improves significantly as the new hotel has a full year's operation in the results and many of the set up costs will not be included.

**Cash flow**

The cash balance has fallen to $0.6 million. It should be noted that Schrute has undertaken a number of activities to raise cash in the year. Investments were sold for $15.5 million, $19 million was raised from a share issue and $20 million has been raised from debt finance. It seems that the vast majority of these funds were spent on the acquisition of Howard and the new hotel.

Looking at the other areas and their impact on cash flow, it can be seen that receivable days have decreased significantly in the year. With no indication of changes in customer terms for the farms, it is likely that this is the effect of Howard being largely cash based and having a positive impact on cash flow.

The inventory turnover period has reduced, which is likely to be due to Howard not having the same level of inventory, as inventory in a hotel may be limited to food and drink. A period of 52 days still seems potentially high for a business involved in the farming industry, and the inventory should be investigated to ensure that none of the produce has perished.

**Conclusion**

It is difficult to judge the success of the business as a whole in this transitional year. There are concerns over the acquisition of Howard. Whilst the revenue has increased significantly, Howard appears to have made a loss and put pressure onto the cash flow of the Schrute group.

The individual results of Howard need to be obtained for a more meaningful comparison to be made. It would then be possible to better understand the impact of the new hotel.

## 397  PITCARN

**(a)     Ratios for the year ended 31 March 20X6**

| | | |
|---|---|---|
| Gross profit margin | 30% | (28,200/94,000) × 100 |
| Operating margin | 6% | (5,600/94,000) × 100 |
| Interest cover | 2.9 times | (5,600/(1,900) |

In producing the consolidated information, Sitor must be added in for the year, with adjustments made to remove the intra-group sale, rent, interest and dividend.

| | 20X6 $000 |
|---|---|
| Revenue (86,000 + 16,000 − 8,000 intra-group) | 94,000 |
| Cost of sales (63,400 + 10,400 − 8,000 intra-group) | (65,800) |
| | |
| Gross profit | 28,200 |
| Other income (3,400 − 300 rent − 1,000 dividend − 500 interest) | 1,600 |
| Operating expenses (21,300 + 3,200 − 300 rent) | (24,200) |
| | |
| Profit from operations | 5,600 |
| Finance costs (1,500 + 900 − 500 intra-group) | (1,900) |

**(b)** Looking at the figures calculated for the Pitcarn group, it seems that performance has deteriorated in terms of revenue, margins and interest cover.

This would suggest that the disposal of Sitor is a mistake, as the group appear to be performing worse without Sitor than when Sitor was included as a subsidiary.

Looking at Sitor's individual results appears to confirm this, as Sitor has profit margins which are higher than the rest of the group, both in terms of gross and operating margin.

A closer examination of Sitor's results highlights an issue to be aware of. Half of Sitor's revenue is made by selling to Pitcarn, and this is done at an extremely high margin of 40%. This is much higher than the margin of 35% made overall, and means that the other half of Sitor's sales must be made at a margin of 30%. This means that the external sales of Sitor are actually made at the same gross margin as the rest of the group.

It is possible that Pitcarn deliberately purchased goods from Sitor at an inflated price in order to demonstrate a stronger performance in Sitor in order to achieve a good selling price.

While this allowed, it highlights the problem with analysing an entity's performance based on its individual financial statements if it is part of a group, as prices can be manipulated within the group to artificially inflate the performance of one part.

A similar fear arises in respect of the operating margin. Sitor uses Pitcarn's properties, and is paying a lower rate than the market rate of rent. This will again artificially inflate the margin made by Sitor, as Pitcarn bear the majority of the property costs without recharging an accurate rate of rent.

It appears that Pitcarn have suffered lower margins in order to make the margins look better in Sitor by paying a high price for goods and not charging a market rate of rent. Pitcarn has taken a further $1.5 million cash out of Sitor during the year, through the receipt of a $1 million dividend and $500,000 interest. The loan agreement should be investigated further in order to assess if the interest charged was at market rates or not.

Following the disposal of Sitor, Pitcarn will lose at least $1.3 million of income through no longer obtaining a dividend or rent from the properties. For a more detailed analysis of future prospects, it will be important to speak to Pitcarn regarding the excess office space and whether there are plans to utilise it themselves or to rent it to a third party. The loan agreement with Sitor should also be examined to see if this will change following the sale. It may be that the interest rate increases now Sitor is no longer in the group, or the loan may need repaying by the new Sitor owners.

The one area where Sitor underperformed relative to the rest of the Pitcarn group is in terms of interest cover, with profits able to cover interest less times. Again, a review of the loan agreement with Pitcarn will be able to assess if this interest rate is at market rate, as Pitcarn may be charging a higher rate of interest than market rates in exchange for the cheaper rent and higher priced goods.

Examination should also be made as to whether Pitcarn will still need Sitor to supply goods. If so, supplies may be harder to obtain now that Sitor is no longer in the group.

Overall, the sale of Sitor appears to be a reasonable move. Whilst Sitor does appear to be making good profits, when the goods and rent with Pitcarn are adjusted to market values it is likely that Sitor would not be making significant profits. As long as Pitcarn is not reliant on Sitor as a supplier, this seems to be a reasonable move and one which may free up space in the premises to pursue more lucrative options.

**(c)** **Gain/loss on disposal**

|  | $000 | $000 |
|---|---:|---:|
| Proceeds |  | 25,000 |
| Net assets at disposal | 17,000 |  |
| (10,000 share capital + 7,000 retained earnings) |  |  |
| Goodwill at disposal (W1) | 5,000 |  |
| Non-controlling interest at disposal (W2) | (1,800) |  |
|  | ——— | (20,200) |
|  |  | ——— |
| **Gain on disposal** |  | **4,800** |
|  |  | ——— |

**Workings**

**(W1) Goodwill**

|  | $000 |
|---|---:|
| Consideration | 17,000 |
| NCI at acquisition | 1,000 |
| Net assets at acquisition | (13,000) |
| (10,000 share capital + 3,000 retained earnings) |  |
|  | ——— |
| Goodwill at acquisition | 5,000 |
|  | ——— |

**(W2) Non-controlling interest at disposal**

|  | $000 |
|---|---:|
| NCI at acquisition | 1,000 |
| NCI share of Sitor's post acquisition retained earnings |  |
| (20% × (7,000 − 3,000)) | 800 |
|  | ——— |
| Non-controlling interest at disposal | 1,800 |
|  | ——— |

## 398   GREGORY

(a)   **Note: References to 20X6 and 20X5 are to the years ending 31 March 20X6 and 20X5 respectively.**

### Comment (1)

"I see the profit for the year has increased by $1m which is up 20% on last year, but I thought it would be more as Tamsin was supposed to be very profitable."

There are two issues with this statement: first, last year's profit is not comparable with the current year's profit because in 20X5 Gregory was a single entity and in 20X6 it is now a group with a subsidiary. A second issue is that the consolidated statement of profit or loss for the year ended 31 March 20X6 only includes six months of the results of Tamsin, and, assuming Tamsin is profitable, future results will include a full year's profit. This latter point may, at least in part, mitigate the CEO's disappointment.

### Comment (2)

"I have calculated the EPS for 20X6 at 13 cents (6, 000/46, 000 × 100 shares) and at 12.5 cents for 20X5 (5,000/40, 000 × 100) and, although the profit has increased 20%, our EPS has barely changed."

The stated EPS calculation for 20X6 is incorrect for two reasons: first, it is the profit attributable to only the equity shareholders of the parent which should be used and second the 6 million new shares were only in issue for six months and should be weighted by $^6/_{12}$. Thus, the correct EPS for 20X6 is 13.3 cents (5,700/43,000 × 100). This gives an increase of 6% (13.3 − 12.5)/12.5) on 20X5 EPS which is still less than the increase in profit. The reason why the EPS may not have increased in line with reported profit is that the acquisition was financed by a share exchange which increased the number of shares in issue. Thus the EPS takes account of the additional consideration used to generate profit, whereas the trend of absolute profit does not take additional consideration into account. This is why the EPS is often said to be a more accurate reflection of performance than the trend of profits.

### Comment (3)

"I am worried that the low price at which we are selling goods to Tamsin is undermining our group's overall profitability."

Assuming the consolidated financial statements have been correctly prepared, all intra-group trading has been eliminated, thus the pricing policy will have had no effect on these financial statements. The comment is incorrect and reflects a misunderstanding of the consolidation process.

### Comment (4)

"I note that our share price is now $2.30, how does this compare with our share price immediately before we bought Tamsin?"

The increase in share capital is 6 million shares, the increase in the share premium is $6m, thus the total proceeds for the 6 million shares was $12m giving a share price of $2 at the date of acquisition of Tamsin. The current price of $2.30 presumably reflects the market's favourable view of Gregory's current and future performance.

**(b)**

|  |  | *20X6* | *20X5* |
|---|---|---|---|
| (i) | Return on capital employed (ROCE) (7,500/74,300 × 100) | 10.1% | 11.3% |
| (ii) | Net asset turnover (46,500/74,300) | 0.63 times | 0.53 times |
| (iii) | Gross profit margin (9,300/46,500 × 100) | 20.0% | 25.7% |
| (iv) | Operating profit margin (7,500/46,500 × 100) | 16.1% | 21.4% |

Looking at the above ratios, it appears that the overall performance of Gregory has declined marginally. The ROCE has fallen from 11.3% to 10.1%, which has been caused by a substantial fall in the gross profit margin (down from 25.7% in 20X5 to 20% in 20X6), over a 22% (5.7%/25.7%) decrease. The group have relatively low operating expenses (at around 4% of revenue), so the poor gross profit margin feeds through to the operating profit margin. The overall decline in the ROCE due to the weaker profit margins has been mitigated by an improvement in net asset turnover, increasing from 0.53 times to 0.63 times. Despite the improvement in net asset turnover, it still seems very low, with only 63 cents of sales generated from every $1 invested in the business, although this will depend on the type of business Gregory and Tamsin are engaged in.

On this analysis, the effect of the acquisition of Tamsin seems to have had a detrimental effect on overall performance, but this may not necessarily be the case, as there could be some distorting factors in the analysis. As mentioned above, the 20X6 results include only six months of Tamsin's results, but the statement of financial position includes the full amount of the consideration for Tamsin. [The consideration has been calculated (see comment (4) above) as $12m for the parent's 75% share plus $3.3m (3,600 − 300 share of post-acquisition profit) for the non-controlling interest's 25%, giving total consideration of $15.3m.] The above factors disproportionately increase the denominator of ROCE which has the effect of worsening the calculated ROCE. This distortion should be corrected in 20X7 when a full year's results for Tamsin will be included in group profit. Another factor is that it could take time to fully integrate the activities of the two entities and more savings and other synergies may be forthcoming such as bulk buying discounts.

The non-controlling interest share in the profit for the year in 20X6 of $300,000 allows a rough calculation of the full year's profit of Tamsin at $2.4m (300,000/25% × $^{12}/_6$, i.e. the $300,000 represents 25% of $^6/_{12}$ of the annual profit). This figure is subject to some uncertainty such as the effect of probable increased post-acquisition depreciation charges. However, a profit of $2.4m on the investment of $15.3m represents a return of 16% (and would be higher if the profit was adjusted to a pre-tax figure) which is much higher than the current year ROCE (at 10.1%) of the group. This implies that the performance of Tamsin is much better than that of Gregory as a separate entity, and that Gregory's performance in 20X6 must have deteriorated considerably from that in 20X5 and this is the real cause of the deteriorating performance of the group.

Another issue potentially affecting the ROCE is that, as a result of the consolidation process, Tamsin's net assets, including goodwill, are included in the statement of financial position at fair value, whereas Gregory's net assets appear to be based on historical cost, as there is no revaluation surplus. As the values of property, plant and equipment have been rising, this effect favourably flatters the 20X5 ratios. This is because the statement of financial position of 20X5 only contains Gregory's assets which, at historical cost, may considerably understate their fair value and, on a comparative basis, overstate 20X5 ROCE.

In summary, although on first impression the acquisition of Tamsin appears to have caused a marginal worsening of the group's performance, the distorting factors and imputation of the non-controlling interest's profit in 20X6 indicate the underlying performance may be better than the ratios portray and the contribution from Tamsin is a very significant positive. Future performance may be even better.

Without information on the separate financial statements of Tamsin, it is difficult to form a more definite view.

| Marking scheme | | Marks |
|---|---|---|
| (a) | 2 marks for each reply to the CEO's observations | 8 |
| (b) | 1 mark for each pair of ratios | 4 |
| | 1 mark per relevant comment on performance up to | 8 |
| | | 12 |
| **Total** | | **20** |

**Examiner's comments**

This is the first time a question combining interpretation with an element of consolidation has been examined and candidates did find this a challenging question.

For part (a) the comments required in response to the Chief Executive Officer (CEO)'s observations were not at the expected standard. Most candidates launched into irrelevant detail regarding ratio movements and did not consider the reason for the difference between the two years' financial statements, specifically that the statement of profit or loss for the second year included the consolidated results of the newly-acquired subsidiary but, crucially, only for six months.

The low margin on intra-group sales was seen by many candidates as, correctly, not affecting the consolidated financial statements or the overall profitability of the group. Some candidates did mention the impact of any unrealised profit on inventories held from such trading, but this was not likely to have a material effect.

For part (b) the four ratio calculations were generally well done although for ROCE, capital employed should include the non-controlling interest as this is part of equity (those who took total assets less current liabilities had no problem with this) and the calculation of net asset turnover (revenue/capital employed) was either omitted or the figures inverted. A minority of candidates attempted to adjust for the intra-group transactions before calculating ratios which was not required as we must assume that intra-group transactions had already been correctly eliminated on consolidation.

> For the comments on comparative performance, the usual observations on past papers continue to apply. To suggest ratios have increased or decreased does not qualify as analysis; suggesting the change is better or worse begins to show understanding, but more than this is required. In many cases the impact of the acquisition (as answered in part (a)) was completely ignored and candidates compared this year and last year results as if they were directly comparing like with like.
>
> The relationship between gross and operating profit margin was often misunderstood. Many candidates stated that the decrease in the operating margin was caused by increased operating costs when in fact operating costs were a lower % of revenue in the second year (despite any one-off costs of the acquisition) and the cause of the decrease was the reduction in the gross profit margin. Very few candidates used the information in the question regarding the non-controlling interest in the subsidiary's profit to determine the subsidiary's possible contribution to the group's profit for the year and thus determine that there could have been a decline in the profit earned by the parent alone in the second year.

## 399   LANDING

(a)   **Archway's restated figures**

On the assumption that Landing purchases Archway, the following adjustments relate to the effects of notes (i) to (iii) in the question and the property revaluation:

|  | $000 |
|---|---|
| Revenue (94,000 × 95%) | 89,300 |
| Cost of sales (see below) | 76,000 |
| Loan interest (10,000 × 8%) | 800 |
| Equity (10,000 + 2,300 RE + 3,000 revaluation) | 15,300 |
| Non-current liabilities: 8% loan notes | 10,000 |

The cost of sales should be first adjusted for the annual licence fee of $1m, reducing this to $72m. Half of these, $36m, are net of a discount of 10% which equates to $4m (36,000/90% – 36,000). Adjusted cost of sales is $76m (73,000 – 1,000 + 4,000).

(b)   These figures would give the following ratios:

| | | |
|---|---|---|
| Annual sales per square metre of floor space | (89,300/12,000) | $7,442 |
| ROCE | (13,300 – 10,000)/(15,300 + 10,000) × 100) | 13% |
| Net asset turnover | (89,300/(15,300 + 10,000)) | 3.5 times |
| Gross profit margin | ((89,300 – 76,000)/89,300 × 100) | 15% |
| Operating profit margin | ((13,300 – 10,000)/89,300 × 100) | 3.7 % |
| Gearing (debt/equity) | (10,000/15,300) | 65.4% |

**(c)    Performance**

|  | Archway as reported | Archway as adjusted | Sector average |
|---|---|---|---|
| Annual sales per square metre of floor space | $7,833 | $7,442 | $8,000 |
| ROCE | 58.5% | 13% | 18.0% |
| Net asset turnover | 5.0 times | 3.5 times | 2.7 times |
| Gross profit margin | 22.3% | 15% | 22.0% |
| Operating profit margin | 11.7% | 3.7% | 6.7% |
| Gearing (debt/equity) | nil | 65.4% | 30.0% |

A comparison of Archway's ratios based upon the reported results compares very favourably to the sector average ratios in almost every instance. ROCE is particularly impressive at 58.5% compared to a sector average of 18%; this represents a return of more than three times the sector average. The superior secondary ratios of profit margin and asset utilisation (net asset turnover) appear to confirm Archway's above average performance. It is only sales per square metre of floor space which is below the sector average. The unadjusted figure is very close to the sector average, as too is the gross profit margin, implying a comparable sales volume performance. However, the reduction in selling prices caused by the removal of the brand premium causes sales per square metre to fall marginally.

As indicated in the question, should Archway be acquired by Landing, many figures particularly related to the statement of profit or loss would be unfavourably impacted as shown above in the workings for Archway's adjusted ratios. When these effects are taken into account and the ratios are recalculated, a very different picture emerges. All the performance ratios, with the exception of net asset turnover, are significantly reduced due to the assumed cessation of the favourable trading arrangements. The most dramatic effect is on the ROCE, which, having been more than three times the sector average, would be 27.8% (18.0 − 13.0)/18.0 × 100) below the sector average (at 13% compared to 18.0%). Analysing the component parts of the ROCE (net asset turnover and profit margins), both aspects are lower when the reported figures are adjusted.

The net asset turnover (although adjusted to a lower multiple) is still considerably higher than the sector average. The fall in this ratio is due to a combination of lower revenues (caused by the loss of the branding) and the increase in capital employed (equal to net assets) due to classifying the loan notes as debt (non-current). Gross margin deteriorates from 22.3% to only 15.0% caused by a combination of lower revenues (referred to above) and the loss of the discount on purchases. The distribution costs and administrative expenses for Archway are less than those of its retail sector in terms of the percentage of sales revenue (at 11.3% compared to 15.3%), which mitigates (slightly) the dramatic reduction in the profit before interest and tax. The reduction in sales per square metre of floor space is caused only by the reduced (5%) volume from the removal of the branded sales.

**Gearing**

The gearing ratio of nil based on the unadjusted figures is not meaningful due to previous debt being classified as a current liability because of its imminent redemption. When this debt is replaced by the 8% loan notes and (more realistically) classified as a non-current liability, Archway's gearing is much higher than the sector average. There is no information as to how the increased interest payable at 8% (double the previous 4%) compares to the sector's average finance cost. If such a figure were available, it may give an indication of Archway's credit status although the doubling of the rate does imply a greater degree of risk in Archway seen by the lender.

**Summary and advice**

Based upon Archway's reported figures, its purchase by Landing would appear to be a good investment. However, when Archway's performance is assessed based on the results and financial position which might be expected under Landing's ownership, the recalculated ratios are generally inferior to Archway's retail sector averages. In an investment decision such as this, an important projected ratio would be the return on the investment (ROI) which Landing might expect. The expected net profit after tax can be calculated as $2m ((3,300 before interest and tax − 800 interest) × 80% post-tax), however, there is no information in the question as to what the purchase consideration of Archway would be. That said, at a (probable) minimum purchase price based on Archway's net asset value (with no goodwill premium), the ROI would only be 7.9% (2,000/25,300 × 100) which is very modest and should be compared to Landing's existing ROI. A purchase price exceeding $25.3m would obviously result in an even lower expected ROI. It is possible that under Landing's management, Archway's profit margins could be improved, perhaps coming to a similar arrangement regarding access to branded sales (or franchising) as currently exists with Cardol, but with a different entity. If so, the purchase of Archway may still be a reasonable acquisition.

| ACCA Marking scheme | | |
|---|---|---:|
| | | *Marks* |
| (a) | Revenue | ½ |
| | Cost of sales | 2 |
| | Loan interest | ½ |
| | Equity | 1½ |
| | Non-current liabilities | ½ |
| | | ― |
| | | 5 |
| | | ― |
| (b) | 1 mark per ratio | 6 |
| | | ― |
| (c) | 1 mark per relevant comment up to | 9 |
| | | ― |
| **Total** | | **20** |
| | | ― |

## 400 FUNJECT CO

(a) **Restated financial information**

**Statement of profit or loss**

|  | 20X4 |
| --- | --- |
|  | $000 |
| Revenue (54,200 – 2,100 (note (i)) | 52,100 |
| Cost of sales (21,500 – 1,200 (note (i)) | (20,300) |
| Gross profit | 31,800 |
| Operating expenses (W1) | (12,212) |
| Profit before tax | 19,588 |

| **(W1) Restatement of operating expenses** | 20X4 |
| --- | --- |
|  | $000 |
| As per question | 11,700 |
| Less:  expenses relating to non-core division | (700) |
| Less: loss on disposal of non-core division | (1,500) |
| Less:  Gamilton management charge (54,200 × 1%) | (542) |
| Add: Funject management charge (31,800 × 10%) | 3,180 |
| Less: rent charged  by Gamilton | (46) |
| Add: commercial rent | 120 |
| Restated operating expenses | 12,212 |

(b) Profit has decreased from $21,000,000 to $19,588,000 and the resulting journal entry will be ($000s):

| Dr Retained earnings (21,000 – 19,588) | $1,412 |
| --- | --- |
| Cr Cash | $1,412 |

Ratio calculations

|  |  | 20X4 |
| --- | --- | --- |
| Gross profit margin | 31,800/52,100 × 100 | 61% |
| Operating profit margin | 19,588/52,100 × 100 | 38% |
| Receivables collection period (days) | (5,700/52,100) × 365 | 40 days |
| Current ratio | (12,900 – 1,412)/(11600) | 1:1 |
| Acid test (quick)ratio | (12,900 – 4,900 – 1,412)/(11,600) | 057:1 |
| Gearing (debt/equity) | 16,700/(9,000 – 1,412) | 220% |

### (c)    Commentary on performance

#### Profitability

The discontinued operation had a gross profit % (GP%) of 43% (900/2,100 × 100) and an operating profit % (OP%) of 10% (200/2,100 × 100).  Before adjusting for the disposal, Aspect Co had a GP% of 60%.  After an adjustment has been made to reflect the disposal, Aspect Co's GP% is 61%, which is higher than the industry average of 45%. Thus, it would appear that the disposal of the non-core division has had a positive impact on the GP% of Aspect Co.  Such a positive comparison of the GP% to the industry average would suggest that Aspect Co has negotiated a very good deal with its suppliers for the cost of goods in comparison to its competitors, as the GP% is 16% (61 – 45) higher than the industry average.

However, when considering the OP%, the financial statements have been adjusted to reflect: (i) the disposal of the discontinued operation, (ii) a new management charge which would be imposed by Funject Co, and (iii) commercial rent charges.  These adjustments result in an OP% of 38%.  So, although the OP% is still 10% (38 – 28) higher than the industry average, it would appear that some of the advantage of having such a good deal with its suppliers is lost when operating costs are incurred. The OP% does not outperform the industry average to the same extent that GP% did. Although the management charge will be eliminated as an intra-group transaction on consolidation, it will still have an impact in the individual financial statements of Aspect Co.  However, there is no indication of what this charge represents, and whether or not it reflects a market value for these costs.  The rent of $120,000 is deemed to be a fair market value which would indicate that the previous rent charge of $46,000 was artificially low.  If Funject Co acquires Aspect Co, it may wish to capitalise on the relationship which Aspect Co has with its supplier of goods but it might also need to investigate the composition of operating costs other than those described above to see if any of these can be avoided or reduced.

#### Liquidity

Aspect Co's receivables collection period appears to be comparable with the KPIs provided (40 days in comparison to 41 days). Terms of trade of 30 days are quite reasonable (though this usually depends on the type of business) and so there appear to be no causes for concern here.

Given that Aspect Co's receivables collection period is comparable to the industry average, the difference in the current ratio (11:1 in comparison to 16:1) can only be explained by either lower current assets other than receivables (for example, cash) or higher current liabilities. As Aspect Co's cash balance does not appear to be low ($23m), this suggests that its liabilities might be higher than average. Perhaps Aspect Co's favourable relationship with its suppliers also extends to longer than average credit terms.  As Aspect Co's acid (quick) ratio (057:1) is much less than the industry average (14:1), this would also suggest that Aspect Co is holding a higher than average level of inventory. This may raise a concern about Aspect Co's ability to sell its inventory.  There is also a current tax bill to consider.  Indeed, if Aspect Co were asked to settle its current liabilities from merely its receivables and bank, it would be unable to do so.  Perhaps Funject Co may wish   to   further   investigate the procedures associated with the purchase and holding of Aspect Co's inventory prior to a takeover.  As a parent company, Funject Co should be able to influence these procedures and have more control over the levels of inventory held.

**Gearing**

Aspect Co appears to be highly-geared but perhaps this is not a huge cause for concern because it appears to be a highly-geared industry (220% compared to 240%). It may be that the proceeds from the sale of the non-core division can be or perhaps were used to repay loans. As the gearing for the industry is higher than that of Aspect Co, it may be that Aspect Co could still increase borrowings in future.  If so, Aspect Co may need to increase working capital efficiency and reduce costs in order to generate enough cash to service higher borrowings.

**Conclusion**

Overall, Aspect's statement of financial position gives little cause for concern: the profit margins appear to be healthy, although further investigation of operating costs and working capital efficiency may be required.  More information also needs to be obtained about the nature of the business and perhaps the financial statements of several years (as opposed to one) would also be beneficial.

| ACCA Marking scheme | | | |
|---|---|---|---|
| | | | Marks |
| (a) | | Adjustment to revenue and cost of sales | 1 |
| | | Disposal of non-core division | 1 |
| | | Management charge (remove old, add new) | 2 |
| | | Rent expense (remove current, add commercial) | 1 |
| | | | — |
| | | | 5 |
| | | | — |
| (b) | | 1 mark per ratio | 5 |
| | | | — |
| (c) | | 1 mark per relevant comment: | |
| | | Profitability | 5 |
| | | Liquidity | 3 |
| | | Gearing | 1 |
| | | Conclusion | 1 |
| | | | — |
| | | | 10 |
| | | | — |
| **Total** | | | **20** |
| | | | — |

# Section 7

# SPECIMEN EXAM QUESTIONS

This exam is divided into three sections:

**Section A**

- 15 objective test (OT) questions, each worth 2 marks.
- 30 marks in total.

**Section B**

- Three OT cases, each containing a scenario which relates to five OT questions, each worth 2 marks.
- 30 marks in total.

**Section C**

- Two constructed response questions, each containing a scenario which relates to one or more requirement(s).
- Each constructed response question is worth 20 marks in total.
- 40 marks in total.

Please note that the live exam is worth a total of 110 marks, 10 marks of which are for questions that do not count towards your final result and are included for quality assurance purposes. This specimen exam is worth a total of 100 marks, reflecting the element of the live exam on which your result will be based.

All questions are compulsory.

Click **Next** to start your exam.

# F7 Financial Reporting - Specimen Exam

## Section A

This section of the exam contains **15 objective test (OT) questions**.

Each question is worth **2 marks** and is compulsory.

This exam section is worth **30 marks** in total.

Select **Next** to continue.

## Q1

**Match the tokens to the appropriate category based on whether or not the costs should be capitalised in the initial carrying amount of an item of plant.**

| Tokens |
| --- |
| The cost of transporting the plant to the factory |
| The cost of a three-week training course for staff to operate the plant |
| The cost of installing a new power supply required to operate the plant |
| The cost of a three-year plant maintenance agreement |

The initial carrying amount of plant should include:

The initial carrying amount of plant should NOT include:

## Q2

When a parent is evaluating the assets of a potential subsidiary, certain intangible assets can be recognised separately from goodwill, even though they have not been recognised in the subsidiary's own statement of financial position.

**Which of the following is an example of an intangible asset of the subsidiary that may be recognised separately from goodwill when preparing consolidated financial statements?**

- ⦾ A new research project which the subsidiary has correctly expensed to profit or loss but the directors of the parent have reliably assessed to have a substantial fair value

- ⦾ A global advertising campaign which was concluded in the previous financial year and from which benefits are expected to flow in the future

- ⦾ A contingent asset of the subsidiary from which the parent believes a flow of future economic benefits is possible

- ⦾ A customer list which the directors are unable to value reliably

### Q3

On 1 October 20X4, Flash Co acquired an item of plant under a five-year lease agreement. The present value of the total lease payments was $25m. The agreement had an implicit finance cost of 10% per annum and required an immediate deposit of $2m and annual rentals of $6m paid on the 30 September each year for five years.

**Calculate the current liability of the lease in Flash Co's statement of financial position as at 30 September 20X5.**

$ [                    ]

### Q4

Financial statements represent transactions in words and numbers. To be useful, financial information must represent faithfully these transactions in terms of how they are reported.

**Only one of the following four statements regarding faithful representation is true. Identify that statement, by clicking on the relevant box in the table below, and mark all of the others as false.**

| | | |
|---|---|---|
| Charging the rental payments for an item of plant to profit or loss where the rental agreement meets the criteria for a right of use asset is an example of faithful representation | TRUE | FALSE |
| Including a convertible loan note in equity on the basis that the holders are likely to choose the equity option on conversion is an example of faithful representation | TRUE | FALSE |
| Derecognising factored trade receivables sold without recourse is an example of faithful representation | TRUE | FALSE |
| Treating redeemable preference shares as part of equity in the statement of financial position is an example of faithful representation | TRUE | FALSE |

## Q5

On 1 October 20X4, Kalatra Co commenced drilling for oil from an undersea oilfield. Kalatra Co is required to dismantle the drilling equipment at the end of its five-year licence. This has an estimated cost of $30m on 30 September 20X9. Kalatra Co's cost of capital is 8% per annum and $1 in five years' time has a present value of $0.68.

**What is the provision which Kalatra Co would report in its statement of financial position as at 30 September 20X5 in respect of its oil operations?**

○ $32,400,000

○ $22,032,000

○ $20,400,000

○ $1,632,000

## Q6

When a single entity makes purchases or sales in a foreign currency, it will be necessary to translate the transactions into its functional currency before the transactions can be included in its financial records.

**In accordance with IAS 21 The Effect of Changes in Foreign Currency Exchange Rates, which TWO of the following foreign currency exchange rates may be used to translate the foreign currency purchases and sales?**

☐ The rate that existed on the day that the purchase or sale took place

☐ The rate that existed at the beginning of the accounting period

☐ An average rate for the year, provided there have been no significant fluctuations throughout the year

☐ The rate that existed at the end of the accounting period

## Q7

On 1 October 20X4, Hoy Co had $2.5m of equity share capital (shares of $0.50 each) in issue. No new shares were issued during the year ended 30 September 20X5, but on that date, there were outstanding share options which had a dilutive effect equivalent to issuing 1.2 million shares for no consideration.

Hoy Co's profit after tax for the year ended 30 September 20X5 was $1,550,000.

**The graph below represents a trend in both basic and diluted earnings per share (EPS) since 20X3. Complete the EPS trend analysis by calculating the diluted EPS for the year ended 30 September 20X5 for Hoy Co and click on the graph to identify its position.**

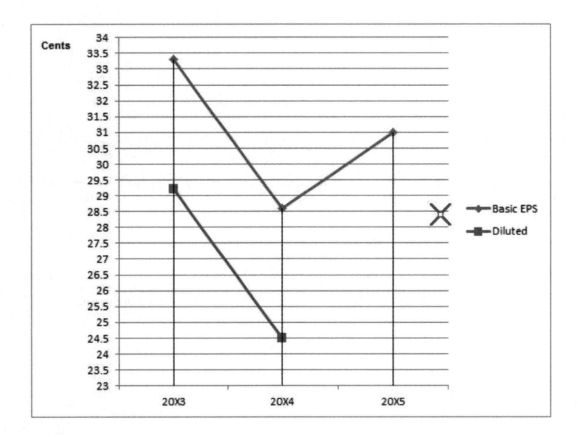

## Q8

Fork Co owns an 80% investment in Spoon Co which it purchased several years ago. The goodwill on acquisition was valued at $1,674,000 and there has been no impairment of that goodwill since the date of acquisition.

On 30 September 20X4, Fork Co disposed of its entire investment in Spoon Co details of which are as follows:

|  | $'000 |
| --- | --- |
| Sales proceeds of Fork Co's entire investment in Spoon Co | 5,580 |
| Cost of Fork Co's entire investment in Spoon Co | 3,720 |

Immediately before the disposal, the consolidated financial statements of Fork Co included the following amounts in respect of Spoon Co:

|  | $'000 |
| --- | --- |
| Carrying amount of the net assets (excluding goodwill) | 4,464 |
| Carrying amount of the non-controlling interests | 900 |

**Calculate the profit/loss on disposal (before tax) that will be recorded in Fork Co's CONSOLIDATED statement of profit or loss for the year ended 30 September 20X4.**

$ _____

## Q9

Consolidated financial statements are presented on the basis that the companies within the group are treated as if they are a single economic entity.

**Which TWO of the following are requirements of preparing consolidated financial statements?**

☐ All subsidiaries must adopt the accounting policies of the parent in their individual financial statements

☐ Subsidiaries with activities which are substantially different to the activities of other members of the group should not be consolidated

☐ All entity financial statements within a group should normally be prepared to the same accounting year end prior to consolidation

☐ Unrealised profits within the group must be eliminated from the consolidated financial statements

## Q10

A parent sells goods to its 80% owned subsidiary during the financial year, some of which remains in inventory at the year end.

**Match the tokens to the appropriate item in the statement of financial position (SOFP) to reflect the adjustment required in the consolidated statement of financial position to eliminate any unrealised profit in inventory.**

## Q11

Caddy Co acquired 240,000 of Ambel Co's 800,000 equity shares for $6 per share on 1 October 20X4. Ambel Co's profit after tax for the year ended 30 September 20X5 was $400,000 and it paid an equity dividend on 20 September 20X5 of $150,000.

**On the assumption that Ambel Co is an associate of Caddy Co, what would be the carrying amount of the investment in Ambel Co in the consolidated statement of financial position of Caddy Co as at 30 September 20X5?**

○ $1,515,000

○ $1,560,000

○ $1,395,000

○ $1,690,000

## Q12

Quartile Co is in the jewellery retail business which can be assumed to be highly seasonal. For the year ended 30 September 20X5, Quartile Co assessed its operating performance by comparing selected accounting ratios with those of its business sector average as provided by an agency.

Assume that the business sector used by the agency is a meaningful representation of Quartile Co's business.

**Which TWO of the following circumstances may invalidate the comparison of Quartile Co's ratios with those of the sector average?**

☐ In the current year, Quartile Co has experienced significant rising costs for its purchases

☐ The sector average figures are compiled from companies whose year ends are between 1 July 20X5 and 30 September 20X5

☐ Quartile Co does not revalue its properties, but is aware that other entities in this sector do

☐ During the year, Quartile Co discovered an error relating to the inventory count at 30 September 20X4. This error was correctly accounted for in the financial statements for the current year ended 30 September 20X5

## Q13

**Which of the following criticisms does NOT apply to historical cost financial statements during a period of rising prices?**

⚪ They contain mixed values; some items are at current values and some are at out of date values

⚪ They are difficult to verify because transactions could have happened many years ago

⚪ They understate assets and overstate profit

⚪ They overstate gearing in the statement of financial position

## Q14

The following information has been taken or calculated from Fowler Co's financial statements for the year ended 30 September 20X5:

| | |
|---|---|
| Cash cycle as at 30 September 20X5 | 70 days |
| Inventory turnover | 6 times |
| Year-end payables at 30 September 20X5 | $230,000 |
| Credit purchases for the year ended 30 September 20X5 | $2,000,000 |
| Cost of sales for the year ended 30 September 20X5 | $1,800,000 |

**Complete the following table, by dragging and dropping the tokens into the appropriate place, in order to reflect the correct calculation for Fowler Co's cash cycle at 30 September 20X5.**

| Tokens | Add/subtract | | Days |
|---|---|---|---|
| Subtract | | | |
| | | Inventory turnover days | C |
| Add | | | |
| 42 days | A | Receivables collection period | D |
| 51 days | | | |
| | B | Trade payables period | E |
| 61 days | | | |
| | | Fowler Co's cash cycle at 30 September 20X5 | 70 |

## Q15

On 1 October 20X4, Pyramid Co acquired 80% of Square Co's 9 million ($1) equity shares. At the date of acquisition, Square Co had an item of plant which had a fair value of $3m in excess of its carrying amount. At the date of acquisition it had a remaining life of five years.

Pyramid Co's policy is to value non-controlling interests at fair value at the date of acquisition. For this purpose, Square Co's shares had a value of $3.50 each at that date. In the year ended 30 September 20X5, Square Co reported a profit of $8m.

**At what amount should the non-controlling interests of Square Co be valued in the consolidated statement of financial position of Pyramid Co as at 30 September 20X5?**

| Select... ▼ |
|---|
| Select... |
| $26,680,000 |
| $7,900,000 |
| $7,780,000 |
| $12,220,000 |

**Section B**

This section of the exam contains **three OT cases**.

Each OT case contains a scenario which relates to **five OT questions**.

Each question is worth **2 marks** and is compulsory.

This exam section is worth **30 marks** in total.

Select **Next** to continue.

Telepath Co has a year end of 30 September and owns an item of plant that it uses to produce and package pharmaceuticals. The plant cost $750,000 on 1 October 20X0 and, at that date, had an estimated useful life of five years. A review of the plant on 1 April 20X3 concluded that the plant would last for a further three and a half years and that its fair value was $560,000. Telepath Co adopts the policy of revaluing its non-current assets to their fair value but does not make an annual transfer from the revaluation surplus to retained earnings to represent the additional depreciation charged due to the revaluation.

On 30 September 20X3, Telepath Co was informed by a major customer that it would no longer be placing orders with Telepath Co. As a result, Telepath Co revised its estimates that net cash inflows earned from the plant for the next three years will be:

| Year ended 30 September: | $'000 |
|---|---|
| 20X4 | 220 |
| 20X5 | 180 |
| 20X6 | 200 |

Telepath Co's cost of capital is 10% which results in the following discount factors:

| Value of $1 at 30 September: | $ |
|---|---|
| 20X4 | 0.91 |
| 20X5 | 0.83 |
| 20X6 | 0.75 |

Telepath Co also owns Rilda Co, a 100% subsidiary, which is treated as a cash generating unit. On 30 September 20X3, there was an impairment to Rilda Co's assets of $3,500,000. The carrying amount of the assets of Rilda Co immediately before the impairment were:

| | $'000 |
|---|---|
| Goodwill | 2,000 |
| Factory building | 4,000 |
| Plant | 3,500 |
| Receivables and cash (at recoverable amount) | 2,500 |
| | **12,000** |

## Q16

Use the tokens to complete the following definitions in accordance with IAS 36 Impairment of Assets.

An asset is impaired if its [        ] is [        ]

than its recoverable amount. In turn, the recoverable amount

of an asset is defined as the higher of its fair value less costs

of disposal and its [        ]

| TOKENS | | |
|---|---|---|
| carrying amount | historical cost | less |
| replacement cost | greater | value in use |

## Q17

**Prior to considering any impairment, what is the carrying amount of Telepath Co's plant and the balance on the revaluation surplus at 30 September 20X3?**

- ⦿ The carrying amount of the plant is $480,000 and the balance on the revaluation surplus is $185,000

- ⦿ The carrying amount of the plant is $300,000 and the balance on the revaluation surplus is $0

- ⦿ The carrying amount of the plant is $480,000 and the balance on the revaluation surplus is $0

- ⦿ The carrying amount of the plant is $300,000 and the balance on the revaluation surplus is $185,000

## Q18

**Calculate the value in use of Telepath Co's plant at 30 September 20X3.**

$ [        ]

**Q19**

**Which of the following are TRUE in accordance with IAS 36 Impairment of Assets?**

(1) A cash generating unit is the smallest identifiable group of assets for which individual cash flows can be identified and measured

(2) When considering the impairment of a cash generating unit, the calculation of the carrying amount and the recoverable amount does not need to be based on exactly the same group of net assets

(3) When it is not possible to calculate the recoverable amount of a single asset then that of its cash generating unit should be measured instead

⊙ 1 only

⊙ 2 and 3

⊙ 3 only

⊙ 1 and 3

**Q20**

**Calculate the carrying amount of Rilda Co's plant at 30 September 20X3 after the impairment loss has been correctly allocated to its assets.**

$ ☐

At a board meeting in June 20X3, Neutron Co's directors made a decision to close down one of its factories by 30 September 20X3 and market both the building and the plant for sale. The decision had been made public, was communicated to all affected parties and was fully implemented by 30 September 20X3.

The directors of Neutron Co have provided the following information relating to the closure:

(1) Of the factory's 250 employees, 50 will be retrained and deployed to other subsidiaries within the Neutron group during the year ended 30 September 20X4, at a cost of $125,000. The remainder accepted redundancy at an average cost of $5,000 each.

(2) The factory's plant had a carrying amount of $2.2m, but is only expected to sell for $500,000, incurring $50,000 of selling costs. The factory itself is expected to sell for a profit of $1.2m.

(3) The company also rented a number of machines in the factory under operating leases which have an average of three years to run after 30 September 20X3. The present value of these future lease payments at 30 September 20X3 was $1m, however, the lessor has stated that they will accept $850,000 if paid on 30 October 20X3 as full settlement.

(4) Penalty payments, due to the non-completion of supply contracts, are estimated to be $200,000, 50% of which is expected to be recovered from Neutron Co's insurers.

## Q21

**Which TWO of the following must exist for an operation to be classified as a discontinued operation in accordance with IFRS 5 Non-current Assets Held for Sale and Discontinued Operations?**

☐ It represents a separate major line of business or geographical area

☐ It is a subsidiary

☐ It has been sold or is classified as held for sale

☐ It is considered not to be capable of making a future profit following a period of losses

## Q22

IFRS 5 Non-current Assets Held for Sale and Discontinued Operations prescribes the recognition criteria for non-current assets held for sale. For an asset or a disposal group to be classified as held for sale, the sale must be highly probable.

**Which TWO of the following must apply for the sale to be considered highly probable?**

☐ A buyer must have been located

☐ The asset must be marketed at a reasonable price

☐ Management must be committed to a plan to sell the asset

☐ The sale must be expected to take place within the next six months

## Q23

Calculate the employee cost associated with the closure and sale of Neutron Co's factory that should be charged to profit or loss for the year ended 30 September 20X3.

$ [                    ]

## Q24

What is the profit or loss on discontinued operations relating to property, plant and equipment for the year ended 30 September 20X3?

⊚ $1.75m loss

⊚ $1.75m profit

⊚ $550,000 loss

⊚ $550,000 profit

## Q25

In respect of the operating leases and penalty payments, what provision is required in the statement of financial position of Neutron Co as at 30 September 20X3?

⊚ $1,100,000

⊚ $1,050,000

⊚ $1,200,000

⊚ $950,000

Speculate Co is preparing its financial statements for the year ended 30 September 20X3. The following issues are relevant:

(1) Financial assets

Shareholding A - a long-term investment in 10,000 of the equity shares of another company. These shares were acquired on 1 October 20X2 at a cost of $3.50 each. Transaction costs of 1% of the purchase price were incurred. On 30 September 20X3 the fair value of these shares is $4.50 each.

Shareholding B – a short-term speculative investment in 2,000 of the equity shares of another company. These shares were acquired on 1 December 20X2 at a cost of $2.50 each. Transaction costs of 1% of the purchase price were incurred. On 30 September 20X3 the fair value of these shares is $3.00 each.

Where possible, Speculate Co makes an irrevocable election for the fair value movements on financial assets to be reported in other comprehensive income.

(2) Taxation

The existing debit balance on the current tax account of $2.4m represents the under/over provision of the tax liability for the year ended 30 September 20X2. A provision of $28m is required for income tax for the year ended 30 September 20X3.

The existing credit balance on the deferred tax account is $2.5m and the provision required at 30 September 20X3 is $4.4m.

(3) Revenue

On 1 October 20X2, Speculate Co sold one of its products for $10m. As part of the sale agreement, Speculate Co is committed to the ongoing servicing of its product until 30 September 20X5 (ie three years after the sale). The sale value of this service has been included in the selling price of $10m. The estimated cost to Speculate Co of the servicing is $600,000 per annum and Speculate Co's gross profit margin on this type of servicing is 25%. Ignore discounting.

## Q26

**Match the financial instrument to its appropriate classification in accordance with IFRS 9 Financial Instruments.**

| Financial instrument | Classification |
|---|---|
| A contract to exchange financial instruments with another entity under conditions that are potentially unfavourable | A financial asset |
| Any contract that evidences a residual interest in the assets of an entity after deducting all of its liabilities | A financial asset |
| Cash | An equity instrument |
| An equity instrument of another entity | A financial liability |

## Q27

In respect of the financial assets of Speculate Co, what amount will be included in other comprehensive income for the year ended 30 September 20X3?

- ◉ $9,650
- ◉ $10,600
- ◉ $10,000
- ◉ $0

## Q28

Calculate the total amount that will be charged to the statement of profit or loss for the year ended 30 September 20X3 in respect of taxation.

$ [                    ]

## Q29

What is the amount of deferred income which Speculate Co should recognise in its statement of financial position as at 30 September 20X3 relating to the contract for supply and servicing of products?

- ◉ $1.2 million
- ◉ $0.6 million
- ◉ $1.5 million
- ◉ $1.6 million

## Q30

Only two of the following statements in respect of Speculate Co's deferred income at 30 September 20X3 are true. Identify these statements, by clicking on the relevant box in the table below and mark all the others as false.

| | | |
|---|---|---|
| The deferred income will be split evenly between the current and non-current liabilities in Speculate Co's statement of financial position as at 30 September 20X3 | TRUE | FALSE |
| The costs associated with the deferred income of Speculate Co should be recognised in the statement of profit or loss at the same time as the revenue is recognised | TRUE | FALSE |
| The deferred income can only be recognised as revenue by Speculate Co when there is a signed written contract of service with its customer | TRUE | FALSE |
| When recognising the revenue associated with the service contract of Speculate Co, the stage of its completion is irrelevant | TRUE | FALSE |

**Section C**

This section of the exam contains **two constructed response questions**.

Each question contains a scenario which relates to one or more requirement(s) which may be split over multiple question screens.

Each question is worth **20 marks** and is compulsory.

This exam section is worth **40 marks** in total.

**Important:** In your live exam please show all notes/workings that you want the marker to see within the spreadsheet or word processing answer areas. Remember, any notes/workings made on the Scratch Pad or on your workings paper will not be marked.

Select **Next** to continue.

## Q31

**This scenario relates to three requirements.**

After preparing a draft statement of profit or loss for the year ended 30 September 20X5 and adding the current year's draft profit (before any adjustments required by notes (1) to (3) below) to retained earnings, the summarised trial balance of Kandy Co as at 30 September 20X5 is:

|  | $'000 | $'000 |
|---|---:|---:|
| Equity shares of $1 each |  | 20,000 |
| Retained earnings as at 30 September 20X5 |  | 15,500 |
| Proceeds of 6% loan note (note (1)) |  | 30,000 |
| Investment properties at fair value (note (2)) | 20,000 |  |
| Land ($5 million) and buildings – at cost (note (2)) | 35,000 |  |
| Plant and equipment – at cost (note (2)) | 58,500 |  |
| Accumulated depreciation at 1 October 20X4: |  |  |
| buildings |  | 20,000 |
| plant and equipment |  | 34,500 |
| Current assets | 68,700 |  |
| Current liabilities |  | 43,400 |
| Deferred tax (notes (2) and (3)) |  | 2,500 |
| Interest paid (note (1)) | 1,800 |  |
| Current tax (note (3)) |  | 1,100 |
| Suspense account (note 2) |  | 17,000 |
|  | **184,000** | **184,000** |

The following notes are relevant:

(1) The loan note was issued on 1 October 20X4 and incurred issue costs of $1 million which were charged to profit or loss. Interest of $1·8 million ($30 million at 6%) was paid on 30 September 20X5. The loan is redeemable on 30 September 20X9 at a substantial premium which gives an effective interest rate of 9% per annum. No other repayments are due until 30 September 20X9.

(2) Non-current assets:
On 1 October 20X4, Kandy Co owned two investment properties. The first property had a carrying amount of $15 million and was sold on 1 December 20X4 for $17 million. The disposal proceeds have been credited to a suspense account in the trial balance above. On 31 December 20X4, the second property became owner occupied and so was transferred to land and buildings at its fair value of $6 million. Its remaining useful life on 31 December 20X4 was considered to be 20 years. Ignore any deferred tax implications of this fair value.

The price of property has increased significantly in recent years and so the directors decided to revalue the land and buildings. The directors accepted the report of an independent surveyor who, on 1 October 20X4, valued the land at $8 million and the buildings at $39 million on that date. This revaluation specifically excludes the transferred investment property described above. The remaining life of these buildings at 1 October 20X4 was 15 years. Kandy Co does not make an annual transfer to retained profits to reflect the realisation of the revaluation gain; however, the revaluation will give rise to a deferred tax liability. The income tax rate applicable to Kandy Co is 20%.

Plant and equipment is depreciated at 12.5% per annum using the reducing balance method. No depreciation has yet been charged on any non-current asset for the year ended 30 September 20X5.

Plant and equipment is depreciated at 12.5% per annum using the reducing balance method. No depreciation has yet been charged on any non-current asset for the year ended 30 September 20X5.

(3) A provision of $2·4 million is required for income tax on the profit for the year to 30 September 20X5. The balance on current tax in the trial balance is the under/over provision of tax for the previous year. In addition to the temporary differences relating to the information in note (2), Kandy Co has further taxable temporary differences of $10 million as at 30 September 20X5.

Required:

(a) Prepare a schedule of adjustments required to the retained earnings of Kandy Co as at 30 September 20X5 as a result of the information in notes (1) to (3).

(8 marks)

(b) Prepare the statement of financial position of Kandy Co as at 30 September 20X5.

Note: The notes to the statement of financial position are not required

(9 marks)

(c) Prepare the extracts from Kandy Co's statement of cash flows for operating and investing activities for the year ended 30 September 20X5 which relate to property, plant and equipment.

(3 marks)

(20 marks)

## Q32

**This scenario relates to three requirements.**

The summarised consolidated financial statements for the year ended 30 September 20X5 (and the comparative figures) for the Tangier group are shown below.

Consolidated statements of profit or loss for the year ended 30 September:

|  | 20X5 | 20X4 |
|---|---|---|
|  | $m | $m |
| Revenue | 2,700 | 1,820 |
| Cost of sales | (1,890) | (1,092) |
| **Gross profit** | **810** | **728** |
| Administrative expense | (345) | (200) |
| Distribution costs | (230) | (130) |
| Finance costs | (40) | (5) |
| **Profit before taxation** | **195** | **393** |
| Income tax expense | (60) | (113) |
| **Profit for the year** | **135** | **280** |

Consolidated statements of financial position as at 30 September:

|  | 20X5 | 20X5 | 20X4 | 20X4 |
|---|---|---|---|---|
|  | $m | $m | $m | $m |
| Non-current assets |  |  |  |  |
| Property, plant and equipment |  | 680 |  | 310 |
| Intangible asset: manufacturing licence |  | 300 |  | 100 |
| goodwill |  | 230 |  | 200 |
|  |  | **1,210** |  | **610** |
| Current assets |  |  |  |  |
| Inventory | 200 |  | 110 |  |
| Trade receivables | 195 |  | 75 |  |
| Bank | 0 | **395** | 120 | **305** |
| Total assets |  | **1,605** |  | **915** |

| Equity and liabilities | | | | |
|---|---|---|---|---|
| Equity shares of $1 each | | 330 | | 250 |
| Other components of equity | | 100 | | 0 |
| Retained earnings | | 375 | | 295 |
| | | **805** | | **545** |
| Non-current liabilities | | | | |
| 5% secured loan notes | 100 | | 100 | |
| 10% secured loan notes | 300 | **400** | 0 | **100** |
| Current liabilities | | | | |
| Bank overdraft | 110 | | 0 | |
| Trade payables | 210 | | 160 | |
| Current tax payable | 80 | **400** | 110 | **270** |
| Total equity and liabilities | | **1,605** | | **915** |

At 1 October 20X4, the Tangier group consisted of the parent, Tangier Co, and two wholly owned subsidiaries which had been owned for many years. On 1 January 20X5, Tangier Co purchased a third 100% owned investment in a subsidiary called Raremetal Co. The consideration paid for Raremetal Co was a combination of cash and shares. The cash payment was partly funded by the issue of 10% loan notes. On 1 January 20X5, Tangier Co also won a tender for a new contract to supply aircraft engines which Tangier Co manufactures under a recently acquired long-term licence. Raremetal Co was purchased with a view to securing the supply of specialised materials used in the manufacture of these engines. The bidding process had been very competitive and Tangier Co had to increase its manufacturing capacity to fulfil the contract.

**Required:**

**(a) Comment on how the new contract and the purchase of Raremetal Co may have affected the comparability of the consolidated financial statements of Tangier Co for the years ended 30 September 20X4 and 20X5.**

(5 marks)

**(b) Calculate appropriate ratios and comment on Tangier Co's profitability and gearing. Your analysis should identify where the new contract and the purchase of Raremetal Co have limited the usefulness of the ratios and your analysis.**

Note: Your ratios should be based on the consolidated financial statements provided and you should not attempt to adjust for the effects of the new contract or the consolidation. Working capital and liquidity ratios are not required.

(12 marks)

**(c) Explain what further information you might require to make your analysis more meaningful.**

(3 marks)

**(20 marks)**

# Section 8

# ANSWERS TO SPECIMEN EXAM QUESTIONS

# SECTION A

### Q1

The correct answer is that the initial carrying amount of plant should include:
(1) the cost of transporting the plant to the factory; and
(2) the cost of installing a new power supply required to operate the plant.

### Q2

The correct answer is the new research project.

### Q3

Current liability = 19,300,000-15,230,000 = $4,070,000

|  | $'000s |
|---|---|
| FV 1 Oct 20X4 | 25,000 |
| Deposit | (2,000) |
|  | 23,000 |
| Interest 10% | 2,300 |
| Payment 30 Sep 20X5 | (6,000) |
|  | 19,300 |
| Interest 10% | 1,930 |
| Payment 30 Sep 20X6 | (6,000) |
| Liability at 30 Sep 20X6 | 15,230 |

### Q4

The correct answer is:
Derecognising factored trade receivables sold without recourse to the seller is an example of faithful representation.

### Q5

Dismantling provision at 1 October is $20.4 million (30,000 x 0.68) discounted. This will increase by an 8% finance cost by 30 September 20X5 = $22,032,000

**Q6**

The correct answer is the rate that existed on the day that the purchase or sale took place or an average rate for the year may be used.

**Q7**

(1,550/(2,500 x 2 + 1,200)) = $0.25

**Q8**

|  | | $'000 |
|---|---|---|
| Sales proceeds | | 5,580 |
| Net assets at disposal | 4,464 | |
| Goodwill at disposal | 1,674 | |
| Less: carrying amount of NCI | (900) | (5,238) |
| | | 342 |

**Q9**

The correct answer is that all entity financial statements within a group should normally be prepared to the same accounting year end prior to consolidation and unrealised profits within the group must be eliminated.

**Q10**

The correct answer is:
DEBIT    Group retained earnings
CREDIT  Inventory

**Q11**

|  | $'000 |
|---|---|
| Cost (240,000 x $6) | 1,440 |
| Share of associate's profit (400 x 240/800) | 120 |
| Less dividend received (150 x 240/800) | (45) |
| | 1,515 |

## Q12

The correct answers are:

- The sector average figures are compiled from companies whose year ends are between 1 July 20X5 and 30 September 20X5
- Quartile Co does not revalue its properties, but is aware that other entities in this sector do

## Q13

The correct answer is:

They are difficult to verify because transactions could have happened many years ago - this is not a vald criticism of historic cost financial statements

## Q14

Inventory turnover is 61 days (365/6)

Trade payables period is 42 days (230,000 x 365/2)

Therefore, receivables collection period is 51 days (70-61 +42)

## Q15

|                                                        | $'000s |
|--------------------------------------------------------|--------|
| FV NCI at 1/10/14 (9000 x 20% x $3.50)                 | 6,300  |
| Post acq'n profit (8000-(3000/5)) = 7,400@20%          | 1,480  |
|                                                        | 7,780  |

## Q16

The correct answer is:

An asset is impaired if its carrying amount is greater than its recoverable amount. In turn, the recoverable amount of an asset is defined as the higher of its fair value less costs of disposal and its value in use.

## Q17

Annual depreciation prior to the revaluation is $150,000 (750/5). At the date of revaluation (1 April 20X3) the carrying amount is $375,000 (750-(150x2.5yrs)). Revalued to $560,000 with a remaining life of 3.5 years results in a depreciation charge of $160,000 per annum which means $80,000 for 6 mths. The carrying amount at 30 September 20X3 is therefore $480,000 (560-80). An alternative calculation is $560,000 - ($560,000/3.5 x 6/12) = $480,000 Revaluation surplus : $560,000-$375,000=$185,000

## Q18

|  | cflow | 10%discount | present value |
|---|---|---|---|
|  | $'000 | $'000 | $'000 |
| 30-Sep-X4 | 220 | 0.91 | 200.2 |
| 30-Sep-X5 | 180 | 0.83 | 149.4 |
| 30-Sep-X6 | 200 | 0.75 | 150 |
|  |  |  | 499.6 |

## Q19

The correct answers are:

- A cash generating unit is the smallest identifiable group of assets for which individual cash flows can be identified and measured; and
- When it is not possible to calculate the recoverable amount of a single asset then that of its cash generating unit should be measured instead

## Q20

|  | Carrying amt before | Impairment loss | Carrying amt after |
|---|---|---|---|
| Goodwill | 2,000 | 2,000 | Nil |
| Property | 4,000 | 800 | 3,200 |
| Plant | 3,500 | 700 | 2,800 |
| Cash and receivables | 2,500 | nil | 2,500 |
|  | 12,000 | 3,500 | 8,500 |

## Q21

The correct answers are:

- It represents a separate major line of business or geographical area
- It has been sold or is classified as held for sale

## Q22

The correct answers are:

- The asset must be marketed at a reasonable price
- Management must be committed to a plan to sell the asset

## Q23

The correct answer is:
200 employees at $5,000 = $1,000,000 redundancy costs. The retraining costs are a future cost.

## Q24

The impairment loss on plant is $1,750,000 (2,200,000 - (500,000 - 50,000))

## Q25

Onerous contract $850,000 + penalty payments $200,000 = $1,050,000. The possible insurance receipt should be ignored as there is no certainty that it would be received and it would not be netted off against the provision anyway.

## Q26

The correct answer is:

- Cash = a financial asset
- An equity instrument of another entity = a finacial asset
- A contract to exchange financial instruments with another entity under conditions that are potentially unfavourable = a financial liability
- Any contract that evidences a residual interest in the assets of an entity after deducting all of its liabilities = an equity instrument

## Q27

The correct answer is:
Shareholding A is not held for trading as an election made - FVTOCI
Shareholding B is held for trading and so FVTPL (transaction costs are not included in carrying amount)
Cost of shareholding A is 10,000 x $3.50 x 1.01 = $35,350
FV at 30 September 20X3 10,000 x $4.50 = $45,000
Gain - 45,000 - 35,350 = $9,650

## Q28

|  | $'000s |
|---|---|
| DT provision required at 30 Sep 20X3 4,400 |  |
| DT provision at 1 October 20X2 | (2,500) |
|  | 1,900 |
| Underprovision for the y/e 30 Sep 20X2 | 2,400 |
| Income tax for the year ended 30 Sep 20X3 | 28,000 |
| Charge for the year ended 30 Sep 20X3 | 32,300 |

## Q29

At 30 September 20X3 there are two more years of servicing work, thus $1.6 million ((600,000 x 2) x 100/75) must be treated as deferred income

## Q30

The correct answers are:
- the deferred income will be split evenly between the current and non-current liabilities in Speculate Co's statement of financial position as at 30 September 20X3; and
- The costs associated with the deferred income of Speculate Co should be recognised in the statement of profit or loss at the same time as the revenue is recognised

## Q31

Note: this spreadsheet is preformatted so that all numbers use a comma separator for $'000s and all negatives are expressed in

**Kandy Co – Schedule of adjustments to retained earnings as at 30 September 20X5**

|  | $'000 |
|---|---|
| Retained earnings per trial balance | 15,500 |
| Adjustments re: |  |
| Issue costs of loan note (w(i)) | 1,000 |
| Loan finance costs [(30,000-1,000)@9%] (w(i)) | (2,610) |
| Gain on disposal of investment property (17,000-15,000) | 2,000 |
| Gain on revaluation of investment property prior to transfer (6,000-5,000) | 1,000 |
| Depreciation of buildings (w (ii)) | (2,825) |
| Depreciation of plant and equipment(w(ii)) | (3,000) |
| Income tax expense (w(iii)) | (800) |
| Adjusted retained earnings | 10,265 |

**Kandy Co – Statement of Financial Position as at 30 September 20X5**

|  | $'000 | $'000 |
|---|---|---|
| **ASSETS** |  |  |
| **Non-current assets** |  |  |
| Property, Plant and Equipment(50,175 + 21,000) (w(ii)) |  | 71,175 |
|  |  |  |
| **Current assets** |  |  |
| Per trial balance |  | 68,700 |
|  |  |  |
| **Total Assets** |  | 139,875 |

**EQUITY AND LIABILITIES**
**Equity**

| | | |
|---|---|---|
| Equity Shares of $1 each | | 20,000 |
| Revaluation Surplus (32,000 - 6,400) (w (ii) and (iii)) | | 25,600 |
| Retained Earnings Part (a) | | 10,265 |
| | | 55,865 |

**Non-current liabilities**

| | | |
|---|---|---|
| 6% loan note (w(i)) | 29,810 | |
| Deferred Tax (w(iii)) | 8,400 | 38,210 |

**Current liabilities**

| | | |
|---|---|---|
| Per trial balance | 43,400 | |
| Current Tax | 2,400 | 45,800 |
| **Total Equity and Liabilities** | | **139,875** |

**Kandy Co – Extracts from the Cash Flow Statement for the year ended 30 September 20X5**

| | $'000 |
|---|---|
| **Cash flows from operating activities:** | |
| Add back depreciation | 5,825 |
| Deduct gain on revaluation of investment property | (1,000) |
| Deduct gain on disposal of investment property | (2,000) |
| **Cash flows from investing activities:** | |
| Investment property disposal proceeds | 17,000 |

**Workings (monetary figures in brackets in $'000)**
**w(i) Loan note**

The issue costs should be deducted from the proceeds of the loan note and not charged as an expense. The finance cost of the loan note, at the effective rate of 9% applied to the carrying amount of the loan note of $29 million (30,000 - 1,000) is $2,610,000. The interest actually paid is $1.8 million. The difference between these amounts of $810,000 (2,610 - 1,800) is added to the carrying amount of the loan note to give $29,810,000 (29,000 + 810) for inclusion as a non-current liability in the statement of financial position.

**w(II) Non-current assets**
**Land and Buildings**
The gain on revaluation and carrying amount of the land and buildings will be:

|  | $'000 |
|---|---|
| Carrying amount at 1 October 20X4 (35,000 - 20,000) | 15,000 |
| Revaluation at that date (8,000 + 39,000) | 47,000 |
| Gain on revaluation | 32,000 |

| Buildings depreciation for the year ended 30 September 20X5: | |
|---|---|
| L&B existing at 1 October 20X4 (39,000/15 years) | 2,600 |
| Transferred investment property (6,000/20 x 9/12) | 225 |
|  | 2,825 |

| Carrying amount at 30 September 20X5 (47,000 + 6,000 - 2,825) | 50,175 |
|---|---|

**Plant and Equipment**

| Carrying amount at 1 October 20X4 (58,500 - 34,500) | 24,000 |
|---|---|
| Depreciation for the year ended 30 September 20X5 (12.5% reducing balance | (3,000) |
|  | 21,000 |

**w(III) Taxation**
**Income Tax Expense**

| Provision for year ended 30 September 20X5 | 2,400 |
|---|---|
| Over-provision in previous year | (1,100) |
| Deferred tax (see below) | (500) |
|  | 800 |

**Deferred Tax**

| Provision required at 30 September 20X5 ((10,000 + 32,000) x 20%) | 8,400 |
|---|---|
| Provision at 1 October 20X4 | (2,500) |
| Movement in provision | 5,900 |
| Charge to revaluation of land and buildings (32,000 x 20%) - SOCIE | (6,400) |
| Balance – credit to profit or loss | (500) |

| Marking scheme | | |
|---|---|---|
| **Part (a)** Schedule of adjustments to retained earnings at 30 Sep 20X5 | | |
|  | **Maximum Ma** | **Awarded** |
| retained earnings per trial balance | ½ | |
| issue costs | 1 | |
| loan finance costs | 1 | |
| gains on investment properties | 1 | |
| depreciation charges | 3 | |
| income tax expense | 1½ | |
|  | **8** | |
| **Part (b)** Statement of financial position as at 30 September 20X5 | | |
| property, plant and equipment | 2 | |
| current assets | ½ | |
| equity shares | ½ | |
| revaluation surplus | 2 | |
| deferred tax | 1 | |
| 6% loan note | 1½ | |
| current liabilities (per trial balance) | ½ | |
| current tax payable | 1 | |
|  | **9** | |
| **Part (c)** Extracts from the statement of cash flows for the year ended 30 September 20X5 | | |
| Cash flows from operating activities: | | |
| add back depreciation | 1 | |
| less gain on revaluation of investment property | ½ | |
| less gain on disposal of investment prop | ½ | |
| Cash flows from investing activities: | | |
| Investment property disposal proceeds | 1 | |
|  | **3** | |

**Q32**

(a) Note: References to '20X5' are in respect of the year ended 30 September 20X5 and '20X4' refers to the year ended 30 September 20X4.

The key matter to note is that the ratios for 20X4 and 20X5 will not be directly comparable because two significant events, the acquisition of Raremetal Co and securing the new contract, have occurred between these dates. This means that the underlying financial statements are not comparable. For example, the 20X4 statement of profit or loss (SOPL) will not include the results of Raremetal Co or the effect of the new contract. However, the 20X5 SOPL will contain nine months of the results of Raremetal Co (although intra-group transactions will have been eliminated) and nine months of the effects of the new contract (which may have resulted in either a net profit or loss). Likewise, the 20X4 statement of financial position does not contain any of Raremetal Co's assets and liabilities, whereas that of 20X5 contains all of the net assets of Raremetal Co and the cost of the licence. This does not mean that comparisons between the two years are not worthwhile, just that they need to be treated with caution. For some ratios, it may be necessary to exclude all of the subsidiaries from the analysis and use the single entity financial statements of Tangier Co as a basis for comparison with the performance of previous years. Similarly, it may still be possible to compare some of the ratios of the Tangier group with those of other groups in the same sector although not all groups will have experienced similar acquisitions.

Assuming there has been no impairment of goodwill, the investment in Raremetal Co has resulted in additional goodwill of $30 million which means that the investment has cost more than the carrying amount of Raremetal Co's net assets. Although there is no indication of the precise cost, it is known to have been achieved by a combination of a share exchange (hence the $180 million new issue of shares) and a cash element (funded from the proceeds of the loan issue and the decrease in the bank balance). Any intra-group sales have been eliminated on consolidation and it is not possible to determine in which individual company any profit on these intra-group sales will be reported; it is therefore difficult to measure any benefits of the investment. Indeed, the benefit of the investment might not be a financial one but merely to secure the supply of raw materials. It would be useful to establish the cost of the investment and the profit (if any) contributed by Raremetal Co so that an assessment of the benefit of the investment might be made.

(b)

| Relevant ratios: | 20X5 | 20X4 |
|---|---|---|
| Gross profit margin % (810/2,700 x 100) | 30·0% | 40·0% |
| Operating profit margin (235/2,700 x 100) | 8·7% | 21·9% |
| ROCE (235/(805 + 400)) | 19·5% | 61·7% |
| Net asset turnover 2,700/(805 + 400) | 2·24 times | 2·82 times |
| Debt/equity (400/805) | 49·7% | 18·3% |
| Interest cover (235/40) | 5·9 times | 79·6 times |

All of the issues identified in (a) make a comparison of ratios difficult and, if more information was available, then some adjustments may be required. For example, if it is established that the investment is not generating any benefits, then it might be argued that the inclusion of the goodwill in the ROCE and asset turnover is

unjustified (it may be impaired and be written off). Goodwill has not been excluded from any of the following ratios.

The increase in revenues of 48·4% (880/1,820 x 100) in 20X5 will be partly due to the consolidation of Raremetal Co and the revenues associated with the new contract. Yet, despite these increased revenues, the company has suffered a dramatic fall in its profitability. This has been caused by a combination of a falling gross profit margin (from 40% in 20X4 to only 30% in 20X5) and markedly higher operating overheads (operating profit margin has fallen from 21.9% in 20X4 to 8.7% in 20X5). Again it is important to note that some of these costs will be attributable to the consolidation of Raremetal Co and some to the new contract. It could be speculated that the 73% increase in administrative expenses may be due to one-off costs associated with the tendering process (consultancy fees, etc) and the acquisition of Raremetal Co and the 77% increase in higher distribution costs could be due to additional freight/packing/insurance cost of the engines, delivery distances may also be longer (even to foreign countries) (although some of this increase may also be due to consolidation).

This is all reflected in the ROCE falling from an impressive 61·7% in 20X4 to only 19·5% in 20X5 (though even this figure is respectable). The fall in the ROCE is attributable to a dramatic fall in profit margin at operating level (from 21·9% in 20X4 to only 8·7% in 20X5) which has been compounded by a reduction in the asset turnover, with only $2·24 being generated from every $1 invested in net assets in 20X5 (from $2·82 in 20X4).

The information in the question points strongly to the possibility (even probability) that the new contract may be responsible for much of the deterioration in Tangier Co's operating performance. For example, it is likely that the new contract may account for some of the increased revenue; however, the bidding process was 'very competitive' which may imply that Tangier Co had to cut its prices (and therefore its profit margin) in order to win the contract.

The costs of fulfilling the contract have also been heavy: investment in property, plant and equipment has increased by $370 million (at carrying amount), representing an increase of 61% (no doubt some of this increase will be due to the acquisition of Raremetal Co). The increase in licence costs to manufacture the new engines has cost $200 million plus any amortisation (which is not identified in the question) and there is also the additional goodwill of $30 million.

An eight-fold increase in finance cost caused by the increased borrowing at double the interest rate of the borrowing in 20X4 and (presumably) some overdraft interest has led to the dramatic fall in the company's interest cover (from 79·6 in 20X4 to only 5·9 in 20X5). The finance cost of the new $300 million 10% loan notes to partly fund the investment in Raremetal Co and any other non-current assets has also increased debt/equity (one form of gearing measure) from 18·3% in 20X4 to 49·7% in 20X5 despite also issuing $180 million in new equity shares. At this level, particularly in view of its large increase from 20X4, it may give debt holders (and others) cause for concern as there is increased risk for all Tangier Co's lenders. If it could be demonstrated that the overdraft could not be cleared for some time, this would be an argument for including it in the calculation of debt/equity, making the 20X5 gearing

level even worse. It is also apparent from the movement in the retained earnings that Tangier Co paid a dividend during 20X5 of $55 million (295,000 + 135,000 − 375,000) which may be a questionable policy when the company is raising additional finance through borrowings and leaves Tangier Co with a substantial overdraft.

Overall, the acquisition of Raremetal Co to secure supplies appears to have been an expensive strategy, perhaps a less expensive one might have been to enter into a long-term supply contract with Raremetal Co.

(c) Further information which would be useful to obtain would therefore include:

(i) The cost of the investment in Raremetal Co, the carrying amount of the assets acquired and whether Tangier Co has carried out a goodwill impairment test as required under IFRS.

(ii) The benefits generated from the investment; for example, Raremetals Co's individual financial statements and details of sales to external customers (not all of these will be measurable in financial terms).

(iii) The above two pieces of information would demonstrate the investment in Raremetal Co had been worthwhile.

(iv) The amount of intra-group sales made during the year and those expected to be made in the short to medium term.

(v) The pricing strategy agreed with Raremetal Co so that the effects on the profits reported in the individual financial statements of Raremetal Co and Tangier Co can be more readily determined.

(vi) More information is needed to establish if the new contract has been detrimental to Tangier Co's performance. The contract was won sometime between 1 October 20X4 and 1 January 20X5 and there is no information of when production/sales started, but clearly there has not been a full year's revenue from the contract. Also there is no information on the length or total value of the contract.

| Marking Scheme | Maximum Marks | Awarded |
|---|---|---|
| **Part (a) comparability** | | |
| A like for like comparison taking account of the consolidation and the contract | 5 | |
| **Part (b) Analysis of results** | | |
| up to 5 marks for ratio calculations | 5 | |
| Profitability | 4½ | |
| Gearing and interest cover | 2½ | |
| | 12 | |
| **Part (c) additional information** | | |
| Any three of the six suggestions provided | 3 | |

# Section 9

# REFERENCES

The Board (2016) *Conceptual Framework for Financial Reporting*. London: IFRS Foundation.

The Board (2016) *IAS 1 Presentation of Financial Statements*. London: IFRS Foundation.

The Board (2016) *IAS 2 Inventories*. London: IFRS Foundation.

The Board (2016) *IAS 7 Statement of Cash Flows*. London: IFRS Foundation.

The Board (2016) *IAS 8 Accounting Policies, Changes in Accounting Estimates and Errors*. London: IFRS Foundation.

The Board (2016) *IAS 10 Events after the Reporting Period*. London: IFRS Foundation.

The Board (2016) *IAS 12 Income Taxes*. London: IFRS Foundation.

The Board (2016) *IAS 16 Property, Plant and Equipment*. London: IFRS Foundation.

The Board (2016) *IAS 20 Accounting for Government Grants and Disclosure of Government Assistance*. London: IFRS Foundation.

The Board (2016) *IAS 21 The Effects of Changes in Foreign Exchange Rates*. London: IFRS Foundation.

The Board (2016) *IAS 23 Borrowing Costs*. London: IFRS Foundation.

The Board (2016) *IAS 27 Separate Financial Statements*. London: IFRS Foundation.

The Board (2016) *IAS 28 Investments in Associates and Joint Ventures*. London: IFRS Foundation.

The Board (2016) *IAS 32 Financial Instruments: Presentation*. London: IFRS Foundation.

The Board (2016) *IAS 33 Earnings per Share*. London: IFRS Foundation.

The Board (2016) *IAS 36 Impairment of Assets*. London: IFRS Foundation.

The Board (2016) *IAS 37 Provisions, Contingent Liabilities and Contingent Assets*. London: IFRS Foundation.

The Board (2016) *IAS 38 Intangible Assets*. London: IFRS Foundation.

The Board (2016) *IAS 40 Investment Property*. London: IFRS Foundation.

The Board (2016) *IAS 41 Agriculture*. London: IFRS Foundation.

The Board (2016) *IFRS 3 Business Combinations*. London: IFRS Foundation.

The Board (2016) *IFRS 5 Non-current Assets Held for Sale and Discontinued Operations*. London: IFRS Foundation.

The Board (2016) *IFRS 7 Financial Instruments: Disclosure*. London: IFRS Foundation.

The Board (2016) *IFRS 9 Financial Instruments*. London: IFRS Foundation.

The Board (2016) *IFRS 10 Consolidated Financial Statements*. London: IFRS Foundation.

The Board (2016) *IFRS 13 Fair Value Measurement*. London: IFRS Foundation.

The Board (2016) *IFRS 15 Revenue from Contracts with Customers*. London: IFRS Foundation.

The Board (2016) *IFRS 16 Leases*. London: IFRS Foundation.

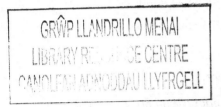